Brewed in Japan

Brewed in Japan

The Evolution of the Japanese
Beer Industry

Jeffrey W. Alexander

UBCPress · Vancouver · Toronto

21 20 19 18 17 16 15 14 13   5 4 3 2 1

Printed in Canada on FSC-certified ancient-forest-free paper
(100% post-consumer recycled) that is processed chlorine- and acid-free.

Library and Archives Canada Cataloguing in Publication

Alexander, Jeffrey W. (Jeffrey William), author
     Brewed in Japan : the evolution of the Japanese beer industry /
Jeffrey W. Alexander.

Includes bibliographical references and index.
Issued in print and electronic formats.
Co-published by: University of Hawai'i Press.
ISBN 978-0-7748-2504-7 (bound); ISBN 978-0-7748-2506-1 (pdf)

     1. Beer industry – Japan – History. I. Title.

HD9397.J32A44 2013   338.4'7663420952   C2013-903782-9
                                                          C2013-903783-7

Canada

UBC Press gratefully acknowledges the financial support for our publishing program of the Government of Canada (through the Canada Book Fund), the Canada Council for the Arts, and the British Columbia Arts Council.

This book has been published with the help of a grant from the Canadian Federation for the Humanities and Social Sciences, through the Awards to Scholarly Publications Program, using funds provided by the Social Sciences and Humanities Research Council of Canada.

Printed and bound in Canada by Friesens
Set in Futura and Warnock by Artegraphica Design Co. Ltd.
Copy editor: Sarah Wight
Proofreader: Grace Yaginuma

UBC Press
The University of British Columbia
2029 West Mall
Vancouver, BC V6T 1Z2
www.ubcpress.ca

For Terry

Contents

Illustrations

Acknowledgments

This project has benefited from the very kind support of many colleagues, agencies, and institutions since it began several years ago. Foremost among them is the Japan Foundation, which in 2008 awarded a research fellowship that enabled me to investigate Japan's brewing industry first-hand and to collect valuable materials in several major cities stretching from Okinawa to Hokkaido. In 2011, the Northeast Asia Council of the Association for Asian Studies awarded a research travel grant that enabled further fieldwork in Japan and helped me to finalize this manuscript. During that visit, the staff at the Tokyo Metropolitan Archives was especially helpful. I must thank the Asahi, Kirin, Sapporo, and Orion brewing companies for their kind responses to my inquiries, as well as the University of Chicago Library, which in 2009 awarded me funding to use its collection of company histories and related industry literature. I must also thank the staff of the Asian Reading Room at the Library of Congress in Washington, DC, for their assistance. Other libraries that generously provided access to their collections include Waseda University, University of Hawai'i, Harvard University, Yale University, University of Wisconsin, University of California, Ohio State University, University of Kansas, and Michigan State University.

I must thank David Edgington, Julian Dierkes, and Masao Nakamura of the Centre for Japanese Research at the University of British Columbia for their support and for David's kind invitation to participate in the CJR Seminar Series in 2009. I also extend my thanks to Ulrike Schaede, Bill Tsutsui, Laura Hein, Teri Bryant, Steven Ericson, Judit Kawaguchi, Bill Sewell, Karen Wigen, and Julia Adeney Thomas for their help and encouragement as this project unfolded. Likewise, Bob Eberhart and the participants in the Stanford Project on Japanese Entrepreneurship (STAJE) deserve thanks for their terrific meetings in 2010, 2011, and 2012. It was there that I met Tom Roehl, to whom I am grateful for his close read of this study. His very informed comments, as well as those of the Midwest Japan Seminar members, are much appreciated. Ken Coates and the members of the Japan Studies Association of Canada also merit special thanks for hosting excellent annual conferences at which much of this material was presented in recent years. I must also thank my colleagues at the University of Wisconsin–Parkside, which extended valuable support for research- and conference-related travel.

Japanese is a difficult language in which to conduct historical research, and even native speakers often cannot read given names, geographic locations, or antiquated kanji aloud with absolute certainty. In this regard, Enokido Keisuke was a terrific help with obscure Japanese names and idioms, and I owe him many thanks for fielding my many "onegai" requests. Japanese names appear in the traditional fashion, with family names first, followed by given names. I take full responsibility for any errors or omissions in my translations.

Finally, my heartfelt thanks go to friends, family, and especially my wife, Carolyne, whose support is never-ending.

Notes for the Reader

- Many of the brewing firms discussed in this book sold brands of beer that were named after their respective companies. In order to distinguish between them, the names of beer brands appear in quotes. For example, from 1949 until 1957, the Nippon Beer Company sold the brand "Nippon Beer."
- The names of beer companies, brewing associations, distribution firms, laws, taxes, and government ministries and agencies appear in English in the text. The glossary provides a complete list of their Japanese names, with dates where relevant, as well as historical eras and conversions for Japanese units of measure.
- The names of publicly traded Japanese companies are generally followed by the term *kabushiki kaisha* (KK). Japan's commercial code formerly translated *kabushiki kaisha* as "business corporation," but today the government recognizes the more literal term "stock company." Although *kabushiki kaisha* is typically translated into English as "Company Incorporated," many Japanese corporations still append the suffix "Ltd." (Limited) to their names in their English-language literature. Therefore, although Japan's four major brewers (Asahi, Kirin, Sapporo, and Suntory) are today incorporated firms that issue stock, I refer to them in English as limited companies (e.g., Kirin Brewery Co., Ltd.).

Brewed in Japan

Introduction:
Beer's Evolution into a Japanese Commodity

Many Westerners believe that beer was invented in Europe, but Japanese brewers are quick to point out to their domestic customers that beer is not a strictly European innovation. To illustrate this point, the visitor's centre at the Kirin brewery near Yokohama features a large rotunda decorated with an elaborate mural depicting beer's global evolution. It begins by illustrating beer's origins as an ancient Egyptian beverage and then portrays its gradual adoption and adaptation by Europeans during the last millennium. Finally, the mural illustrates beer's importation to Japan during the latter half of the nineteenth century and its continuing domestic production. Of course, the message to Japanese consumers is that Europeans did not invent beer, which was brewed in at least some form in other lands thousands of years ago. By extension, therefore, the artist encourages Japanese to feel as entitled as Westerners to brew and enjoy beer, which has become a domestic Japanese commodity just as it did a European one.[1]

Arriving at this proud conclusion, however, took several decades, and it was not fully realized until after the Second World War. Prior to that point, no Japanese brewer, even the largest among them, dared to portray itself as the maker of a totally domestic Japanese product, for it was not possible to brew beer solely with domestically grown malts and hops.[2] Instead, their strict use of authentic German ingredients, recipes, and brewing techniques was advertised heavily as fundamental to brewing high-quality, genuine beers worthy of their German brewmasters' uncompromising standards. As these brewing experts were trained in accordance with the *Reinheitsgebot* (German Beer Purity Law) of 1516, overcoming the lingering perception that domestically brewed beer was an inherently foreign commodity required time and a series of significant transformative pressures. These included the interruption of global trading patterns by two world wars, the formation of a domestic beer cartel, the total reorganization of the industry by Japan's wartime government, the forcible merger and closure of several leading brewers, the seven-year Allied Occupation (1945-52), and an unprecedented economic recovery.

As a business history of Japan's beer brewing industry, this book is concerned chiefly with how its surviving companies overcame the many obstacles to manufacturing, distributing, marketing, and selling this once-foreign beverage to Japanese consumers. My central claim is that, due to the pressures brought on by the Second World War, Japan's beer industry came to be regarded by consumers as the proud producer of a domestic Japanese product instead of a transplanted German one. Importantly, this shift involved the extensive involvement of Japan's government, which intervened at several points to foster, restructure, and reorganize the country's beer industry. Initially gradual, the pace of this transformation was accelerated dramatically in the 1940s by the exigencies of the war era, thus dividing the beer industry's development into two clear phases.

Chapters 1, 2, and 3 examine the first phase, which covers the industry's roughly seventy-five-year development up to the end of the war in August 1945. By the middle of the Meiji era (1868-1912), Japan's beer market was home to over a hundred small domestic firms, but they produced a comparatively expensive and distinctly German niche product for consumption largely by wealthy Japanese.[3] Sales to factory workers and military personnel grew during the Taishō era (1912-26), but participation in the beer market remained rather unprofitable even for the half-dozen large brewers that had managed to survive to that point. Only during the first twenty years of the Shōwa era (1926-89) did they finally manage to establish control over their retail networks, but brewers remained largely dependent on imported ingredients and German engineers for much of that time. It was not until the Second World War that the brewers at last achieved genuine material and technical self-sufficiency. Importantly, however, that independence was realized only through a total reorganization of the industry by the Ministry of Finance into a brandless, revenue-generating arm of Japan's wartime command economy. The story of the first phase of the industry's development thus conveys the significant, lasting influence of its initial German character and the great depth of the technical, logistical, commercial, and economic pressures that faced its major firms between the 1870s and 1945.

The second phase of the beer industry's evolution is explored in Chapters 4, 5, and 6. Japan's postwar era began with a seven-year military occupation that maintained many wartime brewing agencies and regulations, but the war had set the stage for the industry's swift revival and the discovery of its own, domestic identity. Freed from the influence of German brewmasters, Japan's beer makers in the 1950s developed lighter recipes, ads aimed at younger, often female consumers, and commercials starring homegrown Japanese celebrities. Beer consumption grew tremendously through the 1960s and 1970s, during which time packaging became more creative, product lines expanded, and beer advertisements were targeted more carefully toward key consumer subgroups. By the 1980s, Japan's beer industry bore little resemblance to its prewar self, despite the continued involvement of the Ministry of Finance in its carefully negotiated pricing and production regime. This unofficial postwar beer cartel prevented the underselling and excessive competition of the prewar era, but it also bored beer consumers. By the mid-1980s, many of them had grown tired of the market's lengthy domination by "Kirin Lager," and they were eager to try more innovative brews. The status quo was then shattered in 1987 with the debut of Asahi "Super Dry," which transformed Japan's beer market once more. Fully twenty-five years later, Asahi still leads the industry, but the marketplace has been altered radically since the mid-1990s by the government's permission of local craft brewing and by the advent of low-malt beers and related beer-like products. Today, a traditionally trained German brewmaster would hardly recognize Japan's beer industry, which has evolved to produce an array of unique, often seasonal brews for a diverse range of tastes. Japan's beer market is now among the most complex on earth, and its remarkable evolution continues.

Why the Beer Industry?

Like Japanese automobiles, Japanese beers are familiar products to many Westerners. In fact, there are several parallels between the origins, development, export, and eventual international production of these two commodities.[4] Both were introduced to Japan by Westerners, both were first produced there with a good deal of Western technical and material assistance, and both were the purview of wealthier Japanese consumers for quite some time. Likewise, both industries were taken over or regulated by Japanese government agencies during the Second World War era, and both were deeply affected by the war and the subsequent Allied Occupation. Naturally, each of these sectors struggled in the early postwar era, but like Japan's automakers, the surviving beer brewers – Kirin, Asahi, and Nippon (later Sapporo) – came gradually not only to prosper, but to export successfully and ultimately to make their products overseas. Beer brewing also took root in postwar Okinawa, where Orion Breweries was established in 1957. Just as in mainland Japan, however, Orion was forced to struggle against Okinawans' own sense of industrial and commercial inferiority, which viewed their own products as no match for foreign imports. Establishing the quality and merit of indigenous Ryūkyūan wares required significant effort, and Orion's experiences parallel those of mainland Japanese brewers very closely.

For all of the above reasons, Japan's evolving and lucrative beer industry is deserving of historical investigation, especially as relatively little scholarly work has yet been done in English. The leading works include a book chapter by Harald Fuess that explores Japan's prewar brewers; recent work by Penelope Francks that discusses prewar beer sales and Japan's emerging consumer culture; and an article by Stephen R. Smith that studies the shifting postwar patterns of drinking etiquette brought on by Japan's wide-scale adoption of Western alcoholic beverages.[5] Several business case studies have focused on Japan's leading brewers, but they deal chiefly with the industry's sales and marketing trends in the 1970s and 1980s. Given the scarcity of literature in English, this book therefore incorporates a wide variety of Japanese-language source material, some of which has also explored the "Japanization" *(Nihonka)* of beverages that were once thought of as distinctly foreign.[6] There are also many good technical and historical sources that deal with the beer industry in depth, as well as a host of first-person memoirs by former brewing company executives.[7] Some of the most detailed sources, however, come from the leading companies themselves, which, like many Japanese firms, publish official company histories on their major anniversaries.[8] Significantly, major manufacturing companies are among the oldest continuously operating entities in modern Japanese history. Due to their longevity and stability, they offer us remarkably consistent perspectives on Japan's economic, industrial, and even social development since the 1870s.

Despite their substantial contents, however, company histories must be explored carefully, for their authors and editors are typically committees of company insiders, and the finished volumes are promotional in nature. Still, it is worth noting that for the bulk of the twentieth century there were fewer than six beer brewers operating in Japan at any one time, and just two, Kirin and Dai Nippon (Greater Japan), for much of the Second World War era. Although the latter firm split into Asahi and Nippon in 1949, only two other major firms, the liquor distillers Takara and Suntory, would enter Japan's beer market, in 1957 and 1963, respectively. Takara, however, withdrew from the beer market in 1967, leaving Suntory to compete alone against the industry's top three companies until Japan's government decided in 1994 to again permit small-scale brewing. For fifty years this tiny handful of companies thus composed Japan's beer industry, and as they are the only firms that have documented their industry's history in any depth, their official histories are at once both valuable and challenging. For example, we can be confident that the production, pricing, sales, and export data that they contain have already been vetted carefully by the Ministry of Finance, because in Japan, beer is taxed heavily at the point of production. At the same time, however, I have also had to discern what has been omitted or left unsaid, what requires qualification or corroboration by contemporary sources, and what must be situated within the scholarly literature on Japan's late nineteenth and twentieth century development. Therefore, despite their value, I by no means rely on company histories exclusively. I also incorporate contemporary newspaper reports, market analyses, print advertisements, photographs, travel literature, museum collections, technical publications, published memoirs, and scholarly Japanese-language literature.

This book is my humble effort to fill a part of what has for many years been a large hole in the literature on Japan's industrial and commercial history. Naturally, a book on Japan's beer industry may attract a wide variety of readers, including historians, management scholars, general-interest readers, business and industry professionals, and Japan experts of all sorts, and no one book could begin to answer all of their questions. Fortunately, however, beer industry sources also include important details on such themes as living standards, social trends, women, war, leisure, urbanization, and popular culture. I have therefore endeavoured to capture and share much of that detail in order to connect the story of this industry's development with an array of broader issues affecting Japanese society. Still, I must make clear that I am a business historian, and this book is chiefly an industry and product history. It aims to demonstrate how the beer industry began and grew to become one of Japan's largest and most distinct, despite beer's entirely foreign origins. In so doing, it focuses closely on the struggles of the companies involved, their competitive strategies, the influence of Japan's government on their industry, and the reasons for beer's gradual transformation from a foreign luxury item into an affordable, appealing, and popular domestic commodity.

1 Foreign Influences: The Origins of Japan's Beer Brewing Industry, 1868-1906

Japan's domestic beer industry did not begin in earnest until after the collapse of the Tokugawa shogunate (1603-1867) and Japan's gradual acceptance of wider trade and diplomatic relations with Western nations during the subsequent Meiji era (1868-1912). Like many businesses inspired by increased interaction with Westerners, beer brewing began due to the activities of resident foreigners during the 1870s, many of whom longed for the taste of familiar foods and beverages. With the efforts of Dutch, English, German, and American brewers in Yokohama in the 1870s, wealthy Japanese had opportunities to taste this unique Western brew – and their reviews varied widely at the outset. Initial reactions were mixed, for the beverage had little to offer the connoisseur of fine *Nihonshu*, or sake. Beer was initially so prohibitively expensive that very few Japanese could even afford to taste it, and those living outside Japan's largest urban centres could most likely not have found it had they tried. Cities like Tokyo and Yokohama were very much at the cutting edge of imported Western trends and fashions during the 1870s and 1880s, but even there, in the most bustling marketplaces, foreign influences had their limits.[1]

This chapter explores the origins of the Kirin and Sapporo brewing companies and the rising popularity of beer among comparatively wealthy Japanese consumers during the Meiji era. The brewery that would become Kirin in 1907 actually began in late 1869 or early 1870 as a resident foreigner's private business in Yokohama, while Sapporo was founded in 1876 as part of a government-directed industrial development plan on Japan's northernmost main island, Hokkaido. During this period and later, consumer product manufacturing represented an enormous financial, organizational, and logistical challenge, both for resident foreigners and for Japanese entrepreneurs. Some of Japan's earliest beer industry participants had the opportunity to study under brewmasters in Germany before returning to Japan, but contemporary access to new skills and technologies was not unfettered. The late nineteenth century was the era of the "unequal treaties," which derive their name from the terms of the 1858 Treaty of Amity and Commerce between Japan and a variety of Western nations, first among them the United States. These treaties posed unique difficulties for those who wished to found manufacturing companies together with Westerners, or even to purchase such assets from them. Contemporary Japanese law also forbade ordinary citizens from doing business directly with foreigners, which made it impossible for Japanese investors to acquire even bankrupt Western firms located in Yokohama's foreigner district. Kirin's founding, therefore, offers us a rare example of international entrepreneurial cooperation, for in order to circumvent the law, the company was reestablished in 1885 as a Japanese-Western joint venture headquartered in British colonial Hong Kong. Thereafter, wresting ownership from its foreign investors and reestablishing Kirin in Japan in 1907 would require significant effort and the support of the powerful Mitsubishi Corporation.

Japan's breweries in this era maintained and advertised rigid ties to German recipes, processes, and brewmasters, but they also struggled to produce quality products, due chiefly to Japan's underdeveloped agricultural and infrastructural bases. Fledgling brands like "Sapporo," "Kirin," and "Asahi," together with more than a hundred others, faced significant obstacles to acquiring ingredients, accessing sufficient ice to keep their beer chilled, and shipping their heavy liquid product over mountainous terrain. Challenged also by powerful foreign imports from Europe, Japanese brewers fought hard during the 1890s and early 1900s both to expand their domestic market shares and to export their products to neighbouring nations throughout the Asia-Pacific region. All the while, the definitive brew remained the traditional German lager, which resident German brewmasters defended with authority. Their insistence on quality and the use of authentic European ingredients made good business sense at the outset, but their stubbornness had long-term consequences. Decades after the industry's birth, Japanese farmers still produced only a small fraction of the ingredients used by Japanese brewers, while the product's continued German identity stymied its evolution into a domestic commodity in the minds of consumers. Beer advertisements in major Japanese newspapers during the late nineteenth century were often placed by import wholesalers or "Western liquor shops" (*yōshu-ya*), which gave even domestically brewed beer a continued foreign character for many years.[2] At the same time, however, the rising popularity of beer halls, cafés, and outdoor beer gardens in Japan's major cities attracted thousands of consumers, especially members of Japan's burgeoning professional classes.

"Bitter Horse-Piss Wine": The Introduction of Beer to Japan

Although Japan's contact with Europeans began in the sixteenth century with the arrival of the Portuguese, they did not bring beer to Japan. Rather, they imported wine, which Jesuit missionaries served at receptions along with other alcoholic drinks known to the Japanese by such names as *chinta, rōke, kanebu,* and *mirinchu.*[3] Following the unification of Japan under Tokugawa Ieyasu in 1600 and the establishment of his hereditary dictatorship, the Tokugawa shogunate, Ieyasu signed the Christian Expulsion Edict in 1614. The Portuguese were thereby expelled and Christianity was suppressed, leading to the execution of dozens of Japanese converts. The shogunal government then ushered in a policy of national seclusion *(sakoku seisaku),* which grew more pronounced during the 1630s, and came by 1641 to exclude all Europeans from trading with Japan – except for the employees of the Dutch East India Company (Vereenigde Oost-Indische Compagnie, or VOC).

Because these Dutch traders were willing to forgo any attempts at spreading the Christian faith, the shogunate granted the VOC (and later the Dutch government) exclusive access to a single Japanese port city – Nagasaki. Until 1853, only Dutch, Chinese, and Korean ships were permitted to call at Nagasaki, and the Dutch traders were required to live on a man-made, fan-shaped island in the harbour called Deshima. Although religious books and services were strictly forbidden, the Dutch residents of Deshima, who numbered around twenty, did have various recreational opportunities, including games such as badminton and billiards, as well as beer. The words for beer, brandy, wine, and whisky gradually made their way into the Japanese lexicon via the Dutch, for Dutch studies, known in Japanese as *rangaku,* was popular among contemporary Japanese students, intellectuals, and court figures. A Dutch-Japanese dictionary dating to 1810 features the Dutch words *bierglas* and *klein bierglas* (beer glass and small beer glass) rendered into Japanese script.[4] Beer and its related vocabulary were thus introduced to Japan, and when VOC representatives made their compulsory annual trips to Edo (today Tokyo) to pay their respects to the shogun, they brought beer with them as well.[5] In their two-volume work *Oranda iji mondō* (Questions and answers on Holland), contemporary authors Takebe Seian and Sugita Genpaku described an occasion when the Dutch prepared their own food at an inn called the Nagasaki-ya near the centre of Edo: "The wine was made from grapes. Another was made from barley. It was like a barley sake ... It was called *biiru* ... Three men brought their cups together [saying], 'chin chin.'"[6]

Gradually, Dutch wine and beer were shipped to Japanese consumers in the country's urban centres, and adventurous Japanese began to consume Dutch *bier* after meals, in order to aid digestion. Soon, a few pioneering

Japanese began to attempt brewing beer for themselves. The first was a scholar of Dutch medicine living in Sanda, Hyōgo prefecture. Kawamoto Kōmin (1810-71) reportedly found a reference to the brewing process in a Dutch book on new Western science, which he translated into Japanese. Eager to attempt the process himself, Kawamoto is said to have built a kettle in his home for brewing beer.[7]

The next step in beer's introduction to Japan came in the mid-nineteenth century, when Commodore Matthew C. Perry of the US Navy arrived to encourage the shogunate to initiate diplomatic relations with the United States. Although the July 1853 encounter was tense, Perry did succeed in delivering a letter from President Millard Fillmore to "His Majesty the Emperor of Japan."[8] Perry pledged to return to Japan the following year to receive Japan's reply, which he did in March 1854. When the shogunate then agreed to sign the Convention of Kanagawa, known officially as the Nichibei Washin Jōyaku, or Japan-America Treaty of Amity and Friendship, it held a celebratory reception to mark the occasion. At the event, the US delegation presented gifts to the Japanese officials of innovative American products, including a working telegraph, a one-quarter-scale steam locomotive, and three casks of beer. The beer was described by Japanese observers as being an earthen colour, with a large volume of bubbles on top, but reviews of its taste were mixed. Some called it "magic water," while others labelled it "bitter horse-piss wine."[9] Between 1860 and 1870, scholar and statesman Fukuzawa Yukichi published a ten-volume work called *Seiyō jijō* (Conditions in the West) in which he too describes beer. In a passage entitled "Western Things" (literally, "Western food, clothing, shelter"), Fukuzawa writes, "There is a drink called 'beer.' This barley sake *(mugizake)* has an extremely bitter taste."[10] With a history of enjoying mild sakes, sweet plum wines, and similar alcoholic beverages, Japanese were unfamiliar with the bitter, hopped flavours of nineteenth-century beers, but this would soon change.

With the signing of the Japan-America Treaty of Amity and Friendship in 1854, Americans were granted permission to conduct trade in specially designated areas of a handful of Japan's major port cities. As the city of Yokohama opened to foreign settlement on the signing of the United States–Japan Treaty of Amity and Commerce in 1858, arrivals from England, Europe, and America soon settled there in a segregated district between the seashore and Yamate Hill, where they built numbered apartment flats, merchant offices, and so on. At the same time, the national government, or *bakufu*, encouraged Japanese merchants from Kyoto, Osaka, and Edo to move to Yokohama, so about 150 merchants applied to come to the area to set up shops and homes. By the 1860s, the character of Yokohama had already changed a great deal. The foreigners' district of Yokohama was a bustling community that fascinated many contemporary Japanese. The curious homes, clothes, ships, and wares possessed by foreigners inspired a wave of artistic renditions by contemporary Japanese writers and woodblock print *(ukiyoe)* artists. Foreign traders, merchants, and shopkeepers imported a large volume of familiar tastes, including meat, which Japanese at that time traditionally did not eat, and of course beer.

In 1863, the bakufu also began to permit English and French military forces to be stationed at Yokohama. The British "Red Corps" was stationed on Yatoyama in Motomachi, and the French "Blue Corps" at nearby Yatobashi. Under the pretext of protecting their nationals, they conducted elaborate drills and training exercises under the watchful eye of bakufu observers and local residents.

The presence of so many thirsty foreign soldiers led naturally to a rising tide of beer imports from their home countries, the first of which was reportedly the English brand "Bass." In about 1871, a German merchant established the Wagen Company in Yokohama's building No. 57, where he began importing beer. Soon thereafter, a Frenchman established the Couldrie Company in building No. 62, and then the Adecamper Company opened in building No. 95, both of which also imported beer, including German and American brands. Also in the early 1870s, the English import firm Carnaut Company, located in Yamate-chō, began to attract Japanese customers with its imported beers. These shops began to compete by importing and selling their home brands, and although most of them were German, Kirin reports that most of their labels featured the English spelling *beer*. Despite the English spelling, Kirin notes that, among Japanese, the pronunciation of the word *beer* seemed to more closely resemble the German than the English.[11]

As for the beers brewed increasingly in Japan after 1870, their labels too featured the English word *beer*, with the Japanese portion of the label reading *biiru* in *katakana* script. During the Meiji and Taishō eras, most major Japanese brewing firms hired German brewmasters, and thus their products were distinctly German in style.[12] Smaller breweries, however, such as one established at Kōfu, in Yamanashi prefecture, were often dependent on Japanese technicians who had trained either in Europe or at the foreigners' breweries in Japan. A large number of these late-nineteenth-century Japanese brands were produced by wealthy local families that managed their own businesses, families to which Edward E. Pratt refers as *gōnō*, or "wealthy farmers."[13] While not a contemporary term, these wealthy farming families in rural areas had often risen to prominence during the Edo era (the Tokugawa era) due to their proto-industrial handicraft businesses, which included silkworm and sake production, among other things. As the Meiji era arrived, some of these families tried to diversify their operations by brewing beer, which was the latest trend and remained an untaxed industry. Enterprising individuals leapt in as well, seeking to carve out a niche in the growing beer market, which in the 1870s and 1880s presented very few real barriers to entry.

Pratt discusses the beer industry only briefly, but he offers a look at some of the pitfalls that faced entrepreneurs who tried their hands at brewing beer. He relates the story of one Ishikawa Chiyozō, a young sake brewer who sold his "Japan Beer" to shops and taverns in Tokyo and Yokohama over a six-month period in 1888, while facing significant hurdles. These included bottle caps that occasionally cracked under pressure, and the difficulty of collecting on his sales, which amounted to just 1,212 large bottles and 414 small bottles during that half year. Frustrated by the whole affair, Ishikawa abandoned the beer industry after less than two years, and refocused his attention on his sake business instead.[14] Ishikawa's experience is just one of many, many like it that involved pioneering efforts to brew beer by a variety of entrepreneurs, young and old. In his unpublished 1975 dissertation on Japan's prewar beer industry, Joseph Alphonse Laker focuses on the theme of entrepreneurship, and his chapter on early Japanese breweries is a medley of tales about the dreams of small merchant brewers gone awry. One after another, these enterprising men failed to grow sufficient hops, locate enough bottles, or brew beer of sufficient quality, and gradually they went bankrupt, sold out, or drifted off into other businesses.[15] In fact, over 120 Japanese breweries, stretching from the island of Kyushu in the west to the island of Hokkaido in the north, produced beer between 1869 and 1945, but the vast majority disappeared well before the close of the Meiji era in 1912. Exploring these tiny firms is difficult, as very little evidence survives about them, but a lengthy list of their names, brands, locations, and dates of operation appears in the appendix.

Many of the brewmasters working for these small firms moved often from one brewery to the next, or worked at several simultaneously, but nearly all of the breweries failed before long. These Japanese brewmasters had studied with German engineers at larger breweries before moving on to work for rivals or to set up their own companies. This underscores the breadth and flexibility of the domestic beer market during the late nineteenth century, when no single company had yet dreamed of selling its products nationwide. Few firms, in fact, shipped their wares beyond their own areas, largely because of Japan's vastly underdeveloped roadway infrastructure. During the 1870s, Japan's government prioritized the completion of the nation's burgeoning railway system, and though city tramlines and paved roads did expand gradually in the urban centres, Japan's intercity dirt roads languished in a very poor state until the 1960s.[16] Given the very narrow profit margins of small breweries operating in the late nineteenth century and the great cost of shipping a liquid product over the nation's limited rail lines, very few small brewers aimed to sell beer outside their immediate areas. This led to the emergence of a virtually galactic industry, fanning out across Japan's network of urban centres but seldom penetrating the more remote areas of the country, where beer remained a rarity until the twentieth century.

No. 123, Yokohama: The Origins of Kirin Brewery

William Copeland and the Spring Valley Brewery

Although imported beer was plentiful, some Westerners in Yokohama were determined to brew beer locally and thus undercut the market for expensive foreign brands. The most famous among them was William Copeland. Born Johan Martinius Thoresen in Norway in 1834, he changed his name when he immigrated to America as a young man. Copeland then moved to Yokohama in 1864 and set himself up as a brewer in 1869, making his story one of the first detailed accounts that we have of a foreigner who founded and managed his own company in Japan.[17] According to Copeland's signed "Brewery Company" business plan, he first worked for five years during the late 1840s as an apprentice to a German brewmaster in Norway. He married his first wife there, but when exactly she died is unclear. After completing his apprenticeship, Copeland moved to America in the 1850s, where he eventually became a naturalized American citizen. He was thus always treated as an American while in Japan. According to Yokohama's English-language paper, the *Japan Weekly Mail,* Copeland started out in the cartage business along Yokohama's wharf before trying his hand in the city's burgeoning dairy industry.[18] Due to his early presence in the city, his name appears in *The Written History of Yokohama City (Yokohama-shi shi kō)* in a list of Americans and Europeans living there in 1868, at the very beginning of the Meiji era.[19]

Copeland settled in Yamate's Kiyoizumi area, next to Amanuma Pond, which was the site of a natural spring. It was there in 1869 or 1870, at the age of thirty-six, that he founded his new company, naming it the Spring Valley Brewery (Izumi no tani). On both his labels and in his personal letters, Copeland always included the address "No. 123 Bluff, Yokohama," and though he did not use the name Amanuma, his product was known locally as Amanuma *biyazake,* or "Amanuma beer sake." In *The Written History of Yokohama City,* the authors note, "Indeed, Amanuma biyazake is certainly one thing that the British officers and men stationed at the nearby Teppoba training grounds [a rifle range in modern Yamate-chō], as well as the foreign residents of Yokohama count as indispensable."[20] At that time, the bulk of the beer consumed in Japan consisted of foreign brands, and Amanuma beer was pitted against imports like "Bass Ale" and "Bass Stout," as well as German brands. Copeland's three brands, "Lager Beer," "Bavarian Beer," and "Bavarian Bock Beer," were sold principally in casks to Yokohama taverns and beer halls, but he also sold a small amount of bottled beer to foreigners living throughout Yamate and Yamashita-machi.

The labels, which bore a trademark figure of a circle, read, "Brewed and Bottled by Copeland & Co." or "by Copeland and Wiegand," in reference to Emil Wiegand, his sometime business partner. The signatures of both men are visible in a surviving letter and in advertisements, but the details on Wiegand are not at all clear. The nationality of the name is uncertain, and *The Written History of Yokohama City* does not list Wiegand among the foreigners living in the area. In 1878, a brewing technician named Moritani Hisamatsu published a report on yeast manufacturing techniques, in which he mentions a beer brewery at building No. 68 in Yokohama by the name of "Ue-gando" (Wiegand). He may have simply been Copeland's sales and marketing partner, but whatever the case, they seem to have parted ways after a falling out in 1880, after which the Spring Valley Brewery became Copeland's solo venture.[21] The only clue as to Wiegand's fate is found in a letter from Copeland and his head clerk, J.D. Eyton, to a cork shop in San Francisco, which closes with, "Many thanks for information about Wiegand."[22]

The Spring Valley Brewery illustrates the early tax and business regulation regimes facing foreign entrepreneurs during the 1870s. During this period there was of course a national domestic tax on businesses, including breweries, but as a foreigner's enterprise Copeland's firm was not subject to the national Alcohol Tax Law. The early relations between Japan and Western nations were tenuous, and the latter did not wish to grant Japan parity of status at the outset. For this reason, the United States, Great Britain, France, Holland, and others demanded and received the right of extraterritoriality, meaning that, when in Japan, their citizens were not subject to Japanese law. Viewed by Westerners as a sort of "Oriental despotism" (for Japan had not yet embraced the Western principles of the Enlightenment or the rights of man), Japan's laws were not deemed to be equal to those of Western nations, the governments of which reserved the right to regulate and to prosecute their own citizens where necessary, especially in criminal cases. Consular officials thus remained the local authorities inside the foreign settlements, and they often adjudicated legal matters, including crimes, lawsuits, and contracts. As a result, late-nineteenth-century entrepreneurs like William

Copeland found themselves in a sort of regulatory no-man's-land, operating Western businesses on Japanese soil with foreign oversight. As such, Copeland did not require a local business licence and was not required to pay the brewing tax to the government of the local Kanagawa domain.

Still, in 1874, Copeland applied to the Kanagawa domain for a business licence anyway, on receipt of which he fully expected to begin paying local taxes. However, the Kanagawa Ministry of Finance sent Copeland a courtly letter, dated 16 April 1874, in which it claimed to have no jurisdiction over his brewery. The ministry claimed that, according to the 1858 Treaty of Amity and Commerce between the United States and Japan, the rights of extraterritoriality required that such matters as business licences and tax collection for resident foreigners fell within the jurisdiction of their respective countries' consuls general. Consequently, the ministry rejected Copeland's application for a business licence, although he and his associates continued their operations undaunted. Copeland not only brewed beer, he also instructed interested Japanese in the craft of brewing; two of his several apprentices went on in 1873 to found the first brewery in Kōfu. These activities, in turn, inspired other Japanese to attempt to found competing breweries of their own. On 30 May 1875, the *Yokohama Mainichi* newspaper reported that "in the northern village of Honmoku, a certain Mr. Hosaka and other persons are making beer, and selling it, and it has a taste that rivals Western alcohol *(yōshu)*, and yet in spite of its value, if it is still priced cheaply, alongside the foreign-made beers, we recommend that this will continue to be good for Mr. Hosaka."[23]

The Spring Valley Brewery had fared well in its early days, but after Copeland and Wiegand parted ways in 1880, the US consul was required to settle a lawsuit between Copeland and Eyton, his head clerk. Although Copeland won, the suit bankrupted Spring Valley. The brewery's funds were consumed by its debts, and it was unable to weather the recession and deflation of 1882. After its failure in that year, Japan's government challenged the efforts of the US consul general to dispose of the brewery unilaterally, and, remarkably, the two sides argued the case before a Japanese federal court. In its ruling, the court ordered that Copeland's former firm be disposed of by sale, which would soon permit a group of European and Japanese investors to buy the former brewery's assets. Copeland wrote, "I experienced 15 years of success in this country as a brewer of Anglo-German beer,"[24] and though his firm had gone bankrupt, Copeland himself was not finished. In 1886, he moved next door to building No. 212, remodelled his house into a beer garden, and began selling beer next to his old factory, which had been purchased by the Japan Brewery Company, Ltd.

Copeland's beer hall was a truly pioneering effort. Inside the shop were four or five storage cellars for keeping casks of beer, each of which held fifty gallons. The hall drew water through a lead pipe from Amanuma Pond in order to keep the cellars cool, and Copeland served beer in thick glass mugs with handles, known as *jokki*. At first these mugs were made in the West, but later Copeland imported them from China. A small glass cost 10 sen, and a large glass was 20 sen. To curb breakage, Copeland later switched to galvanized metal mugs. The customers who came to drink at Copeland's beer garden were mostly foreign sailors – so many sailors, it seems, that local resident foreigners almost never came. During this period, Copeland also served as a consultant for other local breweries, but he was not able to buy shares in any of them. Finally, in 1889, he gave up on making a comeback in the brewing world, and together with his second wife, Umeko, he moved first to Hawaii and then to Guatemala, where he opened a shop that sold goods made in Japan.[25] He was troubled, however, by chronic rheumatism and heart trouble, and because his funds were scarce, he could not continue to stock his shop. In 1894, Copeland wrote to Umeko saying that he did not want to return to Japan, but they did finally sail back to Yokohama in 1902, his seventy-first year.[26]

At the directors' meeting of The Japan Brewery on 12 February 1902, the company chairman reported:

A few weeks ago, Copeland-kun and his wife, who are poor and dying, returned from South America [sic]. He is the originator of Spring Valley Brewery, the firm that fostered our firm, The Japan Brewery, so I think it is only just that our company should hold out a helping hand ... However, Copeland died suddenly last night. Therefore, I think I'd like the company to cover the funeral expenses and give a gift to his widow as a humble token.[27]

Thereafter, the following passage about the late Copeland appears in the company minutes, dated 11 March: "The director reports that the sum of ¥198.05 was disbursed to cover the funeral and other associated costs, as aid for Copeland's widow, and he read her letter of thanks."[28] Naturally, Copeland's obituary was published in the *Japan Weekly Mail*, which observed:

By the death of Mr. William Copeland, which occurred on Tuesday night, passed away one of the early foreign residents of Yokohama. Mr. Copeland, who was a citizen of the United States, came to Japan in 1864, and first started the drayage business [horse-drawn carts]. He was also the first foreigner to engage in the dairy business and in beer brewing. The Spring Valley Brewery, where he established the latter business, was situated on the site of the present Japan Brewery's works. At that time, however, the Japanese had not acquired the taste for beer and the venture was not attended with much success.[29]

The late professor Katsumata Senkichirō of Waseda University said that Copeland was a tall, very imposing man, who was excellent at his work in better times. He was known for his mild disposition, and he had an attractive character, but his only shortcoming was that he was a bad drunk, which may have contributed to his poor health.[30] His second wife, Umeko, died in 1908; they had no children. William Copeland's grave lies in the famous Yokohama Foreign General Cemetery on Yamate Hill.[31]

Skirting the "Unequal Treaties": The Japan Brewery Company, Ltd.

The formation of the Japan Brewery Company is the story of Japanese investors purchasing, reincorporating, and managing a foreign-owned business during an era when Japanese and foreigners were legally forbidden to do business with one another. Even though foreigners could not yet travel freely within Japan, their presence was already prompting rapid changes in Japanese consumer habits. Specifically, the eating of meat and bread became more widespread during the 1870s and 1880s, and beer drinking had begun to rise fairly quickly as well, fuelling rising domestic production through the turn of the century (see Table 1).

Although much too expensive for the average worker, who could afford only the most inexpensive sake, beer gradually become popular with many urban Japanese bar patrons during the Meiji era. In Japan, urban bars and restaurants date back to the sixteenth century, when simple tea shops *(cha-ya)* served tea and snacks to travellers and passers-by, who often sat on

Table 1

National population and domestic beer production per person, 1887-1902

Year	National production (kL)	Population (000s)	Production per person (mL)
1887	3,158.3	38,703	81
1892	1,517.3	40,508	38
1897	11,854.7	42,400	279
1902	16,423.8	44,964	364

Note: Source data is available only at five-year intervals.
Source: Kirin biiru KK, *Kirin biiru KK gojū nenshi* [Kirin Brewery Company, Ltd.: Fifty-year history] (Tokyo: Kirin biiru KK, 20 March 1957), 235.

benches out front. During the Edo period, these establishments became more specialized, and neighbourhood taverns *(izakaya)*, noodle shops, and expensive restaurants began to emerge. Although Western-style taverns, saloons, hotel bars, beer salons, and "cool-drink bars" *(seiryō inryō)* started out as urban novelties, by the mid-Meiji era they too were steadily more numerous, especially in the business and shopping districts of Japan's largest cities.[32]

The first establishment purported to have called itself an actual *baa* (bar) was the Kamiya Bar, founded in 1880 by a brewer named Kamiya Denbei near the Thunder Gate in Asakusa, Tokyo. A virtual institution, the Kamiya Bar is still in operation today, offering patrons a remarkable glimpse of the city's storied past. In his 1914 classic, *The Nightside of Japan*, Fujimoto Taizō notes that Kamiya's bar "gave satisfaction to drinkers by serving very cheap liquors brewed at his own brewery." Kamiya's customers drank not only beer and whisky, but also the bar's signature cocktail, known as "electric brandy" *(denki bran*, a mix of brandy, gin, wine, curaçao, vermouth, and herbs).[33] Added to proper bars like Kamiya's were simple beer stands at major street crossings and on train station platforms, where busy city folk could pause for a quick glass. Public consumption of alcohol was of course nothing new in Japan. For centuries, urbanites had been familiar with the sight of roadside sake stands and "swinging sellers" *(furi-uri)* dealing cups of sweet sake *(amazake)* to customers on the street. These peddlers sold cool sake in summer and warm sake in winter, walking the streets of Edo shouting "sweet, sweet amazake" while shouldering a pole from which two wooden boxes hung.[34] The box in front carried trays and sake cups, while the one in the rear contained a small furnace and a pot. Although sake peddlers could still be seen in the Meiji era, they were soon eclipsed by urban stand-up bars selling cold beer, which consumers quickly learned was a good deal more refreshing on hot summer days, and also came in larger glasses.

The encouragement of Western eating and drinking habits during the Meiji era was part of a determined effort by Japan's government to convince the Great Powers to accept the Japanese as peers and renegotiate the "unequal treaties." In the quintessential example of this campaign, Inoue Kaoru, Japan's foreign minister from 1879 to 1887, spearheaded the construction of the Rokumeikan (Deer Cry Pavilion) near the Imperial Palace in the Hibiya district of central Tokyo. Designed by British architect Josiah Conder, the Rokumeikan was an opulent, two-storey building famous for its Western parties and balls, to which many high-ranking Japanese were invited in order to demonstrate their familiarity with Western dress, foods, beverages, and decorum. Completed in 1883, it served distinctly Western fare, including French food, American cocktails, English cigarettes, and, of course, German beer. Although the "Rokumeikan era" ended by 1889 after failing to convince the Great Powers to renegotiate the treaties, it did expose hundreds of wealthy Japanese to fine Western foods and beverages, and it cemented the idea of German beer as the premier, authentic brew.[35]

Because beer was growing steadily more popular with wealthy Japanese consumers, and locally made beer was less expensive than imported beers, Japan's domestic brewing industry appeared to have a bright future. When William Copeland's Spring Valley Brewery factory was sold at the beginning of 1885, annual beer imports totalled over 2,500 *koku* (451 kL; 1 koku equalled roughly 278.3 litres until 1891, when a smaller koku unit was introduced that equalled 180.39 litres) and domestic consumption was holding steady. Copeland's factory had produced a high-quality product, and as other local brewers were earning profits, a group of Japanese investors decided to move in and buy Copeland's plant after it failed.

However, Japanese citizens were not free to purchase the assets of resident foreigners, and Japanese were not permitted to go into business with foreigners. Therefore, in order for interested Japanese to be permitted to acquire Copeland's former brewery, Thomas Blake Glover, who was a special adviser to Mitsubishi, and a Mr. M. Kirkwood, who worked for the Japanese Ministry of Justice, each made frequent trips between Tokyo and Yokohama to negotiate the deal. Due to the restrictions of the "unequal treaties," concluding the sale required remarkable creativity and a certain sleight of hand.[36]

Glover and Kirkwood examined the treaties closely, and concluded that yes, Japanese citizens were indeed forbidden to conduct business with foreigners – *in Japan*. The treaty said nothing about Japanese doing business with foreigners overseas, and the very nature of the treaties gave Japan no jurisdiction over its citizens' actions there. Glover and Kirkwood therefore encouraged interested Japanese investors to amass the capital necessary to purchase shares in a newly incorporated brewery that was to be registered in British Hong Kong. They also recruited a group of British and European directors and asked them to register the new brewery in Hong Kong as a native English firm, in which Japanese citizens, with the blessing of their Ministry of Justice, could purchase shares. In early May 1885, a group of resident foreigners held an establishment preparation conference *(setsuritsu junbikai)*, where a proposal was drafted calling for the founding of a completely furnished, suitably sized beer brewery in Yokohama. The draft proposal featured no Japanese names, but the true purpose of the meeting was to permit interested Japanese investors to examine the former Spring Valley Brewery and to assess its viability. By this point, two-thirds of the necessary capital had already been pledged by the Japanese, and a host of questions and suggestions was fielded from the Japanese attendees. Together with the foreigners, the Japanese examined the former brewery's founding, its assets, the impact of the 1882 recession, and the federal court order that the firm was to be disposed of by sale. On 26 June 1885, the consultants prepared a provisional prospectus and formally announced an initial public offering (IPO) of shares.[37]

The foreign ownership and Hong Kong incorporation were essentially a legal fiction through which Japanese and local foreign investors secured tacit interest in the new firm. In order for the investors to assume legitimate, public control over the company and to profit fully, Japan would have to succeed in revising or abolishing the "unequal treaties." If that could be accomplished, then the fledgling company would benefit from the following opportunities:

- Resident foreigners would be able to live and work together with Japanese.
- Foreigners with passports would be permitted to do business and travel freely within Japan.
- Foreigners would be able to sell their assets to Japanese.
- The tariff on imported beer could be raised to 25 or 30 percent from the current, fixed level of under 5 percent.
- The firm could open sales agencies in every major city and dispatch salesmen nationwide.

The "unequal treaties" did not permit Japan to set its own trade tariffs, which were fixed very low to benefit foreign imports (see Table 2). The prospective investors in the Japan Brewery knew that if the country were enabled to raise its tariffs on imported beer, the result would be a boon for domestic brewers. Higher tariffs would put a significant dent in the current volume of imported beer, which was then valued at over HK$100,000 annually.[38]

The Japanese investors also knew, however, that the domestic beer market had great potential only if consumers could be assured of finding a high-quality product at a sensible price. In this arena, the investors had a series of specific concerns and requirements, many of which involved the importation of foreign machinery and access to sufficient water. The prospectus identified the following priorities:

- The company had to employ the best brewing techniques from England, Germany, and the United States, and offer sufficient salaries.
- The very same site occupied by the former Spring Valley Brewing Company had to be acquired, because it had a clean water supply.

Table 2

Imports of alcoholic beverages, 1880-90

Year	Beer Volume (kL)	Cost (¥)	Wine (kL)	Brandy, whisky, and liqueurs (kL)
1880	530.0	133,387	585.9	120.9
1881	405.2	95,949	375.8	120.9
1882	405.0	95,641	353.2	91.6
1883	451.0	103,707	415.3	86.8
1884	453.3	105,640	361.9	84.2
1885	567.7	131,247	338.4	122.7
1886	810.9	183,189	587.9	146.1
1887	1,633.1	378,745	1,022.1	280.1
1888	1,552.4	459,421	663.1	125.7
1889	801.8	220,628	503.3	105.0
1890	611.9	154,800	754.4	97.0

Source: Kirin biiru KK, *Kirin biiru KK gojū nenshi* [Kirin Brewery Company, Ltd.: Fifty-year history] (Tokyo: Kirin biiru KK, 20 March 1957), 232.

- The company must commission an architect from London to design the facility.
- The firm must acquire the most up-to-date machinery and steam equipment.
- A capable sales agent must be enlisted to market the product effectively.

The investors therefore weighed the costs necessary to establish and operate the brewery against the potential sales and revenues. The estimated costs included the site, the building, machinery and equipment, packing materials, and wagons and draft horses.[39] As for projected revenues, the planned equipment was expected to produce 2,900 koku (523 kL) of beer in eight months' time. In that era, brewing work typically stopped from June through September, during which time machinery was repaired and summer demand was met with casks in storage in the cellar. (In an age before air conditioning, hot summer weather was not the ideal atmosphere for brewing new beer, for the sake both of the product and of the workers.) At that time, the beer made by Japanese breweries was typically of a lower grade than foreign imports, and one gallon of Japanese beer sold for about 50 sen. For example, the beer produced by Sakurada Beer sold for ¥20 for a thirty-six-gallon cask, so one gallon cost about 55 sen. The investors assumed that their beer, being of better quality, would sell for HK$0.40 per gallon, and as they aimed to produce just over 115,000 British gallons per year, they expected to generate total revenues of HK$46,656 annually. The investors' faith in these numbers, added to the former Spring Valley Brewery's track record of profitability, encouraged them to vote to approve the founding proposal.[40]

The IPO of shares was issued in Hong Kong dollars, and the prospectus was sent to potential investors following the 26 June meeting. Exactly five hundred shares would be issued, generating a total of HK$50,000 in capital stock. Investors were given until 6 July to apply, and at the first directors' meeting on 8 July, a provisional board of directors was established to oversee the firm. The board consisted of James Dodds of Butterfield and Swire as chair, Carl Rhodes of Carl Rhodes and Company as deputy chair, F. Grosser of Grosser and Company, Edgar Abbot, and W.H. Talbot as special secretary. At the meeting, the directors named the firm the Japan Brewery, agreed to establish it officially in Hong Kong as a limited liability company and a native English firm, recorded HK$35,000 in paid-in capital, and agreed to find a qualified German brewmaster. At their second meeting on 13 July, the directors agreed that prospective investors must pay HK$5 per share at application time, HK$5 per share at assignment time, and HK$10 per share every month thereafter. A survey was also commissioned of the 6,998.4-square-metre site for purchase, and on 21 July the formal application was made to register the company in Hong Kong. Temporary offices were established at No. 70, on Main Street in Yokohama, in the office of Carl Rhodes and Company, which was the leading German merchant office in Yokohama.[41]

By March 1886, 492 out of the initial 500 shares had been sold, and an additional 258 shares were sold to Japanese investors exclusively, making the new firm's IPO so successful that fully HK$75,000 in capital stock was raised, HK$25,000 more than originally planned. Thomas Glover of Mitsubishi handled the sales, and by August, the purchasers included the Mitsubishi conglomerate, Dai-ichi Bank, the Takada Company, nine private Japanese individuals, and the Ōkura Trading Company, which was established in 1873 as the Ōkura Group by Baron Ōkura Kihachirō (1837-1928). The board of directors and an auditor hosted an annual shareholders' meeting, so although it was officially known as a limited liability company by name, the classification "company incorporated" in fact applied. Although the "unequal treaties" were not renegotiated successfully until the eve of the First Sino-Japanese War in 1894, the reincorporation of the Japan Brewery outmanoeuvred the treaty's restrictions on doing business with foreigners. By definition, the treaty had no jurisdiction over a company established in British Hong Kong.[42]

German Influence and the Launch of the Kirin Beer Brand

The fledgling brewery's prospectus was approved at the board of directors' meeting on 21 July 1885, where Carl Rhodes was named the new company's chief managing director. Fellow Germans H. Bell and O. Heinemann were also appointed directors, and as agreed, the management took steps to hire a German brewing expert. Hermann Heckert was thus invited from Hamburg and arrived in Yokohama to take up his new post on 5 July 1887. By August, however, the yeast that he had ordered from Germany had still not arrived, so he grudgingly sent away for American yeast from San Francisco instead. All the remaining ingredients and equipment were imported from Germany, including the machinery, rubber hoses, malted barley, and hops. (Malt is the thick, sugary liquid derived from germinated cereal grains, on which yeast feeds during the brewing process. The germinating and drying process known as "malting" develops the enzymes that convert the grain's starches into sugars, after which the grains are mashed. Hops are the female flower clusters used to stabilize beer during fermentation and to give it a variety of bitter or tangy flavours.) Even the glass bottles were imported from Germany, and early attempts to substitute locally made bottles often met with failure. For example, in 1888, the Shinagawa Glass Company made bottles in Tokyo with German technicians and machinery, putting out up to nine thousand bottles daily, most of which were purchased by the Japan Brewery Company. Though briefly profitable, the firm was bankrupted by the recession of 1892, and unable to find a buyer, it closed its doors in that year.[43] Although much of the brewing equipment and supplies were also made in Japan, and malts could be ordered much more cheaply from the United States, the Japan Brewery went to the trouble to import these items from Germany in order to produce a truly German beer (see Table 3).[44] Even the architecture of Japanese beer breweries was influenced heavily by German brick factory designs, though their designers were typically British.[45]

Table 3 demonstrates that while imports of malts and hops fluctuated from year to year, they rose overall in concert with Japan's overall beer production. The brewers' continuing use of European ingredients and adherence to German brewing methods became their industry's hallmark and the virtual gold standard among domestic brewing companies of the era. In 2011, Kirin Brewery's CEO, Katō Kazuyasu, noted that "although Spring Valley had eventually disappeared, the Japan Brewery Company shared its primary objective of brewing authentic German beer. Veteran German brewmasters were recruited and the most advanced equipment and steaming systems of the time were acquired, all under the mantra of providing Japanese consumers with the most authentic quality and satisfying taste possible."[46] Despite the

Table 3

National imports of malts and hops, 1883-1913

Year	Volume of malts (kL)	Volume of hops (kg)
1883	n.d.	2,070
1884	n.d.	2,062
1885	n.d.	5,714
1886	n.d.	1,114
1887	n.d.	23,500
1888	n.d.	35,116
1889	n.d.	16,090
1890	n.d.	18,342
1891	n.d.	11,610
1892	n.d.	9,658
1893	n.d.	13,579
1894	n.d.	14,730
1895	n.d.	32,820
1896	368,119.9	47,074
1897	419,284.3	50,166
1898	548,832.2	55,017
1899	769,306.2	78,483
1900	1,017,856.2	85,390
1901	1,188,128.3	108,999
1902	538,673.4	45,508
1903	479,530.4	65,818
1904	672,825.5	84,967
1905	742,180.6	86,738
1906	1,202,618.6	158,463
1907	1,147,160.8	145,422
1908	1,312,334.5	132,813
1909	683,915.5	96,342
1910	684,317.8	78,342
1911	474,645.2	122,863
1912	757,674.1	124,753
1913	1,120,474.4	152,333

Source: Kirin biiru KK, *Kirin biiru KK gojū nenshi* [Kirin Brewery Company, Ltd.: Fifty-year history] (Tokyo: Kirin biiru KK, 20 March 1957), 232.

steady growth of Japanese beer makers, producing a truly "Japanese" product was a liability in the eyes of both brewers and consumers. Domestic beers had to appear as German as possible in order to compete with the high quality and reputation of European imports. Hermann Heckert's insistence on these high standards made production more costly than necessary, but it was likewise expected to increase the cachet of the product, along with the company's reputation.[47]

The dependence of Japanese breweries on imported ingredients was also noted by marketplace reporters in both China and Great Britain. In 1889, the *Chinese Times* of Tianjin commented that "efforts are now being made to produce malts and hops of suitable quality in Japan, so as to obviate the necessity for importing these articles, from which, the report avers, the *lager bier* of the Japan Brewery Company is solely made."[48] In 1896, Great Britain's official *Board of Trade Journal* likewise underscored Japan's continuing reliance on German brewmasters:

The chief expert of the Yebisu Beer Brewing Company [Nippon Beer Co., discussed below] has been sent to Germany for two years to study the condition of the German brewing industry with its latest improvements. In a speech on the occasion of a farewell banquet given to this gentleman, and reported in the "Japan Weekly Mail," a director of the Company observed that the brewers of Japan have not only succeeded in nearly putting a stop to the import of most malt liquors into Japan, but now export their produce to China and Singapore, and even as far as Bombay. In fact, the supply is hardly adequate to meet the growing demand ... Of the various fermenting industries of Japan, beer brewing is generally admitted to be one of the most profitable, and this even though malt is imported from abroad. The profits would therefore be very much greater were this material produced at home. The Yebisu Beer Company is paying earnest attention to this point, and is manufacturing malt experimentally from German barley with the latest appliances available. It was for the purpose of investigating this important branch of the industry that the Company decided to despatch its expert to Germany. Success in producing malt in Japan would mark an epoch in the history of beer brewing in the country.[49]

Despite these early forays, Japan's efforts at self-sufficiency would take many years to bear fruit, and expanded domestic production of malts and hops would not deter Japan's brewers from adhering strictly to German recipes, processes, and equipment. In addition, any use of domestic ingredients would very seldom be advertised.

Ironically, in spite of the low tariffs on imported beer, the Japan Brewery's early success was due in part to the "unequal treaties" with the Great Powers. Because the treaties forbade Japanese and foreigners from living together, and foreigners could not travel without special permission, foreign sales agents could not be dispatched to the interior of the country. As a result, the brewery directors hatched a plan to sell their beer at branch stores nationwide, and Glover, the Mitsubishi adviser who had helped found the company, became their point man once more. Glover recommended that the Japan Brewery conclude a sales agency contract with the Japanese retailer Meidi-ya, which could help to promote the brand domestically. An importer and purveyor of foreign goods and beverages since 1885, Meidi-ya is still in business today, and has sixteen supermarket outlets across Japan and one in Amsterdam. Its survival is a significant carry-over from the era of exclusive trade relations between the Dutch and Japanese governments during the Edo period, and thus the story of its founding is well worth examining. Its early operations speak directly to the significant challenges facing a growing number of retail firms during the Meiji era – how to distribute and sell beer to Japanese consumers.

Meidi-ya's first director, Isono Hakaru, found himself heading up the retailer due to his international experience. In 1880, Isono and fellow student Masujima Rokuichirō were sent to London on a business scholarship sponsored by Mitsubishi. Although an expensive investment, training personnel in this manner was routine for major Japanese companies of the Meiji era and later. In London, the two studied and worked in business for six years, returning in 1885 to Japan, where Isono was hired by Mitsubishi's shipping division in Kobe. Mitsubishi had been considering founding a distribution firm in Yokohama specifically to deliver foodstuffs to the many Japanese shipping companies operating there. In 1885, Mitsubishi's president, Iwasaki Yanosuke, and the head of its Yokohama shipping branch, Kondō Yasuhira, agreed to found just such a firm, which was named Meidi-ya. Isono's international experience, his excellent written and spoken English, and the trust he had already established with foreigners made him an ideal candidate to head up the new retail company. Mitsubishi's adviser, Thomas Glover, nominated Isono for the job so enthusiastically that when shareholders demanded that a guarantor stand in as a safeguard, Iwasaki and Kondō personally put up ¥50,000, enabling them to write his contract to be their agent. Naturally, Glover also recommended that Meidi-ya become the sole sales agent for "Kirin Beer." Although Meidi-ya began with just one outlet in Yokohama, that would change swiftly as new branch stores were opened in major cities across Japan.[50]

In the interim, however, Meidi-ya and the Japan Brewery had to cooperate with partner retailers. When the *Yokohama Mainichi* newspaper advertised the launch of "Kirin Beer" from 29 to 31 May 1888, it touted both beer's growing importance and the company's skilled German brewmaster, Hermann Heckert. Nevertheless, the ad listed just *five* sales agencies in only *two* cities where individual consumers, bar owners, or other retailers might purchase "Kirin Beer," underscoring the truly tiny scale of even a major product launch in this era. The firm's sales agencies were:

- Meidi-ya, Yokohama, Kitanakadōri, 4-chōme
- Nishijima-ya, Yokohama, Sakaimachi, 1-chōme
- Miura-ya, Tokyo, Kyōbashi, Owarichō, 2-chōme
- Kame-ya, Tokyo, Kanda-ku, Awajimachi, 2-chōme
- Ise-ya, Tokyo, Hongokuchō, 4-chōme.

In addition, the brewery maintained Copeland's former office at building No. 123, Yamate in Yokohama's foreigner district as its branch store, which we may think of today as a sort of factory outlet. The ad specified the prices for "Kirin Beer," which were competitive, but slightly higher than those of contemporary rivals. A one-gallon cask sold for 60 sen, four dozen large bottles cost ¥8.50, and eight dozen small bottles cost ¥10.50.[51]

"Kirin"'s launch is also illustrative of early efforts to attract consumers with eye-catching labels and logos, many of which imitated the style of contemporary European imports. The Japan Brewery decided initially to feature the rays of the rising sun on its label, but in 1889 the new firm adopted its familiar label and eventual namesake: "Kirin," the giraffe-like unicorn, or "Qilin," from Chinese mythology. The Kirin label design was owned initially by Meidi-ya, but in 1897 it was formally transferred to the brewing company, which has maintained it ever since. Kirin notes that the idea for the unicorn design came from "Guinness Stout," which had been imported to Japan since 1868 and featured a cat on its seal. This had given William Copeland the idea to put a billy goat on the label of his "Bock Beer," which in turn inspired several Japanese brewers to put animals on their own labels.[52] These included "Shibutani Beer," which had a dog; a beer in Kobe that bore a fox; another in Tokyo that featured the head of a rooster; and two that featured lions, Osaka's "Lion Beer" and Chiba's "Noda Beer." The labels of other brands featured a wide variety of images such as sailing ships, cannons, beer barrels, roses, Mt. Fuji, swords, *daruma* dolls, and even a long-nosed *tengu* goblin.[53]

Despite the wide array of competitors, "Kirin"'s reputation as a leading brand was soon well established. In 1891, the *London and China Telegraph* published the firm's report to its shareholders, which boasted:

> The result of the company's business during the past year must be considered satisfactory. Beer is still regarded as a luxury in this country, and the demand for it must greatly be influenced by any causes that affect the prosperity of the people at large. The fact of an increase in the sales conclusively proves the popularity of Kirin beer and its superiority to any other beer; in this connection the directors have pleasure in mentioning that the highest medal awarded to beer at the Japanese National Exhibition of 1890 was gained by Kirin, as

well as the *Jiji Shimpō* [newspaper] Gold Medal for the best beer brewed in Japan.[54]

The Japan Brewery remained officially an English company with a head office at Queens Road No. 15 in Victoria, Hong Kong. None of its managers were Japanese, and its contract sales agent, Meidi-ya, marketed "Kirin Beer" as much to English visitors as it did to Japanese consumers. As a purveyor of imported goods, Meidi-ya even took out whole-page ads in Basil Hall Chamberlain's *A Handbook for Travellers in Japan*, which was printed in several editions in London.[55] Throughout the period, the company also continued to celebrate its German brewmaster, reporting at its eleventh shareholders' meeting in 1895 that its beer "was suitably exhibited at the Kyoto Exhibition of 1895, and carried off the highest medal and certificate awarded to beers, a result on which the company has to congratulate its chief brewer, Mr. Heckert, and its general agents."[56]

It was not until 19 July 1889 that a Japanese person, Shibusawa Eiichi, the founder of the Tokyo Stock Exchange, was brought into the brewery's managing lineup. Shibusawa was an industrialist who is often referred to today as the father of Japanese capitalism. He was instrumental in bringing Western business practices to Japan during the Meiji era, and he introduced many important economic reforms, including modern banks and joint stock corporations. Shibusawa never attended any of the Japan Brewery's leadership meetings, but his signature, in kanji script, can be found in the meeting records, which were otherwise kept exclusively in English. Shibusawa apparently quit the directorship in about 1893 and was thereon paid ¥100; there is no reason recorded for the payment, though we may surmise that it was retirement compensation. The only Japanese person who actually attended directors' meetings was Masujima Rokuichirō, a legal adviser. Given the firm's foreign management, the director of Meidi-ya, Isono Hakaru, played a critical role in connecting the firm to the Japanese market. In December 1897, however, he died suddenly of pneumonia, and the brewery's directors found themselves uncertain whether or how to continue their relationship with Meidi-ya. A call was issued for outside applicants to serve as agents, but when Toyokawa Ryōhei of Mitsubishi offered to continue his guarantee for Meidi-ya's new chosen director, Kōmei Genjirō, the arrangement with Meidi-ya continued. Furthermore, the Japan Brewery soon decided to make the firm its sole contract sales agency *(tokyūyakuten keiyaku)*. The relationship would grow so close that, later, Kōmei would become both the president of Meidi-ya and the director of the renamed Kirin Brewery Company, Ltd.[57]

Turning Japanese: The Founding of the Kirin Brewery Company, Ltd.

After the "unequal treaties" between Japan and the West were revised in 1894, the legal fiction of foreign ownership of the Japan Brewery was unnecessary. Still, although the brewery was located in Yokohama, reestablishing it as a Japanese company proved to be a tricky process. The first step came in 1897, when Japan joined the international gold standard and thus fixed the value of the yen. Consequently, the Japan Brewery, which had been set up on the Hong Kong dollar, had to transfer its capital stock into yen. The company's foreign directors first planned to exchange every HK$100 worth of stock for two ¥50 stock certificates, but the British colonial government of Hong Kong would not approve the exchange. As a result, the Hong Kong dollar–based company was broken up and a new yen-based company was established in its place, also in Hong Kong and under foreign management. The prefix "The" was added to its name, making it *The Japan Brewery*, in order to distinguish between the former and revised firms. By 1899, the company's capital stock had grown to ¥600,000, and a total of nine thousand shares totalling ¥450,000 had been paid up in full.[58]

The company enjoyed steady growth alongside other firms in the industry, although the Russo-Japanese War of 1904-5 did present significant challenges. When The Japan Brewery's year-end financials were reported in the *Japan Weekly Mail* on 4 February 1905, it indicated that while net profits remained above ¥64,000 for the year, stronger headwinds were beginning to blow. The managers reported, "From the 1st of January 1905, the Government has raised the Excise Tax on Beer, and the Income and Business Taxes; the Import Duty on Malts and Hops is doubled, and the Duties on other brewing materials are largely increased. Competition has become keener than before, probably caused by over-production and the decrease in consumption."[59] Faced with these circumstances, the directors agreed that both their brewery and their supply of capital demanded expansion.[60]

Fortunately, an opportunity came in 1905 to purchase the firm and finally establish it in Japan as a Japanese enterprise, thus realizing the plan that had been initiated in 1885. The effort began when Magoshi Kyōhei wrote to The Japan Brewery's chair, James Dodds, offering to buy the brewery. Born in Okayama prefecture in 1844, Magoshi joined the Mitsui trading company in 1876 and ultimately rose to become its Yokohama branch manager.[61] In 1892, he began working with Nippon (Japan) Beer, the brewer of "Yebisu Beer," and in 1896 he retired from Mitsui in order to devote his full attention to the brewery. In 1900, he became Nippon Beer's president, by which time he was known as the Beer King of the Orient *(Tōyō no biiru ō)*.[62] Magoshi's original letter does not survive, but his offer to purchase The Japan Brewery was clearly interesting enough to bring Dodds to Tokyo several times for negotiations. Those talks were challenging, for while Magoshi spoke of his aim to unify Japan's beer industry and make it profitable under the "Kirin" brand, The Japan Brewery's finances did not warrant a sale or merger. Though its shareholders were not earning particularly rich profits, the company's future looked bright, and they were not inclined to sell. Dodds was therefore unmoved by Magoshi's offer, even though his chief occupation, that of brewery director, was not making him a fortune. Perhaps this was because, as Kirin records, Dodds was earning some money on the side by "exporting the antiques of ruined Tokyo nobility" and saving the profits in anticipation of returning home to England.[63] As he looked to the future, unsure of whether to sell, Dodds discussed Magoshi's offer with Kōmei Genjirō, director of the Meidi-ya sales agency.

For some time already, Kōmei had lamented The Japan Brewery's dependence on foreign directors, and when he heard of the possibility of purchasing the firm, he consulted with the president of the Mitsubishi conglomerate, Iwasaki Hisaya. Iwasaki was about to head off on an inspection tour of China, so he invited Kōmei to join him, during which time the two discussed the situation and Iwasaki was persuaded to support the initiative. In the fall of 1906, Kōmei engaged in frequent negotiations, after which a formal purchase application was issued, stating that the project sponsors wished to buy The Japan Brewery for ¥2 million and reestablish it as the Kirin Brewery Company, Ltd.[64] When the offer was presented to the shareholders at a special meeting on 18 December 1906, they gave it their unanimous consent. On 16 January, Kōmei and two company representatives met to sign the agreement, in which the purchasers promised "to do everything possible to deliver to The Japan Brewery 20,250 shares with a face value of ¥50 as soon as possible."[65] The remaining ¥987,500 would be paid in cash. On 22 January 1907, a founding general meeting was held in Kōjimachi, Tokyo, on the top floor of the Mitsubishi Joint Stock Company. There, the shareholders voted to accept the brewery's financial reports, resolved to shoulder the founding expenses, and elected managing officers. The firm's new managing director was Kōmei Genjirō.

On 13 February 1907, at the ninth shareholders' meeting of The Japan Brewery, a special resolution to break up the firm was called for under the Company Ordinances of Hong Kong.[66] On 23 February, the Kirin Brewery Company, Ltd., was formally established in Yokohama. The cash portion of the purchase offer came in the form of corporate bonds, with which the outgoing directors settled the firm's outstanding renovation bills. The details of the purchase were registered with the Yokohama district court on 28 February, and on 1 March 1907 the property and assets of The Japan Brewery, which were valued at ¥2,010,000, were formally transferred to the new firm. On the same day, the Yokohama Tax Office cancelled the former firm's beer brewing licence *(biiru seizō menkyo)*, and the licence application submitted by the new firm was granted.[67]

The company's shareholders had also voted to award a collective bonus payment of ¥20,000 to the directors for their efforts to date. What Kirin's histories do not record, however, was that the bonus payment was met by an objection from J.H. Rosenthal, a shareholder who, according to a report in the *Japan Weekly Mail*, challenged the payment in Yokohama District Court on the very same day, 13 February. This was still relatively new territory for the Japanese legal system, which had only regained jurisdiction over foreigners' civil and criminal activities in 1894 (Japan's new Criminal Code did not even go into effect until 1 October 1908). Despite the objection, the payment and the rest of the special resolution dissolving the company was passed at a special shareholders' meeting on 18 February. Rosenthal and five of his fellow shareholders further questioned the legality of passing such a resolution at a special meeting, rather than at a general shareholders' meeting. Another shareholder, who was also a lawyer, argued that Rosenthal's objection should not be admitted "either by British law or Japanese," but the court agreed to hear the case.[68] On 2 November 1908, Judge Miyake of Yokohama District Court found for Rosenthal, thus nullifying the collective payment to the former company's directors.[69]

As for sales, at the first directors' conference on 13 April 1907, Kirin Brewery again signed a contract for sole sales agency with Meidi-ya, the details of which were as follows:

1 Meidi-ya shall be the sole representative shop both in this country and overseas.
2 The price for four dozen large bottles is ¥11.70, while export is ¥11.35, and the price of a gallon of draft is ¥1.10.
3 The sales of the above are to be on a fixed payment rate.
4 Both companies are to share the advertising costs fifty-fifty annually.
5 It is to be the absolute responsibility of Meidi-ya to handle delivery of products sold.
6 The term of the contract shall be for five years, and if a notice of cancellation is not given six months before that, it shall continue for an additional year.

On 23 April, the process of transferring The Japan Brewery's trademark rights was complete, and operational control was entirely in the hands of the new management by 5 May. Although at the first shareholders' meeting in February the name of the firm had been given as Kirin bakushu kabushiki kaisha (KK), on 5 May the liquidator, a Mr. Bernard, wrote the name in English – Kirin Beer KK – and "biiru" remained in the company's official name thereafter.[70]

Despite the symbolism of the purchase, foreigners still held the vast majority of the shares. Although the liquidator, Mr. Bernard, did not record the individual shareholders' names, in Kirin's first operational report, entitled *Founding Data (Sōritsu jikō)*, their nationalities are listed as follows:

- Foreigners: 95 names, 14,393 shares, ¥719,650
- Chinese: 9 names, 1,582 shares, ¥79,100
- Japanese: 33 names, 4,275 shares, ¥213,750
- Total: 137 names, 20,250 shares, ¥1,012,500.

The new firm thus remained 71 percent foreign-owned, but it was finally a Japanese company both geographically and legally, and its managing director was a Japanese citizen. The legacy of the "unequal treaties" echoed for some time after their revision in 1894, but the "Kirin" brand was at last repatriated.[71] The reorganization also came at a critical time, for, as will be examined in depth in Chapter 2, in June 1905, the *Japan Weekly Mail* reported that rivals Sapporo, Osaka, and Nippon Beer were planning to merge and form a nationwide brewing giant.[72]

Snow Country: The Origins of "Sapporo Beer"

Sapporo's Establishment in Hokkaido
The "Sapporo Beer" label claims that it is "Japan's Oldest Brand," but this claim requires qualification. While "Sapporo" is certainly the oldest brand name produced today, it has not been sold continuously since the firm's founding in Sapporo, Hokkaido, in 1876. More important than its age, however, is the manner in which the firm came to be – as part of a government colonization program spearheaded by Japan's powerful Home Office, which was itself created in 1873. One of the central figures in the young Meiji government was Ōkubo Toshimichi (1830-78), the Lord of the Home Office, known more commonly as the Home Minister. In 1874, Ōkubo issued a memorial on the encouragement of industry *(kangyō kenpakusho)*, which he cited as critical to the strength of the country, arguing that the wealth of a

country's people is determined by its products. His principal desire was the achievement of the policy of "rich nation, strong army" *(fukkoku kyōhei),* an important theme that has been explored by many Western scholars, most notably Richard Samuels.[73] Throughout his service to the government, Ōkubo maintained that an integral step toward national strengthening was encouragement of industry *(shokusan kōgyō seisaku).* The importance of encouraging industry continued to grow with time, due in large part to the government's policy of "northern defence" *(hokuhen no bōbi)* against possible southerly advances by Russia. Security was thus the chief impetus behind the new government's policy of industrial development on Hokkaido, the northernmost of Japan's home islands (known formerly as Yezo or Yesso). At that time, Hokkaido was seen as a vast wilderness; and in pursuit of modernization and enrichment, the Meiji government began planning and creating a second, little Japan on the island. Ōkubo's vision placed the onus for Japan's industrial progress, including that of the beer industry, squarely on the shoulders of the government.[74]

Throughout the 1870s and 1880s, dozens of foreign experts and consultants, known as *oyatoi gaikokujin* (hired foreigners), were brought to Japan to train Japanese technicians and to lead the development of Japan's first industrial plants, infrastructure, and agricultural projects. Japan's early brewers likewise employed many German engineers, but Hokkaido's undeveloped lands offered unique potential for agricultural experimentation as well.[75] As William Wray notes, "Hokkaido was already the focus of intensive study by Japan's new imperial government, which established the Hokkaido Colonization Office (Kaitakushi) in Tokyo in 1869."[76] In 1871, an American adviser to the Colonization Office named Horace Capron (1804-85) reported to its director *(chokuwan),* Kuroda Kiyotaka (1840-1900), that the government should begin cultivating American strains of barley, wheat, rye, and hops on Hokkaido's rich lands. Capron noted that the climate and raw materials in Hokkaido were ideal for growing grains, and he also discovered several species of wild hops. He and others began experimenting with these hops in 1874, and their work generated promising results. In his official report to Kuroda, Capron summarized his assessment of Hokkaido's wild hops:

> Near Saru is one of the head-quarters of the Ainos [indigenous Ainu people], consisting of seven villages with a population of about five hundred inhabitants. Their occupation is principally fishing and hunting; but I found some traces of agriculture, or rather garden culture, along the banks of the river on the good rich soil. Millet and beans formed the principal crops. Wild hops grow frequently in this soil; the specimens I saw looked very much like foreign

ones, and I think would improve by cultivation. Foreign hops imported there would certainly succeed well if the Ainos could be induced after proper instruction to devote themselves to this profitable article of commerce. Of all the localities I have seen during my stay in Hokkaido none seems in my opinion more favourable to the cultivation of hardy foreign fruit as far as both position and soil are concerned.[77]

Kuroda, who would rise to become minister of agriculture and commerce in 1887 and Japan's second prime minister from 1888 to 1889, did not take Capron's suggestions lightly. Convinced that beer was indeed the "beverage of the new era" *(shinjidai no nomimono)*, he spearheaded the plan to develop agriculture in Hokkaido and to capitalize on its produce by establishing a beer brewery in Tokyo.[78]

Pleased with Capron's reports and advice concerning this and many more plans for developing Hokkaido, Japan's Meiji emperor granted him an official audience on 28 March 1875. There, the emperor delivered an address that was translated by the Colonization Office as follows:

Address of the Emperor to Commissioner Capron

Since your engagement with the Kaitakushi, intrusted as you have been with the work for the settlement and development of the Island of Hokkaido (Yesso) you have so assiduously and faithfully executed your responsible duties, and advised the Chokuwan [Kuroda], that the important work of the department has been successfully carried out and it is daily progressing to our satisfaction. Indeed your services were valuable and deserve my high appreciation and it is hardly a matter of doubt, that the future progress of the Island, the fruit of your labor, will much advance the happiness of my whole Empire.

Now, on your return to your country, on the termination of your engagement, I have to acknowledge your valuable services, and wish to express my good wishes for your future prosperity and happiness.[79]

The emperor's address demonstrates the close attention paid by the young imperial government to the development of Hokkaido and the establishment of local coal mines, farms, railways, and food mills. Capron soon sailed home for America, after which Kuroda turned to the business of founding a brewery. Several Japanese were already studying the brewing process in Germany, including one Nakagawa Seibei.[80] Nakagawa's story underscores the challenges and opportunities that faced overseas Japanese students during the early Meiji era, when the country was steadily dispatching studious young men to Europe and America.

In the early 1870s, there were roughly a hundred Japanese students in Germany, most of whom were studying to be doctors, engineers, and military officers. In 1872, Nakagawa travelled to Europe unofficially, without government assistance; in order to support himself while learning a foreign skill he was resigned to working as a domestic servant. He sailed to Germany via England, and when he arrived at the North Sea port of Bremerhaven, he met a fellow Japanese student named Aoki Shūzō. Aoki took Nakagawa under his wing, offered to assist him financially, and advised him to study beer brewing. With Aoki supervising his studies and financing his tuition, the Japanese government agreed to pay the deposit for Nakagawa's enrolment, which underscores the government's interest in this particular industrial skill set. In the summer of 1873, Nakagawa was sent to the Berliner Brauerei-Gesellschaft Tivoli, which had a factory in Fürstenwalde on the Spree River, fifty-five kilometres east of Berlin. He studied there for twenty-six months, learning the entire brewing process, and on 1 May 1875, the Berliner Brauerei conferred on him a certificate of study. German influence on Japan's beer industry was thus not simply a one-way affair headed up by German brewmasters in Japan; it was also initiated by ambitious Japanese students in Europe, at least one of whom had both private and government backing.[81]

In the meantime, Nakagawa's sponsor, Aoki, had become Japan's special ambassador extraordinary and plenipotentiary *(tokumeizenkenkōshi)* to Germany. When Nakagawa's studies were complete, Aoki advised him to return to Japan. In June 1875, Aoki sent a letter to Kuroda Kiyotaka at the Hokkaido Colonization Office, in which he suggested a link between the cultivation of the beer industry in Hokkaido and the cultivation of industry broadly – and he further recommended that Kuroda hire Nakagawa as a brewmaster. Coincidentally, that April a shipment of hops seedlings had arrived in the port of Yokohama from England, and the preparation of the necessary fields in Hokkaido had begun. Kuroda was soon dispatched to the Sapporo central government office, and on 13 May, the hops seedlings were planted there in a 1.35-square-kilometre field. Encouraged, Kuroda sent a report to the office in Tokyo that the preparations were complete. His conclusions would prove to be premature, but his enthusiasm was apparent.[82]

On his return to Japan, Nakagawa took up a position at the Hokkaido Colonization Office, where he was assigned to direct the agricultural section on 24 August 1875. His exact title was "beer brewer" *(bakushu shōzō jin)*, and his salary was ¥50 per month as a ninth-grade civil servant (out of fifteen grades).[83] Besides Nakagawa, very few Japanese really knew the proper taste of beer or how to brew it, so he alone was tasked with drawing up a plan for a fully operational brewery. The job included compiling a list of necessary machinery, supplies, ingredients, and so on, which he submitted to his superior, Murahashi Hisanari, who was a seventh-grade civil servant. Murahashi, in turn, attached it as a circular memo for approval by the directors of the Hokkaido Colonization Office. Nakagawa's needs included

- two items from overseas – hops and yeast
- seven items from Yokohama, including a truck for carrying malts, a barley separator, a malt crusher, and other machinery
- six items from Tokyo, including four kettles, a hoist, and bottles.

He assured his boss that this equipment could outfit a small-scale brewery that could produce 72 koku (13 kL) of beer each year. As for the hops and yeast, Nakagawa contacted his former sponsor, Aoki Shūzō, to have them shipped from Germany. When they had still not arrived by June 1876, Nakagawa advised Murahashi to order them from the United States, but the German supplies arrived at last in July. They were unloaded at Otaru Harbour, in Hokkaido, shortly after the location of the actual brewery was finally decided.[84]

From the outset, the plan had been to build the plant on government land in Tokyo, not in Hokkaido. Although there was a local government office in Sapporo, most of the management of the Hokkaido Colonization Office actually worked under Kuroda Kiyotaka at its main office in Tokyo. Hokkaido was expected to be a useful agricultural base. As the cultivation efforts in Hokkaido continued to go smoothly, however, Murahashi began to question the utility of locating the brewery in the nation's capital. As he grew more familiar with Nakagawa's brewing experience, Murahashi came to recognize the importance of snow – and especially of *ice* – to maintaining the composition of beer during storage and transit. In an age before refrigeration, ice was an essential ingredient that Tokyo could not furnish but that Japan's northernmost island possessed in great quantities and could generate for free. Furthermore, it seemed to Murahashi that the goals of encouraging both industry and agriculture in Hokkaido would be better achieved by building the brewery there. Although preparations for the brewery in Tokyo continued, Murahashi circulated a memo in December 1875 advocating the Hokkaido plan.[85]

Murahashi's memo, entitled "Hokkaido Construction Inquiry," made the following points:

1   Hokkaido had ample wood and a climate ideally suited for making beer.
2   Refrigeration was one of the most important requirements to brew German-style beer, and Hokkaido's large supply of ice and snow meant this would not be a concern.
3   The decision to relocate the equipment from Tokyo to Hokkaido would prove to be economical.

Also, because construction in Hokkaido could begin the next spring, Murahashi closed by pointing out that it was essential for the Colonization Office to decide quickly and begin searching for a suitable water source. The memo was speedily circulated, because the start date of construction in Tokyo was fast approaching, and to Murahashi's great satisfaction, it won the approval of Kuroda Kiyotaka and the other development project managers. Kuroda put his seal on the memo, and with his brush wrote the date "27 December" and the kanji character 北 (north), which was a strong endorsement for the Hokkaido plan. On 28 February 1876, Murahashi determined that the brewery's construction would top ¥8,348, and he therefore sought a temporary advance until the end of the building phase.[86]

Even before setting off for Sapporo, Murahashi ordered the local project managers there to accelerate their experimental hops production program. At the end of April 1876, the project managers visited the residence of *oyatoi gaikokujin* (hired foreigners) agricultural expert Edwin Dun (1848-1931) in Sapporo to ask for his assistance with the cultivation of hops. Murahashi set sail for Sapporo in late May in order to select suitable sites for not only the brewery but also a winery and a spinning plant for which he was also responsible. At that time, Sapporo was home to roughly twenty-six hundred people living in about nine hundred households.[87] Designed with the aid of hired foreigners, it featured a grid plan of streets at right angles, resembling an American city. At its heart was a main street on an east-west axis, north of which stood the major government offices, and south of which stood the residents' houses. Murahashi decided to build the spinning plant and the wine and beer breweries next to the central government office. The beer brewery was located near Gangi-dōri, near present-day North Nijō, in east 4-chōme, next to the Toyohira River.[88]

Nakagawa took charge of drafting the plans for the brewery, which was to be constructed on a 3,600 *tsubo* site (1.2 hectares; 1 tsubo = 3.3 square metres). While awaiting the arrival of the raw materials and equipment, the construction team broke ground on 27 June 1876. The machinery was installed by 8 September, and three fifteen-metre lead pipes were hooked up to a series of well pumps to provide the water needed to brew 250 koku (45 kL) per year.

The brewery, which was referred to contemporarily as the Hokkaido Colonization Office Brewery *(Kaitakushi jōzōsho)*, was finished on 23 September 1876, shortly after the winery and the spinning mill. (Hereafter, until its sale to private investors in 1886, the beer brewing operation is referred to simply as the "Sapporo" brewery, after its location and the name of its brand.) A ceremony was held on that date to mark the grand opening of all three facilities, and all of the key personnel from the Sapporo central government office came out in their best attire, along with all of the men and women who worked at the three plants.[89] Almost 130 years later, in commemoration of his efforts to convince Japan's government to establish the country's first public brewery in Sapporo instead of Tokyo, a bronze bust of Murahashi Hisanari was unveiled in the garden of the Hokkaido governor's official residence in Sapporo in 2005.[90]

Targeting Japan's Elite Consumers: Sapporo Begins Brewing

Nakagawa Seibei's efforts to produce Sapporo's first batch of beer came at a remarkable time for Japan and its young imperial government. Although brewing operations began in September 1876, getting under way proved challenging, because both the volume and quality of native barley grown in Hokkaido were deemed insufficient. Instead, local farmers had to grow a few American species, as well as a species grown on the government's experimental farms in Tokyo. During the initial brewing process, Nakagawa used hops imported from America as well as Germany, and the yeast that he had ordered from Germany. Hokkaido experienced an especially mild winter that year, and as the harbour at Otaru did not freeze over, Murahashi hoped to ship out the first batch of beer in mid-January 1877. The yeast, however, did not start brewing as expected, which caused a delay, and by January, the project managers at the Tokyo office were growing anxious for the shipments to begin.

Finally, in late May, the plant succeeded in producing beer. Here is where we find evidence of just how unprepared the firm was to sell its new product (a theme that Sapporo's histories do not discuss, but which we may easily infer). To begin with, the plant did not even have any bottles on hand. On 28 May, the brewery sent a telegram to Tokyo, ordering five thousand large empty bottles. Because there were as yet no glass bottle plants in Japan, the Tokyo office began placing orders and gathering foreign-made bottles. Soon afterward, Murahashi had to cable the Tokyo office and order more bottles, as well as a shipment of wooden casks. Only at this point did the brewers begin to wrestle with a name for their product, settling on "Sapporo Cold Beer." Their plan was to focus their print advertisements on the theme of German brewing laws, which were famous for assuring purity. The term "lager beer" was settled on as well, which the managers decided should be sold as mature, aged beer, as in Germany. The description "cold beer" *(hiya bakushu)*, however, did not exactly reflect the concept of properly aged beer, so on 6 June, the directors decided to change the name to "Sapporo Cold-Brewed Beer" *(hiyazei bakushu)*, and not a moment too soon. A government ship named the *Hakodate-maru* was dispatched from Tokyo to collect the first batch. When it called at Otaru Harbour on 20 June, the beer was loaded aboard together with a large volume of ice, lest the precious cargo spoil during the hot journey back to the nation's capital. As Nakagawa Seibei studied traditional brewing in Germany, he was not taught to heat-treat (pasteurize) the beer after bottling, which is a process that kills the yeast and halts the fermentation process. Owing to the presence of active yeast inside the bottles, unheated beer was prone to changes in taste and quality, especially at the height of summer. Preservation and shipping were therefore major problems in that era. Consequently, the first batch, totalling twenty dozen large bottles and nine casks, amounting to 7 koku (13 kL), was shipped to Tokyo on ice.[91]

The ship landed in Tokyo on 23 June 1877, and the beer was promptly stored in a cold warehouse in Hakosaki. The fledgling brewery's managers intended to target Japan's most elite consumers, so their first beer shipment would serve as gifts to key government ministries and agencies. The aim was to establish beer as a beverage worthy of Japan's ruling class by encouraging them to drink it. Therefore, on 26 June, the officers of the Hokkaido Colonization Office presented a box of beer to government ministers and several senior officials in the Imperial Household Ministry. Afterward, the ministry continued to order more beer, both for ministry officials and reportedly even for members of the imperial family, including the queen mother. Nakagawa Seibei also sent a special request on 12 June, asking the Tokyo Industrial Encouragement Office to deliver a report to the Tokyo household of his former benefactor, Ambassador Aoki Shūzō, who was still serving in Berlin. Nakagawa's report said that he had become a brewmaster due to Aoki's guidance and support while in Europe, and owing to his deep debt of gratitude, Nakagawa wished that he could send him a taste of the first batch.[92]

Sapporo's directors also targeted another branch of Japan's ruling class – the senior leadership of the nation's new Imperial Japanese Army. On 5 July, the *Hakodate-maru* set sail from Sapporo to Tokyo with another 18 koku (3.2 kL) of beer, a portion of which was sent to army headquarters in Kyoto. At that time, from January to September 1877, the army was waging the Southwestern War against the rebellious western province of Satsuma. Known to Westerners as the Satsuma Rebellion, the conflict pitted Japan's imperial forces against the traditionalist leader Saigō Takamori (1828-77), who himself had helped to put the imperial government in power in the late 1860s. In support of the war effort, Kuroda Kiyotaka and other senior government officials were sent to the front to assist the army staff officers, and Kuroda arranged to bring "Sapporo Beer" with him. Another 37 koku (6.7 kL) was soon shipped to the front via Tokyo, arriving at Kagoshima, the capital of Satsuma province, on 10 July. Not long afterward, more beer was sent to the Imperial Household Ministry and the senior officers at Imperial Army headquarters. Sapporo also sent five dozen bottles to the development office in nearby Hakodate, also on Hokkaido.

Surprisingly, however, it was only at that point that Sapporo's directors actually drafted a cursory plan to begin selling their beer. They began by shipping three koku (0.5 kL) to Hakodate on 5 July. Before the Meiji Restoration, Hakodate had been one of the first ports opened to Westerners, and as the population was even larger than that of Sapporo, foreign ships called there often. News of Hokkaido's new brewery was even reported in 1879 in the esteemed British journal *Nature*, which assessed its prospects as follows:

> In a note on brewing contained in a report on Sapporo and Ishcari [River] (Japan) we read that the beer is poor, weak stuff that will not keep. In course of time, however, it is fully expected that the art of brewing will succeed, more especially as a native director has spent several years in America and Europe devoting his attention to brewing. The hops used, it seems, are imported, and foreign hop seed has been sown, the plants raised from which appear to be doing well. The wild hops, which are found in great abundance on the road from Morarau to Sapporo, and have been found to be unsuitable for brewing in their wild state, are now being cultivated, as it is supposed that by care and attention they will prove to be as good if not better than foreign hops. Consequently, great pains are now being taken with these hop plantations.[93]

Despite the above assessment of Sapporo's early product, on 29 August, Murahashi received word that the beer was running short in Hakodate due to the great volume being sold to thirsty sailors arriving aboard foreign warships. The brewery stepped up production in response to their demands, but if "Sapporo Cold-Brewed Beer" was to survive, its producers needed to devise a genuine program for domestic sales in Tokyo and beyond.[94]

Sapporo's Early Marketing and Sales

While planning "Sapporo Beer"'s Tokyo debut, the brewery's directors consulted with the owner of a shop in Ueno Park and asked him about the prices of the city's competing brands. On 12 July 1878, chief engineer Nakagawa Seibei drew up a survey on beer prices in the Tokyo-Yokohama market, which he reported as follows:

1   London and Bass large casks (50 gallons), each equivalent to approximately 330 bottles at 10 sen per bottle: 30 Western silver dollars *(yōgin)*.
2   London and Bass casks, each holding about four dozen bottles: ¥9.50. Lowest price for a large bottle: 25 sen.
3   Yokohama; Amanuma American-made beer *(Beikoku jinsei bakushu)*. Large bottle: 20 sen, small: 15 sen.
4   Tokyo; Koishikawa Beer, discounted by retailers. 1 dozen bottles: ¥1.75, large bottle: 17 sen, small: 11 sen.
5   Tokyo; Shinbashi Araganema Beer, discounted by retailers. 1 dozen bottles: ¥1.75, large bottle: 17 sen, small: 11 sen.[95]

In comparison, quality sake at that time sold for an average of 4.5 sen per *shō* (1.8 litres), making it by far the least expensive alcoholic beverage on the market. Bass beer sold on draft remained the least expensive beer at just 13 sen per glass, which gave Bass the upper hand in the Tokyo area.[96] In order to cover its costs, Sapporo would have to set its prices lower than the foreign bottled imports, but higher than Bass draft.[97]

In its first real public debut, "Sapporo Cold-Brewed Beer" appeared as one of five entrants in the First Domestic Industrial Encouragement Exhibition *(Dai ikkai naikoku kangyō hakurankai)*, held in Ueno, Tokyo, in late June and July 1877. Several such exhibitions were staged in Japan during the late nineteenth century, in order to promote technical capability in domestic manufacturing. They provided not only publicity for participant firms, but sometimes cash prizes and even the adoption of their wares by government ministries or agencies. Often, members of Japan's nobility and the imperial family attended, and industry leaders vied for the title of "best in show." After the exhibition, in September 1877, Sapporo staged an official product launch in Tokyo, called a *haraisage* (put up for sale). To announce the sale, the development office placed five advertisements in each of three Tokyo newspapers, including the *Yūbin Yōchi Shimbun*. The ads featured the following prices:

• Big bottle: 16 sen each, ¥1.60 per dozen, ¥15.20 per ten dozen
• Small bottle: 10 sen each, ¥1 per dozen, ¥9.50 per ten dozen

In addition to the newspaper ads, Sapporo also printed a handbill for distribution by its sales staff that stressed the difference between Sapporo's "cold-brewed" beer and other beers. In July 1878, Kuroda Kiyotaka reported in a company circular memo that the handbill was "easy enough even for women and children to understand," and so he advocated that the phrase "cold-brewed beer" should continue to be stressed by sales representatives. He also advised that the company's ads should claim that beer is recommended for consumption even by those worried about weak digestion.[98]

The inaccuracy of this claim notwithstanding, sales of "Sapporo Cold-Brewed Beer" rose steadily over the next two years, even though beer remained largely an unknown quantity for most consumers. Sapporo therefore had to explain to most attendees of fairs and exhibitions just what beer was. As Penelope Francks points out, although some traditional modes of life faded away during the early Meiji years, Japanese wares and luxury products often remained true to their original designs, and remained very popular with consumers.[99] Western goods were merely one part of a rising tide of consumer product manufacturing during the late nineteenth century, much of which actually introduced traditional Japanese products to rural households in unprecedented volumes. Still, like many Western commodities, beer gradually carved a niche in Japan's shifting beverage market, becoming a staple in sophisticated urban inns and teahouses, as well as at a growing number of urban saloons, taverns, beer salons, and restaurants. But whether it was served in a traditionally Japanese or a Western-style establishment, domestically produced beer remained a staunchly Western product by virtue of its German brewmasters and its largely European ingredients.[100]

In 1882, the Hokkaido Colonization Office was abolished and three prefectures were created in Hokkaido: Sapporo, Hakodate, and Nemuro. Four years later, in 1886, these three prefectures were themselves abolished and replaced by the Hokkaido Government.[101] In the same year, the former Colonization Office in Sapporo was sold to the Ōkura Trading Company, which was then betting heavily on Japan's growing beer industry. As noted above, Ōkura also purchased shares in the newly founded Japan Brewery in Yokohama in 1886. In December 1887, however, a group of entrepreneurs led by pioneering businessmen Shibusawa Eiichi and Asano Sōichirō bought the plant from the Ōkura Trading Company and reestablished it in 1888 as the Sapporo Breweries Company, Limited.[102] Even further intertwining these two firms' early histories, Shibusawa would join the board of directors of the Japan Brewery Company in 1889. Also in that year, Sapporo Breweries imitated its chief domestic rivals by bringing aboard a German brewmaster named Max Pormann, who would later be instrumental in setting up the

Osaka Beer Company in 1889.[103] Pormann helped Sapporo to further refine its brewing processes, and the firm was careful to note his expertise in its contemporary advertisements for "Sapporo Beer."[104]

Sapporo's managers also refined their brand image by focusing on the label and chose to use the familiar image of a star inside a circle, which symbolized the pioneering North Star. By the 1880s, the quality of the labels was prioritized so highly that the directors arranged to print them at the federal currency office of the Ministry of Finance. Furthermore, the designers chose to affix the label rather high on the side of the bottle, leaving a space beneath to enable "polite handling" of the product. Whether served by a beautiful geisha at one of Kyoto's top teahouses, or simply by a fashionable urban homeowner, this positioning of the label permitted servers to pour "Sapporo Beer" for their guests without obscuring the brand name or logo. Indeed, no such opportunity to showcase the brand was left to chance. For a time, Sapporo even affixed a third, supporting label between the neck and bottle labels, on which the date of production was printed. The best hosts would, of course, strive to serve only the freshest beer.[105]

In the 1890s, Sapporo also began working with advertising traders, who aided the firm in publicizing store openings and big sales. Despite its modest advertising, however, Sapporo's product was well received by consumers. In surveys conducted by the Hokkaido Colonization Office, habitual drinkers reported that they liked the coldness *(reitan)* of the product, which they said had a different flavour than that of imported beers. On the subject of flavour, a late-nineteenth-century American music critic and travel writer named Henry Theophilus Finck described his impressions of "Sapporo Beer," which he first tried near Fukushima during a guided tour of northern Japan in 1894:

> Although there was water, water everywhere, and Yabi and the runners had their tea every hour or two, I had not a drop to drink till we came to the inn where we lunched. I made up for lost time by drinking two bottles of beer, with but slender assistance from my friend, who did not care much for that bitter beverage. I was sorry not to be able to get any more of the Sapporo beer, which I had found much better and more Germanic than the products of Tōkyō and Yokohama breweries; although I was glad enough to find that the latter are now to be found in every Japanese village, at a price varying from twenty-two to thirty cents per quart bottle.[106]

Despite Finck's relief that he could find beer in many Japanese villages, the number of public establishments where a person could drink beer was still quite small at that time, and those that did exist typically sold foreign-made beers, often more cheaply than domestic brews. In order for Japan's domestic brewers to compete effectively against imported brands, Japan would have to reestablish sovereign control over its borders and raise its import duties.

Culling the Herd: The Beer Tax and the Dawn of the Beer Sales War

Until 1894, the "unequal treaties" left Japan unable to control its own trade tariffs, and the *ad valorem* tax on imported beer was just 5 percent. Kirin notes that the result of this low tariff barrier was a wave of imported Western foods and beverages. Even with low tariffs, imported beer was twice the cost of domestic beer, but the imports prospered, and they soon encroached on the market for sake.[107] In response, domestic beer brewers had essentially three ways to compete. The first was by raising import tariffs, but as Japan still did not have tariff autonomy at that time, such action was impossible. The second option was a domestic beer industry protection policy *(hodō seisaku)*. This policy had already been pursued since 1875, when the Meiji government chose not to tax the beer industry, but even this was not a sufficient means of import prevention *(bōatsu)*. The third option was to make imports appear inferior, but because domestic beer sold for less than half the cost of imported beer through the 1880s, consumers continued to regard the more expensive foreign imports as superior in quality. This only underscored the importance for Japanese brewers of adhering strictly to German recipes using imported ingredients. The brewers that maintained this policy were rewarded with steadily increasing sales, while foreign imports dropped off dramatically between 1890 and 1900.[108]

The breweries that cultivated successful recipes and manufacturing processes gradually challenged the dominant Western brands. On 13 and 15 June 1890, the *Tokyo Nichi Nichi* newspaper wrote about the transformation of Japan's beer market and the manner in which brands like Kirin had already begun to challenge foreign brands. In an article entitled "On Kirin Beer," the paper reported:

Well now, as for the start of the sale of Kirin Beer, it began back in 1888, and already by that time a number of years had passed since the establishment of the beer industry in this country, back when the imports of foreign beer on the left and right were not a moderate force. On the contrary, imports of foreign beer increased more and more every year, and in 1878, they amounted to over ¥460,000, which was a very large sum. But then, this Kirin Beer became known to the world. Its sales rose immensely and in 1889, the imports of

Table 4

Imports of alcoholic beverages, 1890-1906

Year	Beer Volume (kL)	Beer Cost (¥)	Wine (kL)	Brandy, whisky, and liqueurs (kL)
1890	611.9	154,800	754.4	97.0
1891	451.9	114,279	914.8	102.1
1892	464.0	128,514	947.0	97.6
1893	347.3	104,928	1,179.6	102.3
1894	152.1	50,161	1,454.3	173.2
1895	235.2	76,635	2,232.7	853.4
1896	238.5	66,760	2,552.9	158.0
1897	154.8	51,102	2,228.9	188.0
1898	191.0	64,799	3,558.0	361.0
1899	117.1	34,631	1,529.3	99.0
1900	100.1	42,700	1,626.6	208.9
1901	72.3	33,474	1,854.0	146.8
1902	87.3	40,012	1,590.1	162.2
1903	49.8	22,895	1,321.5	189.4
1904	53.9	23,497	1,178.8	266.6
1905	49.6	24,859	1,876.2	338.2
1906	65.3	32,026	2,120.3	511.6

Note: Shaded area denotes higher import tariffs in effect.

Source: Kirin biiru KK, *Kirin biiru KK gojū nenshi* [Kirin Brewery Company, Ltd.: Fifty-year history] (Tokyo: Kirin biiru KK, 20 March 1957), 232.

foreign beer dropped below their majority [market share] of the previous year, and in that period the price of foreign beers dropped sharply to half of what it was before.[109]

When Japan finally achieved tariff autonomy with the revision of the "unequal treaties" in 1894, it did not raise import duties immediately. In 1897, the government finally passed a specific duty tax known as Law No. 14, which raised the tariff on foreign beers to 25 percent. A dozen small bottles of imported beer were taxed 38.5 sen, and on large bottles the tax was 51.5 sen. In 1901, the tax rate was raised to 30 percent, which amounted to 10.4 sen for every litre, and ¥18.76 per koku. The result was a sharp drop in imports of foreign beer, which had already fallen steadily since 1887 (see Table 4). Significantly, the new import tariffs did not apply to wine, brandy, whisky, or liqueurs, which were not yet brewed in Japan in significant quantities.

The new tariffs on imports were a welcome development for Japan's domestic brewers, but this new protective measure came at a dear price, for in

Table 5

Changes in beer production and sales tax rates and beer prices (¥), 1901-18

Date tax rate took effect	Tax rate		Minimum retailers' price per large bottle	Notes
	Production tax per koku	Sales tax per large bottle		
1 October 1901	7.0	0.025	0.19	Establishment of Beer Tax
1 April 1904	7.50	0.027	0.20	Special Tax
1 January 1905	8.00	0.029	–	Special Emergency Tax
16 March 1908- 31 March 1918	10.00	0.036	0.22	

Source: Kirin biiru KK, *Kirin biiru KK gojū nenshi* (Kirin Brewery Company, Ltd.: Fifty-year history) (Tokyo: Kirin biiru KK, 20 March 1957), 248-49.

1901 the government also imposed a new domestic beer production tax, which totalled ¥7 per koku. The tax was raised to ¥7.50 per koku in 1904, and continued to climb to reach ¥10 per koku in 1908 (see Table 5). This new tax was a death knell for the vast majority of Japan's small brewing firms, many of which simply ceased operations overnight, completely unable to foot the tax bill.[110] Roughly seventy brewers were in business prior to Japan's domestic beer tax of 1901, brewing approximately a hundred brands, but the survivors of that industry cull were limited to the companies in Table 6.

The new tax was not imposed at the point of sale, but at the point of bottling – meaning that the weakest firms could not afford to finish the product in their kettles without devastating their own finances. Those driven out were generally small firms or sole operators, which did not have the flexibility to endure such wildly fluctuating business conditions profitably. Wealthy rural families and individual entrepreneurs who had once rushed into the industry intent on serving only their local areas panicked when the wave broke, and they fled the beer business in droves. Mitsuuroko Beer, for example, which had been brewed in Kōfu since 1874, was pulled from the market as soon as the new tax was imposed. Thus, the weak firms fell prey not to the strong, but to the determined tax policy of the Ministry of Finance, and in the end the larger companies annexed many of their smaller rivals. (See the appendix for a list of Japan's beer brewers and their brands, many of which left the industry due to the new production tax.)[111]

From the fray emerged four market leaders (see Figure 1 for a timeline of Japan's leading domestic brewers):

Table 6

Beer companies, locations, and production volumes, 1901

Brand	Company	Location	Production (koku)	Production (kL)
Yebisu Beer	Nippon Beer Co., Inc.	Tokyo	32,956	5,945.0
Asahi Beer	Osaka Beer Co., Inc.	Osaka	29,658	5,350.0
Kirin Beer	Japan Brewery Co., Ltd.	Yokohama	15,800	2,850.2
Sapporo Beer	Sapporo Breweries Co., Ltd.	Sapporo	13,591	2,451.7
Kabuto Beer	Marusan Beer Brewery Co., Inc.	Aichi	7,839	1,414.1
Tokyo Beer	Tokyo Beer Co., Inc.	Kanagawa	3,500	631.4
Asada Beer	Asada Brewery Co., Inc.	Tokyo	600	108.2
Others	16 plants		17,486	3,154.3
Total	32 plants		121,430	21,904.8

Source: Kirin biiru KK, *Kirin biiru KK gojū nenshi* [Kirin Brewery Company, Ltd.: Fifty-year history] (Tokyo: Kirin biiru KK, 20 March 1957), 54.

- The Japan Brewery Co., Inc.: brewer of "Kirin Beer" in Yokohama
- Sapporo Breweries, Ltd.: brewer of "Sapporo Beer" in Sapporo City
- Nippon Beer Co., Inc.: brewer of "Yebisu Beer" in Tokyo
- Osaka Beer Co., Inc.: brewer of "Asahi Beer" in Osaka.

None of these firms could boast a truly nationwide reach in 1901, but even by 1890 the top three brewers had earned significant market share and recognition by Japanese consumers, as well as the attention of the press. In an article on beer exports on 13 and 15 June 1890, the *Tokyo Nichi Nichi* reported that "this Kirin Beer especially was curbing imports of foreign beer, and the road for exports of Japanese beer was opening up for the first time. It was shipping to Korea, Vladivostok, Taiwan, Shanghai, Tianjin, Shandong, Fuzhou, Amoy, Manila, Saigon, Singapore, Batavia; plus Colombo and Calcutta, which was just under the equator."[112] Exports boomed again following the Sino-Japanese War of 1894-95, and by 1900, achieving a modest share of the East Asian beer market began to look like a distinct possibility to Japan's leading brewers. In 1903, at the Fifth National Industrial Encouragement Exhibition, "Kirin Lager" was awarded a certificate of merit, and its brewer, The Japan Brewery Company, was officially commended for "curbing imports and charging ahead with exports" *(yunyū no bōatsu, yushutsu no sakigake).*[113] Kirin was thus named a "formidable beer exporter" *(biiru yushutsu no kai)*

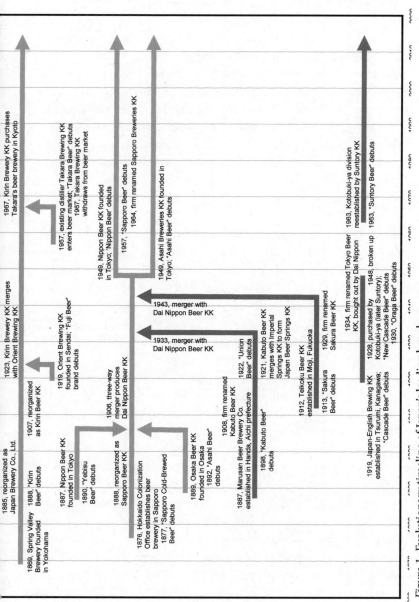

Figure 1 Evolutionary timeline of Japan's leading beer brewers

Source: Kirin Beer K.K., *Biiru to bunmei kaika no Yokohama: Kopurando seitan 150-nen kinen* (Tokyo, JP: Kirin Beer K.K., 1984), 68–69.

by Japan's government; Japanese brands had begun to take on Western beers in neighbouring parts of Asia.

Corroborating this claim, in 1907 the US beer industry trade publication *American Brewer's Review* reported:

> The establishing of foreign breweries at Shanghai and in northern China, such as the Anglo-German Brewing Company, at Kiaochow [today Jiaozhou], has interfered and will continue to interfere somewhat with the sale of Japanese beers in their local districts, but in Korea and Manchuria there is an opportunity which the Japanese are not slow to grasp. The relatively low price of the beverage, the nearness of the market, and cheap transportation, and the fact that the Japanese already in those districts will use and introduce among the native element a demand for the commodity, give Japan every advantage over foreign competition.[114]

Despite the increased competition and opportunity for export sales, however, Japanese beer was still not marketed as a fully Japanese product. The brewers were very consciously producing a transplanted Western product, and they continued to advertise their European ingredients, methods, and brewmasters very heavily, especially in the newspapers.[115]

Reaching New Professional Consumers: Beer Halls and Early Beer Marketing

At home in Japan, competition in the beer market was also intensifying, and it began to weigh on the profit margins of the four market leaders. All of them were matched closely in terms of production equipment, and as domestic demand increased (see Table 1 above), they competed more fiercely with each passing season. To advance both sales and brand awareness, Osaka Beer opened an Asahi Beer Hall in nearby Kyoto in June 1896, where staff served cold beer to the thirsty tourists who flocked to the popular city during the hot summer months.[116] Soon the phrase "beer hall" became familiar throughout Japan's major cities. Although the word "beer" had long since been written in Japan's phonetic *katakana* script as *biiru*, the *ru* was dropped when saying or writing the English phrase "beer hall." The preferred form thus became *biya-hōru*, which rolled off the tongue much more easily.[117] On 6 August 1899, the *Yomiuri* newspaper reported that Nippon Beer had just opened Tokyo's first beer hall – the Yebisu Beer Hall, near Shinbashi Bridge.[118] This venture by Magoshi Kyōhei was both a retail and marketing opportunity that effectively "killed two birds with one stone" *(isseki nichō)*, promoting the Yebisu brand and its sales simultaneously.[119] Soon afterward, the city of Tokyo announced the grand opening of the Tokyo Beer Hall in Asakusa Park, which it advertised in the *Asahi* newspaper in November 1899.[120] Guests were promised "Western food" *(yōshoku)*, and cups of beer costing 10 sen for large, 5 sen for small. Not to be left out, Kirin advertised the launch of its own Kirin Beer Hall in Tokyo just days later.[121] It also constructed a temporary Kirin Beer Hall for the Nagoya Fair in 1900, designed to resemble Kinkakuji, Kyoto's famous Golden Pavilion. The fair was hosted by three cities and over twenty surrounding prefectures, making it an excellent venue for Kirin to expand awareness of its brand. In 1904, Sapporo too opened a beer garden during the months of April and May, after which it established a permanent beer garden in a park along the Sumida River, not far from the famous Tsukiji fish market.[122] Contemporary Tokyo resident Arthur Lloyd described the scene as he sailed past by boat:

> On both sides of the river are to be seen noblemen's mansions, with beautifully laid-out gardens, and some of the most noted restaurants in Tokyo lie on either hand of us. It is a sign of the times, of the coming reign of materialism, that one of these noble and beautiful gardens has recently passed into the hands of the Sapporo Beer-Brewing Company. Thanks to the kindness of German brewers, Japan now possesses several excellent brands of beer, and the Japanese has not required much instruction in the art of beer-drinking. He does not, however, quite understand yet how to handle his beer, and frequently allows it to get too hot in summer or too cold in winter.[123]

More beer halls and gardens were advertised each year thereafter, enabling the leading brewers to ship increasing volumes of beer to Japan's major cities. Despite the rapid growth, however, they still struggled to earn significant revenues. Osaka, Nippon, and Sapporo were particularly strained, and the accelerated production, which was driven by an emerging price war, began to overwhelm their employees. Osaka Beer's postwar successor firm, Asahi Breweries, refers to the era as an "East-West free-for-all fight" *(tōzai konsen)*, due to the geographical divide between the Tokyo- and Osaka-based firms. As a result, the three companies began to consider an alternative to this increasingly fierce domestic market competition.[124] The first attempt to broker a ceasefire was made not by the breweries' directors, but by a group of their factory employees. In early 1900, workers from Sapporo Breweries, Osaka Beer, and Nippon Beer met quietly in Tokyo at the Celestial Hill tea ceremony cottage (Hoshiboshioka charyō), where they staged the first Beer Industry

Workers Roundtable Conference *(Dai ikkai biiru gyōsha kondankai)*. Their discussions were preliminary, and though they failed to reach a conclusion, they agreed to meet again the following year. In 1901, the companies' varying interests and relationships continued to complicate the discussion, which again ended without reaching a consensus on how to staunch the bleeding. All the while, President Magoshi of Nippon Beer continued to ramp up his promotional efforts, targeting Japan's elite consumers even more directly.

Magoshi's marketing strategies were simple but innovative. He was the first to place great importance on advertising, and he took a variety of approaches to reach new beer consumers.[125] First, whenever his firm delivered the first shipment of the year to any city or town, his deliverymen would ride in aboard horse-drawn wagons, sporting traditional *happi* coats emblazoned with the company's logo. For the traditional *shōgatsu* holiday at New Year's, Magoshi also brought a *hanabi* expert to Tokyo from Nagoya to surprise the crowds with fireworks. Significantly, he claimed that Japan's emerging beer consumers could be divided into four key groups: geisha, actors *(yakusha)*, scholars *(gakusha)*, and doctors *(isha)*. Magoshi believed that by earning the endorsement of geisha and actors he could earn wider recognition through word of mouth *(kuchikomi)*; through acceptance by scholars he could earn added prestige; and through sales to doctors he hoped to receive publicity that beer was good for health *(kenkō ni yoi biiru)*. Indeed, Magoshi strove to expand acceptance and consumption of beer by medical professionals especially. In 1903, he invited thirteen hundred attendees of Japan's second annual national medical conference to visit his brewery. Hundreds of medical professors, army and navy doctors, and hospital chiefs came to tour the Nippon Beer plant and to sample its wares. Soon thereafter, over three thousand attendees of a pharmacology conference held at the Koishikawa Botanical Gardens came to be entertained at Nippon Beer's Tokyo branch office over a period of seven days. In 1904, Britain's *Strand Magazine* published a photograph of the giant wooden "Yebisu" beer barrel that Magoshi erected for Japan's fifth and final Industrial Encouragement Exhibition in Osaka in 1903. Measuring fifteen metres high by nine metres in diameter and with walls half a metre thick, the interior was fitted out as a beer hall with a large counter and ten round tables that could accommodate five or six thirsty patrons at a time.[126] In these ways, Magoshi's plan to give beer wider recognition among Japan's rising professional classes carried knowledge of "Yebisu Beer" home to nearly every corner of Japan, where the product was often unavailable. By capitalizing on the aspirations of rural elites, especially those who had visited Tokyo, "Yebisu" earned significant cachet during the early twentieth century.[127]

Conclusions

Beer consumption was quite limited in the early Meiji era, confined initially to the foreigners' district of Yokohama and then chiefly to Japan's major cities. Yokohama was truly Japan's front door during the waning years of the Tokugawa shogunate and the dawning imperial age. Few ordinary people did business directly with foreigners during the late nineteenth century, but curious Japanese gradually came to try Western food and drink, and as more foreign sailors called at Yokohama, beer breweries were soon established there. After the collapse of the shogunate in 1867 and Japan's abolition of the caste system in 1871, entrepreneurial Japanese of any social background were free to go into business, and many pursued investment opportunities brought by the country's efforts at industrialization. Breweries were among the first such opportunities to present themselves, especially because pioneers like William Copeland had already laid the industry's foundations. As these pioneers failed or retired, Japanese were eager to step in and try their hands at producing this exotic new beverage, especially as there were few barriers to entering this market. Most such efforts were small, independent breweries, often run by enterprising landowners who were experienced at brewing sake or miso, but a few were much larger operations; a handful of them survived the nineteenth century.

By the early twentieth century, beer found its way into urban taverns, hotels, and traditional inns and teahouses, where for many years it remained the province of the relatively wealthy. Slowly, Japanese of means came to accept and to enjoy the taste of beer, and many establishments earned prestige from serving this unique Western beverage. Given beer's comparatively high cost, brewers were obligated to target a wealthy clientele at the outset. In order to showcase its wares to Japan's ruling class, Sapporo shipped its first batches from Otaru Harbour directly to government bureaucrats, senior military officers, and members of the royal family. These elite consumers enjoyed the new product, and they ordered more. Clever brewers like Magoshi Kyōhei likewise targeted their early marketing efforts toward Japan's new professional classes: doctors, scholars, and entertainers. Magoshi staged free tastings and tours at his brewery in Tokyo, confident that these celebrities and emerging technocrats would lend an air of sophistication to beer consumption. As these talented and educated modern figures returned to their respective corners of Japan, they brought with them not only knowledge of beer, but often a continued demand for it. Still, though it was brewed in Japan, beer's prestige was derived from its undeniably European heritage, which demanded strict adherence to quality ingredients and German purity laws.

As Japan's brewers worked to expand their customer base during the Meiji era, they faced a series of daunting technological, financial, and logistical challenges. The tasks of sourcing water and ingredients, delivering them to the plant, producing a quality product, shipping it capably, and earning a profit were extremely difficult. Most Japanese industries experienced similar growing pains during this period, and the brewers' histories reveal, often unintentionally, just how unprepared they were to bottle, ship, market, price, and sell their products at the outset. Sapporo's founders in particular had no real business plan when the Hokkaido Colonization Office laid in its first batch, and even as the brewery did so it rather inexplicably lacked the necessary bottles. Sapporo's brief market survey, tracking contemporary competitors' prices in Tokyo, was hardly the sort of product launch that we might expect to see associated with a costly government development plan.

Standing in sharp contrast to Sapporo's somewhat haphazard bureaucratic direction prior to its sale to private investors in 1886 was the significant private-sector role played by Mitsubishi in the purchase and establishment of Kirin Brewery. Mitsubishi's involvement, led by Iwasaki Yanosuke, was extensive. The sprawling conglomerate first served as a sponsor of the Japan Brewery Company when it was formed in 1885; it purchased stock in that firm; it founded Meidi-ya, the distribution company that both owned the "Kirin" trademark and eventually became the brewery's sole contract sales agent; it sponsored the purchase of the Japan Brewery Company from its foreign directors; and finally, it installed the director of Meidi-ya as the brewery's new managing director at a meeting held on the top floor of Mitsubishi's Joint Stock Company in 1907. Without Mitsubishi's sponsorship it is unclear whether or how Japanese investors would have purchased the brewery from foreigners and reestablished it in Japan. For all of the negative press generated about *zaibatsu* (financial cliques) in the early twentieth century, Mitsubishi's steady campaign to take control of the Japan Brewery was successful. It further demonstrates that although Japanese firms were still relatively weak, they were actively planning for the time when they would become strong internationally. Mitsubishi's support for Kirin would continue to benefit the brewery in the years to come.

The initial challenges that faced both Kirin and Sapporo are also important because they qualify the idea that Meiji-era Japan was "fast" becoming a modern, industrialized nation. Writing on Meiji Japan generally hails the "rapid" strides made at this time by business and industry, which positioned the country to begin acting as a regional power. Often, such studies focus principally on the country's military and diplomatic goals, and they examine industrial growth as an engine or component of that broader outcome.[128] These are, of course, extremely valuable works and Meiji-era progress was certainly swift in many respects, but when we look more closely, we see that companies in the brewing industry were only modestly successful, and that the scale of their success was relative. While the general trend was certainly forward, the individual advances could be slow, halting, or have unintended consequences.

For example, until the Great War, Japan's leading brewers lacked the ability to brew beer exclusively with locally sourced ingredients, and they also lacked the technology to ship their fragile product with any real confidence. Japan's road and rail networks were still in their infancy during the 1870s, and the nation's means of acquiring, producing, and distributing critical resources such as coal, steel, lumber, and foodstuffs were vastly underdeveloped. Steady progress was made during the 1880s and 1890s, but even so, the logistical distance between a manufacturing company and its domestic consumers was often measured in weeks or even months, rather than in days. The launch of a new product was not an instantaneous, national affair as it was by the late 1950s or 1960s. Instead, Meiji-era Japanese producers of even staple commodities such as soap, tobacco, and miso had to roll out their wares slowly, often in just one city or region at a time. Building a dealer network or a web of contract sales agents was a painstaking, unfamiliar process beset by dozens of potential pitfalls – and its corollary was the concurrent challenge posed by the desire for steady, reliable acquisition of quality manufacturing materials.

Complicating matters significantly was the government's brutal new beer production tax, which took effect in 1901. After Japan finally succeeded in renegotiating the terms of the "unequal treaties" in 1894, it gained control over its own import tariffs. In 1897, Japan's beer breweries received an increased protective tariff against foreign imports – rising from 5 to 25 percent. However, Japan's government sought to capitalize on the new advantage given to its domestic beer industry by taxing production at the source, rather than at the point of sale. When the new tax was levied, dozens of small brewers were wiped out, unable even to bottle their latest batches without incurring deep losses and bankrupting themselves (see appendix). The annual *Japan Times Year Book* later reported that "the enactment of Beer Brewing Law [sic] of 1901, the economic panic of 1910, and the consequent reduction of production to the minimum output of 1,000 *koku* per year drove small concerns out of business."[129] Here we see the double-edged sword of a protectionist trade agenda that also selected for the largest, most capable companies. Japan scholars often note that many of the earliest Meiji-era entrepreneurs were ruined as they set about investing in new ventures, for even the most daring and progressive among them were often too inexperienced to survive.[130] Indeed, most of Japan's early brewers were too small or were simply dabbling in the market, and when faced with the government's press for increased revenues and more competitive participants amidst difficult economic conditions, they simply fled. The message from the Ministry of Finance was clear – only the strongest participants were welcome to continue operating in the new century.

Through it all, Japan's largest domestic brewers were careful to advertise the authenticity of their strictly German recipes, ingredients, and brewmasters, for although they were Japanese firms, none of them wished to be seen as producers of imitation products. Instead, they wished to be seen as technologically capable of brewing beer that matched the calibre of the European imports. Japan's government attempted to inspire greater use of domestically grown ingredients, and the brewers did establish experimental hops plantations and procure domestic barley through contract-farming arrangements, but these limited efforts were not generally advertised. Beer was made, marketed, and sold in Japan as a proudly German-styled commodity into the late 1930s, until the hostilities and deprivations of the Second World War prompted Japan's domestic brewers to cast aside the pretense that foreign wares were naturally better. Before then, however, the surviving brewers had to find a way to control their dealers, many of whom were locked in a bitter sales war. Lacking control over the marketplace, the beer producers soon found themselves at the mercy of unscrupulous wholesalers and retailers, whose continued underselling would drive the exhausted brewers to distraction.

2 Keeping Up Appearances: Maintaining Beer's German Authenticity, 1906-36

The thirty-year period between the Russo-Japanese War and Japan's invasion of China in 1937 was characterized by significant social, economic, and technological change. Japan's regional military victories over China in 1894-95 and Russia in 1904-5 had quickly raised Japan's stature in the western Pacific, and it concluded a defensive alliance with Great Britain. Japan's economic fortunes were also on the rise, but while the future looked promising, doing business in East Asia actually grew more difficult for Japanese companies in the early twentieth century. European manufacturers, financial firms, and service firms continued to expand in Asia during the 1900s and early 1910s, which hampered the growth of several Japanese export industries – the beer industry among them. European brewers continued to dominate the East Asian export marketplace, where Japanese beers experienced difficulty establishing brand recognition. Japanese brewers thus faced significant pressure to maintain the authentic German character and quality of their brands in order to avoid the perception that they were second-class domestic imitations.

The outbreak of the First World War in 1914 changed the situation entirely. Japanese manufacturers, banks, and shipping companies were granted a sudden reprieve, and they moved swiftly into the vacuum left by their powerful European rivals. The Great War completely changed the trajectory of Japan's industrial growth, prompting both increased production and newfound strength in the domestic market. Although Japan declared war on Germany in 1914, the fighting between the two was brief and limited to East Asia and the Pacific. It therefore did not alter the high regard in which Japanese consumers held German beer. Even during the war, Japan's brewmasters remained German, including one who was captured by the Japanese army at the German settlement in Qingdao, China, in 1914. In addition to a German-American malthouse expert who aided Kirin during the war, this continuing German influence gave Japanese brewers the technical skills necessary to compete in the East Asian export market.

While the boom in the beer industry carried on into 1920, the eventual aftermath was a crippling domestic price war that claimed several makers and left the largest producers exhausted. This severe marketplace competition was compounded by the devastating earthquake that struck Tokyo and Yokohama in 1923, which was a catastrophe for virtually every major company in the populous Kantō area. During the early twentieth century, Japanese wholesalers and retailers did not pay for beer on delivery; instead, they paid remittances to the brewers on its final sale to consumers. This system gave brewers no means of controlling independent urban retailers, and when those shops cut their prices in an effort to keep up with their neighbourhood competitors, the remittances owed to the brewers were cut as well. The only real winners were Japanese consumers, who watched as beer prices fell swiftly during the 1920s and early 1930s, amidst a general recession and economic deflation. Beer consumption climbed steadily during the interwar era, driven upward by rising wages, changing tastes, and a steady rise in the number of working-class beer consumers. Rising beer sales naturally spurred more production, but they also threatened to bankrupt the breweries, which faced ever more difficulty getting paid.

Finally, however, the continuing price war between the brewers was resolved in the early 1930s by the creation of a powerful domestic beer cartel designed to control both production and prices. Curbing the rampant underselling by rebellious retailers would take time, as would the defeat of unscrupulous rival producers, but by 1936, two breweries would emerge victorious: Kirin and Dai Nippon. Their production and sales cartel reestablished control over the domestic marketplace just as Japan plunged into the Second World War.

Oligopoly Dawns: The Merger and Growth of Dai Nippon Beer, 1906-13

On 2 January 1905, Russian troops surrendered Port Arthur, on China's Liaodong Peninsula, to Japanese forces after a siege that had begun the previous summer. Six days later, the *Asahi* newspaper reported that Sapporo Breweries planned to celebrate the Russian surrender with a special week-long sales promotion in which it would give away silk handkerchiefs.[1] Sapporo's symbolic gifts proved premature, for the war did not end until September, but after it did, the city of Tokyo held a reception in Hibiya Park for members of the Imperial Japanese Navy, who were served great quantities of "Sapporo," "Yebisu," and "Kirin" beer.[2] Beer's prestige was aided greatly by the war, especially as domestic brands were served aboard Japanese Navy ships, but the year-long flurry of patriotic beer advertising was merely a front. Japan's brewers were nowhere near ready to produce their product solely with domestically sourced ingredients or without the aid of skilled German technicians, who would continue working in Japan for decades. The navy reception did, however, mark the start of an economic boom that fuelled increased beer sales nationwide, and with it came a more earnest desire on the part of Japan's brewers to end their own hostilities. The severe competition between Sapporo Breweries, Osaka Beer, and Nippon Beer had not been allayed by the preliminary meetings of their employees in 1900 and 1901, and thus by 1906 a merger appeared to be the best option.

The opportunity finally came when the minister of agriculture and commerce, Count Kiyōra Keigo (1850-1942), and Nippon Beer president Magoshi Kyōhei stepped in to mediate negotiations among the three firms and the corporate conglomerate Mitsui Trading Company. Mitsui sought a role in the beer industry in response to its rival Mitsubishi's support of the Kirin brewery, and as Magoshi had previously headed Mitsui's Yokohama branch, he had no difficulty bringing Mitsui into the deal, which took the shape of a joint venture.[3] Sapporo cites three principal aims for the merger, the first of which was the avoidance of excessive "petty competition" *(kagyū kakujō no kyōsō)*, which was eroding all of the brewers' returns. The second aim was the expansion of Japan's overseas market share, which was suffering due to stiff competition from European brands. Third, Japan's government had begun to encourage self-sufficiency *(jikyūjisoku)* in resources and manufacturing, especially of critical materials, and a larger brewer was deemed more capable of making the necessary investments in this arena.[4] Producing sufficient grain, malts, hops, bottles, and so forth domestically was intended to leave Japan's beer industry less vulnerable to shortages or a stoppage of global trade, such as might occur in wartime. These three aims served to unite the feuding brewers, which merged to form the Dai Nippon (Greater Japan) Beer Company, Inc., on 26 March 1906 under Magoshi Kyōhei's very capable leadership. Although the above aims are plausible, closer examination uncovers discrepancies between the stated aims of the merger and Sapporo's more practical and immediate goals.[5]

To begin with, despite the intention to end the petty competition among Japan's jumble of small beer retailers, the merger did little to reorganize the actual marketplace, aside from uniting several existing brands. In fact, the competition among retailers was accelerating. As for the merger's second aim, improving export sales, the creation of Dai Nippon gave the Mitsui Trading Company full control over the brewer's export sales. Similarly, just prior to Kirin's reincorporation in 1907, it too began to export beer through its sales agency, Meidi-ya, which had been founded by Mitsubishi.

Table 7

Japan's total beer exports, 1906-13

Year	Volume (kL)
1906	5,413.3
1907	4,529.8
1908	4,001.6
1909	3,288.5
1910	3,234.6
1911	2,380.8
1912	2,391.1
1913	2,614.4

Source: Kirin biiru KK, *Kirin biiru KK gojū nenshi* [Kirin Brewery Company, Ltd.: Fifty-year history] (Tokyo: Kirin biiru KK, 20 March 1957), 233.

On 29 January 1909, Kirin even amended the first article of their contract to add the phrase *kaigai* (overseas, foreign), thus granting Meidi-ya complete control over export sales.[6] In spite of the change, however, exports plummeted. Japan's overseas market share actually declined steadily until the First World War began, by which point Japan's total export volume was less than half of what it had been in 1906 (see Table 7). Until 1914, the spheres of influence in the East Asian beer market remained dominated by European producers:

• China, Guangdong Leased Territory: English beer
• South China, Shanghai, Hong Kong: German and English beer
• India: English beer
• Dutch East Indies: (mainland) Dutch beer
• South Seas: European beer.[7]

The third aim, achieving brewing self-sufficiency, although a logical long-term goal vis-à-vis national security, was by no means possible in the first decade of the twentieth century. Dai Nippon's founding directors initially had no such plan for their new company. They proposed to produce a truly German beer using only German engineers and imported German malts and hops, but Japan's government rejected this plan during the merger negotiations. Instead, the Ministry of Agriculture and Commerce forced the new brewing giant to prioritize, at least in principle, domestic ingredients and expertise. This was a significant turning point in the continuing standoff between domestic brewers over the authenticity and foreignness of their product. Still, it was neither a rapid nor a complete transformation.[8] (I will return to the issue of increasing manufacturing self-sufficiency in Chapter 3.)

Following their thirty-year reliance on German ingredients, techniques, and brewmasters, no company wished to be the first to claim that its beer was a totally Japanese product, for the perception that imported beer was superior was deeply entrenched in the minds of Japanese consumers. Kirin continued to emphasize in its advertisements the German expertise behind its brand, and given its refusal to join Dai Nippon's three-way merger in 1906, the perceived authenticity of the Kirin brand posed a potential threat to the new brewing giant. Kirin's unwillingness to cultivate a domestic consumer product identity effectively forced Dai Nippon to drag its feet on its own conversion process, and it therefore transitioned to using domestically sourced ingredients only very slowly and reluctantly. Consequently, imports of malts to Japan would fluctuate until the mid-1920s, and the volume of imported hops would balloon through the mid-1930s (see Table 8).

It is useful to consider the more immediate, practical motives behind the three-way merger that produced the massive Dai Nippon brewing company in 1906. According to Sapporo, the purpose of the merger was the achievement of greater stability across Japan's beer industry, but this is not corroborated by rival Kirin or by the Japanese literature on the industry's development. Not surprisingly, Kirin contends that the merger was much more self-interested. In the simplest terms, the Sapporo, Osaka, and Nippon brewing companies sought to create the largest, most productive, and most geographically dominant firm, to combine their stable of nearly a dozen brands, and to reach a mutual market-sharing agreement on production and sales.[9] Given the difficulty and costs associated with shipping individual brands across Japan's home islands, the merger presented a terrific opportunity to tie together three of Japan's leading firms and their respective regional markets. Then, as now, shipping a heavy liquid product like beer over great distances was best avoided by brewing locally. Whereas Sapporo had been isolated in Hokkaido, Dai Nippon now boasted manufacturing plants in Sapporo, Tokyo (Meguro and Azumabashi), and Suita City, near Osaka, which created a powerful web of brewing and bottling facilities that minimized transportation costs.[10] With such a commanding reach, Dai Nippon was poised to brew and ship its beer with relative ease, while its rivals faced steep transportation costs. The company's market share circa 1907 was a stark indication of Dai Nippon's newfound strength: it controlled fully 72 percent of Japan's domestic beer market, while its chief rival, Kirin, commanded just 20 percent, and the remaining competitors held just 8 percent.[11]

Table 8

National imports of malts and hops, 1914-36

Year	Volume of malts (kL)	Volume of hops (kg)
1914	1,306,438.5	190,117
1915	687,249.8	154,677
1916	1,283,096.0	185,527
1917	2,435,210.9	314,577
1918	1,523,177.1	259,018
1919	1,488,776.7	491,943
1920	1,887,312.3	677,850
1921	352,103.2	295,988
1922	1,226,471.6	341,972
1923	827,954.0	419,263
1924	1,960,027.5	548,496
1925	445,274.7	408,676
1926	184,376.6	359,015
1927	137,240.7	458,641
1928	136,934.0	454,457
1929	416,069.5	373,193
1930	227,994.9	525,201
1931	184,557.0	315,596
1932	29,133.0	427,965
1933	7,937.2	414,557
1934	–	400,348
1935	90.2	423,141
1936	92,467.9	712,020

Note: Figures recorded originally in *kin* were converted to kilograms by the author, where 1 kin = approximately 600 grams.

Source: Kirin biiru KK, *Kirin biiru KK gojū nenshi* [Kirin Brewery Company, Ltd.: Fifty-year history] (Tokyo: Kirin biiru KK, 20 March 1957), 232.

Not only was Dai Nippon able to save on shipping costs, its consolidated production and transportation network helped to eliminate wasteful spending. Kirin, on the other hand, shouldered the entire cost of shipping its product to the stores of its sole contract sales agent. Meidi-ya had its head sales office in Yokohama, as well as new branches in Tokyo, Osaka, Kobe, and Moji, which did serve as a unified sales network, but Kirin's contractual obligation to cover all of its own transportation costs was a significant liability. Kirin's partnership with Meidi-ya is a clear example of its continuing inability to manage its sales or to control its own market effectively. Furthermore, Kirin continued to maintain its focus on product quality and strictly German production methods, which kept its product costs very high. At that time,

Table 9

National market share of Kirin Brewery, 1906-13

Year	Production by Kirin Brewery (kL)	National production (kL)	Kirin's market share (%)
1906	5,731.0	28,748.2	19.9
1907	7,128.5	36,284.4	19.6
1908	5,913.7	29,475.0	20.1
1909	5,321.3	27,208.4	19.6
1910	5,298.1	28,094.1	18.9
1911	5,499.5	32,228.5	17.1
1912	6,014.2	35,429.3	17.0
1913	6,707.8	40,002.0	16.8

Source: Kirin biiru KK, *Kirin biiru KK gojū nenshi* [Kirin Brewery Company, Ltd.: Fifty-year history] (Tokyo: Kirin biiru KK, 20 March 1957), 231. Data to 1906 comes from *Dai Nippon yōshu kankitsu enkakushi* [Great Japan Western alcohol bottling history], and data for 1907-13 comes from Ministry of Finance, *Shuzeikyoku nenpō* [Tax Bureau Annual Report].

"Kirin Beer" sold generally for between 1 and 3 sen more than its chief rivals, but this did not generate especially significant revenue for the firm. Still, the higher price point did help to maintain "Kirin Beer"'s image as a premium product, and though Kirin retained a smaller market share for quite some time, it remained modestly profitable. Plus, its financial position was secure, for at the time of its reincorporation as Kirin Brewery Company in 1907, the profits of the previous era amounted to ¥200,000, and its proportion of paid-up capital hit 80 percent, totalling ¥2.5 million.[12] At the time of Kirin's reincorporation, the post–Russo-Japanese War boom fuelled an increase in the company's production figures, and volume increased 20 percent between 1906 and 1907. Soon afterward, however, Japan's beer market began to take a turn. An economic slump following the initial postwar boom erased nearly all of Kirin's gains in 1908, after which Kirin's market share slid through 1913 (see Table 9).

During the same period, however, Dai Nippon Beer fared very well. National beer production rose nearly 30 percent between 1906 and 1913, and Dai Nippon's proportion of market share increased overall, topping 80 percent. Kirin found itself slipping further and further behind, and, desperate to recover, its directors hired several managers from Japan's Imperial Commercial Bank to produce an analysis of the national beer industry. What they learned speaks to the extreme difficulties faced by Kirin in the early twentieth century, and underscores the genuine technical and marketing incapability of some companies during that era.[13]

Still Doing Things the Old-Fashioned Way: The Travails of Kirin Brewery

In 1907, Kirin was caught between a rock and a hard place. After the merger and launch of Dai Nippon Beer in 1906, Kirin suddenly found its proportion of national market share challenged not by three chief rivals, but by one goliath with a large stable of popular, quality brands. For thirty years Kirin had nurtured a reputation for fastidious, uncompromising adherence to strict German recipes, ingredients, and techniques. This approach was predicated on the notion that domestic Japanese beers were inferior (as they once had been) and that only a truly German-style product could be considered a premium brand. But now Kirin's commitment to its expensive German processes was both limiting its profits and curbing its ability to transition to less costly ingredients and techniques. Its hallmark approach to quality had become an albatross, and its resident German engineers were fast becoming liabilities. When interviewed in 2011, Kirin's CEO, Katō Kazuyasu, explained, "The singular pursuit of authentic German beer quality remained the primary mission, however, and beer continued to be brewed with imported ingredients under German brewmaster supervision. The public's perception of Kirin as a producer of 'real' German beer helped it quickly close the lead that Dai Nippon Beer Company had gained in the time since its merger."[14] But Katō's final assertion is doubtful: Kirin did not actually close the lead against Dai Nippon. Instead, Kirin's histories describe the era from its reincorporation in 1907 through 1913 as one of "suffering," as it faced financial and technical difficulties, as well as marketing and environmental challenges.[15]

Kirin's chief error was its failure to adopt more modern or efficient machines or processes. Kirin's head German engineer took a hardline, conservative approach to his craft, and he absolutely refused to adopt new machines, techniques, or ingredients. Kirin's directors were thus hamstrung by their determination to continue using traditional brewing methods, which were firmly entrenched throughout the production process and were the basis for all of its employees' training. The company's management team, dominated as it was by its German brewmaster, continued to prioritize the production of a high-quality German-style product, however costly. This burdened Kirin's payroll especially, which prevented significant capital reinvestment in new machinery. Furthermore, Kirin's brewmaster detested English and American ingredients, and he refused to use them altogether. Kirin records that its directors and employees were therefore totally unaware that US malts and hops were far cheaper than German ingredients. The company's rigid quality standards helped it justify its slightly higher price in the marketplace, which offset its production costs but did not generate significant returns.[16]

As an example of its adherence to increasingly outdated techniques, Kirin continued to seal its bottles using corks well into the twentieth century, even though rival Dai Nippon Beer adopted the bottle cap in 1907. For many years, the "Kirin" brand had been well known for having long corks, similar to those used in champagne bottles. Using corks was highly inefficient. They tended to pop out while the bottles were being heat pasteurized, which necessitated the placement of a metal clamp over the mouth of each bottle in order to hold the cork inside. After pasteurization, the clamps had to be removed, which was another tedious process for the bottling line workers. Placing and removing the clamps took a total of nearly four hours, so Kirin's bottling operation could only be performed twice a day. Despite their brewmaster's objections, Kirin used corks manufactured by the London Crown Cork Company – one of the few examples of Kirin's success in overruling its stubborn brewmaster. Then, in 1912, Kirin's directors aimed to begin using so-called Goldy Corks – a new aluminum crown cork resembling a modern bottle cap, which was produced in Germany. Although these caps were visually appealing and had earned praise in Germany, they proved somewhat difficult to use, and the brewmaster again opposed them adamantly. Nevertheless, Kirin placed an order for both 1,440,000 regular corks and 500,000 Goldy Corks, at which point Kirin's managing director issued an order to use the latter as well, stating that he would take personal responsibility for any difficulties. Kirin's directors had won this round, but their labels still had to be affixed to the bottles by hand, for the firm would not begin using an automated bottle-labelling machine until 1917.[17]

Another problem for Kirin stemmed from the location of its factory, which was inconveniently situated in Yamate-chō in the southeast of Yokohama. The site was located in a valley between two enormous hills, over which all deliveries and shipments had to pass. This example of Japan's mountainous topography beset many companies in Yokohama at that time. Kirin had to ship its heavy liquid malts from the port over Yatozaka Hill by horse-drawn wagon. Likewise, the wagons delivered their heavy liquid product back to the port in the same fashion. The problem was compounded during the Russo-Japanese War of 1904-5, when all of the company's horses were requisitioned by the military and the carts had to be pushed back and forth over Yatozaka Hill by teams of men. Thirty-five years after Copeland had founded his brewery, reliance on such rudimentary labour hardly seems representative of the "rapid" Meiji-era industrialization hailed by so many Japan scholars. Even after the war against Russia, Japan's urban transportation network remained woefully underdeveloped for many years, significantly hindering commercial growth. Yokohama was of course a thriving metropolis and a major seaport, but many parts of the city remained out of reach of the rail and tramlines until the 1920s and later, forcing companies there to improvise.[18] The situation improved somewhat once the Yokohama tramway's Yamate Tunnel opened in 1911, but Kirin notes that the new artery was not the fundamental improvement that its directors had expected. Still, the firm would not purchase its first pair of motorized delivery trucks until 1919, and it continued to use horses for several years afterward. Kirin records that foreign beer companies maintained fleets of excellent draft horses lined up proudly, and, determined to appear every inch the European brewer, Kirin too kept ten horses in the barn, always ready to deliver beer.[19]

This brings us to a more noteworthy anachronism: until the Great War, Kirin chose to ship its fragile glass bottles in baskets made of handwoven bamboo. Each was divided on the inside to separate either two dozen or four dozen bottles, but the baskets themselves were often damaged during handling. This necessitated the employment of two or three full-time basket weavers at the factory, to make or repair baskets as needed. Kirin also used large wooden boxes, which it first purchased ready-made, but the company ultimately built these boxes from sets of precut boards at its own factory during the Japan Brewery era (1885-1907). The boxes did not have lids, however, and therefore were no more functional than the baskets, so Kirin preferred to use the latter to ship its bottles until the Great War. Although many of the traditional products once made by Japanese craftsmen (such as wooden barrels, buckets, clogs, and paper lanterns and umbrellas) were by that time rivalled by mass-produced designs, at least a few traditional artisans clearly remained of use to modern industry, if only after a fashion.

Stormy Weather: Beer Sales versus Mother Nature

Beer advertising grew increasingly important during the late Meiji and Taishō eras. During Kirin's reincorporation, the company pioneered new methods of generating brand awareness and reaching out to new consumers, and the advent of the motorcar proved to be a useful tool. In 1906, the vice-president of the Meidi-ya sales agency, Isono Chōzō, returned from abroad after purchasing a remarkable new PR machine – a delivery truck shaped like a beer bottle, with the cap facing forward. Built by the Scottish automobile company Argyll, it arrived in Yokohama six months later, at the cost of ¥4,000. Company artists painted the bottle-body with the "Kirin" beer label, and it was put to use as an advertising and promotional wagon, delivering beer samples far and wide. Kirin contends that this truck was Japan's very first such promotional vehicle, and there is good evidence to support this claim. Licence plates for motor vehicles became mandatory just then, and Kirin's bottle-shaped truck received Japan's very first plate from the Tokyo Metropolitan Police Department: registration No. 1.

Naturally, Kirin's bottle-truck raised eyebrows and interest throughout Tokyo and Yokohama. It was also dispatched on field trips throughout the surrounding Kantō region and even into the northern Tōhoku region of Japan's main island, Honshu, in order to call on local retailers and consumers. On 9 June 1912, it departed from Tokyo's Akihabara Station bound for Aomori, the northernmost prefecture of Tōhoku, with one driver and one assistant, plus a representative from Meidi-ya. For thirty-six days, the three men bounced along the rough country roads, visiting a long list of small towns and cities, distributing beer samples and enlivening the countryside with their amusing vehicle. Not to be outdone, Dai Nippon Beer imported Japan's fourth-ever licensed truck at the identical cost of ¥4,000, to which it attached a painted signboard.[20]

The year 1907 was fairly prosperous for Japan's beer industry due to the postwar economic boom, and both Dai Nippon and Kirin reached their increased annual production and sales goals. Still, no marketing campaign could begin to control the weather, which is a variable that is seldom considered by studies of Japan's early industrialization. Beer sales were impeded in August as unusually heavy rains triggered serious flooding that interrupted shipping, especially to customers outside of Tokyo and Yokohama. Most of Japan's intercity roads remained unpaved for much of the twentieth century, and it was not until 1919 that a bill aimed at creating a national roadway infrastructure was introduced by Japan's government. The resulting Road Law passed in 1920, at which point Japan's Home Ministry launched its Thirty-Year Provincial Capital and Prefectural Road Improvement Plan.[21] *Thirty years* was the estimated time needed to pave the country's intercity roads and erect bridges over its major rivers, which was a plan that did not anticipate costly interruptions by Japan's continental and Pacific wars of the late 1930s and early 1940s. Those conflicts and resulting defeat and occupation through 1952 consumed the lion's share of Japan's state budget, thus retarding the country's highway infrastructure until the 1960s. Torrential rains were, therefore, a serious barrier to commercial growth in the early twentieth century because they washed away the roads or turned them into miles of muddy ruts.

The difficulties caused by severe rains were then compounded in mid-1908 by very cool summer weather, which both slowed beer sales and contributed to a poor harvest, leading to problems caused by inferior ingredients. During the same period, loan accounts at district banks began sliding into delinquency, a trend that had begun as early as January 1907 but intensified the following year. The recession in the general economy was naturally followed by a recession in the beer industry, as consumers' discretionary spending declined. The combination of poor weather, bad materials, and the economic downturn dealt Kirin a serious blow. Due to the cool, wet summer, a large volume of "Kirin" beer was returned to the company by its sales agency, Meidi-ya, which was not contractually responsible for unsold product. Kirin's net profit for 1908 barely reached ¥84,000, and despite a slight upturn in 1909, heavy rains again triggered terrible flooding in August 1910, hindering shipments once more and leading to cancelled orders throughout Kantō and Tōhoku. Although a drop in the cost of charcoal earlier that year helped to lower production costs, the poor weather seriously affected beer sales.[22]

Amidst these difficulties, Kirin's directors invested in an expanded advertising program in conjunction with Meidi-ya. At its directors' conference on 15 January 1908, Kirin resolved to spend ¥55,000 on the new marketing campaign, splitting the cost evenly with its sales firm. A host of ads and publicity campaigns followed, designed to catch the eye of consumers and promote Kirin's new products. The publicity was essential, for rival Dai Nippon Beer was also focusing its substantial resources on advertising. In December 1910, for example, Kirin launched a new "Bock Ale," which it made from caramel malts imported from Germany. Around the same time, Kirin also began selling a second new brand called "Munich Beer," which was produced using imported Pilzen malts, boasted higher alcohol content, and was sold in an attractive, long-necked bottle. Both new products were light brown in colour, placing them between Kirin's existing lager and stout. Sales grew slightly in 1911, and not only did Japan's economy recover somewhat in 1912, the weather improved as well, which boosted sales once more. That summer, Dai Nippon staged a combination Yebisu-Sapporo Beer Hall, where it sold large draft beers for only 5 sen, and 3 sen for small, which was just half the price that draft beer had cost when beer halls had first begun opening at the turn of the century.[23]

Despite all of this innovation and aggressive pricing, competition from European brands continued to stymie export sales for all of Japan's brewers. Contemporary market reporters followed the struggle carefully. When the German ambassador to Japan addressed a beer conference staged by the Japan-Germany Society (Nichidoku Kyōkai) in 1912, the *Asahi* newspaper covered the event, even though the gathering elicited little more than pleasantries.[24] This phase of friendly competition would change, however, with the outbreak of the First World War in August 1914. The start of hostilities in Europe abruptly halted exports of European beer to East Asia, giving Japan's brewers their first opportunity to ply the waters of the western Pacific virtually unopposed.[25]

Continuing German Influence and the First World War, 1914-18

The Great War was a boon to Japanese industrial, finance, and service companies, for while the Western powers were preoccupied with the fighting both in Europe and abroad, Japanese companies rushed in to fill the void. As William Wray writes, orders for goods and services poured into Japan, especially from countries in the Asia-Pacific region, prompting Japanese policymakers and financiers to view the war as an economic opportunity that "comes along once in a thousand years."[26] Naturally, Dai Nippon and Kirin shared this opinion. In the first half of 1914, Kirin was hit especially hard by deteriorating sales amidst intense domestic competition, but by the latter half of the year, Japan's weather improved dramatically, and English and German beers were no longer available in Asia. Suddenly, Japanese beer was in great demand, and business boomed. Furthermore, like many German nationals working abroad, Kirin's troublesome German brewmaster was ordered home to aid his country with the war effort. This freed Kirin's management to try new things, and plans were soon laid to expand operations, to use additional Japanese equipment, and, faced with a dearth of German ingredients, to attempt to use cheaper substitutes.

In 1914, Japan's leading brewers numbered just four: Kirin, Dai Nippon, Kabuto Beer, and Teikoku (Imperial) Beer. Combat operations for Japanese forces were limited during the First World War, but Japan did enter the conflict on the side of the Entente Powers, declaring war on Imperial Germany and its allies in August 1914. After seizing Germany's colonies in Micronesia in early October, Japanese forces teamed up with the British to defeat German forces during the Siege of Qingdao, China, in October and November. On its seizure of the territory and its forts, Japan set about reorganizing the small district, fully anticipating (wrongly) that it would keep the outpost following the war. Already by February 1915, the *Asahi* newspaper reported that Dai Nippon Beer aimed to purchase the settlement's brewery, founded in 1903 as the Germania-Brauerei but known by that time as the Anglo-German Beer Company.[27] The firm was liquidated in September 1916 under the supervision of the Japanese military administration, and the foreign shareholders were paid out. On 23 December 1916, the *North China Herald* reported:

> The beer brewery at Tsingtao, which was run jointly by British and German capital, was compelled by the Japan-German War to suspend operations. The brewery has since been left idle. The Dai Nippon Beer Co. has decided to

purchase its interests, and a contract has been concluded with the British concerned for the buying of the whole of its interest ... for the sum of ¥1,700,000. The Dai Nippon Co., will shortly set about resuming operations at Tsingtao, and it is intended to place the first brew on the market at the beginning of May next. At first the brewery will have a capacity of 30,000 cases a year, but its maximum capacity is 50,000 cases. The taste and flavour of the beer will be the same as when the brewery was under German control, but brewing materials will be supplied from Japan.[28]

With that, Dai Nippon assumed control of the brewery and continued to produce its now-famous brand.

The acquisition of "Tsingtao Beer" came just as demand for Japanese beer was rising throughout Asia due to the sudden absence of European imports. In June 1916, US consul general to Japan George H. Seldmore sent the following report from the *Japan Advertiser* to Washington:

> The Dai Nippon Brewery Co. has purchased the plant of the Tsingtau Brewery Co. [and] by this transaction the former company has eliminated strong competition in the Chinese market ... It is reported that since the outbreak of war, the increase in the demand for Japanese beer for export has been remarkable. The Dai Nippon Brewery Co. alone has already exported this year about 80,000 cases to China, 30,000 to Chosen [Korea], 20,000 to Rangoon, 25,000 to Calcutta, 60,000 to Bombay, 20,000 to Singapore, and 20,000 to Java, or more than 250,000 cases in all in the five months. The figures this year are treble those in the corresponding period of last year, and are more than eight times larger than the amount in the corresponding period the year before last. It is also remarkable to note that quite recently the Dai Nippon Brewery Co. has received an order from Egypt for 10,000 cases.[29]

Importantly, some of Tsingtao's German technicians, including the brewmaster, named Streichel, were kept on as prisoners of war by the Japanese. The German nationals were glad not to be recalled to Germany, where they faced the prospect of being sent to the front. Instead, Streichel and his comrades continued brewing beer for their new Japanese plant managers for the duration of the war, cementing a relationship between Dai Nippon and the Tsingtao brand and allowing continued access to German brewmasters and their technical skill despite the state of war between the two nations.[30]

Poor weather in late summer 1915 curbed both domestic sales and exports for a spell, but as 1916 arrived, the war in Europe became deadlocked and

Japanese exports of all kinds grew dramatically. Later in the year, Kirin's exports surged so much that even running its plant at peak capacity was not enough to keep pace with the rising demand. In 1916, the *Straits Times*, published in British Singapore, noted that Japan's beer brewers were steadily conquering the global market for beer in the absence of steady European exports. The paper reported that while Japan had exported 92,300 cases of beer between January and June 1915 (each containing four dozen large bottles), its brewers shipped 166,000 cases during the same period in 1916 – a 45 percent increase, year over year. The report explained:

> The beer trade of Japan is one of those industries which have materially bene-fited from the war. Exports have been steadily on the increase since the early part of last year. Four-fifths of the export is represented by the products of the Dai Nippon Beer Co. ... The marked increase in regard to India, the South Seas, and Australia is worth notice, as these places were irrigated with German beer before the war. It is stated that the popularity of Japanese beer has lately specially increased, and while the export has hitherto been made exclusively through the Mitsui bussan kaisha and other exporters, foreign importers have now come to deal direct with the brewery. As a matter of fact, it is said, a British merchant in India has come all the way to Japan to open direct con-nections. Another notable fact is that there has been a remarkable increase in the demand from Egypt and South Africa.[31]

This report was echoed by an article in the *Japan Chronicle*, which was forwarded from Yokohama to the US Bureau of Foreign and Domestic Commerce by US Vice-Consul M.D. Kirjassoff in mid-October 1916. In November, the bureau reprinted a verbatim excerpt in its daily *Commerce Reports*:

> A Japanese official sent to Bombay to inspect the commercial situation made a report to the Tokyo Government in which he said that among Japanese products imported by India beer was one which had increased remarkably since the outbreak of war and had the brightest prospects. "The largest Japanese exporter of beer to India," he said, "is the Dai Nippon Beer Co., followed by the Kabuto and Sakura Beer Cos. It is satisfactory to note that they station their agents in India and are making vigorous efforts to extend their markets." The imports of beer into Bombay from April, 1915, to March, 1916, totalled 228,000 gallons, Japanese imports amounting to 62,000 gallons, or about 27 per cent of the total. In 1912-13 the total received from Japan was not more than 3 gallons; 22 gallons were shipped in 1913-14, and 8,100 gallons

in 1914-15. "It will be seen," stated the report mentioned, "what a great difference the war has made in Japan's beer trade. It is expected that in the current year the figure will double that for the preceding year."[32]

Despite these rosy reports, however, the writer for the *Straits Times* could not resist concluding that "it is doubtful whether the present state of prosperity can be maintained after the war, and the Japanese merchants concerned are described as stating that much depends on the improvement of the quality of Japanese beer."[33] It was thus clear to Western observers that the wartime boom in Japan's beer exports would very likely be temporary, for brewing industry professionals around the world were keenly aware of Japan's continuing reliance on foreign ingredients. The October 1915 edition of the *Western Brewer* observed that while Japan's beer production was up, its reliance on imported hops was substantial. Based in Chicago and boasting the largest circulation of any brewing trade journal in the world, it reported:

> According to a recent report from the United States Vice-Consul at Yokohama, the beer brewed in Japan during the year ending February 28, 1915, amounted to 11,415,523 gallons. Of the total output the Dai Nippon Brewery Co., Ltd., with breweries at Meguro, Azumbashi and Hodogaya, all in the vicinity of Tokio [sic], and at Sapporo, Hokkaido and Suita, near Osaka, brews over 7,000,000 gallons, and the Kirin Beer Co., of Yokohama, about 2,000,000 gallons. The remainder is brewed by the Kabuto Beer Co., of Handa, near Nagoya, and by the Sakura Beer Co., of Moji. The Dai Nippon Brewery Co. is the only one that raises sufficient hops for its own uses. The other breweries are largely dependent upon imports for their supply.[34]

The US Bureau of Foreign and Domestic Commerce drew similar conclusions, and further noted that "some hops are grown in Japan in the Hokkaido, but the quantity is inconsiderable and the quality inferior, those imported from Germany being regarded as the best."[35] The bureau's reporting was accurate. Dai Nippon's hops plantations were nowhere near productive or capable enough to make the company self-sufficient – that lofty goal would not be reached until the 1940s.

Not everyone was impressed, however, that Japan's breweries were capitalizing on the absence of competition in global beer markets brought on by the First World War. Japan's rising beer exports did not sit well with Christian missionaries working in East Asia, who denounced the trade as a social evil and a further obstacle to their "civilizing mission." At the 1916 National

Missionary Congress in Washington, DC, speaker Amos Wilder roundly criticized Japan's beer industry:

> It is abhorrent business, super-adding to the burdens of undeveloped and pagan lands the additional curse of alcoholism. It is regrettable that Japan is taking in drink noticeably; beer-brewing is one of the features of Western civilization now rooted in that country, which is even engaged in export trade, Japanese beer now being a feature of Chinese cities. One notes in China the gradual appearance of the Western saloon, the windows filled with gaudy bottles containing deadly concoctions.[36]

Japan's brewers paid such denunciations no heed. Rather than be left behind by its rivals Dai Nippon, Kabuto, and Teikoku, Kirin's sales agent, Meidi-ya, dispatched a team of inspectors to survey Asia's regional beer marketplace in 1916, led by its vice-president, Isono Chōzō. Their journey through colonial Asia was remarkable, for the ports listed on their itinerary mirror the territorial ambitions of the Empire of Japan. The group set off early in the year, travelling by steamship first to British-held Singapore, then to Kuala Lumpur in modern Malaysia, followed by Rangoon in Burma (today Yangon, Myanmar). Next they journeyed to India, stopping in Calcutta (Kolkata), Bombay (Mumbai), Madras (Chennai), and Ceylon (Sri Lanka), but their trip was cut short in Batavia (then part of the Dutch East Indies, now Indonesia). There, the members of the group contracted malaria and sought medical care, which curtailed their southern tour. Still, what they learned about the East, Southeast, and South Asian beer markets was significant, and underscores their prior failure to make significant investments in expanding sales in those arenas.[37]

During their trip, Isono and his team concluded exchange deals with a variety of local businesses, such as the Patterson and Simon Company in Singapore, a smaller firm in Kuala Lumpur called the Patterson and Hampstead Company, and the Balthazar Company in Rangoon. No business negotiations were conducted in Bombay or Madras, but in Calcutta, Isono signed a sole agency contract with the Lipton Company, and his account of the negotiations offers an extremely rare and candid look at dealing with a very British tea company in British India:

> In Calcutta, the manager of the Lipton's Company office, which specialized in purchasing tea, had an extremely sharp tongue. This man held a tasting for the two of us at which we tested single samples. He gathered up all of the beers

sold in the Calcutta market and he poured them into numbered cups. I said, "this one is the best, and the second best is this one." Next, the manager taste-tested them, and he agreed exactly with my opinion on which were the first and second best. When we checked the numbers to see, we found that Kirin Beer was the first one, and the second was Key Brand from Bremen [Beck's]. Now, I knew the taste of Kirin Beer more than any, especially because the beer sample was fresh. At any rate, both the manager and I drank and drew the same conclusion as to which one was the best. When we talked about the price of ours, it's no wonder we entered into an agency agreement.[38]

Having passed the test, Isono continued on to sign a second sales contract at the Lipton Company office in Ceylon, where "Kirin Beer" was similarly well received. Kirin's reps were proud that their German-style lager had stacked up against its European rivals so strongly. The team did not hold any negotiations in Batavia due to their illness, but with the aid of the Mitsubishi Company, Meidi-ya later struck a deal with a local import firm there.

After their recovery, Isono and his group sailed home via China, where they visited Hong Kong, Shanghai, and Hankow (in modern Wuhan). In Hong Kong, sales of "Kirin Beer" were handled by a firm called the Honda Company (Honda yōkō, where "yōkō" meant, literally, a store in Japanese-occupied China operated by a foreigner). By 1916, Japan was flexing its muscles in China, and just the year before, the foreign minister, Katō Takaaki, had issued Japan's infamous "Twenty-One Demands" to China. Via those demands, Japanese companies sought increased trade rights and access to markets and resources throughout China, especially in Shandong Province, southern Manchuria, and the Yangtze River Valley. For Kirin, however, taking advantage of such an opportunity required not only added production capacity but a reliable means of shipping beer. Recently freed from the grip of its iron-willed German brewmaster and flush with orders from abroad, Kirin's directors moved swiftly to expand and modernize their operations.

Ever since its founding, rival firm Dai Nippon Beer had converted grain grown in Hokkaido into malts at both its Suita plant (formerly Osaka Beer) and at its Meguro plant in Tokyo (formerly Nippon Beer), but never in large enough quantities to satisfy its needs entirely. Kirin, of course, had no malting equipment, because it had always relied on German malts exclusively, even though this was expensive. German malts had to be shipped to Japan via the Indian Ocean, which was a very hot and humid climate in the summer months. The malts therefore had to be sealed in large, moisture-resistant boxes made of strong tin sheeting, which were both costly and heavy. Once they arrived in Yokohama, they then had to be delivered to the brewery over

Yatozaka Hill by wagon, which was another huge cost disadvantage compared to other breweries. Cognizant of the burden, Isono Chōzō of Meidi-ya had suggested in 1895 that the brewery begin processing its own malts domestically, but Kirin's directors did not approve of the plan because their German engineers were adamantly opposed to it. With the arrival of the Great War and the recall of its German brewmaster, however, Kirin decided in the fall of 1916 to begin producing its own malts.[39] Although significant at the time, these efforts were but a shadow of the manufacturing self-sufficiency that would be required during the Second World War.

Making malts required a significant investment in new machinery and facilities, and for that Kirin would have to convince not only its shareholders, but also Mitsubishi Bank. During a dramatic meeting, Kirin's director, Ida Kiyozō, persuaded Mitsubishi Bank representative Kirishima Shōichi of the brewery's financial obligation to produce its own malts. Kirishima, who Kirin records "even looked like the head of a bank," was able in turn to persuade Kirin's shareholders of the plan's legitimacy.[40] The only alternative, which Kirin considered a plan of last resort, was to use caramel malts from a company in Osaka, which would require using capital stock to pay for the necessary testing. Instead, Kirin opted to reorganize the corporation and found the Japan Malts Manufacturing Company. This was a symbolic step forward, but the technical challenges had only just begun. Due to the collapse of global commerce caused by the Great War, Kirin was unable to import sufficient barley or any malting machinery from Germany or England, so the Mitsubishi shipyard in Kobe agreed to produce half of the necessary equipment. Kirin engineer Asano Toshirō brokered the deal and assisted Mitsubishi with the unique machine specifications. Then, Kirin sent Asano to visit breweries and malts producers in the United States, just as engineers from rivals Dai Nippon and Kabuto were doing, for making the journey across the Pacific to America was far safer than attempting to visit Europe. Furthermore, the threat of alcohol prohibition was looming ever larger in the United States by that time, prompting many American breweries to sell their machinery and exit the industry. Visits by Japanese brewing reps therefore caught the attention of the *Brewer's Journal* (which would itself be shuttered in 1920 as a consequence of Prohibition). In January 1917, the journal reported that "large orders for brewing machinery are being placed with Milwaukee concerns by the Dai Nippon Brewing Co., Sapporo, Japan, and the Kabuto Beer Brewery Co., Ltd., Tokyo, Japan, whose representatives, Juji Kasahara and K. Tachiki, were recently in Milwaukee. They have been in this country for some time and are inspecting leading breweries and malting plants."[41]

While in America, Asano inspected breweries and a barley processing plant, and he arranged to purchase some American-made malts-processing equipment as well. Because Kirin had no trained malts production staff, foreign expertise was again recruited in order to establish a malthouse and train the required workers. German nationals were largely unavailable due to the war, so in August 1917, a skilled American brewer and malts producer named August Groeschel was brought to Yokohama on a one-year contract. His great-grandson, Jeff Haas, reports that Groeschel was a German-American born and raised in southeast Wisconsin.[42] Groeschel's father had operated a small brewery there, where he trained his son to make beer and malts. In Japan, however, Groeschel faced several obstacles, including a serious shortage of suitable barley that required imports from Australia, heavy rains that delayed the malthouse construction, continuing difficulty importing the necessary machinery, and work schedules that favoured traditional Sunday holidays over continuous malts production. On the final point, an exasperated Groeschel wrote home to his family in Wisconsin, lamenting that his employers and staff "have no idea what it is to run a malthouse."[43] At first, the workers found the handling of the drum-shaped germination can very troublesome, but with Groeschel's guidance, they were soon able to produce quality malts. As a result, Kirin's malts costs fell dramatically, which led to a major rise in profits.[44] His tenure at Kirin was challenging, but as the photographs shared by the Haas-Groeschel family attest, Groeschel also found time to relax with his colleagues and enjoy the fruits of their labour (see Figure 2). When his first twelve-month contract expired, Kirin renewed it and, given his worsening health, at a slower pace than before, but he soon fell gravely ill. He passed away on 8 December 1918 and was buried in the Yokohama Foreign General Cemetery on Yamate Hill, where his headstone rightly describes him as a "maltster" (see Figure 3).[45]

At the same time that Kirin was building its new malthouse, rising export demand and a limited water supply at its Yokohama plant prompted the firm to construct an entirely new brewery. Surveys were conducted and it was decided that brewing beer nearer to Osaka in the Kansai region was essential to meeting Kirin's rising domestic and export sales targets. As a result, a 25,000 tsubo (8.3 hectare) site was chosen in the small village of Shio, in the Kawabe district of Hyōgo prefecture, which Kirin purchased in February 1917. In order to fund the construction of what would soon be named the Kanzaki plant, the directors resolved at a special shareholders' meeting on 10 February to double Kirin's capital stock from ¥2.5 million to ¥5 million by issuing a corporate bond. The new plant boasted brewing machinery and bottling equipment imported from the United States, for Kirin notes that

Figure 2 August Groeschel (centre), at a teahouse with colleagues from the Kirin Brewery Company, 1917. *Courtesy of Jeff Haas.*

Figure 3 Grave of August Groeschel, Yokohama Foreign General Cemetery, Yamate Hill, December 1918. *Courtesy of Jeff Haas.*

Japanese machine technology at that time was "a poor 10 percent" of what it would later become.[46] The cost to construct and furnish the Kanzaki plant totalled roughly ¥3 million, but it could produce 1,800 koku (325 kL) of beer annually, and it could store up to 30,000 koku (5,412 kL) in its warehouse. Engineer Asano Toshirō took a position at the new plant, and brewing operations commenced there on 28 June 1917. With 170 workers and one bottling line, Asano struggled to fine-tune the machinery and keep the plant running despite a variety of glitches and mechanical failures.[47]

Supplying the new plant with water proved to be troublesome, and the plant also necessitated the construction of one of Japan's first wastewater purification facilities. This episode hints at the environmental challenges that would face Japanese industry in the future. As well water was initially very limited at the Kanzaki plant site, the brewery drew water from the nearby Kanzaki River and purified it in a large filtration pond on its factory grounds. Maintaining this reservoir also helped to purify the often stagnant river water. As for sewerage, however, the brewery proved initially to be an unwelcome neighbour. At that time, the wastewater generated when breweries washed out their tanks and kettles was usually filtered for other uses, including irrigating nearby fields. The yeast particles, which were high in nitrogen, would greatly enhance the quality of fertilizer when added to regular manure. The problem, however, was that not only did it make weeds grow furiously, it smelled like dead fish, which nauseated the local farmers and prompted numerous complaints. For that reason, Kirin asked an eminent scholar from Kyushu University, a Dr. Nishida, to build a wastewater treatment facility. Kirin was perhaps the first beer company in Japan to construct such a system; when the city of Osaka had trouble with its own wastewater purification facility, it sent engineers to investigate the facilities at the Kanzaki plant.[48]

In another, unexpected example of technology transfer, engineer Asano delivered an innovation that he learned about during his inspection tour of breweries in the United States. There, he had observed US bottlers shipping their wares in specialized wooden boxes known as crates, which had lids that opened up and closed again. On his return to Japan, Asano informed Kirin's directors about these crates, which were still unknown to the firm even in 1916. Cautiously, Kirin began to experiment with them. Some employees feared that the new crates would be damaged aboard the ships, wagons, and trucks that carried their bottles beyond Yokohama, so they proceeded very slowly. Lacking confidence, Kirin's carpenters built their first crates using five double-width boards with only narrow spaces between them, in hopes that they could withstand the journey. After the first delivery shipped

Table 10

Japan's total beer exports, 1914-23

Year	Volume (kL)
1914	3,440.9
1915	5,070.9
1916	9,967.8
1917	15,673.2
1918	20,242.6
1919	17,011.5
1920	7,586.5
1921	9,725.5
1922	5,963.0
1923	4,277.0

Source: Kirin biiru KK, *Kirin biiru KK gojū nenshi* [Kirin Brewery Company, Ltd.: Fifty-year history] (Tokyo: Kirin biiru KK, 20 March 1957), 233.

out, the plant managers waited anxiously to hear the results from the Meidiya shop in Osaka. They were relieved to learn that there had been no accidents, even after three wagonloads were delivered. Owing to the war and Asano's US inspection tour, Kirin had at last managed to lower its transportation costs and shorten its reach to Japan's westernmost prefectures – two developments that had appeared impossible in early 1914.[49]

Fuelled by the First World War production boom, Japan's overall manufacturing strength grew rapidly, and in 1916 national beer production rose 36 percent over that of 1915. In 1917, it rose a further 25 percent, and another 30 percent in 1918. Much of this increase is attributable to the leap in export sales, which peaked late in the war but then fell sharply during the early 1920s (see Table 10).[50]

Domestic beer sales in Japan were never truly threatened by the possibility of alcohol prohibition, despite the existence of the Japan Woman's Christian Temperance Union (WCTU) since the 1880s. Yasutake Rumi notes that not only were Japanese WCTU members uncomfortable with using the word "Christian" in their name, they also "never agreed with World WCTU missionaries about the merits of emphasizing the temperance cause." Yasutake writes that, because drinking sake had long been an important cultural ritual, Japan WCTU members felt that advocating temperance challenged tradition and triggered "public reproach" of female social activism.[51] Consequently, she asserts, the Japan WCTU never required prospective members to pledge total abstinence from alcohol in order to join the organization, despite pressure from World WCTU missionaries. Conversely, Elizabeth Dorn Lublin claims that Japan WCTU members were indeed committed to the cause of abstinence from alcohol, although she too acknowledges a pervasive adult resistance to the campaign.[52] Absent any real social resistance to beer consumption, domestic beer sales continued to rise into the 1920s.

The Roaring Twenties: Rising Beer Sales after the Great War, 1918-23

On 11 November 1918, the remaining belligerents signed an armistice to end the First World War, at which point Japan's economy was struck by a brief panic. There had been such rapid growth during the war that Japanese investors fully expected falling profits and a drop in production to inevitably follow the peace. Surprisingly, however, the momentum of the war years continued. Japan's domestic beer consumption also remained strong through 1920, even among factory workers. Business at bars, taverns, and beer gardens was healthy, and as more establishments opened throughout Japan's largest cities, their amenities improved as well. Throughout 1920, newspaper ads for the new Crystal Café located at the "Famous Yebisu Beer Garden" informed Westerners that it was the "Only 1st Class Bar and Restaurant in the City." From noon to two p.m., patrons could enjoy a "Special Crystal Tiffin" (light lunch) consisting of three dishes and a glass of beer for ¥1, and the ads proudly boasted "up to date Toilet service."[53] In October 1921, Dai Nippon launched a beer garden on the Ginza, Tokyo's famed shopping street.[54]

In 1922, the *Japan Advertiser* published news of a beer market analysis by the Nomura Banking Corporation, which found:

> The beer industry has not suffered the general depression which has marked other lines of business after the war ... In fact, profits have tripled since the war period, due to the fact that beer drinking has replaced sake to a great extent, and is becoming more popular among the poorer classes. Increased purchasing power of the laboring man, brought on by higher wages, has made him more extravagant and led to his choice of beer instead of the cheaper sake, according to the bank report, and now the consumption ratio between the two liquors is 7 to 1 [beer to sake, by volume].[55]

Of course, a glass of beer has a much larger volume than a cup of sake, but the ratio of 7:1 clearly indicates beer's impressive sales growth during and after the Great War. Although many Japanese workers continued to drink sake, which was less expensive, the overall ratio was a significant milestone for domestic beer producers. The report went on to note that while both Dai Nippon and Kirin were enjoying rising production volumes, Japan's smaller

Table 11

National population and domestic beer production per person, 1907-32

Year	National production (kL)	Population (000s)	Production per person (mL)
1907	36,284.4	47,416	763.2
1912	35,429.3	50,577	698.4
1917	76,212.1	54,134	1,404
1920	99,230.6	55,391	1,787
1925	143,213.8	59,179	2,416
1926	146,772.5	60,210	2,432
1927	144,876.4	61,140	2,365
1928	161,068.8	62,070	2,590
1929	163,281.6	62,930	2,588
1930	148,026.0	63,872	2,313
1931	137,069.5	64,870	2,108
1932	138,402.2	65,890	2,095

Note: Source data is available only at five-year intervals to 1925.
Source: Kirin biiru KK, *Kirin biiru KK gojū nenshi* [Kirin Brewery Company, Ltd.: Fifty-year history] (Tokyo: Kirin biiru KK, 20 March 1957), 235.

brewers, such as Sakura, were losing market share to the veteran firms. On the whole, however, the period immediately following the armistice was one of solid growth fuelled by steadily increasing domestic demand in the continued absence of European imports (see Table 11).

Japan's brewers knew that their free hand in Asia would not last forever. Steadily, Europe's leading brands returned to recover Asian markets that had been lost during the conflict. For that reason, and due also to a sharp appreciation of the yen and to stiffening domestic competition, Japan's postwar beer exports retreated for much of the next fifteen years (see Table 12).[56]

Despite the decline in exports, domestic sales were strong enough to warrant the construction of new plants in order to keep pace with demand. Already by January 1919 Kirin had finished installing an array of new machines at its original Yamate plant in Yokohama, including equipment just imported from Germany. Significantly, mere months after the November armistice and just as the negotiations at Versailles got under way, Kirin had already rekindled its relationships with the German brewing world. Free to travel once more, a German engineer named Litner journeyed to Japan in January to assist with the set-up, and Kirin's updated factory was soon up and running. Despite the improvements, however, Kirin soon required even more production capacity. When its senior managing director, Kōmei Genjirō, passed away in late 1919, he was succeeded in January 1920 by Isono Chōzō,

Table 12

Japan's regional beer exports (kL), 1918-32

Year	China	English colonies	Straits colonies	Dutch colonies	Other areas	Total
1918						20,242.6
1919						17,011.5
1920						7,586.5
1921						9,725.5
1922						5,963.0
1923						4,277.0
1924						3,854.4
1925						3,130.1
1926	1,896.8	688.2	295.5	697.4	472.6	4,050.5
1927	4,247.1	804.4	399.4	656.1	622.2	6,729.1
1928	4,434.3	1,006.8	291.0	1,012.7	654.3	7,399.1
1929	3,750.5	1,454.5	235.0	891.3	732.0	7,063.4
1930	3,404.0	1,375.5	340.4	751.7	1,097.7	6,969.2
1931	2,954.6	1,362.1	270.8	510.1	1,511.3	6,608.9
1932	7,587.4	1,871.5	233.1	1,597.5	1,123.5	7,001.3

Note: All regional groupings are as in the original source. Contemporary English colonies included Hong Kong, while "Straits colonies" refers to the former British crown colony on the Strait of Malacca comprising Singapore, Penang, Labuan, and Malacca. Dutch colonies included the Dutch East Indies (modern Indonesia). All of these regions were occupied by Japanese forces during the war. "Other areas" include the Philippines and the many islands in the western Pacific, to which exports fell during the war as these territories were lost by Japan.

Source: Kirin biiru KK, *Kirin biiru KK gojū nenshi* [Kirin Brewery Company, Ltd.: Fifty-year history] (Tokyo: Kirin biiru KK, 20 March 1957), 233.

the vice-president of Meidi-ya. Kirin began to consider expanding further, and Orient Brewing's new plant in Sendai City became an increasingly attractive target for a possible merger – especially because it was so well equipped.[57]

When it was founded in 1919, the Orient Brewing Company was able to lower the cost to equip a modern brewery because of the US prohibition of beverage alcohol production in that year. As Prohibition swiftly shuttered breweries across the United States, some of them were forced to sell their production machinery. In October 1921, the *Japan Advertiser* reported that "the brewing industry in Japan has been making great strides in recent months largely due to the bargain sales in brewing machinery and equipment following the enactment of prohibition in the United States."[58] Orient was among the Japanese brewers to capitalize on this fire sale. Founded in Sendai, the largest city in Tōhoku, with ¥2 million in capital stock, Orient purchased an array of American brewing machinery made useless by the new US law. Construction of Orient's new plant began in May 1920, and on 10 October 1921, the company launched its new brand, "Fuji Beer." The brewery's employees were quite inexperienced, and their chief engineer, who was hired from rival firm Kabuto Beer, had spent less than five years in the industry. However, the new company soon bolstered its technical abilities by hiring Mr. Streichel, the German former prisoner of war who had been a brewing engineer at Tsingtao Beer during the Great War.[59]

As soon as Orient Brewing opened, however, the firm found itself caught in the midst of a fierce business war in the Tōhoku region, and although its directors advertised their new brand widely, sales did not meet expectations. As operations floundered, Orient's managers entered into talks to sell their plant to Japan's leading brewer, Dai Nippon Beer. Dai Nippon's director, Magoshi Kyōhei, inspected the troubled Orient Brewing plant in October 1922, but the plant did not meet his expectations and the negotiations failed. Orient then approached Kirin Brewery, whose representative inspected and found that the plant's equipment was sufficient. He recommended that Kirin buy the plant, whose location would offer Kirin greater reach into the Tōhoku marketplace. Given the cost savings of shipping beer north from Sendai instead of from Yokohama, Kirin's directors approved the purchase plan.[60] Kirin's shareholders were also pleased and voted to approve the merger, for it greatly relieved the existing pressure on the Kirin brand, which faced complaints due to frequent shortages. Renewed competition from European imports was also a growing concern; the first postwar shipment of German beer, totalling fifty thousand bottles, arrived in Kobe in early 1923.[61] Japan's brewers were therefore forced to lower their prices in order to stay competitive. This would soon be the least of their problems. Before summer's end, disaster struck.

Hell on Earth: The Great Kantō Earthquake and Its Aftermath, 1923-26

On 1 September 1923, the Great Kantō Earthquake struck the cities of Tokyo and Yokohama, devastating towns and villages throughout the surrounding Kantō plain and beyond. Six prefectures were significantly affected by the quake, which caused over three million casualties and killed over 150,000 people, due mostly to fires.[62] The duration of the seismic event, which measured 7.9 on the Richter scale, is uncertain, but various accounts place it at between four and ten minutes. The quake was so terrible that its description features prominently in virtually every history published by cities, municipalities, and major companies that operated in the region. Countless shops, homes, and businesses were simply erased by the quake and the resultant firestorm, because it struck at 11:58 a.m., just as gas stoves and braziers throughout the region were red hot, preparing lunch for office workers, factory employees, and schoolchildren throughout the region. Many small and medium-sized businesses never recovered, because their managers, workers, and owners were killed within minutes. Kirin's original plant at Yamate, in Yokohama, collapsed and burned. For beer brewers operating inside German- and British-influenced brick facilities, which were the most prone to toppling over, the earthquake was particularly devastating. Kirin's record of the events is truly woeful, and parallels many of the themes in Gregory Clancey's recent work on Japan as an "earthquake nation" ill suited to adopting such fragile brick constructions.[63]

In 1923, Kirin possessed some of the oldest German-styled brick architecture in Japan, and the destruction of its Yamate plant was, therefore, virtually total. On 1 September, the factory was in the care of chief engineer Imaida when the earthquake struck, toppling the high brick walls and bringing down the fermentation, finishing, bottling, and storage facilities simultaneously. An enormous volume of both unfinished and finished beer rushed out into the factory and the surrounding neighbourhood as the kettles ruptured and hundreds of casks and crates of bottled beer were shattered. The remains of the factory were soon engulfed in flames, and Imaida himself was narrowly rescued by fellow employees. As soon as he was pulled from the rubble, he rushed to the company dormitory, which, like the company's head office, was located right next to the factory. (Traditionally, and even today, major manufacturing companies in Japan operate dormitories for unmarried male employees, and some firms even construct family housing for married employees. These living arrangements keep employees near to the plant while strengthening the sense of community among the workers.) Sadly, Kirin's family dormitory was crushed when the brick factory collapsed on top of it, killing all of the workers' wives and young children, who were at home having lunch at that hour. While Imaida surveyed the ruined dormitory, the remains of the factory, and the responsibility to conduct the rescue operations, fell to engineer Ōtsuka Yoshio. Two office workers and twenty-four factory employees had been killed by the earthquake, and Ōtsuka gathered up all of the surviving employees and sent them home immediately to find their own families. He asked them to reconvene in the afternoon, when they set about cleaning up the beer that had spilled out of the warehouse. Much of the factory burned into the night and was destroyed completely. Even Kirin's unique bottle-shaped PR truck, which it had imported in 1906, was lost in the fire.[64]

The next morning, survivors from the surrounding neighbourhood of Chiyozakichō assembled at the Kirin site and helped to unearth the victims buried in the rubble of the plant. The food supply was totally disrupted by the disaster, so the surviving managers ordered that the remaining stores of grain be distributed to the local citizens. (At the first meeting of the Yokohama City Council after the disaster, one of Kirin's inspectors suggested that the firm would be glad to distribute its few surviving casks of beer to the local populace, as there was no building in which to store them.) Like most of the company officials, the president of the company, Itami Nirō, lived in Tokyo. As the railway and tramlines were torn up by the earthquake, and the roads were strewn with rubble, he was unable to come to the plant in person. Nevertheless, Nirō ordered an office employee to go to the company's bank, withdraw ¥50,000 in cash, and bring it back to the plant site immediately. Banks were among the few buildings to survive the earthquake and fire, because they were often constructed of stone and reinforced concrete as well as brick, giving them added strength. In a contemporary photograph of then Crown Prince Hirohito, he and his retinue are seen surveying the devastated city of Yokohama from atop the Yokohama Specie Bank, which had survived largely intact. Remarkably, Kirin's office staffer was able to make the withdrawal as ordered, and on his return to the plant site the money was divided among all of the surviving employees in order to aid their recovery.[65]

In the disaster, Kirin lost its main plant, head office, employee dormitory, and nearly all of its equipment and materials. As its surviving officials lived principally in Tokyo, which became a much more remote location, a make-shift head office was set up at Yaesu in Kōjimachi, Tokyo, where Kirin already operated a company store. When the quake losses were finally tallied in early 1924, Kirin's losses amounted to ¥1,410,188.04, which totalled roughly 10 percent of its capital stock.[66] Fortunately for Kirin, the company had just acquired Orient Brewing in Sendai in May 1923, which, together with its Kanzaki plant in Hyōgo prefecture, enabled Kirin to keep production on track. Much worse was the tremendous loss of life suffered throughout the Kantō region, for the victims included Kirin's Meidi-ya sales agents, retailers, and customers. As an independent entity, Meidi-ya had to bear the brunt of its own recovery, which was a heavy blow. Its losses included product that toppled from shelves and smashed, as well as some stores that were destroyed completely, killing their owners. Many of Meidi-ya's shops, known as *tenpo*, were family run and included sleeping quarters in the back. The losses totalled over ¥2.35 million, which erased nearly all of Meidi-ya's capital stock of ¥2.5 million.[67]

As for Kirin's rivals, their experiences of the earthquake were mixed. Dai Nippon's losses were rather light; though its beer warehouse at Azumabashi, Tokyo, was totally destroyed, its factories at Meguro and Hodogaya suffered only minor damage. The only part of the latter plant that had to be reconstructed was, not surprisingly, its bottle manufacturing facility. By 1925, Dai Nippon had already opened a new plant in Nagoya in response to the steady increase in demand, and its capital stock reached an impressive ¥80 million by 1928. On the other hand, the Japan-English Brewery Company, which sold the brand "Cascade Beer," suffered the most serious blow among Japan's makers, when measured to scale. The earthquake destroyed the company's plant and spilled all of its stored beer, costing ¥302,000, which equalled the total value of its property plus the previous year's earnings. The firm's recovery was therefore difficult, and continued operational difficulties forced its directors to put the factory up for auction in 1928. A retail store called Kotobuki-ya purchased the troubled brewer and took over its operations. (Originally established in 1899 by Torii Shinjirō as the Torii shōten, a seller of imported liquors and later distiller of "Suntory Whisky," it had been renamed Kotobuki-ya in 1921.) Finally, in contrast, the Japan Beer Springs Company in distant Handa City, near Nagoya, was relatively unscathed. Formed in 1921 by area brewers Kabuto Beer and Imperial Springs, the firm had begun selling the brand "Union Beer" the following year (see Figure 1). Although Japan Beer Springs lost its Tokyo head office in the earthquake, its Handa plant managed to continue supplying the beer markets of Tokyo and Yokohama during their recovery. Significantly, the factory, which was originally built as the Marusan Beer Brewery in 1887 and renamed Kabuto in 1908, has since been designated a National Tangible Cultural Property because it is the largest surviving red-brick building from Japan's Meiji era. Despite these variable outcomes, the Great Kantō Earthquake inflicted roughly ¥6 million worth of damage to Japan's beer industry, and national output fell by roughly 30 percent.[68]

Following the destruction of its Yamate plant in Yokohama, Kirin commissioned a group of technical engineers from the Shimizu Group to come and inspect the damage. Their report concluded that the cost to rebuild would be roughly the same as building a new plant. Furthermore, clearing away all of the brick rubble would be costly, and the firm had long since realized that the site was too small to permit expansion. Although an obvious blow, the loss of the Yamate plant proved to be an opportunity in the long run, for it prompted the construction of a new plant on a larger site. This would end the company's long-time difficulties with shipping, water supply, and production capacity at a stroke, as well as providing an opportunity to purchase new equipment and machinery. Consequently, when Kirin settled the account for the losses incurred in 1923, it included the cost of the plant. In the interim, the value of its land had risen, which helped lighten the debt repayment load by ¥200,000.[69]

Selecting a new site was a challenge, for while relocating to Tokyo had its appeal, the firm had a long relationship with Yokohama. After considering several possible locations, Kirin learned of a site where a group of industrialists had planned to build a sugar refinery. Located in Namamugi-chō, to the south of Yokohama, it had been seriously damaged during the earthquake, and its owners were willing to sell in order to recover some of their investment. It faced a canal, was close to the Hikikomi railway line, and totalled 307,000 tsubo (101.5 hectares). It also stood just a few hundred yards from the site where a group of samurai from the western province of Satsuma had slain a British tourist named Charles Lenox Richardson in 1862, which led to the Anglo-Satsuma War of 1863 (and the first grave in the Yokohama Foreign General Cemetery). Despite Namamugi's infamy, Kirin's directors again commissioned engineers from the Shimizu Group to inspect the site, which faced the former Tōkaidō Road stretching from Osaka to Tokyo. Test drilling revealed a single sheet of bedrock at a depth of just over two metres, which could easily support the weight of a brewery, so Kirin decided to purchase the entire property. To Kirin's chagrin, however, the Namamugi site was unable to draw from Yokohama's water supply. Kirin therefore agreed to buy a 600 tsubo (1,984 square metre) site in the nearby town of Koyasu-chō, which did have access to Yokohama's water supply. There, Kirin set up its new head office, after which the Yokohama City Council agreed to grant the Namamugi plant access to its water supply.[70]

In June 1925, Kirin broke ground and began constructing a brand new factory with machinery imported entirely from Germany and the United States. The City of Yokohama then agreed to make Namamugi a part of the city's Tsurumi ward, which made it unnecessary to maintain an office in nearby Koyasu-chō. Kirin therefore moved its head office to its new plant site in September. The brewery was finished in April 1926, and with two hundred employees on two bottling lines, and a storage capacity of nearly 5,000 kL of beer, Kirin's new factory was a significant investment. The timing was right, however, for despite a brief drop in national production, demand rose steadily in the years following the 1923 earthquake, and Kirin's output continued to climb. Research on the use of crates continued as well, and gradually all of Kirin's facilities came to use crates to ship beer. The new machinery, especially the bottling line, incorporated a great deal of European and American equipment and technical skill. Kirin even dispatched engineers to study at breweries in Europe, which, although costly, was a worthwhile investment. On their return, the consistency of Kirin's product quality improved, by preventing the occasional cloudiness of its beer. This step forward also satisfied Japan's beer brewing laws, which regulated the colour, taste, and alcohol content of individual beer types, ranging from lighter lagers and pilsners to darker stouts and black beers.[71] Pleased with its state-of-the-art brewery, Kirin proceeded to plunge headlong into a sales war fuelled by accelerating beer production and declining prices.[72]

Targeting New Consumers: Beer Posters, Soft Drinks, and Pharmaceuticals

Through the 1920s and 1930s, beer and soft-drink advertising produced by Japan's leading brewers included newspaper ads, flyers, leaflets, logo-bearing automobiles, hot-air balloons, and especially posters. These large, full-colour posters were commissioned as original paintings, many of which featured beautiful, anonymous women *(reijin)* dressed in colourful kimono or, alternatively, sporting the latest Western fashions and hairstyles. Kendall H. Brown and Sharon Minichiello note that "images of geisha were used indiscriminately to sell everything from beer to kimono throughout the Meiji and Taishō periods and were effective marketing tools for songbooks as well."[73] Dai Nippon, Kirin, and Asahi in particular commissioned many posters via two or three of Japan's leading printing companies, which came to pitch designs directly to the breweries' senior managers. The directors generally expected to see models with particular appearances, and the firms would often request the work of specific painters. They also welcomed modern printing techniques such as lithography *(sekiban)* and plate-making *(seihanga)*, which were growing popular with consumers at that time.

In a report on Japanese poster advertisements appearing in the New York–based publication the *National Lithographer,* the author notes that in these posters,

> the things advertised comprise coffee, biscuits, perfumery, cigarettes, beer, etc., besides transportation: and pretty Japanese ladies lend the charm of their faces and figures to attract attention, just as many of our own advertisers use such pictures ... There are several large hangers advertising such celebrated Japanese "lager beers" as are brewed by the Asahi, Sapporo and Kirin breweries – and they use the words "lager beer" as if they were true disciples of Gambrinus [a legendary king of Flanders and unofficial patron saint of beer and beer brewing]. Again the pretty lady is utilized to call attention to these brews and the labelled bottles plainly indicate their contents.[74]

The artists often remain anonymous because either they added no signatures, or only very faint outlines survive. Artists who worked in the early Shōwa age are somewhat easier to identify, and some can be linked to particular poster themes or styles. Generally, however, the early Shōwa age was an era in which portrait rights and copyrights were not observed, especially internationally. Artists in Japan simply copied Western advertisements and replaced the faces with those of Japanese women, thus rendering their works more modified copies than original paintings.

Their themes are captivating nonetheless. Looking at the posters in chronological order, it is easy to see how their chosen styles and imagery changed over time. In the 1890s and early 1900s, beer is seen served by countless reijin in traditional Japanese settings, and the image of Japan's top geisha, Manryō (1894-1973), appeared among the many posters in this vein. The traditionally dressed Japanese beauty remained a popular subject for posters in later decades too (see Figure 4), but those dating to the mid-1920s and 1930s increasingly featured modern Japanese women in Western clothing, resembling contemporary Hollywood film actresses.[75] These posters featured scenes of beer being enjoyed in trendy cafés by so-called modern girls *(moga)*, typically sporting fashionable Western clothes and hairstyles, as well as women in nightclubs and cabarets wearing sequined and even backless dresses (see Figure 5).[76] A third major trend in poster advertising simply showcased bottles of beer next to modern Western technologies and entertainments, including airplanes, racehorses, sailboats, and dancing girls (see Figure 6). Juxtaposed with these images, beer and other Western products like soda and biscuits were often associated with a new elite culture, especially by those still aspiring to afford them.[77]

Once they were hung in bars, taverns, and Japan's increasingly popular café bars (which often served meals; see Figure 7) and cool-drink bars (which generally did not), the brewers monitored the performance of each poster. Those that were found to boost sales were hung more frequently and for longer periods, up to year-round, while less influential posters were retired sooner. Oddly, however, the posters were hung most commonly in bars where patrons were already drinking, rather than in locales that might reach new consumers. Historian of Japan Donald Keene writes that Edward Seidensticker, the long-time resident of Tokyo and author of *Low City, High City* and *Tokyo Rising,* much preferred the city's back streets, where glimpses of the city's prewar life could still sometimes be found. Seidensticker, he writes, "liked old drinking places like Kagiya, a crowded, smoky bar that dated back to the 1840s and was decorated with posters advertising Meiji-period brands

Figure 4 Traditional Japanese "beauties" (*reijin*) portrayed in beer poster advertisements. From left: Sapporo Beer, 1918; Kirin Beer, 1926; Kirin Beer, 1938. *Courtesy of Sapporo Breweries, Ltd., and Kirin Brewery Co., Ltd.*

Figure 5 Japanese "modern girls" (*moga*) portrayed in beer poster advertisements. From left: Kirin Beer, 1927; Sapporo Beer, 1931; Kirin Beer, 1932. *Courtesy of Sapporo Breweries, Ltd., and Kirin Brewery Co., Ltd.*

Figure 6 Western imagery featured in beer poster advertisements. From left: Sapporo Beer, 1914; Sapporo Beer 1930; Asahi Beer, 1937. *Courtesy of Sapporo Breweries, Ltd., and Asahi Breweries, Ltd.*

Figure 7 Counter of a Western liquor "café" bar, 1934. *Courtesy of the Mainichi Newspapers.*

of beer. I shared his enthusiasm for Kagiya, and also his grief when it was torn down to widen a road."[78] The racy slip dresses and wavy, pincurl hairstyles worn by the women in Taishō-era beer posters continue to capture the imaginations of style, art, and fashion commentators. Throughout 2012, the *Nihon Keizai Shimbun* (Japan economic times) ran a popular series of articles on the women featured in Taishō posters, which focused closely on the themes of liberty, urbanism, modernity, and Western living captured by the artists.[79] Consumers at the time could not have possibly failed to appreciate the brewers' equation of beer with freedom and modern living.

In addition to trendy forms of advertising, Japan's leading beer brewers focused on product diversification during the latter half of the 1920s, experimenting with the manufacture of soft drinks, bottles, and even vitamin drinks and supplements. Kirin Brewery was the first Japanese beer company to begin producing soft drinks, which in the 1920s was a growing and lucrative consumer market. Kirin's sales agency, Meidi-ya, had already negotiated to purchase the trademarks for two popular sodas: "Tansan" (meaning "carbonated") and "Diamond Lemon," which were produced by the Nunobiki Mineral

Springs Company. The cost to acquire those brands, however, was dear. Meidi-ya had to pay ¥1.1 million for the factory, the machines, and a "goodwill" fee *(norendai)*. The last of these was considered payment for the name and reputation of the firm, over and above its tangible assets, which, though an appreciable concept, lacks an exact parallel in the West. Kirin, meanwhile, already possessed the factory, most of the equipment, and the reputation necessary to introduce its own soft drinks competitively. At its shareholders' meeting on 28 January 1927, the second of Kirin's articles of association was updated, and to its business purposes was added the phrase "maker and seller of soft drinks." On 31 August 1927, the company began to assembling a soft-drink factory inside its Yokohama plant, and production began on 11 March 1928. Just five days later, "Kirin Lemon" went on sale.[80]

At the outset, Kirin's Yokohama plant had an annual production capacity of 400,000 crates of "Kirin Lemon," at twenty-four bottles each, and the new product soon earned favourable reviews. Quickly, the company released new flavours such as "Kirin Cider," "Kirin Citron," and in 1929, "Kirin Tansan." Coloured bottles were less expensive, but Kirin was committed to using the highest grade of materials, and it was therefore the first Japanese soft-drink maker to use clear glass bottles. That innovation was received very well by consumers, and it therefore fuelled not only the soft-drink industry, but Japan's burgeoning bottle manufacturers as well. This prompted rapid investment by Kirin in its own bottle production facility. Bottle manufacturing had not begun in Japan until 1893, and though several bottle makers were founded in such cities as Suita, Yokohama, and Sapporo prior to the 1920s, it was some time before Japan's leading beer manufacturers began to produce their own bottles. In 1920, Dai Nippon Beer merged with the Japan Glass Company, which had until then provided bottles to both Dai Nippon and Kirin. The two brewers had discussed cooperative management of the bottle plant, but Dai Nippon's acquisition suddenly threatened Kirin's supply of bottles. Although Kirin was still able to purchase bottles from the company after its acquisition, the brewery's directors realized just how important it was to possess their own bottle manufacturing facility. As a result, the company began building a bottle plant at its Yokohama plant in September 1928, which was completed in October 1929. Based on machinery imported from England, it was expanded in October 1934, by which point it had an annual production rate of eighteen million bottles.[81]

In addition to beer and soft drinks, by the 1920s some Japanese brewers were selling vitamin drinks made from beer yeast, including a popular brand named "Ebios," which was introduced by Dai Nippon in 1930. Not to be outdone, Kirin Brewery updated its articles of association once more, on

28 July 1932, to list the firm's purpose as a maker and seller of "beer and other beverages," as well as "chemical products and medicines." In October 1933, Kirin established a pharmaceutical manufacturing division *(seiyakusho)* at its Yokohama plant, which began producing patent medicines such as Yeast Medicine Amitaze (Kōbozai Amitaze), in both powdered and tablet forms. Still, while all of this diversification necessitated new departments and even new manufacturing facilities, in the long run the core beer market mattered most.

The Invisible Hand: Broken Gentlemen's Agreements and the Beer Sales War

Following the First World War, Japan's economic situation tightened up, foreign exchange was prohibited, and wages and prices remained high. This environment fuelled the continued growth of the market leaders, but the end result was a beer sales war *(biiru hanbaisen)*.[82] By the late 1920s, alcohol consumption by ordinary workers was rising alongside that of meat, eggs, and milk, although vegetables and fish remained the leading commodities purchased by both salaried and factory workers (see Table 13).[83] Sake remained the leading alcoholic drink for the average Japanese consumer, but beer made steady inroads, and factory workers too came to drink it more regularly as living standards rose through the late 1920s and into the 1930s. For many younger consumers, beer was becoming the preferred choice over sake,

Table 13

Food and beverage expenditures by salaried and factory workers, 1926-27

Foods and beverages, listed in descending order from staples to luxuries	Salaried workers (% of spending)	Factory workers (% of spending)
Total food and beverages	31.49	37.92
Grain staples	11.09	15.23
Fish	3.02	3.31
Meat	1.12	1.91
Dairy products	1.04	0.80
Vegetables and dried foods	4.51	5.29
Seasonings	2.78	3.20
Sweets and fruit	2.91	2.43
Alcoholic beverages	1.59	2.60
Other beverages	0.52	0.47
Restaurant meals	2.91	2.68

Source: Naikaku tōkei-kyoku (Government Statistics Office), 1926, 1927, as appearing in Hazama Hiroshi, "Historical Changes in the Life Style of Industrial Workers," in *Japanese Industrialization and Its Social Consequences*, ed. Hugh Patrick with Larry Meissner (Berkeley: University of California Press, 1976), 38.

especially in the growing number of urban cafés and restaurants. As Penelope Francks notes, Western foods grew more popular during this era and more Japanese found themselves eating meal "sets" comprising white rice with side dishes, instead of cheaper, more traditional fare.[84]

As Kirin celebrated its fiftieth anniversary in brewing in 1921, its sales growth was steady and its shares were rising 5 to 10 percent each year. Even after the catastrophe of the Great Kantō Earthquake in 1923, Kirin's finances remained healthy, and its recently acquired plant in Sendai served as a solid foundation for further growth. Dai Nippon Beer enjoyed a steady 30 percent rise in its share price each year during the early 1920s, and it likewise invested its funds toward the construction of new factories. Although the brewing giant erected and equipped a new plant in Nagoya in 1925, it still had surplus funds remaining. Also in 1925, Japan Beer Springs, the brewer of "Union Beer," built a new factory near the Tokyo market in Kawaguchi. By the time that Kirin opened its new plant in Yokohama in 1926, the increased production capacity had begun to generate a surplus, which triggered a drop in prices that soon spiralled into a market collapse. Importantly, however, the sudden drop in prices was not dictated by the manufacturers; the industry leaders had failed to control their own market and thereby secure their own profits.[85]

At that time, Japan's brewers sold their products to their wholesalers and special contract stores, which then supplied small retailers like shops and taverns, which in turn served consumers. As noted previously, the wholesalers and retailers were required to remit payments to the manufacturers only after the beer was sold. As the market tightened in the 1920s, these same dealers and retailers, who had little regard for the manufacturers' desired profit margins, dropped their prices. The price collapse therefore benefited the consumers while it burned the manufacturers. Kirin, for example, was tied to its sales agency, Meidi-ya, by contract, which it renewed for a further six years in April 1922. In the contract, Kirin agreed to a system of compensation that would reimburse the brewer based on a rate of high-volume sales. This system was appropriate during an era of fair competition when prices were stable, but as the competition intensified, the credit arrangement through which Kirin supplied Meidi-ya became more tenuous, and the falling prices triggered by oversupply soon ate up the returns owed to Kirin. Even special incentives and generous subsidies by Kirin aimed at opening up new markets and boosting sales could not prompt Meidi-ya to try any harder.[86]

Meidi-ya had chosen to devote itself to paying off its own earthquake debts at the very time that Kirin needed to expand its sales in order to pay for the reconstruction of its plant at Yokohama. Due to the disaster, Meidi-ya had over ¥2.3 million in bad credit claims to sort out, as well as a series of branch stores to reconstruct. Another major weakness of the market was the nature of the sales agreements made between dealers like Meidi-ya and the various small retailers and shop owners, which were simply "gentlemen's agreements" (*shinshiteki kyōtei* or *shinshi keiyaku*). These verbal contracts were un-supported by documentation, signatures, or collateral. Problems concerning the agreed-on price of beer cropped up at retail outlets in Tokyo in July 1924, including at one of Kirin's own special contract stores, but the brewer was unable to intervene. The price of beer was falling across the country, and as the shop owners tried to stay competitive, the beer market steadily collapsed.[87]

Despite the value of having a buffer between itself and its sole dealer's debts, Kirin's relationship with Meidi-ya had clearly run its course, for the market continued to deteriorate and Kirin's profits were growing worrisomely thin. The cost of Meidi-ya's sales staff payroll was a burdensome form of value-added that left little space for Kirin to target cost savings. At its own plants, the cost of Kirin's payroll was compounded by the payments on its enormous array of fixed assets, especially its new plant in Yokohama. Also, the superheated market competition and falling prices meant there was no way for the brewer to curtail its labour costs, for its entire workforce was working full-time to meet the rising demand for beer. Kirin's high payroll costs soon forced the company to postpone further investments in new machinery, and even to delay payments on its existing equipment for several years. Indeed, during the late 1920s, Kirin notes, it became a challenge for Japan's beer companies to continue operating and to settle their accounts, for doing both at the same time required a degree of financial stability that the beer market did not offer.[88]

Dealers and retailers began to offer deep discounts as a means of generating capital, slashing their prices and underselling the breweries altogether. Kirin's directors hoped that if they stopped sending rebate money to the dealers, they could block the underselling, but this tactic had no effect. As an eco-nomic recession gripped Japan and deflation set in, many retailers fell deeply into debt and neglected their payments to the brewers. Some even closed up shop and fled with the proceeds of their fire sales. These undersellers, thieves, and runaways were referred to as "locusts" *(batta)* by the brewing companies, which were hemorrhaging cash. Worse, the brewers appeared powerless to stop the excessive retail competition, which drained the financial reserves that they had amassed during and after the Great War. Here, the

Table 14

Changes in beer production and sales tax rates and beer prices (¥), 1918-37

Date tax rate took effect	Tax rate		Manufacturers' price per large bottle	Minimum retailers' price per large bottle
	Production tax per koku	Sales tax per large bottle		
1 April 1918	12.00	0.043	–	0.30
1 August 1920	18.00	0.064	–	0.44
1 April 1926-1937	25.00	0.089	0.302	0.38

Source: Kirin biiru KK, *Kirin biiru KK gojū nenshi* [Kirin Brewery Company, Ltd.: Fifty-year history] (Tokyo: Kirin biiru KK, 20 March 1957), 248-49.

companies' perspective on the marketplace competition does not take into account the retailers' point of view, which must surely have been equally desperate. The mid-1920s was a difficult economic period when deflation drove down prices for many consumer goods, even as taxes continued to rise (see Table 14). Price wars between retailers were probably inevitable, especially as they were not required to remit payments to the brewers until after the product was sold. Nevertheless, it was growing increasingly clear that Kirin Brewery had to lean more heavily on its sole sales agent. Drastic measures were required.[89]

In May 1926, Kirin proposed a turnaround plan stipulating that even if Meidi-ya did not manage to sell beer profitably, and did not reach its sales goals, it would still pay Kirin a fixed sum. However, due to the rising production rates and the increasing overabundance of supply, neither company could be certain that the current sales figures could be maintained. In addition, Japan's government had recently announced a tax hike of 3 sen per bottle.[90] Caught between a rock and a hard place, Meidi-ya refused Kirin's proposal, and the two firms were at an impasse. Kirin's chief creditor, Mitsubishi Bank, attempted to relieve the situation by suggesting that the two companies organize a separate joint venture staffed by employees from both firms. Kirin, however, concluded establishing a separate organization would not be a fundamentally different arrangement. Hence, Kirin's directors had but one option remaining – to reestablish direct control over sales.[91]

In the fall of 1926, Kirin's management concluded that any further hesitation would damage the company's welfare. Twenty years after its reincorporation in 1907, the brewer at last resolved to become a unified manufacturer and distributor. This decision by a Japanese manufacturing company to end the relationship with its long-time dealer is rather unusual, given the preponderant focus of the literature on vertical ties, loyalty, and the general reluctance of Japanese firms to break even unprofitable arrangements. Nevertheless, Kirin moved swiftly. Every fifth year, Kirin's president, Itami Nirō, and Meidi-ya's director, Isono Chōzō, exchanged formal letters in which they renewed their sales agency arrangement, but on 16 November 1926, Itami's letter informed Isono that Kirin intended to cancel the contract and to begin dealing directly with its existing customers on the last day of 1926.[92]

Accordingly, sales operations were transferred from Meidi-ya to Kirin on 1 January 1927, and at Kirin's fortieth shareholders' meeting on 28 January, its articles of association were revised once more to include its new branch offices: "Article 3: The company's main office is in Yokohama City, and its branch offices are in Tokyo, Yokohama, Osaka, Nagoya, Fukuoka, Sendai, and Keijō" (the Japanese name for Seoul, the capital of Chōsen, or colonial Korea).[93] On 12 February, the Yokohama district court formally registered one Kirin branch store in each of these cities, all of which were supervised by the Yokohama head office.[94] Later, in April 1928, Kirin opened a new office in the Yaesu Building in Kōjimachi, Tokyo, to which all of the business of its head office was transferred. More importantly, Kirin was now required to establish a new department to manage its system of direct sales, which also required staffing.

At first, one of Kirin's directors, Arata Takema, proposed establishing an entirely new sales organization, but his colleagues deemed that plan too impractical. Remarkably, Kirin chose instead to poach the beer sales staff of Meidi-ya, and transferred them summarily into its own employee ranks. For years, Meidi-ya's sales staff had cultivated relationships with Kirin's many retailers, and Kirin's directors did not wish to jeopardize that community. Nearly all of the Meidi-ya staffers who were connected to beer sales were thus transferred into Kirin's new business department and permitted to keep their former positions. Significantly, this even included Meidi-ya's director, Isono Chōzō. Isono was made the first managing director of Kirin's new business department, where his only loyalty was now to Kirin itself. Kirin thus not only abandoned its long-time sales agency, which Mitsubishi had essentially founded for Kirin's benefit (see Chapter 1), but took Meidi-ya's most experienced staff members as well.[95]

Meanwhile, Japan's beer market was becoming more chaotic with each passing month. National beer production rose again in 1927 as the Japan Beer Springs Company, the maker of "Union Beer," opened another plant in Nishinomiya, near Osaka. At the same time, Dai Nippon Beer shocked the industry by announcing that it had voted to double its capital stock, which hinted at plans for further expansion. Soon, Japan experienced a financial panic *(kinkyū kyōkō),* which prompted action on the part of the leading brewers, who finally declared a truce in their brutal sales war. The era of Japan's beer cartel was dawning.[96]

Voluntary Restrictions: Japan's Beer Cartel Forms, 1928-36

This chapter closes with a study of the negotiated process through which Japan's competing brewers agreed to fix their respective market shares and annual production targets in order to end Japan's endemic beer sales war. The leading brewers had staged a "friendly beer conference" *(biiru konwakai)* in 1923, but it was not until early 1928 that Dai Nippon, Kirin, and Japan Beer Springs at last came to a "three-company agreement" *(sansha kyōtei)* on nationwide production and sales. On 28 February 1929, these three firms were joined by Kyushu's only brewer, Sakura Beer, which had recently changed its name from Teikoku Beer to reflect the name of its brand. Sakura too had experienced severe market difficulties during the 1920s. Its capital stock fell from ¥10 million in 1926 to just ¥4 million in 1929, due chiefly to the costly failure of its parent company, Suzuki shōten.[97] Together, the four largest survivors of Japan's beer sales war concluded a four-company agreement *(yonsha kyōtei)* and attempted to rein in the runaway competition.[98]

Their first attempt at combatting the widespread underselling was an agreement to fix the retail price of a box (four dozen bottles) of beer at ¥19.50. However, in a clear example of the brewers' failure to control their own market, Japan's many beer retailers simply ignored this decree. These "locust shops" *(batta-ya)* continued to set the price of beer unilaterally, and as they were locked in a heated war with one another, the market price simply continued to fall, just as it had been doing for years. In Tokyo, the average price of a box fell as follows:

- 1927: ¥18.60
- 1928: ¥17.30
- 1929: ¥16.40
- 1930: ¥15.30.

In order to break the control of the retailers, the four companies agreed to sponsor the formation of the Tokyo Alcoholic Beverage Wholesalers League. In May 1929, with the cooperation of the beer companies, the league began denying promotional rebate money to those dealers who defaulted on their payments or undersold their peers. Then, in 1930, the league conducted an investigation into the problem of continued underselling and the outstanding remittances owed to the beer manufacturers. It concluded that Kirin and Dai Nippon should fix the price of a box of beer at below ¥16.30 and work to maintain that market price by advertising the product to consumers at that price. If they did so, the league's report concluded that the beer companies would be able to collect the appropriate remittances.

Despite his advancing years, president Magoshi Kyōhei worked with his team at Dai Nippon to implement the league's recommendations. By June 1931, the brewers were indeed able to raise the market price to ¥16.50, but Kirin records that while the entire campaign was unprecedented, its actual effects were not terribly noticeable. Although the wholesalers were organized, they had real no control over shop-level retailers, and the chronic underselling continued. Although the sales tax on beer continued to rise, the league was forced to lower its official minimum retail prices for beer, which put further pressure on the brewers.[99]

Additionally, Kirin faced a challenge from the unscrupulous new manufacturer Kotobuki-ya, which bought out the Japan-English Brewing Company, maker of "Cascade Beer," in 1928 and began selling "New Cascade Beer." In 1930, Kotobuki-ya changed the name of its brand to "Oraga Beer."[100] This, however, was not the only thing that Kotobuki-ya changed. While it had begun by selling its beer in bottles that featured its own marque on the label, in 1931 the company began purchasing and using old Kirin bottles instead. Refilling used bottles was nothing new in Japan, but Kotobuki-ya did not bother to remove the "Kirin Beer" labels. Instead, it simply refilled the bottles with "Oraga Beer," affixed an "Oraga" label to the other side, and shipped them out. "Oraga Beer" was not yet selling in very large quantities, but Kirin was worried about the damage that this clear trademark infringement was doing to its reputation. Kirin soon filed suit against Kotobuki-ya, which lost and was forced to scrape the "Kirin Beer" label off of every bottle it had in stock, which, though only fair, must have been a tedious process.[101]

In spite of the continued challenges from undersellers and competitors, Kirin's profit margin began to rise slowly in the early 1930s, due chiefly to its takeover of sales. As sales increased, Kirin was able to amass funds for reinvestment in new equipment. The broader economy also began to improve after Japan's invasion of Manchuria on 18 September 1931, followed two days later by Great Britain's abandonment of the gold standard. When newly elected Prime Minister Inukai Tsuyoshi (1855-1932) formed his cabinet on 30 December, Japan prohibited gold exports and lowered the foreign exchange rate in an effort to breathe life into the nation's economy. The price of beer soon stopped falling, and the four leading brewers were actually able to raise the official price of a box of beer by a full ¥1. However, the prices of other commodities rose even further, and as beer underselling remained problematic, the outlook in the beer world remained chronically bearish.[102]

On 21 February 1932, the heads of the leading beer manufacturers met with representatives from both the Tokyo Alcoholic Beverage Wholesalers League and the Tokyo Alcoholic Beverage Sales Association. At the meeting, the latter group, which represented shop-level retailers, agreed to cooperate with the brewers and wholesalers and form the Tokyo Beer Cooperative Association. This new association resolved not to deliver any more products to underselling retailers, who were to be shunned. This strategy, however, had little influence over the vast number of retailers throughout the Tokyo area, many of whom simply ignored the demands of the new cooperative association. The undersellers knew well that despite the protests of the manufacturers, both sides had a vested interest in keeping the beer moving, and the association's pledge to shun the retailers turned out to be an empty threat. If the leading brewers were really going to take control of Japan's beer market, they were going to have to use heavier artillery. Selling beer profitably clearly required genuine control over every level of the sales chain – and in all markets beyond Tokyo. For the manufacturers, an important option remained: the merger or acquisition of nearly all of the remaining brewers and the imposition of a sweeping new system of retail control. A powerful beer cartel was soon to emerge.[103]

By 1928, Dai Nippon's president, Magoshi Kyōhei, was one of the wealthiest men in Japan and a Crown member of Japan's appointed upper house, the House of Peers.[104] In 1932, however, his health began to decline and he sought to shore up Dai Nippon's capital stock in preparation for the arrival of a new president. During his tenure, Magoshi had always maintained that the ideal level for Dai Nippon Beer's capital stock was ¥100 million, but in the early 1930s the company's stock hovered at just ¥80 million. Magoshi knew that if his firm were to combine with Japan Beer Springs, the brewer of "Union Beer," Dai Nippon's stock would indeed hit ¥100 million. Therefore, Dai Nippon sent its mediator, Iwasaki Hisaya, to open negotiations with its smaller rival. Rather than be secretive about the plan, Japan Beer Springs in turn sent its own representative, Metsu Kaichirō, to inform Kirin's directors of the ongoing merger talks. Metsu told Kirin that if Dai Nippon Beer and Japan Beer Springs did indeed merge, Magoshi of Dai Nippon gave his solemn promise *(katai yakusoku)* that the colossal new company would compete with Kirin on equal terms.

On 20 April 1933, however, Magoshi passed away at the age of ninety. In accordance with his wishes, Ōhashi Shintarō succeeded him as Dai Nippon's president, but Magoshi's death and the resultant management shakeup at Dai Nippon left the merger negotiations adrift. The president of Mitsubishi Bank, Katō Takeo, agreed to step in and mediate renewed merger talks privately.

Publicly, the ostensible mediator was the minister of commerce and industry, Nakajima Kumakichi, who, along with Katō's quiet efforts, brokered a temporary agreement on 21 June 1933. Thus, Japan's government gave its explicit approval to the merger, which was concluded on 19 July.[105]

After the merger with Japan Beer Springs, Dai Nippon boasted an impressive array of assets, brands, and financial strength, but the beer sales war had already made it clear that size alone would not enable control of the beer market. For this reason, in summer 1933, Dai Nippon embarked on the second phase of its plan – negotiations with Kirin over the creation of a formal beer cartel. Cartels were already in existence throughout Japan's steel, weaving, banking, and machinery sectors. Nakamura Takafusa notes that during the interwar era, "every industry formed cartels, striving to reduce output and maintain prices."[106] The formation of the prewar beer cartel was thus an obvious response to the problem of superheated sales triggered by rampant underselling. In order to reach such an agreement, Dai Nippon proposed that the two brewers enter into a comprehensive cooperative beer sales agreement *(bakushu kyōdō hanbai keiyaku)*, which it further proposed to manage by co-founding a new sales agency, the Cooperative Beer Sales Company. The revolutionary plan, which would ultimately necessitate the involvement or takeover of both remaining brewers, Sakura and Kotobukiya, was an unprecedented market-sharing arrangement. Its terms read as follows:

1   Each company will invest ¥2 million in the establishment of the Cooperative Beer Sales Company, Inc.
2   Both companies will sell all of the beer that they produce through the new sales company.
3   All advertising will be done via the sales company, and all expenses related to shipping will be borne by the companies themselves.
4   Production will be based on each company's respective sales numbers: Dai Nippon Beer's share is 70.12 percent and Kirin Brewery's share is 29.08 percent.
5   If excess volumes are produced, compensation will be paid to the other party.
6   The practical business of sales, such as their sales network, orders, special contract stores, etc., will be handled by each company, just as before.
7   During the term of the agreement, building new factories or improving existing ones without consulting the other party is not permitted.
8   The same is true for factories overseas, and for similar plans.
9   This agreement will remain in effect for a period of five years.

This sweeping arrangement was simple and clear. The relative proportions of market share, which formed an almost perfect 70:30 split, were based on the sales then commanded by the two firms, and were not a division of the whole market – at least not yet.[107]

The resulting Cooperative Beer Sales Company was established on 12 August 1933 with a head office in Kyōbashi, Tokyo. The managing directors were Isono Chōzō, formerly of Meidi-ya and the director of Kirin's business department, and Takahashi Ryūtarō of Dai Nippon Beer, who would later become that company's president. Together, they charted a course for the future of Japan's beer market that would tolerate neither underselling retailers nor uncooperative brewers. With their sights thus set on rivals Sakura and Kotobuki-ya, the dawn of a new beer industry was at hand. In early 1934, Kotobuki-ya reorganized and became the Tokyo Beer Company, and Dai Nippon simply bought all of its shares in a swift, albeit civil, takeover. The shares were transferred to the Cooperative Beer Sales Company in July 1934, and future production by the little firm was thereafter shared in the 70:30 sales ratio already agreed on by Dai Nippon and Kirin.

This complex process gave rise to a special-contract sales network *(tokuyaku hanbaimō)* more extensive than that of any other Japanese food or beverage producer. The growing fleet of special chain stores *(tokuyakuten)* more than doubled from 212 stores in 1933 to 499 in 1938.[108] The number of bars and cafés also grew dramatically through the 1930s, many of them sponsored by the brewers. The owners of these establishments naturally represented a large vested interest that was opposed to Japan's temperance movement, which also continued to grow throughout the interwar years. Although the Japan WCTU was still a relatively small group, in 1934 the Japan Temperance League boasted fully 3,300 branches and a membership of 300,000.[109] Despite their growing ranks, however, any hopes of convincing Japan's parliament to enact prohibition would be dashed by the coming war. Given the rising consumption of beer and the precious tax revenue that it generated, the government would choose to protect and control the industry, rather than abolish it.

Despite its remote location in Moji, Kyushu, little Sakura Beer could hardly escape Dai Nippon's immense gravity for very long. In 1935, Sakura Beer and the Cooperative Beer Sales Company effectively replicated the agreement between the two market leaders by each investing in and establishing the Sakura Beer Sales Company. The two sides agreed that all "Sakura Beer" would be sold through the new sales firm, and Sakura was guaranteed annual sales of one million boxes of beer, each containing twenty-four bottles. If that sales figure could not be met, the Cooperative Beer Sales Company, which was owned jointly by Kirin and Dai Nippon, would pay Sakura compensation.

Table 15

Domestic market share of leading brands (%), 1935-39

Year	Asahi	Kirin	Yebisu	Sapporo	Sakura	Union	Kabuto	Oraga
1935	27.7	28.2	19.5	8.7	8.1	5.6	1.4	0.8
1936	28.8	28.4	21.5	8.4	7.0	4.0	1.2	0.7
1937	29.8	27.9	22.4	8.6	7.0	2.8	0.9	0.6
1938	31.4	27.0	24.5	8.8	6.4	1.0	0.4	0.5
1939	32.2	26.0	25.3	8.9	6.4	0.7	0.1	0.4
Avg.	30.0	27.5	22.6	8.7	7.0	2.8	0.8	0.6

Note: Asahi, Yebisu, and Sapporo were all brewed by Dai Nippon biiru. Union was produced by Japan Beer Springs. Kirin, Sakura, Kabuto, and Oraga were brewed by eponymous firms.
Source: Sapporo biiru KK, *Sapporo 120 nenshi* [120-year history of Sapporo Breweries] (Tokyo: Sapporo biiru KK, 1996), 297.

This deal was effectively a compromise in which Sakura, unwilling to be acquired outright, preserved its nominal independence by signing a truce with the leading brewers' goliath sales company.

In a parallel to the establishment of the Cooperative Beer Sales Company on Japan's mainland, the colonial government on Taiwan issued orders in 1933 to create the Taiwan Alcoholic Beverage Monopoly. Thereafter, all beer was sold under the authority of the Taiwan governor general's office. In the home islands, however, government intervention had been unnecessary. The leading brewers had essentially agreed to share the market and the spoils, and even to permit increased production, provided that their proportional market shares were maintained (see Table 15). Kirin opened a new brewery in Hiroshima in late 1936, and Dai Nippon too constructed additional facilities, but in accordance with their agreement, each sought the blessing of the other before doing so. Kirin Brewery therefore claims that by the mid-1930s Japan's beer industry was "already conducting itself in perfect order" with the quasi-wartime system *(jun senji taisei)* of manufacturing directives that would begin in 1937.[110] The company underlines that the changes made to the beer industry were not mandated by the Ministry of Commerce and Industry, but were instituted voluntarily by the industry itself in order to halt a long-standing and exhausting business war. Still, the jumble of small retailers in Japan's urban centres had yet to be fully controlled. Achieving that goal would take national mobilization for war.

Conclusions

Beer consumption rose steadily during the first four decades of the twentieth century, in concert with Japan's gradually rising standards of living. The increases were incremental, but over time, beer became affordable for middle-class and even working-class men and women, even if just on occasion. Beer's availability at urban retail stores, taverns, bars, and cool-drink shops expanded steadily, and trucks bearing the brewers' names and logos trundled along Japan's dirt roads, making deliveries to shops and taverns in rural areas as well. High points in Japan's imperial rise, such as its victory over the Russian Navy in 1904, also provided patriotic opportunities for the brewers to advertise beer alongside Japan's national Hinomaru and naval ensign flags.[111] Kirin and Dai Nippon earned significant cachet as suppliers to the Imperial Japanese Navy, whose officers and sailors drank exclusively domestic brews aboard the emperor's state-of-the-art warships. Throughout the late Meiji era, consumers were steadily targeted by posters showcasing elegant beauties in Western fashions and technological innovations like airplanes and automobiles. As a beverage, beer's identity was undoubtedly modern, but its flavour and heritage remained distinctly German during the early twentieth century, due chiefly to the technical skills and continuing influence of German brewmasters.

The Taishō era presented significant export opportunities for Japan's brewing firms, which, like many other companies, suddenly found themselves without European competitors in the East Asian marketplace during the Great War. Preoccupied with the demands of total war on the home front, European manufacturers, financial firms, and service companies abandoned their Asian markets, leaving behind an empty playing field for their Japanese rivals. This ideal combination of wartime circumstances – no significant combat, no competitors, and the lucrative opportunity to supply Entente forces – gave Japan a free hand in the East Asian marketplace for over four years. Like many Japanese banking, insurance, shipping, and manufacturing firms during that era, Japan's brewers were quick to fill the void left by European brands, which had long since dominated the regional market for beer. Despite the ferocity of the Great War and its significant disruption of global trade, however, Japan's relationship with German brewing firms, technicians, and equipment suppliers was swiftly rekindled in 1919. The Great Powers quickly reclaimed much of the East Asian marketplace, but Japan's domestic beer sales boom carried on through the 1920s. Although their facilities were badly damaged by the Great Kantō Earthquake in 1923, both Kirin and Dai Nippon emerged by 1926 stronger than before, armed with more modern plants, equipment, and bottling lines staffed by both men and women. In that year, Kirin's new brewery at Namamugi was advertised as a modern symbol of the region's recovery and the bright future ahead of its many manufacturers. Like their peers in the machinery and munitions sectors, which were swiftly reconstructed after the disaster (often with support from Japan's military), Japan's major brewers soon began producing record volumes.[112]

Despite the market's growth, however, this period in the development of Japan's beer industry also qualifies our perspective on Japanese industry and commerce in several ways. First, the industry demonstrates the very limited reach of contemporary consumer product manufacturers. Although the top beer makers boasted large plants and commanded significant market share, their product remained relatively unusual in Japan's most distant rural areas, where it was also prohibitively expensive for most consumers. Japan's top-ography remained a significant barrier to the spread of commerce beyond the Kantō plain, despite improved transportation technology. The rugged hills and limited roadway infrastructure that had for centuries shielded the capital of Edo from potential insurrection were not overcome suddenly by the arrival of the railroad or the motorcar. Similarly, factories located just over Yatozaka Hill from Yokohama's wharves were rendered no closer to the port by the advent of the locomotive. Teams of horses, or sometimes men, were still pulling heavy wagons to and from Kirin's factory gates sixty years after the arrival of the steam engine in Japan in 1854. Compounding these challenges to the brewers' reach was the annual threat of especially rainy weather, which could turn the country's dirt roads into miles of muddy ruts, inhibiting transport and depressing sales.

Second, modern manufacturing methods did not immediately eclipse traditional modes of production. Kirin records that wooden crates with lids were unknown to the firm even in 1916. Instead, inside its brewery ware-houses, basket makers trained in the Edo era could still be found weaving away as late as the First World War, producing bamboo baskets for packing and shipping bottles. Indeed, sending a liquid product in glass bottles aboard ship from Tokyo to Osaka was still risky at that time. Skills and techniques were improving, but the obstacles remained significant, and although the progress was steady, it was not always swift. As before, these themes are further qualifications of the idea that Japan was industrializing rapidly. Forward progress was being made, but individual companies sometimes took decades to achieve significant advances.

Finally, this chapter gives us a glimpse of the underside of doing business in Japan. In the popular Western imagination, Japanese companies and salary-men are sometimes portrayed as more "honourable" than their Western rivals, but they were not modern-day versions of the archetypical samurai. Japanese manufacturers and retailers were no less capable of cheating, cutting corners, or breaking laws than their Western contemporaries. In the 1920s, an intense and protracted price war between small beer retailers threatened to exhaust Japan's leading producers, who struggled desperately to keep up with demand as the sagging economy drove consumer prices down. Several attempts by the brewers to establish control over pricing failed, swallowing virtually their entire profit margins. This fruitless, decade-long beer sales war was truly won only by beer consumers. The intense market competition was fuelled by competitive shop owners and underselling wholesalers, referred to by the brewers as "locusts," some of whom even stole from their suppliers and fled without paying the brewers. Scholarly discussions of such outcomes are far less common than those that focus on the often communitarian nature of business in Japan, but they are essential to our understanding of what it was like to compete and survive in the complex prewar marketplace.

For over ten years, even explicit price-fixing and market-sharing agreements among the brewers did little to counter a flawed business model that demanded payments from retailers only after beer was sold to consumers. Rather than change their business model, however, the brewers combatted the undersellers through retail federations and various enforcement mechanisms. That lengthy struggle, made worse by a lengthy recession, involved none of the themes of loyalty between suppliers, dealers, and consumers that are referenced so often by casual Western observers of Japanese business. The phrase "beer sales war" was no euphemism. The continuing price war finally subsided in the early 1930s with the creation of a sweeping and powerful beer cartel designed to control both production and prices.

Influenced very likely by the popularity of cartels in other industrial sectors, the three major brewers agreed in 1933 to form a cartel to curb excessive competition, to eliminate underselling dealers, and to fix both prices and production targets. Brokered ostensibly by the Ministry of Commerce and Industry, the deal, known as the Cooperative Beer Sales Agreement, was actually mediated by the president of Mitsubishi Bank. As part of the deal, both Dai Nippon and Kirin agreed not to build new breweries or even improve existing ones without consulting the other party first, a remarkable voluntary limitation that fixed their market shares and drove their remaining competitors out of business. This explicit collusion between competing manufacturing firms was orchestrated in the name of market stability and securing modest profits. Enacted voluntarily in order to halt a lengthy and exhausting business war, this uniquely Japanese agreement succeeded in raising and stabilizing the price of beer, and it drove out the "locusts" and their underselling ways. Then, in 1937, Japan entered into a ruinous war in China. Although terribly destructive, that conflict and the coming Second World War would prompt changes that finally domesticated Japan's brewing industry and patriated beer as a thoroughly Japanese commodity.

3 Brewing Self-Sufficiency: Beer, Empire, and the Wartime Command Economy, 1937-45

During the war era, Japan's beer industry faced a host of new challenges that would influence the lives of consumers more strongly with each passing year. By examining the brewers' wartime operations, it becomes possible to answer such questions as, With the general prohibition of luxury goods, was beer still available for consumption, and if so, what did it cost? Were the bars, taverns, and restaurants still operating, in spite of the increased rationing? And finally, how could the purchase and open consumption of beer be reconciled with the increasing sacrifices asked of ordinary Japanese, especially toward the end of the war when rationing became more severe? On these points, the sources are clear. Not only was rationed beer available until the spring of 1945 in a generic, highly controlled fashion, it served as a key source of wartime tax revenue. Because it generated essential funds for the war effort, beer was available for purchase in bars, restaurants, and even for home consumption until very late in the war. Likewise, beer remained available to military personnel, as well as for public celebrations and soldiers' send-off ceremonies. Ensuring beer's continued availability was also a valuable way for Japan's military government to maintain living standards and boost morale among workers, especially as the war situation deteriorated.

Until 1945, beer was brewed throughout the Japanese Empire, often by the same firms, which gives this industry a broad, imperial dimension. Kirin and Dai Nippon each established an array of breweries throughout Japan's colonies, and the latter firm had even founded a brewery at Balintawak in the Philippines in 1938.[1] In addition, the industry's management by the Ministry of Finance is a unique intersection between wartime agriculture, food policy, manufacturing, distribution control, and tax revenue. Sources on the brewing industry speak to the immense difficulties facing Japanese manufacturing firms during the war years, as well as the manner in which their production and distribution systems were totally reorganized by Japan's government in the name of tighter control and increased efficiency. Japan's beer industry serves as a uniquely detailed example of the manner in which wartime government administrators took over, controlled, and totally reorganized the production, distribution, and taxation of a consumer commodity.

Beer rationing would gradually come to an end by the late 1940s, but many of the industry's wartime representative associations would survive in a modified fashion, having demonstrated their obvious utility as forums for communication between the brewers. In this respect, the case of the beer industry strongly supports Chalmers Johnson's argument for the significance of wartime institutional development in Japan's postwar economic growth.[2] It also supports Nakamura Takafusa's claim that "many social and economic institutions, technologies, life styles, and customs were created during the war and were inherited in the postwar period. Even if they were not created with a long-term perspective at the time, in the end they defined the postwar patterns of companies, industrial organizations, and life styles."[3] Importantly, meeting the demands of the Ministry of Finance freed Japan's brewing industry from its reliance on German recipes, ingredients, and engineers, thus enabling beer's transformation into a thoroughly Japanese consumer product.

Barley versus Rice: Beer, Sake, and Wartime Food Supply Policies

The year 1937 was a challenging one in which to serve as a captain of industry in Japan. Following Dai Nippon Beer's shareholders' meeting on 28 January 1937, a new managing director, Takahashi Ryūtarō, assumed office, and his predecessor, Ōhashi Shintarō, graduated to the role of company chairman. Takahashi was born in Ehime prefecture in July 1875 and studied at Munich University from 1899 to 1904. On returning to Japan, he joined the Osaka Beer Company, which merged with Nippon Beer and Sapporo Breweries to form Dai Nippon Beer in 1906. As chairman, Ōhashi took charge of government office relations, while Takahashi assumed control of all other company affairs. These two men had served as the firm's management core since the death of former president Magoshi Kyōhei in April 1933, but the office of president had remained vacant since his passing. At the directors' meeting on 19 February, it was agreed that Takahashi would also assume the role of president. His tenure, which carried on into the Second World War, would prove to be the most challenging yet for any Dai Nippon president.[4]

Sapporo Breweries (the successor of Dai Nippon) records that market equilibrium was achieved between Japan's leading brewers after the recession and the sales rivalry of the early Shōwa era passed.[5] Dai Nippon's rival, Kirin, likewise describes the mid-1930s as relatively tranquil for Japan's beer industry.[6] However, war broke out between Japan and China on 7 July 1937 after Japanese troops exchanged fire with Chinese forces at the Marco Polo Bridge (Lugouqiao) near Beijing, triggering a planned invasion of North China by Japan's Kwantung Army. Having spent the last six years preparing Manchuria as its forward base of operations, Japan's forces were well prepared for the invasion, and could rely on relatively short supply lines connecting their operations with Manchuria's developing industrial base. Japan's government and private Japanese investors had established and cultivated farms, collieries, foundries, mills, and a wide array of manufacturing enterprises in the years since Japan's annexation of Manchuria in 1931. Beer breweries were among the many enterprises set up in Manchuria, as well as in Korea after the latter's annexation by Japan in 1910.[7] I will focus more closely on some of these firms below.

In August 1937, roughly six months after assuming office, Takahashi Ryūtarō of Dai Nippon Beer set out on an inspection tour of the brewing industry in America and Europe. It was a difficult time for any Japanese executive abroad, for foreign newspapers strongly denounced Japan's invasion and sided with the Chinese, who were generally perceived in the West to be the victims of Japanese aggression. Nevertheless, Takahashi recognized that the deteriorating international political situation threatened the Japanese beer industry. If Europe slid into war, Germany would in all likelihood be unable to export hops, on which Japanese brewers were still very dependent. Takahashi therefore wished to identify ways in which his company might achieve self-sufficiency in brewing materials. Crossing the Pacific by ship, Takahashi and a colleague visited beer company offices and breweries throughout the United States en route to the east coast, whence they sailed to England and visited breweries in London. Next, they travelled to Paris before visiting Germany, which had always been regarded by Japanese brewers as the font of European brewing wisdom. In Berlin, Munich, and other German cities, Takahashi minutely inspected brewers' ingredients, techniques, and markets before returning to Japan in December. His inspection of Western breweries enabled him to deliver a series of lectures about the latest brewing techniques, equipment, and technicians. Particularly interesting to Japan's brewers was the use in America, Germany, and Austria of brewing machinery and storage tanks made of nickel alloys, for their nonreactive surfaces did not interfere with the brewing process.[8] Meanwhile, all sectors of Japan's strategic industries began ramping up production, and legislation to transform their operational targets and priorities was already under consideration. Even for Japan's beer industry, the war era had arrived.[9]

After fire was exchanged by forces of the Imperial Japanese Army and Chinese Nationalist troops in July 1937, Japan's government announced a general plan to keep the conflict localized, referring to the situation as the North China Incident *(Hokushi jihen)*. Military operations expanded step by step, however, until the war came to be known as the China Incident *(Shina jihen)*. In the interim, in order to raise funds to pay for the widening operation, Japan's government established a special North China Incident Tax. However, because the majority of the increasing military spending was funded by war loans, there was already debate among policy-makers over the risk of runaway inflation.[10] The government therefore advised citizens to economize, to spend wisely, and to maintain healthy savings accounts. Civic campaigns admonished families to live like the paragons of diligence and thrift from the Edo era. As Sheldon Garon notes, these savings campaigns featured the tireless young Ninomiya Sontoku (1787-1856), whose work ethic and frugality had delivered him from poverty and ultimately made him a financial planner sought after by provincial lords.[11] Housewives especially were advised to maximize their budgets through careful shopping and cooking. Despite these efforts, the government's rigorous new economic controls over trade and currency exchange led to significant supply shortages. This, in combination with the growing activity of small and medium-sized commercial firms, as well as military subcontractors, triggered sharp increases in both wages and prices. Importantly, this changing economic situation stimulated beer consumption, which was a key source of tax revenue for the central government. Beer manufacturing and consumption were not yet subject to controls, which led naturally to a boom in beer sales that its makers enjoyed to the fullest.[12]

Already by that time, however, there were ominous signs concerning Japan's domestic food supply. From 1934, the rice harvests in Tōhoku, the northern portion of Japan's largest island, had been very poor. At the same time, the standards of living in Korea and Taiwan were rising, increasing the rate of rice consumption there and decreasing exports from these colonies to Japan's home islands. Furthermore, as military operations continued and munitions manufacturing geared up in earnest, rural farming villages began to suffer shortages of manpower. Not only did this erase the rice surplus enjoyed by Japan since the late Taishō period, there were soon signs of a rice shortage. Consequently, the availability of rice for sake brewing was sharply curtailed, and the production of sake peaked at 4.37 million koku (788,300 kL) in 1937.[13]

Naturally, having less sake encouraged consumers' taste for beer, the production of which continued to increase. Despite the rise in beer consumption, however, the 1939-40 edition of the trade publication the *Japan Year Book* noted that beer continued to play second fiddle to sake in Japan:

> This is easy to explain. Most of [Japan's] people take saké, the production of which is about 4.5 times as large as beer. Saké is the standard drink, only a very small quantity of which is enough for average man [sic]. In other countries, beer is a staple, an article of food. But in Japan it is something of a luxury, reserved for the people of middle and upper classes. A bottle of beer, which contains about one-fifth of a gallon of beer, sells about at 50 or 60 sen, which is too high for average Japanese farmers or wage-earners. If the Japanese of these classes take as much beer as the Belgians do they would spend greater portion [sic] of their income on beer.[14]

Still, while beer cost more than sake, it would very soon find itself on top. Already by 1938, Japan's government was faced with a widening war in China, and it soon enacted legislation to mobilize labour and institute both price and profit controls. With the passage of the National General Mobilization Law in April 1938, Japan's economy and industries became increasingly state-directed and state-controlled. At noon on 18 September 1939, the government issued a revised National General Mobilization Law, known as the 9-18 Stop or the 9-18 Price Freeze Order. The "stop" fixed prices on a wide array of raw materials and consumer commodities, including beer. Fixed beer prices, which I will examine in more depth below, were thus combined with the fixed market shares to which the beer producers had already agreed voluntarily in 1933.[15]

After 1939, government-ordered reductions in sake production came to be enforced very strictly. Rice was deemed an essential grade-A foodstuff, and the 1939 sake production year (October 1939-September 1940) witnessed a more than 40 percent drop from the previous year. Very swiftly, the business of sake production became unprofitable, and by the end of 1940, all sake brewers' operations were terminated. While the *existing supply* of sake would be rationed and consumed for the remainder of the war era, the government's decision to shutter Japan's many sake brewers and forbid further production came as a significant psychological blow. The industry boasted multiple operations in all of Japan's former Edo-era domains, which had operated proudly for centuries.[16]

With the closure of the sake industry, the beer industry suddenly took the lead, for its main ingredient was barley, a grade-B foodstuff. In 1939, Japan's brewers produced a combined 313,000 kL of beer, a record amount that was not surpassed until 1953 (see Table 16). Production in that year of

Table 16

National population and domestic beer production per person, 1933-45

Year	National production (kL)	Population (000s)	Production per person (mL)
1933	195,301.0	66,880	2,914
1934	175,158.3	67,690	2,581
1935	189,168.1	68,662	2,749
1936	218,432.8	69,590	3,132
1937	227,503.2	70,040	3,242
1938	266,327.3	70,530	3,767
1939	312,875.3	70,850	4,406
1940	264,380.7	71,400	3,695
1941	264,451.9	71,600	3,685
1942	261,645.8	72,300	3,611
1943	212,317.4	73,300	2,891
1944	158,827.8	73,800	2,147
1945	83,299.8	72,200	1,152

Source: Kirin biiru KK, *Kirin biiru KK gojū nenshi* [Kirin Brewery Company, Ltd.: Fifty-year history] (Tokyo: Kirin biiru KK, 20 March 1957), 235.

Dai Nippon's three brands, "Yebisu," "Sapporo," and "Asahi," totalled 210,000 kL, giving Dai Nippon a 66.4 percent market share (see Table 15, above). Due to the rising price of raw materials, however, the company's profits began to slide that year, and like that of all corporations, its profit margin was capped by the government at 12 percent – a limit that was further reduced to 11 percent in 1940. In that year, due to the pressures and restrictions of the war era, national beer production fell 15 percent below its 1939 peak, and exports likewise declined (see Table 17).[17]

When war broke out between Great Britain and Germany in September 1939, Japan's industries began to anticipate the coming world conflict. Japan's food supply had already begun to dwindle after 1937, and as funds for the war effort came to be raised through war loans, the existing alcohol tax structure became less relevant and effective. Therefore, in March 1940, the Finance Ministry revised the system and a new Alcohol Tax Law was issued. This process illustrates Japan's wartime efforts to regulate and maximize its increasingly desperate food supply – a system that would remain in effect well into the postwar Occupation era. The national war effort required enormous expenditures for supplies and matériel, which triggered a shift from a quasi-wartime tax system to a genuine wartime tax system. With the exception of 1942, the tax levied on beer increased every year between 1937 and 1945. On 1 April 1937, the brewing tax of 25 yen per koku of beer was

Table 17

Japan's regional beer exports (kL), 1937-45

Year	China	English colonies	Straits colonies	Dutch colonies	Other areas	Total
1937	15,100.4	3,061.0	536.3	447.5	5,203.2	24,348.5
1938	36,535.8	2,342.5	269.3	241.4	3,992.6	43,381.6
1939	25,545.6	2,844.4	296.7	382.2	3,229.2	32,298.1
1940	19,071.2	1,389.2	202.4	304.9	2,309.9	23,277.5
1941	17,454.9	642.5	80.5	255.4	1,714.8	20,148.1
1942	6,806.3			70.4	840.1	7,716.7
1943	2,470.1			76.5	487.1	3,033.6
1944	626.7				88.2	714.9
1945					6.0	6.0

Note: All regional groupings are as in the original source. Contemporary English colonies included Hong Kong, while "Straits colonies" refers to the former British crown colony on the Strait of Malacca comprising Singapore, Penang, Labuan, and Malacca. Dutch colonies included the Dutch East Indies (modern Indonesia). All of these regions were occupied by Japanese forces during the war. "Other areas" include the Philippines and the many islands in the western Pacific, to which exports fell during the war as these territories were lost by Japan.

Source: Kirin biiru KK, *Kirin biiru KK gojū nenshi* [Kirin Brewery Company, Ltd.: Fifty-year history] (Tokyo: Kirin biiru KK, 20 March 1957), 233.

increased to 35 yen by the Temporary Tax Increase Notification Law, and then on 1 April 1938 it was increased by another 5 yen per koku through a commodity tax called the China Incident Special Tax Law. On 1 April 1939, this commodity tax was doubled to 10 yen, raising the total brewing tax to 45 yen per koku. Moreover, on 29 March 1940, the new Alcohol Tax Law was promulgated, which formed the framework for Japan's postwar alcohol tax system.[18]

The new Alcohol Tax Law abolished all of the older taxes.[19] From 1 April 1940, the brewing tax was replaced by a beer Storage and Shipping Tax of ¥59.30 per koku. At the same time, however, the volume of beer that was permitted to be produced was reduced. Further restrictions were placed on the ingredients used to brew beer, which, added to the price rise due to the tax increase, severely affected the brewing industry. In 1940, an unprecedented system of compulsory rice delivery and rationing was initiated. In June 1941, various types of barley also became subject to production controls, and the long-time system of barley contract farming, through which the brewers secured future supplies from specific farms, ground to a halt.[20] Naturally, it remained permissible to substitute ingredients for malts, including less than 50 percent of rice, corn, potatoes, flour, sugar, or sorghum. However, the Finance Ministry specified that brewers were not allowed to enhance the taste or colour of their beers by adding bitters or colouring agents.[21] Despite these restrictions, the Finance Ministry kept the beer industry in business, for its bureaucrats had already identified the importance of the tax revenue generated by beer sales.

Grown in Japan: Hops, Barley, and the Steady Achievement of Material Self-Sufficiency

During the interwar era, when Japan had enjoyed reasonably stable harvests, the government's agricultural and financial administrators encouraged increased production of alcoholic beverages because they generated tax revenue. The war era, however, required a more carefully managed balance between production of ingredients, manufacturing, distribution, and taxation. Genuine competition in the beer industry soon died off with the advent of the beer distribution control system in mid-1940 (examined in detail below). As a result, brewing firms no longer had to spend money on promotional campaigns or advertising, and fixed profits were guaranteed. Given these circumstances, Dai Nippon Beer's profits increased yearly from 1940 to 1944, and its ratio of profits to paid-in capital increased 20 percent between 1941 and the end of the war in 1945. With these surplus funds, the company acquired extensive land between 1940 and 1944 in preparation for future barley and hops production and research activities. The company's purchases and the ultimate fate of these lands offer insight into Dai Nippon's long-term development program.

Beer Barley and Japan's Dwindling Food Supply

Unlike edible barley and wheat, which were generally ground into flour, coarse beer barley served primarily as the chief ingredient in beer and whisky. In the late 1930s, the best strains of beer barley used by the brewing companies were typically grown in rice paddies as a secondary winter crop, and their production therefore had only a minimal impact on the rice supply. Since the early seventeenth century, Japanese farmers had aimed to make the most efficient use of their rice paddies, and often eked out "new fields" (*shinden*) that were unknown to the tax authorities by draining marshes or by further terracing the hillsides.[22] If northern climes made the cultivation of two rice crops each year unfeasible, farmers often planted heartier grains during the winter months in order to make continued use of the land. Nevertheless, as the war era unfolded, the strain placed on Japan's food supply increased, and beer barley production too began to decline. In the fall of 1940, barley became a quasi-controlled B-grade foodstuff, and although agricultural prices were controlled by the government, contract farming of barley continued until 1943. In the interim, general-purpose wheat flour for household use came under government control in June 1941, and in July 1942 new controls were instituted with the passage of the Food Provisions Control Law.[23]

By the fall of 1943, beer barley was diverted increasingly to food provisions, and contract farming by the brewers was halted; thus the quasi-control over its use graduated to full control. At that time, Japan's various administrative divisions (the prefectures plus Hokkaido, Osaka, and Kyoto) ordered that all barley planting and purchasing was to be handled by the All Japan Agricultural Business Association. The beer companies were thereafter required to purchase their crops from this association, and their purchasing activities too grew more and more regimented. On 29 April 1943, the *Yomiuri* newspaper reported the formation of a new Japan Beer Brewers Association, and the presidents of Dai Nippon Beer and Kirin Brewery assumed the role of its chairman and president, respectively.[24] In June, this regulatory body established a new firm known as the Japan Beer Ingredients Company, through which Dai Nippon Beer purchased just over 142,000 koku (approximately 25,260 metric tonnes) of crops over the 1944 production year – a roughly 60 percent drop from 1943. The new ingredients firm would operate until the end of May 1948, exercising sole authority over the purchase of beer barley, hops, and other minor ingredients during the rationing era. After the war, guidance concerning beer barley cultivation continued to be provided by the All Japan Agricultural Business Association until 1952, when contract farming arranged by the brewers was at last permitted to resume.[25]

The "Hops Crisis" and Japan's Self-Sufficiency System

Ever since the merger that founded Dai Nippon Beer in 1906, the company's plans for domestic hop production had enjoyed little success. The company's annual production between 1925 and 1935 was roughly 30 to 40 tonnes, only 10 percent of the hops it used each year. Over many years of intense competition, companies such as Kirin Brewery, which used only imported hops, often boasted about the higher quality and authenticity of their products. This served naturally as a disincentive for rival firms to produce hops domestically. Dai Nippon too struggled with the idea for many years, but in 1933 and 1934 there was a spike in the price of hops grown in Germany and Czechoslovakia, and as international relations worsened after 1936, Japanese brewers faced the threat of interrupted supplies. As the suspension of European exports loomed, all of the leading beer companies began to examine the issue more closely.

In January 1937, an import permission system began, and in September a more comprehensive Import and Export Quality Temporary Measures Law was promulgated. This law was one of the so-called Three Control Laws passed in that month, along with the Temporary Funds Adjustment Law and an update to the Munitions Industry Mobilization Law. These three laws gave the government control over money, things, and people *(kane, mono, hito)*, and enabled it to more completely regulate the lifestyles of the populace, putting Japan on the road to full controls. The new import and export law in particular gave the government immediate control over trade, enabling it to limit or halt exports if necessary. As hops were not a munitions supply, their import was restricted severely and immediately. Dai Nippon Beer therefore drew up plans for self-sufficient domestic production of hops and presented them to the Ministry of Finance and the Ministry of Commerce and Industry. It also petitioned the government for permission to import foreign hops due to their importance for beer production, and in this manner succeeded in acquiring 528 tonnes of hops.

For its mass-production plan, Dai Nippon Beer had already established a foothold in Nagano prefecture and Hokkaido, where it developed hops farms. In Nagano prefecture, the firm already had 37 hectares in 1937, which expanded to 113 hectares in 1938, to 250 hectares in 1939, and ultimately to 400 hectares in all. At the same time, in Nakano-machi, a warehouse equipped with hops-drying and compressing equipment was set up. In 1941, a second drying facility was added, giving Dai Nippon a total drying capacity of six hundred tonnes of hops at a time. For guidance with the growing, drying, and compressing of the hops, brewery employees trained as agricultural technicians were stationed at the fields to oversee the operations. In Hokkaido, Dai Nippon had 4.2 hectares under direct company management in Yamahana and 10.2 hectares more under contract near Sapporo.

Dai Nippon records that by 1940 the residents of the farming villages in Nagano and Hokkaido were growing desperate and were therefore pleased to grow hops in exchange for cash. In the interim, Dai Nippon president Takahashi Ryūtarō again travelled to Europe to visit the world's leading hops-producing country, Czechoslovakia, as well as other European hops producers. During his trip, he invited the hop farming expert Heinrich Hilsher to come to Japan on an inspection tour. Hilsher accepted the invitation, and after examining Dai Nippon's entire hops farming, drying, and compressing operations, he developed a plan for improving their quality and stability. However, supplies and manpower grew scarce during the war with China. Dai Nippon therefore sent further funds, supplies, and company reinforcements to the hops farms, determined to realize the goals of its self-sufficiency program in spite of the increased wartime difficulties. By 1940, the firm boasted 91.2 hectares of hops farms in Hokkaido, and new farms were soon established in Yamagata prefecture, Tottori prefecture, and Qingdao, China. Dai Nippon's land acquisitions during the Second World War were as follows:

1   September 1941: purchased 8,255,700 tsubo (2,729.3 ha) in Abemaki, a mountainous forested area in Hiba, Hiroshima prefecture. This Abemaki cork orchard was reestablished as the Shōhara Forest. In September 1949, Dai Nippon Beer's section reverted to Asahi Breweries' control.

2   May 1942: purchased 38,621 tsubo (12.8 ha) in the Seijō plantation *(Seijō nōen)*, Tokyo, for both public welfare and barley research. In 1946, this farm was reestablished as the Seijō Barley Testing Grounds *(Seijō ōmugi shikenji)*.

3   July 1942: purchased 8,804 tsubo (2.9 ha) in Shinkotonihojō, Hokkaido for barley research.

4   Mid-1942: purchased 9,000 tsubo (3.0 ha) in the Mozume garden *(Mozume hojō)* in Kyoto for barley cultivation research in cooperation with Kyoto University. In September 1949, Dai Nippon Beer's section reverted to Asahi Breweries' control.

5   September 1942: purchased 19,975 tsubo (6.6 ha) in Furusato, Nagano prefecture, for hops research.

6   January 1944: purchased 376,898 tsubo (124.6 ha) of mountainous forest in Teinezōrinji, suburban Sapporo, in order to raise and hang hop trellises amidst the larch trees.

Through these efforts, Dai Nippon did indeed realize its goal of achieving 100 percent domestic hop production by 1942. Kirin Brewery, meanwhile, had begun producing hops in Korea (Chōsen) in 1934, but the harvests were not sufficient to supply its annual usage. Kirin therefore undertook domestic production in Yamanashi, Yamagata, and Fukushima prefectures in 1939, going to great lengths to import the delicate hops seedlings from the United States. In spite of these efforts, Kirin's supply of hops worsened steadily as wartime controls tightened. Because Dai Nippon Beer had developed its mass-production system so intensively, Kirin and others were able to purchase hops from Dai Nippon Beer.[26]

No Ticket, No Beer: Fixed Prices, Rationing, and Distribution Controls

The manner in which the Japanese government selected three, and ultimately two, beer manufacturers to serve as the nation's sole suppliers during the war is a significant example of Japan's efforts at achieving industrial rationalization *(sangyō gōrika)*. In pursuing this goal, government ministries and research agencies sought generally to encourage the "scientific" management of Japan's manufacturing enterprises after 1917.[27] The demands of the military for the nation's achievement of industrial self-sufficiency extended even to the brewing industry, and its forced reduction to just two companies by the end of the war was typical of the wartime planned economy.[28] Between 1937 and 1941, the government passed a series of industrial management laws dealing with the production of motor vehicles, aircraft, ships, machine tools, chemicals, heavy machinery, and foodstuffs. These laws and their component ordinances required manufacturing firms to submit annual production targets for approval by a government licensing system designed to satisfy both public and military interests. The goal was industrial efficiency through the elimination of companies producing goods deemed by bureaucrats to be luxurious or redundant.[29] Most studies of this conversion process have focused on Japan's heavy and chemical industries.[30] Its specific impact on the manufacturers of such articles as foodstuffs, however, is less studied.

By the 1930s, Tokyo's alcohol retailers had begun to take steps to cull the enormous jumble of small shops that were fuelling excess competition within the industry. In 1936, the Tokyo Alcohol and Soy Sauce Association League decided on preventative measures – a plan they called their Hundred-Metre Distance Restriction Plan *(Hyaku kome kyori seigen an)*. According to this plan, if any new stores resembling liquor shops opened within a hundred metres of existing retailers, the league agreed not to sell the new shops any product – a commitment that delivered the desired results. Soon thereafter, Japan's government went to great lengths to investigate and control individual retailers, and even to put them out of business if necessary. Initially, the Finance Ministry implemented a retail licensing system in April 1938 in order to eliminate abuses and redundancy in the alcohol wholesale and retail sectors. A wholesaling licence cost ¥14,500, and a retailing licence cost between ¥337,000 and ¥352,800. Licence applicants were subject to a strict examination by Finance Ministry agents – both of their personal lives and of their professional conduct as retail managers. The licensing system aimed to eliminate excess shops and maintain secure sources of tax revenue, which were compatible goals. While many smaller shops were indeed put out of business, licensing weeded out unscrupulous retailers with questionable tax files. The licensing system also effectively established a controlled distribution network for beer and a unified system of beer sales.[31]

Meanwhile, as exports and foreign exchange came under official controls and raw materials were prioritized according to their utility for munitions production, a grave shortage of commodities quickly developed. Consumers faced inflation due to the rising cost of everything from foodstuffs to finished goods, and the government intervened in order to suppress rising prices. In July 1938, the government began to issue notices that set price limits for every commodity, based on the commodities-related rules promulgated in the Import and Export Quality Temporary Measures Law. In September 1939, the price of nearly everything in Japan was frozen through the 9-18 Stop decree, which went into effect on 20 October.[32] Officially priced products were labelled with a single kanji character meaning "public" or "government," which appeared in a circle as 公. This "mark" was referred to generally by consumers and retailers as a *marukō*. Through this system, beer became subject to price controls at the start of March 1939. Those controls actually went into effect in Tokyo in May of that year, in Osaka in June, and in other prefectures after that point.[33]

In 1941, the Finance Ministry differentiated and fixed the official prices for beer at every level of the distribution chain: brewers, wholesalers, retailers, bars, and restaurants. The prices were differentiated further for sales in Tokyo, thirteen other cities, and the various rural areas of the country in which beer was available. Towns and villages near major stations were within the distribution network, but beyond the rail lines, Japan's roads were still quite poor, and shipping beer was both difficult and costly. The most remote parts of Japan had seldom seen shipments of beer even during the interwar era. Nevertheless, where beer was available to consumers, it became subject to local price controls at every stage of sale.[34]

The enforcement of household beer consumption limits began in the Keihin region, comprising Tokyo, Yokohama, and Kawasaki, in June 1940, but this early phase of distribution control only foreshadowed more dramatic changes to come.[35] As US-Japan diplomatic relations deteriorated, the government of Prime Minister Fumimaro Konoe (July 1940–October 1941) sought further price controls, including of those on alcohol. On 22 November 1941, the government promulgated Law No. 88, which specified that such controls were needed because progressive increases in military spending were contributing to rising inflation and swallowing up consumers' purchasing power. At the same time, nationwide material shortages were becoming more severe, so in addition to the tax increase, the law also included wider alcohol consumption limits. In accordance with Law No. 88, it was announced that the price of beer would be fixed at ¥87.80 per koku, effective 1 December (see Table 18).[36] Thereafter, the beer Storage and Shipping Tax rose steeply as the war continued, reaching ¥177.80 on 1 April 1943, ¥280 on 1 April 1944, and finally ¥450 on 1 April 1945. From 1941, the goal of the tax was the provision

Table 18

Changes in beer production and sales tax rates and beer prices (¥), 1937-45

| Date tax rate took effect | Tax rate | | Price/large bottle | | Notes |
	Production tax per koku	Sales tax per large bottle	Manufac-turers	Retailers	
1 April 1937	35.00	0.125	0.338	0.37	
1 April 1938	40.00	0.142	0.357	0.39	¥5 hidden excise tax
1 April 1939	45.00	0.160	0.372	0.41	¥10 hidden excise tax
1 April 1940	59.30	0.211	0.422	0.46	Beer Tax on production is replaced by the Storage and Shipping Tax
8 October 1940	–	–	0.428	0.47	
1 December 1941	87.80	0.313	0.528	0.57	
1 April 1943	177.80	0.624	0.850	0.90	Unified beer distribution system begins; brand trade-marksales end
1 April 1944	280.00	0.983	1.218	1.30	
10 December 1944	–	–	1.238	1.35	
1 April 1945	450.00	1.580	1.860	2.00	

Source: Kirin biiru KK, *Kirin biiru KK gojū nenshi* [Kirin Brewery Company, Ltd.: Fifty-year history] (Tokyo: Kirin biiru KK, 20 March 1957), 248-49.

of funds for war matériel, but it caused such vicious price inflation that consumption was actually restrained. The competing goals of maintaining consumption rates and raising tax revenues could not be realized in concert.[37]

Enforcing the new prices required the simultaneous introduction of a beer distribution control system, which was itself based on proposed beer manufacturing restrictions. The government's efforts to control alcohol production, distribution, sale, and taxation thus entailed a wholesale revision both of alcohol policy and the infrastructure of Japan's beer industry. Unable to simply increase tax revenue without added controls, Japan's government was obliged to totally redesign the beer industry, and the program unfolded as follows.[38]

At the outset, the usual number of domestic beers was sold outside the entrances of small shops, as well as in Japan's many restaurants and bars, just as before. Starting with the Tokyo and Yokohama region, however, the sale of beer (and other alcoholic beverages) for household use was managed from June 1940 according to a ticket system *(kippu sei)*. Each household received a fixed number of tickets, which could be exchanged for the purchase of beer. The system was revised the next year by the introduction of a passbook system, which avoided the printing of additional tickets and thus reduced costs. As consumers purchased beer, their passbooks were stamped, up to the current household limit set by the government.[39] On 26 May 1943, the *Yomiuri* newspaper reported that the allotted monthly alcohol rations were set at 5 *gō* of sake (5 x 0.18 L = 900 mL), and three large bottles of beer per household. (The *Yomiuri* article does not specify whether the allotted "large" bottles were of the 3.51 gō [633.169 mL] or the 4 gō [721.56 mL] variety, though both were distributed commonly during the war and were usually described as 633 mL and 720 mL, respectively.)[40]

In addition, the government also aimed to operate occasional beer halls in order to boost morale in Japan's major cities. For example, on 16 May 1943, the *Yomiuri* reported that a special beer hall would open in Tokyo that evening at six, where patrons could purchase some beer, sake, and a small amount of traditional *oden* stew.[41] Until 1944, meal-ticket restaurants, cafeterias, officer clubs, and even underground restaurants continued operating, and beer was available at many of these establishments, both legally and sometimes illegally. Although Japan's most expensive restaurants and bars were closed by the government's Outline on Decisive War Emergency Measures in late February 1944, cheap restaurants and bars continued operating. On 5 May 1944, the *Asahi* newspaper reported that the government would open a series of "people's bars" *(kokumin sakaba)* in major cities once or twice a week.[42] Thereafter, news reports updated readers on when these bars were scheduled to open. On those days, for brief periods after six p.m., locals could line up to purchase a single shot of whisky, a bottle of beer, or a few small cups of cheap sake.[43] These bars were gloomy affairs, often surrounded by rubble left behind by Allied air raids, but despite the bombing, drinkers in Japan's cities fared somewhat better than those in rural regions, where beer was often unavailable.

As the beer industry became a focus of tax revenue generation, the rationing system likewise guaranteed the continued existence of alcohol wholesalers and retailers. Table 19 outlines the maximum prices allowed by the beer manufacturers and the Cooperative Beer Sales Company from 1 December 1941. The fixed prices for manufacturers and wholesalers were enforced at

Table 19

Maximum beer prices (¥) from 1 December 1941

		Maximum price			
Volume	Location	Manufacturers	Wholesalers	Retailers	Bar and restaurant
4 gō (720 mL) bottle	Tokyo, Kawasaki, Yokohama, Nagoya, Kyoto, Suita, Toyonaka, Ikeda, Osaka, Fuse, Sakai, Amazaki, Nishinomiya, Kobe	25.35 (4 dozen)	25.50 (4 dozen)	0.57 each	0.80 each
	Elsewhere	25.50 (4 dozen)	25.80 (4 dozen)	0.58 each	0.80 each
2 gō (360 mL) bottle	Nationwide	13.90 (4 dozen)	14.00 (4 dozen)	0.31 each	0.45 each
2 L bottle	Nationwide	1.61 each	1.66 each	1.81 each	2.40 each
Cask	Nationwide	0.78/L	0.81/L	0.86/L	1.15/L

Source: Kirin biiru KK, *Kirin biiru KK gojū nenshi* [Kirin Brewery Company, Ltd.: Fifty-year history] (Tokyo: Kirin biiru KK, 20 March 1957), 142-43.

freight train delivery stations and near ship gangways, where beer was unloaded and sold. The remaining figures are the fixed prices that faced consumers at shops, bars, and restaurants. Kirin notes that in smaller towns, local government officials, rather than shop owners, were free to decide what price was appropriate, up to the specified maximums.[44]

By the time Japan launched the Pacific War against the United States on 8 December 1941 (Tokyo time), access to the ingredients needed to make beer was already tightly restricted. Beer production naturally declined, and the government therefore called for further distribution controls in the form of a national sales system. The establishment of a unified sales company played a leading role in the government's new distribution control system, but the company was aided by a parallel organization. Formed originally in October 1938 at the request of the Ministry of Agriculture and Forestry, the Japan Beer Ingredients Association was an independent control group composed of Dai Nippon Beer, Kirin Brewery, Sakura Beer, and Tokyo Beer (the last of which had been a subsidiary of Dai Nippon Beer since 1934). These firms were later joined by the overseas companies Takasuna Beer, Chōsen Beer, and Shōwa Kirin Beer.[45] (Chōsen Beer and Shōwa Kirin Beer, which were colonial Korean subsidiaries of Dai Nippon and Kirin, respectively, are examined further below.) The association's name was changed to the Japan Beer Association in March 1939, and in June 1942, the government asked its member firms to devise a single, unified manufacturing and distribution control system.[46]

In September 1942, Dai Nippon, Kirin, Sakura, and Tokyo Beer followed the orders of the Finance Ministry and transformed their collective distribution department, the Cooperative Beer Sales Company, into the Central Beer Sales Company. Established by Dai Nippon and Kirin with ¥5 million in capital stock, the new firm amounted to a unified distribution machine made up of the member companies' distributorships and company-owned stores. This single sales company had headquarters in each of seven national districts: Sapporo in Hokkaido, Sendai in Tōhoku, Tokyo in Kantō, Nagoya in Chūbu, Osaka in Kansai, Kumamoto City in Kyushu, and finally Hiroshima City, which represented China. The chair of the Central Beer Sales Company was Takahashi Ryūtarō of Dai Nippon Beer, the president was Isono Chōzō of Kirin Brewery, and the managing directors were Shibata Shō of Dai Nippon, Suwa Fujinosuke of Kirin, and Aki Junzō of Sakura Beer. At the same time, all of Kirin and Sapporo's company-owned shops were closed save for one in Tokyo and one in Osaka, where beer and soft-drink sales were permitted to continue. The district sales companies provided a place to sell products, to stay in touch with retailers, to differentiate between commercial- and home-use beer, and to ensure proper distribution.[47]

From top to bottom, the sales and distribution system functioned as illustrated in Figure 8. First, the Central Beer Sales Company drew up a sales plan in conjunction with the Japan Beer Brewers Association, which itself drafted a corollary production plan. The Central Beer Sales Company then determined the distribution volume for the individual areas and shipped the product to the respective regional beer sales companies, which in turn shipped out the various orders to retail and commercial businesses. The daily activities of the shipping office in each regional company were divided between the order processing and delivery departments. In cities, commercial-use beer was delivered by specialized distributors who were familiar with the maze of restaurants, taverns, and bars throughout their districts.

In order to avoid redundancy and overlap in the shipping network, the various brewers' distribution areas centred on their respective factories.

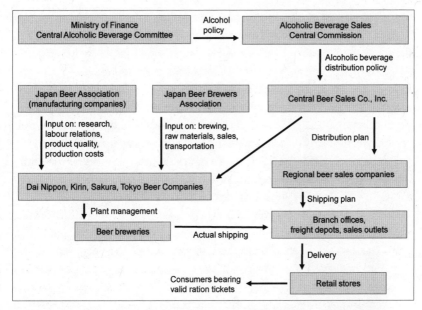

Figure 8 Structure of the unified, controlled beer distribution system, 1943
Source: Created by the author from data appearing in Kirin Beer K.K., *Kirin biiru K.K. gojū nenshi [Kirin Beer Company, Incorporated: 50-Year History]* (Tokyo, JP: Kirin Beer K.K. 20 March 1957).

Consequently, companies with fewer plants, such as Kirin Brewery, lost ground in the capital region, Kyushu, and Hokkaido. All firms, however, continued to supply beer to the military, especially the Imperial Japanese Navy, through direct sales and delivery to ports and naval bases. The volume of beer delivered to the navy during the war is remarkable. Between April 1942 and March 1943, Dai Nippon, Kirin, and Sakura delivered a combined total of roughly twenty million large bottles. In the following year to March 1944, the volume fell to 12.88 million bottles, but the navy took delivery of 2.17 million bottles of beer even during the final months of the war, between April and August 1945 – when the bulk of its ships were fast being sunk by Allied air power. These deliveries represented roughly 5 percent of national production, and the army received approximately the same volumes during the same periods.[48] A great deal of this beer ended up on the ocean floor, and divers exploring the wrecks of Japanese naval vessels, such as those sunk at Truk Lagoon (today Chuuk Lagoon) on 17 February 1944, have photographed huge piles of beer bottles. Visitors to the aircraft ferry ship *Fujikawa-maru* can see hundreds of them spilling out of the stricken vessel's hold, each bearing the name Dai Nippon Beer Brewery in raised letters.[49]

The Japan Beer Association served as a bridge between the Central Sales Company and the brewing companies. In November 1942, the director of the Japan Beer Association and president of Dai Nippon Beer, Takahashi Ryūtarō, delivered a speech to the group's members entitled "On the Reorganization of the Japan Beer Association." It outlined the four criteria integral to the achievement of unified distribution: an agreement on secure production figures; a synthesis of the mixed transportation network; a concrete distribution plan; and stable, centralized management. Thus, on the government's orders, the Japan Beer Association took control of the entire industry's production, materials, pricing, and distribution programs, and assumed a leadership role in its member firms' swift amalgamation.

Furthermore, on 15 March 1943, the government passed the Alcoholic Beverages Industry Group Control Law, known simply as the Alcohol Group Law. This law established firm government control over production and distribution of every kind of alcoholic beverage in Japan. Article 4 of the law established the Japan Beer Brewers Association, which reinforced government control over materials, production, product sales, and transportation (see Figure 8). The Alcohol Group Law also turned the Japan Beer Association into a corporate entity. Its articles set forth key goals: conducting research into beer production and sales, adjusting labour relations, lowering manufacturing costs, and improving product quality, among other forms of broad industry guidance. Although separate agencies, the Japan Beer Association and the Japan Beer Brewers Association shared the same office in the Komei Building on the Ginza in Tokyo, and their officials held posts in both groups in an interwoven fashion.[50]

The enforcement of the Alcohol Group Law also brought other changes to the industry, particularly with regard to the purchase of ingredients. Formerly, brewing company presidents had had a great deal of authority over the securing of ingredients, storage, product sales, and shipping, as well as the power to start new brands, suspend or transfer production, and purchase rival brands. The new law, however, placed all of the decisions under the jurisdiction of the Finance Ministry, which was a significant change in policy. Whereas the relationship between the beer companies and their ingredients suppliers had formerly come under the jurisdiction of the Ministry of Agriculture and Forestry, from June 1943 the Finance Ministry assumed direct control. Under the new regime, the only way for brewers to acquire ingredients like barley, hops, and starch was through a formal application. From this point, the Japan Beer Brewers Association was required to negotiate with the Finance Ministry for ingredient allotments, production ratios, and so on, on behalf of the individual brewers. Due also to the decreasing availability of ingredients and materials, there was a surplus of beer manufacturing equipment. Consequently, in July 1943, Sakura Beer and Dai Nippon Beer were combined forcibly by the government's enterprise equipment ordinance *(seibirei)*, and in October Kirin's bottle production plant at Tomita was closed by the same ordinance. Nevertheless, only two plants were actually closed at this point, Sapporo Breweries' Handa plant and Tokyo Beer's Tsurumi plant.[51]

As for retail control, Section 2, Article 10 of the Alcohol Group Law bound up all alcoholic beverage wholesalers and retailers together into an integrated national Retail Sales Association, thus realizing fully unified distribution routes. On 1 April 1943, the differences between fixed prices in Tokyo and the other regions passed away, and unified official prices *(marukō)* went into effect. Customers were also required to return empty beer bottles and caps to the point of sale in order to be eligible to buy more beer. A similar system was developed to regulate the delivery of beer to restaurants and bars. In addition, there were separate allotments delineated as special beer rations for formal ceremonies, for send-off parties for soldiers leaving for the front, and so on. As the war continued, additional allotments were sometimes made for workers in the munitions industries, known as *kakaku tokuhai bakushu* (special ration price beer).[52] Due to the wartime "controlled distribution" (i.e., rationing) system, beer remained a part of daily life for many Japanese, especially in the cities. On 30 November 1944, the *Yomiuri* newspaper reported price increases for beer and sake at the country's remaining sales outlets, and even as late as 6 June it published a propaganda article entitled "Thanks for Beer Rations" *(Orei ni biiru haikyū).*[53]

At the same time, Japan's beer brewers faced a labour shortage. Kirin's history admits that the country was "intoxicated" by its initial military successes in December 1941, but notes also that the feeling of security soon vanished as the brewers' employees were drafted into the military in large numbers in 1942 and 1943. Because the brewing firms were still operating under civilian control, their managers believed that they could maintain a core workforce by transferring and seconding personnel or by stationing them overseas. Following Japan's defeat by US Marines at Guadalcanal in February 1943, however, government control over the brewers' operations tightened very quickly.[54] On 1 April 1943, the Finance Ministry issued Notice No. 139 concerning the sale of alcoholic beverages, increasing the price of beer as summarized in Table 20.

The Central Beer Sales Company's prices were kept within the range of the maximum prices listed in Table 20, for which the regional beer sales companies had received approval from the finance minister. However, these prices were subject to a bottle deposit surcharge. "Special price" beer was still being

Table 20

Maximum beer prices from 1 April 1943

Volume	Maximum price (¥)			
	Manufacturers	Regional sales companies	Retailers	Bar and restaurant
Large (720 mL) bottle	40.80 (4 dozen)	41.16 (4 dozen)	43.20 (4 dozen)	1.12 each
Large bottle, special price	25.44 (4 dozen)	27.36 (4 dozen)	27.36 (4 dozen)	–
Small (360 mL) bottle	21.84 (4 dozen)	22.02 (4 dozen)	23.04 (4 dozen)	0.62 each
2 L bottle	2.60 each	2.65 each	2.80 each	3.39 each
Cask	1.28/L	1.31/L	1.36/L	1.65/L
Cask, special price	0.78/L	0.86/L	0.86/L	–

Source: Kirin biiru KK, *Kirin biiru KK gojū nenshi* [Kirin Brewery Company, Ltd.: Fifty-year history] (Tokyo: Kirin biiru KK, 20 March 1957), 146.

shipped in limited quantities at this time to workers in strategically important industries, and its price was lower due to a special reduction in the beer Storage and Shipping Tax. In addition, Kirin Brewery was able to add surcharges to the maximum prices for black beer *(kuro biiru)*, stout *(sutauto)*, and vitamin beer *(bitamin biiru)*, as listed in Table 21. If consumers could afford them, these beers could indeed fortify their increasingly meagre diet with much-needed calories and vitamins.[55]

One Bottle, One Recipe, One Brand: The Advent of Wartime "Beer"

Some of the last beer-garden events of the war were staged in Tokyo on 15 March and 22 May 1943, when Kirin Beer Halls hosted outdoor musical events to draw crowds to the Ginza. At the same time, material shortages

Table 21

Additional cost added to maximum prices from 1 April 1943

Volume	Unit	Black beer (¥)	Stout and vitamin beer (¥)
Large bottle	per bottle	0.02	0.10
Small bottle	per bottle	0.01	0.05
Cask	per litre	0.03	–

Source: Kirin biiru KK, *Kirin biiru KK gojū nenshi* [Kirin Brewery Company, Ltd.: Fifty-year history] (Tokyo: Kirin biiru KK, 20 March 1957), 147.

prompted the abandonment of separate brand labels, which had by 1943 become a virtual fiction. These efforts at further streamlining the industry and creating a single beer firm were a significant challenge for the breweries, which were proud of their individual brands and logos. Nevertheless, in March 1943, as the central and regional beer sales companies began operating, the Finance Ministry decided to abolish individual labels and unify beer production under a single brand.

In May 1943, all brand labels were replaced by a unified label that featured only the word "Beer" (麦酒 *bakushu*) flanked by ears of wheat, as well as the individual brewing companies' names in tiny characters. The simple new label was printed in three formats and in three colours, to distinguish the three permitted uses of beer: household use, business use, and special ration price *(kaki-yō, gyōmu-yō, kakaku tokuhai)*. On 22 April 1943, the *Asahi* newspaper reported that this new, brandless "Beer" was served to groups of day-labourers, and on 29 April it published a photograph of munitions workers lining up to receive glasses of special ration beer.[56] Of course, these reports too were pure propaganda aimed at bolstering the government's image amidst a generally worsening war situation, especially as the beer was doled out in addition to the workers' allotted monthly household rations. In 1944, brewing companies' names were removed from the generic beer labels, which now read simply "Beer." By the war's end, the labels no longer distinguished between the three uses, and due to further cutbacks, they were printed in just one colour.[57]

Given the generic approach to labelling, it was only logical that the makers would also use bottles communally. By 1943, using beer bottles of differing shapes was unrealistic, especially given the pressing need to return and reuse them. Like individual brands and labels, specialized bottles gave way to a single, common-use beer bottle *(biiru bin kyōyō)*. In fact, the roots of this practice stretched back to late 1939, when a beer bottle "link-system" started to be enforced by the brewing companies. The system began in Tokyo and Osaka in December of that year, at which point persons not returning empty bottles were not allowed to buy more beer. As for bottle shapes, until 1944, Dai Nippon Beer's large, 3.51 gō (633.17 mL) bottle was nicknamed the "tense-shoulders form" *(katahari-kata)*, while Kirin Brewery's bottle, which resembled a champagne bottle, was known as the "sloping shoulders form" *(nadegata-kata)*. Although slight, there was also a difference in the capacity of the two bottle forms, which, from the standpoint of tax collection, made little sense. Therefore, in August 1944, the latter form, which held 633.17 mL, became the standard bottle format. With these measures, the beer industry became a faceless, almost entirely government-managed system, and the individual companies had essentially no identity. No actual "market" existed for beer in the consumer-driven sense. Pressed by material shortages and its reliance on alcohol tax revenue, Japan's government effectively became a state brewer, bottler, shipper, and price setter of beer.[58]

It would not be until well after the war, on 1 December 1949, that the revival of individual beer brands, labels, and trademarks was officially permitted. The common-use beer bottle, however, persisted, having demonstrated its utility to beer brewers, shippers, retailers, and collectors. Bottle-return programs would persist as well – another example of the long-term influence of the war era and the systemic efficiency that it had demanded. Despite these changes, however, at the level of small retailers the industry's sales structure retained much of its original shape, enabling a reasonably smooth reversion back to the prewar distribution system. Having learned to discipline the retail network before the war, the brewing companies were not inclined to maintain the centralized distribution apparatus created by the government. Beer sales from 1950 were once more aimed at serving the companies and their consumers' best interests, rather than those of the state.[59]

From Beijing to Batavia: Overseas Operations during the Second World War

From the 1910s through the 1930s, the concept of the Japanese Empire in Northeast Asia was as fundamentally real and justified to most Japanese as the idea of the American West was to Americans. Few Americans living on the eastern seaboard of the United States in 1910 would have questioned US sovereignty over California, Oregon, or Washington State. Likewise, the same could be said of Japanese attitudes in 1930 toward Formosa (today Taiwan), which had been a colony of Japan since 1895, or toward Korea, which Japan had annexed formally in 1910 and referred to as Chōsen. For clear examples of these viewpoints, one need look no further than Japanese shipping advertisements or Japan Tourist Bureau brochures from the interwar era to see how important, tangible, and close the growing Japanese Empire seemed to the average citizen. A vast collection of such shipping, rail, and tourist advertisements may be found in any edition of the annual *Japan Year Book*.[60] This business directory about Japan and its colonies, which was also translated into English, was written especially for the interest and information of foreign traders and investors, and its advertisements illustrate just how connected Japan was to its regional holdings.

The enthusiasm of ordinary Japanese for their country's imperial reach intensified after Japan invaded Manchuria in September 1931, after which point the dream of visiting Japan's new western frontier appealed to more and more of the emperor's subjects.[61] For many, the nation's colonial ambitions seemed to be key to realizing Japan's destiny, and the country's leading brewers played a significant part in building this grand future. As Norman Smith illustrates, their activities in Korea, Manchuria, and elsewhere through the war era offer a different perspective on Japan's growing empire and the efforts of manufacturers to supply and market beer to a growing overseas population of settlers, soldiers, traders, and consular officials.[62] Soon after Manchuria's annexation in 1931, the materials, equipment, and ingredients for brewing were naturally shipped from the home islands to Manchuria via Korea. Soldiers throughout Japan's empire, as well as its sailors at sea, deserved beer, whatever the cost. As a case in point, Louise Young notes an April 1932 "Kirin Beer" advertisement in the *Osaka Mainichi* newspaper that featured a sketch of the famous "three human bombs" *(nikudan sanyū shi)*, who had, according to the army, sacrificed themselves during the recent fighting in Shanghai.[63] In Kirin's rendering, however, rather than a bomb, the three soldiers carried a giant bottle of "Kirin Beer" toward the wire fence that was holding back the Japanese advance.[64]

In keeping with Japan's national drive toward self-sufficiency, Japanese brewers in Korea and Manchuria were called on to produce their ingredients locally, but the effort proceeded quite slowly. In Korea, Kirin began experimenting with the cultivation of beer barley in fields along the Chūsei southern road *(nandō)*, and reaped a modest harvest. As for hops, the head of Kirin Brewery's agricultural testing ground, Yugawa Matao (who became the postwar head of Kirin's scientific research institute), delivered an address to management in 1935 entitled "Hops Must Give Its Regards to Korea" *(Hoppu wa yoroshiku Chōsen ni tsukuru beshi)*. Soon thereafter, Kirin selected a spot for hops farming in northern Korea called Kankyō, Keizan. The topography proved suitable and Kirin achieved fairly good results – so good in fact that Kirin's technicians believed that even the company's domestic products would in future use Korean hops. Late in the Second World War, however, as Japanese shipping was sunk at a rapid pace by US submarines, the brewers were forced to take self-sufficiency much more seriously. Given their late start, they achieved only a 10 percent improvement in local ingredient production by the end of the war.[65]

The 1939 edition of the encyclopedic business directory the *Japan-Manchukuo Year Book* described the growth of Manchuria's beer market:

> Beer Brewing was carried on many years ago in Imienpo and Harbin in North Manchuria and Dairen [modern Dalian] in South Manchuria. The breweries in Dairen had long been closed down under the pressure of Japanese imports.

Figure 9 Japanese Army soldiers in China drinking beer during the Second Sino-Japanese War, 1 January 1940. *Courtesy of the Mainichi Newspapers.*

Two breweries in North Manchuria had been the only breweries in existence in Manchuria until the Manchurian incident of 1931. Since then, the demand for beer has greatly increased due to the growth in the number of Japanese settlers ... The demand for beer in Manchuria was 170,000 dozens, valued at ¥360,000 in 1926. Imports of beer, including ale, porter and stout amounted to ¥3,826,000 in 1936 ... The beer brewing industry has shown a steady expansion and production has increased by over 30 per cent. in the five years up to 1937. Total output in 1937 was in excess of 1,300,000 koku (koku = 47.65 US gallons). Beer exports in 1936 amounted in value to ¥5,912,000. The principle [sic] markets are Kwantung Province, Manchoukuo, British India and China.[66]

Among the firms involved, Dai Nippon Beer and Kirin Brewery began to construct new breweries in order to meet the rising wave of demand for beer, especially by the many Japanese soldiers in China (see Figure 9). The following company profiles showcase this significant trend.

Regards to Korea: Shōwa Kirin Beer Company and Chōsen Beer Company
In the 1920s, Kirin began opening up the Korean marketplace to beer sales simply by importing beer that it brewed in Japan. Kirin received a rebate for

the domestic beer tax, since the product was not sold in Japan, which made the shipment of beer to the Korean peninsula quite lucrative. Later, an import tax was imposed by the office of the Japanese governor of Korea, but it was still lower than the beer consumption tax charged in Japan in the 1920s and early 1930s, and Kirin notes that it had domestically grown ingredients on hand in the home islands, so its exports to the Korean market remained comparatively inexpensive to produce. Changes came, however, when Kirin's rival, Dai Nippon Beer, began drawing up plans to construct a brewery in the suburbs of Seoul, a city known to the Japanese at that time as Keijō. In 1932, Kirin learned that Dai Nippon acquired part of a large plot of land from Kanebō, Ltd., a long-time maker of textiles and cosmetics. As Dai Nippon appeared determined to build a factory on the site, Kirin's agents began to search for a comparable plot of land, and the race to dominate the Korean beer market was on.[67]

On 30 December 1932, Kirin's managing director, Isono Chōzō, set out from Tokyo for Seoul and began searching for a suitable site. At this time, Seoul was a bustling urban metropolis that, like much of Korea's industrial and commercial infrastructure, had for twenty years been the focus of substantial Japanese government and corporate investment. Whether this investment benefited the Korean people as much as it did Japanese industrialists remains a hotly debated issue. In this context, however, it will suffice to say that Isono's inspection tour was merely one of many such efforts by a variety of Japanese manufacturing firms. Once in Seoul, Isono learned of the availability of a brick factory located right next to the Dai Nippon site. Isono inspected the plant immediately, and discovered that it was very close to a railway station, giving it excellent potential. With the construction of Dai Nippon's new plant imminent, Isono leapt at the chance to buy the brick factory and convert it into a brewery. Kirin shipped a portion of the machinery from its Sendai plant to Seoul and completed its installation in December 1933.[68]

Kirin planned to operate its new plant simply as an overseas extension of the parent company, but at the suggestion of the governor general of Korea, General Ugaki Kazushige, a separate company named Shōwa Kirin Beer Company was established in December 1933. With ¥2 million in capital stock and ¥200,000 in paid-in capital, it produced "Kirin" brand beer identical to that in Japan. As a subsidiary of Kirin Brewery, the new firm was likewise affiliated with the Mitsubishi conglomerate. Kirin sent a management team under president Itami Nirō to take charge, and not a moment too soon, for in April 1934, Dai Nippon Beer finished constructing its new plant nearby. Named Chōsen Beer, Dai Nippon's wholly owned Korean subsidiary was thus affiliated with the Mitsui group.[69] Chōsen Beer had an annual production capacity of 40,000 koku (7,216 kL), and began shipping product by the end of that year. Shōwa Kirin Beer also shipped its first product in 1934, and its production level rose from 1,875 kL in that year to a peak of 11,059 kL in 1939. After that point, production hovered between 7,825 kL and 9,810 kL until 1945, when it was halted at its 1934 level by the war's end. In the spring of 1945, both Shōwa Kirin Beer and Chōsen Beer received orders from Japan's military to cease producing beer and to switch abruptly into distillers of fuel alcohol. The former firm negotiated and succeeded in continuing to devote half of its operations to beer production, but by the time the necessary equipment was converted to alcohol production, the war had already ended.[70]

New Frontiers: Establishing the Manchuria Beer Company

According to Japan's Department of Railways, there were five beer breweries operating in Harbin, Manchuria, in 1920, all of which were managed by Russians or Germans.[71] Seeking a share of the beer market in Japan's new colonial state of Manchukuo, Kirin Brewery and Dai Nippon Beer collaborated to found the Manchuria Beer Company in the district of Hōten in 1934. Hōten, near Mukden (modern Shenyang), would grow by the end of the Second World War to become a major focus of industrial activity, as well as the site of a notorious prisoner-of-war and forced-labour camp. Thousands of Manchurian and later Allied prisoners of war were forced to work in Japanese automobile, aircraft, munitions, and machine plants there. In the final stages of the war, these factories were bombed by American B-29s, and many of the POWs were liberated by US paratroopers.[72] In 1934, however, Hōten had not yet attained such industrial significance or notoriety. At that time, the government of Manchukuo aimed to develop Manchurian industries comparable to the ones in Japan, so it insisted on collaborative efforts for the sake of rapid infrastructural growth. Kirin and Dai Nippon therefore worked together to found the Manchuria Beer Company, which had capital stock of ¥2 million. Its two parent companies split the investment fifty-fifty, and the first managing directors were Isono Chōzō (Kirin's managing director) and Takahashi Ryūtarō (Dai Nippon's managing director, and president from February 1937).

From 1934, business conditions in Manchuria heated up dramatically and a flurry of land acquisitions led to an economic bubble. Land that had cost ¥4.60 per tsubo in 1934 shot up to ¥100 per tsubo by the summer of 1935. Given the speculation and the rising inflation, companies were forced to exercise extreme caution when moving capital out of Japan's home islands. Typically, all capital needed for construction or factory purchases would have been taken out of the profits earned from beer exported to Manchuria. Fortunately for the new joint brewing venture, however, Manchuria Beer's first factory was exempt from the local beer tax, due chiefly to the confused legal wrangling that accompanied Manchukuo's colonial development. The brewery site at Hōten was located inside the "railway zone" that was controlled by Japan's Manshū tetsudō, or South Manchuria Railway (SMR). The SMR's line stretched 701 kilometres north from the port of Dalian to Hsinking (renamed Shinkyō by the Japanese, and known today as Changchun), and its zone extended for sixty-two metres on either side of the tracks. Given the role played by the SMR as Japan's chief agent of indirect colonization in Manchuria, the railway zone fell under the administrative authority of Japan's extraterritorial rights *(chigaihōken)*, and thus also Japanese Corporate Law. Consequently, the colonial government of Manchukuo could not impose the local beer tax on the new firm. Nevertheless, the SMR reported that the local government cooperated with the brewery to cultivate suitable barley and hops in the region; hops were first grown in Manchuria in 1918.[73]

Because it would be difficult to brew both Kirin and Dai Nippon beer in the same factory, Kirin agreed that the proposed new plant would produce only "Sapporo Beer," which was Dai Nippon's product. In exchange, the site would be subdivided and 4.8 hectares would be set aside for the construction of a second plant reserved exclusively for the production of "Kirin Beer." In this way, Manchuria Beer was a cooperative enterprise, but given the two factories on the site, each firm expected to retain its individual management techniques and operate separate sales networks. The first plant was completed in mid-1935, and the second in November 1936. In April 1937, Kirin began shipping "Kirin Beer" from its branch store in Hōten. In that year, however, Manchukuo's colonial administration forced the brewery to reincorporate within the jurisdiction of Manchukuo, rather than under the Corporate Law of Japan. Manchuria Beer therefore became a public limited company subject to colonial taxation.[74]

By that time, the two plants had become known as the *Man-ni* or the "Manchuria Two," and although their brewing processes differed substantially, cooperation between their operations staffs was essential. For example, the Hōten region boasted good-quality water, but when the groundwater supply suddenly ran out in 1938, the entire staff gathered to discuss what measures should be taken. All agreed that the plants should truck in water from the city of Fushun, fifty kilometres to the east. Other challenges included wholesale price controls, which were in effect throughout Manchukuo. In every place that four-bottle boxes of Kirin were sold for ¥20, rival brands were selling for just ¥15. Nevertheless, the two plants managed gradually to establish brand

Table 22

Volume of "Kirin Beer" produced by Manchuria Beer Company, 1937-43

Year	Beer produced (kL)
1937	4,438
1938	7,703
1939	9,939
1940	9,976
1941	10,517
1942	10,751
1943	12,050

Source: Kirin biiru KK, *Kirin biiru KK gojū nenshi* [Kirin Brewery Company, Ltd.: Fifty-year history] (Tokyo: Kirin biiru KK, 20 March 1957), 128.

recognition throughout Manchukuo, but the effort required flexibility. Because Manchurian people did not know the Japanese word that had been created for beer (*bakushu* 麦酒), Kirin instead printed neck labels with its name in phonetic kana script (キリン), which was rather easily read.[75] This speaks to the significant challenge facing Japanese product manufacturers aiming to distribute their wares throughout Manchukuo, where enthusiasm for the Japanese colonial presence among the Manchurian populace was very low. Still, in Manchuria as in Korea, beer sales to Japanese colonists, soldiers, and consular staff remained high enough to warrant both local production and continued imports of beer from all three of Japan's wartime brewers, Dai Nippon, Kirin, and Sakura.[76] Table 22 illustrates the volume of "Kirin Beer" produced by the Manchuria Beer Company's second plant from 1937 to 1943, and Table 23 details the volumes produced by both of its plants and by its regional rivals in 1943.

Kirin and Dai Nippon were also not the only Japanese companies brewing beer in Manchukuo. They were joined by several others, including the Asia Beer Company, which was founded by Moriwaki Matsuichirō.[77] Having recently retired as managing director of Sakura Beer, Moriwaki decided to seek his fortune in Japan's new colonial west by founding a beer company in Manchuria. By chance, Moriwaki met a wealthy man who had just sold a coal mine in Kyushu, and together with a group of investors, they founded the Asia Beer Company in Hōten in 1936. The fledgling firm had a capital stock of ¥1 million, but it fared very poorly, and its owners sold the company to Kirin on 28 December 1938 for just ¥150,000. Kirin installed a new managing director, Ōgawa Gentarō, but continued to brew and ship the same product,

Table 23

Breweries in Manchuria and their production volume, 1943

Company	Production volume (kL)
Manchuria Beer, plant 1	12,905.7
Manchuria Beer, plant 2	12,049.4
Asia Beer	4,675.0
Harbin Beer, plant 1	4,642.5
Harbin Beer, plant 2	828.0
Harbin Beer, plant 3	462.5
Harbin Beer, plant 4	148.5
Oriental	443.3
Harbin – other	71.0
Marekko	35.7
Crown (Ōkan)	69.0
Total	36,330.6

Source: Kirin biiru KK, *Kirin biiru KK gojū nenshi* [Kirin Brewery Company, Ltd.: Fifty-year history] (Tokyo: Kirin biiru KK, 20 March 1957), 131.

"Asia Beer." Turning a profit proved to be very challenging, due to Asia Beer's significant liabilities, and just as its prospects began to look more favourable, the firm was forced to convert to the manufacture of fuel alcohol in April 1945.

Southern Advance: Operations in Taiwan, China, Southeast Asia, and the Dutch East Indies

Beyond brewing, the leading Japanese beer producers were ordered by both the government and the military to get involved in other business operations in either China or Southeast Asia during the Second World War. This development has many parallels: the leading firms in many industries were similarly ordered to establish or penetrate existing Chinese and Southeast Asian markets for everything from iron ore to foodstuffs. Recent work by Daqing Yang has highlighted the efforts of Japan's telegraph and wireless companies to establish control over communications throughout Japan's wartime imperium, including Indonesia, Thailand, Singapore, and Burma.[78] Similarly, Japanese brewers' overseas operational experience was already significant, and their directors were encouraged by the regional military authorities to either participate in existing brewing operations or to branch out and submit new proposals. Already in 1938, the *China Weekly Review* reported that "plans to open breweries in North China were announced last week by officials of two Japanese brewing companies, Ryutaro Takahashi, president of the Japan [Nippon] Brewery Company and Chozo Isono, managing director of the Kirin Brewing Company."[79] Kirin Brewery's activities in particular speak to the potentially lucrative business opportunities offered by Japan's imperial expansion. At the same time, these activities speak to the effort of Japan's government and military to "rationalize" corporate activity by grouping companies together. Kirin's operations in China and Manchuria included the following:

• In 1940, Kirin acquired an interest in the Takasuna Beer Company, located in Taipei, Taiwan, which was a city referred to by the Japanese contemporarily as Taihoku. In 1933, Japan's colonial government had granted Takasuna a monopoly over the alcoholic beverage market in Taiwan, and Kirin had always provided the firm with technical assistance. When Kirin took control of a portion of the shares, Kirin's director, Orita Shō, became the director of both firms, and the relationship between the two firms grew even closer.

• In 1942, Japan's military seized the beverage maker Crystal Limited from its British managers and entrusted it to both Kirin Brewery and the Mitsubishi Trading Company.[80] They renamed it the Shanhaiguan Brackish Water Company because it had facilities both in the former British Concession at Tianjin and in Shanhaiguan (Shanhai Pass, Qinhuandao, Hebei Province). The company remained a maker of soft drinks.

• In 1943, Kirin Brewery acquired half of the shares and managing control of the Dalian Soy Sauce Company, located at Tai-Shan Machi 2, in Dalian City. The company produced a peak annual output of 2,165 kL of soy sauce and 500,000 *kan* (1,875,000 kg) of tofu.

• Also in 1943, Kirin purchased the Sanwa Bottle Manufacturing Company in Jinan, Shandong Province, from local Japanese owners. Kirin operated Sanwa until the end of the war.

• In 1944, Kirin began aiding the management of East Asia Industries in Jilin City, Manchuria. The firm had three plants that produced cider, carbonic acid gas, and bottles. Kirin did not, however, take total control of this firm.

• In 1945, Japan's military and government suggested that Kirin should begin participating in the management of the Peking Beer Company in suburban Peking. (The modern name Beijing was not adopted formally until 1949.) Located between Peking and Tongzhou (the gateway to eastern Peking), the brewery was managed originally by Dai Nippon Beer and the Ōkura Group. Just prior to the end of the war, Kirin was ordered to hold the stock together with the Mitsubishi Trading Company, but its operations had only just begun when the war ended.[81]

The operations of both Kirin and Dai Nippon in Southeast Asia offer details on the commercial and industrial dimensions of Japan's efforts to conquer the Philippines and the Dutch East Indies from late 1941.[82] After occupying these regions, the goal of Japan's military was again the achievement of regional self-sufficiency in manufacturing, for the supply lines from Japan's home islands were very long. As a part of this effort, after Japanese forces seized the local breweries, Japan's domestic beer companies or their overseas subsidiaries were entrusted with their management. Kirin's direct charges included the Heineken Brewery in Surabaya, Java, and the Malayan Brewery in Singapore. For its part, Dai Nippon Beer managed the Archipel (Archipelago) Brouwerij Companie, which had been established by German investors in 1931 in Batavia (now Jakarta), Java. Kirin and Dai Nippon sent the technicians and managers needed to operate the plants, along with a shipment of ingredients and equipment from their domestic factories. Bottles frequently ran short, and though Archipel was capable of issuing eighty thousand bottles per month by February 1943, it often had to suspend production until bottles could be found. This prompted the firm to offer five cents for used bottles.[83] Kirin eventually dispatched technicians to Singapore and Java to begin semi-automated bottle-manufacturing operations. In order to expand production, plans were made to ship fully automated bottle-making equipment from Kirin's bottle plant at Tomita, but the war came to an end before it could be sent.

The effort exerted to bring the Dutch and Philippine breweries back online was substantial, especially at such a distance from Japan, but the bulk of the beer produced was consumed by Japan's military personnel. Although Kirin operated in Indonesia and the Philippines for less than three full years, its

Table 24

Volume and proportion of overseas production by Dai Nippon Beer, 1940-44

Year	Domestic production (kL)	Overseas production (kL)	Total (kL)	Percentage of overseas production
1940	174,821	24,561	199,382	12.3
1941	175,182	27,812	202,994	13.7
1942	173,737	32,147	205,884	15.6
1943	144,118	33,050	177,168	18.7
1944	124,795	27,090	151,885	17.8

Source: Sapporo biiru KK, *Sapporo 120 nenshi* [120-year history of Sapporo Breweries] (Tokyo: Sapporo biiru KK, 1996), 313.

records indicate that it did, in fact, turn a profit. Whether the same is true of the Mandalay Beer Brewery in Burma is unclear, but the records of Japan's military administration there indicate that Kirin's subsidiary Takasuna Beer began managing the Mandalay brewery via Taiwan in October 1942.[84] When these various breweries fell to the Allies in 1945, the Kirin and Dai Nippon technicians turned over operational control of their plants, and their staffers were eventually repatriated to the home islands.[85] Although most sources on the Pacific War deal principally with military operations, the beer industry offers a rare glimpse into Japan's wartime management of civilian manufacturing plants in occupied areas, both on the Asian continent and throughout the western Pacific. Table 24 details the volume and proportion of overseas production by Dai Nippon Beer between 1940 and 1944.

Drastic Measures: Plant Closures, Forced Conversions, and the War's End

As the war intensified, Japan's military and the government directed a steady stream of plant mergers, conversions, and closures aimed at streamlining domestic industry. Under the National General Mobilization Law, companies were legally compelled in May 1942 to integrate their business operations for the benefit of improving the nation's war potential and demonstrating unity within the national economy. Already from 1940, the government had been organizing small and medium-sized enterprises (SMEs), and it had a policy of dismantling many of them. Inefficient SMEs were reorganized or liquidated, and their workers were appropriated and redirected toward vital national industries. Based on the government's enterprise reorganization plan, roughly half of the nation's sake brewers were diverted or abolished. Compared to the sake industry, beer brewers were treated comparatively gently. However, as the war situation continued to grow more serious, the Finance Ministry, together with the Ministry of Commerce and Industry, began to streamline the beer industry as well.

Japan's shortage of raw materials grew more serious midway through 1942, and by June 1943 the government ordered such metal objects as bed frames, stoves, chairs, doors, and lockers be turned over for use by the nation's war industries. Dai Nippon Beer boasted three bronze statues of founders and past presidents on its premises, all of which were given to the military. Owing to the war situation, domestic beer production began to drop sharply in 1943. In that year, production fell 19 percent versus 1942, down to 212,000 kL.[86] Tighter control over brewing company operations was enforced in June 1943, when the government decided that its enterprise-organization targets would be extended to include large enterprises. In September of that year, the Finance Ministry ordered the beer industry to turn over control of two of its factories.

Dai Nippon Beer's Handa plant (formerly belonging to Japan Beer Springs Company) stopped production in November 1943, and on 30 March 1944 it was sold to Nakajima Aircraft for ¥5.45 million. Dai Nippon circulated an internal company memo that discussed selling off the plant's brewing equipment to Peking Beer or Harbin Beer, but whether the sale was actually carried out is unclear, and unlikely. Meanwhile, a contract to sell Tokyo Beer's Tsurumi factory to Oki Electric Industries for ¥4.2 million was concluded on 14 February 1944.[87] Both purchasers were, of course, munitions firms.

Finally, Kyushu's Sakura Beer was eliminated from the industry by way of a forced merger with the market leader, Dai Nippon Beer. In 1942, production at Sakura Beer's only plant was roughly 18,000 kL, which represented nearly 7 percent of national market share. The firm was significantly weakened, however, by the forced production restrictions that had gone into effect in 1940, which had triggered a steep drop in business. Before long, Sakura had simply too many employees and too much equipment, and officials from the Finance Ministry stepped in to broker a solution. A merger contract was ironed out in July 1943 and approved by the ministry in September. Under the deal, Dai Nippon Beer's capital stock rose to ¥97.75 million and it acquired Sakura's plant at Moji, thus ending a thirty-year run that had begun as Teikoku Beer in 1912.[88] Through the merger with Sakura Beer, Dai Nippon also acquired control of Sakura's partner firms, China Beer and Sakura Grape Wine.

Beer sales were also controlled more rigidly toward the end of the war. On 12 July 1944, the nation's Central Beer Sales Company was renamed the Beer Distribution Control Company, and the regional beer sales companies were converted into its branch offices. Sales were also stunted, naturally, by the extreme scarcity of civilian labour, as the munitions industry was consuming much of Japan's workforce.[89] In 1944, Saipan and Guam fell to the United States, and the mainland came under severe attacks from American B-29s. Due to the bombing, many offices, factories, schoolchildren, and some adult civilians were evacuated from major cities, and the number of damaged buildings in the cities began to rise. In March 1944, the remains of Dai Nippon's Materials, Distribution, and East Asia departments were moved from its bombed head office in the Kyōbashi ward of Tokyo to its plant in nearby Meguro ward. National beer production fell to 159,000 kL in 1944, and the intensity of the US bombing campaign increased in 1945. In the middle of the night on 9 March, Dai Nippon's Azumabashi plant was destroyed in an attack that levelled most of Tokyo's lower town (*shitamachi*). Next, in an attack on Yamanote, Tokyo, on 24 and 25 May, roughly 2.2 hectares of the company's plant at Meguro was destroyed, and the malts in its silos burned. In a major early dawn raid on Nagoya on 19 March, Dai Nippon's brewery was destroyed when most of its wooden buildings burned down. Beyond the plant grounds, the workers' dormitories and houses were also damaged or destroyed. The same plant was bombed again in a lighter raid on 25 March, and in larger raids on 14 and 17 May, damaging it still further. On 28 July, Dai Nippon's Kawaguchi plant was also damaged in a bombing raid. Bombing continued almost incessantly until the end of the war, killing many of the company's workers and their families.

Surviving workers laboured to clean up the damage to Dai Nippon's factories and perform makeshift repairs, but resuming normal brewing operations proved to be remarkably difficult. In May 1945, the government informed Dai Nippon Beer that it intended to shutter Japan's beer breweries, and an internal company memo detailed the Finance Ministry's secret plan to halt beer distribution by September. The government's plan ordered both Dai Nippon and Kirin to

1   stop preparing ingredients immediately
2   finish the beer already brewing
3   convert to production of fuel alcohol or other things using the ingredients on hand
4   scrap unused machinery.

Japan produced just 83,000 kL of beer in 1945, of which Kirin produced 17,498 kL. Overall, national beer production fell in 1945 to just 26.6 percent of Japan's peak production year, 1939, and Kirin was producing just 21.1 percent of its 1939 volume. In July 1945, Kirin and Dai Nippon's individual factories were informed of the government's new plan via a circular entitled "Production Conversion Summary." In it, Dai Nippon's Meguro plant was ordered to begin producing basic pharmaceuticals, its Kawaguchi plant fuel alcohol, its Niihama-shi plant butanol, and its Moji plant salt. Kirin's plants received similar orders, such as the production of special military-use whisky and fuel alcohol. Sapporo Breweries, the modern successor to Dai Nippon, records that Japan's surrender on 15 August saved Japan's beer industry from imminent ruin. At war's end, Dai Nippon Beer still had nine factories and Kirin Brewery had four, and these thirteen factories had an annual production capacity of about 240,000 kL.[90]

On the continent, however, Japanese breweries in both Korea and Manchuria were turned over to the Allies after Japan's surrender. Kirin's factories in Korea fell to the administration of the US Army, and its plants in Manchuria fell to the Soviet Army. Kirin notes that its employees made an effort to put everything in order before handing over their facilities and all related documents to Allied forces. For a time, both Kirin and Dai Nippon employees were required to remain at their posts and continue brewing and shipping beer just as before. Gradually, however, the Japanese staffers were repatriated to Japan, and the company officers were forced to manage the breweries using local workers before they themselves were sent home. On 25 March 1946, *Life* magazine reported that Japanese hostesses were working to entertain Soviet officers at banquets staged by the Chinese Communists, where the tables were laden with an array of foods and drinks, including Japanese beer.[91] Significantly, Kirin's management learned that the "Kirin Beer" brand was still being brewed and sold in Northeast China as late as 1954.[92]

Conclusions

Between 1937 and the spring of 1945, beer brewing and distribution came under increasing restrictions, but while beer was carefully rationed, its supply to Japanese consumers was essentially uninterrupted. Commercially, beer was sold throughout the country in Japan's countless neighbourhood pubs and taverns, and even late in the war at occasional "people's bars." Beer ration tickets were generally required, and quantities were limited, but beer prices remained fixed and consumers were not faced with speculation in the official marketplace. As for home consumption, it too continued, regulated carefully by household beer ration tickets and later by a passbook system designed to ensure that no family could purchase more than its share. Beer was likewise brewed throughout Japan's wartime territorial holdings. Soldiers were served beer at the front until the closing phases of the war (often to the detriment of noncombatants), and the sailors of the Imperial Japanese Navy enjoyed beer bottled and shipped directly to Japan's major naval bases through mid-1945. Indeed, the consumption of beer by military personnel throughout Japan's wartime empire would prove vital to the brewing industry's postwar recovery, for returning veterans soon demanded beer even in remote corners of Japan, where it had often been rare or unavailable before the war.

An array of significant transformative pressures affected the beer industry during this period, including dietary and nutritional concerns, rationing and product distribution, colonial business ventures, and prices and living standards. The government's efforts to achieve material and industrial self-sufficiency throughout Japanese industry applied also to the manufacture of beer, and necessitated expanded programs of domestic barley and hops cultivation as well as malts production. As the economic controls of the Second World War era intensified, however, Japan's brewers were also required to transform the way that they purchased ingredients, manufactured and shipped their products, and set prices. Like many wartime manufacturing sectors, the beer industry was essentially reduced to a revenue-generating arm of the nation's command economy. It became a source of tax revenue for the government, and as such its direction fell increasingly to the Ministry of Finance – an arrangement that would have important long-term repercussions.

Dependent on the tax revenues generated by brewing and sales, Japan's government directed brewers to ship their product under the single, generic label *"Bakushu"* (Beer) right through the spring of 1945. Because the fixed price of beer did not rise again after 1943, the rising taxes on beer were effectively a cash grab – a tax on the brewers that could not be passed on to consumers. Despite the drain of their capital reserves, Japan's beer industry was preserved, defended, and streamlined by the government's control, and many of these modifications survived the war era. Most importantly, the elimination of smaller brewers by the government's enterprise curtailment policy left Dai Nippon and Kirin as the only domestic beer-brewing companies by 1943. Although Dai Nippon would be broken up during the Allied Occupation of Japan as a part of Occupation General Headquarter's (GHQ) policy of eliminating excessive concentrations of corporate control, the brewers that disappeared during the war never returned. Nor, for that matter, would the industry's long-time dependence on German ingredients, technicians, and product identity. Within a few years, Japan's prewar system of contract farming would resume, and Japan's brewers would once again achieve material self-sufficiency.

In addition to culling the competing brewers, the implementation of Japan's wartime controlled distribution system also transformed beer sales. The wartime distribution system permitted tighter control, vetting, and supervision of both wholesalers and retailers by the Ministry of Finance in order to ensure legal beer distribution and thorough revenue collection. While the control of wholesalers and retailers was relaxed after the war and the brewers returned to using their individual brands and labels, the wartime distribution control system persisted during the Occupation. The Beer Distribution Control Company carried on, dropping the term "control" *(tōsei)*, until March 1948, when its affairs were transferred to a new organization, the Alcohol Distribution Public Corporation. Other components of the wartime control system persisted as well. Chief among these was the maintenance of the bottle-return system, which had been inspired by necessity but continued due to its obvious practicality. Similarly, the single "sloping-shoulders" beer bottle design was maintained as the industry standard, which enabled all firms to collect and reuse one another's bottles – obviating the need to hunt for and ship branded bottles back to their home breweries.[93]

The efforts of the Ministry of Finance to regulate beer recipes, production, distribution, taxation, and so on left a deep impression on Japan's surviving brewers that extended far beyond the war years. Although the wartime Japan Beer Brewers Association was broken up in January 1948, the Japan Beer Association simply changed its name to the Incorporated Beer Association in April of that year. The Japanese word used for "association" was *konwakai*, or "friendly get-together," which illustrates the group's postwar discussion-oriented mandate. In time, these organizations would grow into industry representative bodies, enabling continued discussion with government, farmers, and retailers. These lasting changes underscore not only the modernizing effects of Japan's prescribed wartime manufacturing regime, but also its success at decoupling the beer industry from its foreign founders, teachers, and influences. Rivalled only by the brewers' formation of a production and sales cartel in the 1930s, the wartime reorganization and management of the beer industry by the Ministry of Finance left the deepest, most lasting impression on the industry's character. In order to survive, however, Japan's brewers would have to pick up the pieces of their demolished plants and overcome the severe privation of the immediate postwar era.[94]

4 "The Taste of Home": Beer as Postwar Japanese Commodity, 1945-72

The war crippled Japanese industrial and commercial networks in nearly all respects, but while Japan's material losses were significant, its civilian casualties were certainly more tragic. The beer industry was remarkably well integrated into the national economy, and it employed thousands of workers across the country. Its reach extended from farms and plantations to manufacturing plants, through a vast distribution network, and down to the smallest bars and retail shops. Its human losses too were significant, especially in its urban factories. The beer industry's postwar recovery is worthy of close inspection because it took place during a period of severe deprivation, food shortages, and widespread civilian starvation – during which time Allied Occupation personnel were erecting base housing, stocking up their PXs, and eating and drinking well.[1] The beer industry thus lay at the crossroads of these two contrasting agendas for Japan's postwar government: struggling to feed an impoverished civilian populace, while at the same time paying handsomely to ensure that Allied forces were supplied with all of the comforts of home. Here we find jarring clashes between Japan's postwar domestic, security, and industrial policies. As Kenneth Pyle notes, the uncomfortable combination of occupation and poverty was rife with such contradictions.[2]

Japan's modern beer industry had been significantly reshaped during the war years. Nearly every one of its networks and systems was redesigned by the Ministry of Finance or its subordinate industrial groups, including those that regulated farming, materials, recipes, manufacturing, bottling, distribution, rationing, sales, and taxation. Most of those systems continued to operate and evolve after the war's deadly conclusion, which is a testament to the considerable achievements of Japan's wartime economic and industrial policymakers. One very significant break, however, was the interruption of Japan's relationship with Germany during the Allied Occupation of Japan (1945-52). Both countries remained isolated from one another during the Occupation era, during which time Japan was demilitarized, its constitution was rewritten, and its foreign policy was realigned through the conclusion of a sweeping security pact with the United States. Whether this process of "Americanization" was truly welcome in Japan may be debated, but it is certainly fair to say that during the early postwar era, virtually nobody in Japan was celebrating German products, techniques, or manufacturing processes.[3] The unique relationship between Japan's brewers and German brewmasters was now severed, and the idea of advertising a product's strict adherence to German purity laws had been rendered unthinkable. The urgent wartime campaign to achieve self-sufficiency in beer production was a success, but its most significant long-term impact was the permanent decoupling of Japan's brewing culture from its formerly integral German heritage. Even the aforementioned Japan-Germany Society would not be reestablished until after Japan regained its sovereignty in April 1952.

Like firms in many industries, Japan's two surviving brewing companies struggled to stay afloat amidst the intense pressures of the immediate postwar era. The chief architects of the Allied Occupation soon realized, as had Japan's wartime military government, the great value of continued beer production and sales. Although Occupation General Headquarters (GHQ) aimed to democratize Japan both politically and economically by enfranchising workers, smashing monopolies, and abolishing controlled distribution networks, those processes also involved a great deal of input from Japanese managers and bureaucrats. Much of the literature on postwar Japan, the Allied Occupation, and the role of GHQ focuses on the autocratic power wielded by the Supreme Commander of the Allied Powers (SCAP) General Douglas MacArthur. Despite SCAP's profound influence, it handled some manufacturing sectors less severely than others, permitting their managers to play more active roles in drafting both their companies' and their industries' futures. The beer industry was one such sector.

End of Empire: Wartime Losses, Reparations, and Recovery

Dai Nippon Beer and Kirin Brewery, the only two brewers to survive the war era, were impacted deeply by the conflict. Naturally, as in every other Japanese industry that had operated facilities throughout the former Japanese Empire, all of their overseas plants were lost at a stroke on Japan's surrender in August 1945. Dai Nippon had led the beer industry's advance into the overseas marketplace, and its successor firm notes that since the mid-1930s, those facilities had become "a pillar of our operations."[4] All of its overseas plants and their contents were seized by Allied forces, be they Nationalist Chinese, Soviet, British, or American. For Dai Nippon, those immediate subsidiaries included Tsingtao Beer (Qingdao), Chōsen Beer (Korea), Manchuria Beer

(Manchukuo), Peking Beer (Beijing), Takasuna Beer (Taiwan), and Balin-tawak Beer (Quezon City, Philippines) – six major firms that managed forty breweries throughout China and Southeast Asia.

Similarly, Kirin Brewery lost all of the overseas assets it had been accumulating since 1932 and which it valued in 1945 at roughly ¥1.35 million. More importantly, Kirin notes that it lost many talented employees who had been drafted into Japan's army and navy late in the war, whom its surviving employees continued to mourn well into the postwar era. On the other hand, it acknowledges that while the personnel who had been sent overseas on company business had "tasted hardships," they were very fortunate to have been pulled to safety by war's end.[5]

Both companies suffered significant losses throughout Japan's home islands as well. Unlike the sake industry, which had been sharply curtailed by strict production directives and whose many small, rural breweries had escaped Allied bombing raids, Kirin and Dai Nippon were not so fortunate. Kirin's main office and its flagship store in Tokyo were bombed by Allied aircraft in three major raids on 25 May 1945, burning both facilities to the ground. Office employees were able to save the firm's most important records, but Kirin lost a wide array of reference books and other such materials in the blaze. Kirin's bottling plant at Yokohama as well as its cask-filling plant at Amazaki were also bombed, damaging the machinery and idling both plants for a short time. Significantly, however, Kirin's brewery in Hiroshima survived the atomic bombing of that city on 6 August. Amazingly, the firm records that although the windows and the slate roof of the plant were damaged by the atomic blast wave, the building was just outside the most severely impacted portion of the city. Its production machinery was not damaged, and it resumed operations within six months. Kirin's flagship plant at Namamugi, Yokohama, was also spared significant damage due to its location on the periphery of that port city, the heart of which was bombed heavily by US B-29s in the spring of 1945. Overall, Kirin's wartime losses totalled ¥943,484, and it was able to salvage all but 10 percent of its production equipment.[6]

Although Kirin's productive capacity was not permanently affected, it was, like Dai Nippon, crippled in the immediate postwar period by severe manufacturing restrictions, ingredient shortages, transportation problems, and a widespread lack of fuel. In 1945, industry-wide beer production of 83,000 kL was just 25 percent of its high point of 1939. In 1939, Kirin had claimed 26 percent market share, but by 1945 that had fallen to 21 percent at just 17,498 kL, as strict production and supply controls impeded the company's ability to improve its position. Still, Kirin's management opted to repair its war-damaged plants as quickly as possible, and by mid-1948, the costs associated with both the loss of its overseas assets and its domestic repairs were paid off in full.[7] Dai Nippon Beer, however, fared much worse. Its domestic losses were principally its plants in Nagoya and in Meguro, Tokyo, which were severely damaged. Toward the end of the war, Dai Nippon had been ordered by Japan's military government to halt the production of beer and to convert several of its plants to the production of fuel alcohol and other wartime necessities. Still, it took less than two weeks from Japan's surrender on 15 August for the government to order the plants' reconstruction. On 30 August the government decided to scrap the beer factory conversion plan and, faced with the urgent need to raise tax revenue, it ordered the continuation of beer production on 8 September. As Dai Nippon's conversion to military production had only just taken place, switching back to beer manufacturing was not a major obstacle for its engineers. In September 1945, the government permitted the sale of raw ingredients to the beer industry, but Dai Nippon did not receive priority for allotments of fuel, which, like electricity, was in desperately short supply.[8]

Kirin began its recovery by pulling machinery out of its three plants at Amazaki, Sendai, and Hiroshima in order to increase the output of its flagship brewery in Yokohama. Dai Nippon too began sifting through the ashes of its ruined facilities in search of salvageable production equipment. Among the wreckage was a functional grinding machine for processing grain, along with a few other pieces of equipment, which were moved to its Azumabashi plant in Tokyo. Their installation was complete in mid-February 1946, and the brewmasters laid in their first batch later that month. In 1947, Dai Nippon purchased a nearby warplane hangar from the former Nakajima Aircraft Company, which it converted into a manufacturing plant by October. (At the time of writing, that site is the headquarters of the Asahi Soft Drinks Company, Inc.) As for its Nagoya plant, Dai Nippon contracted the Taisei Construction Company to reconstruct the facility, but the build did not commence until November 1946. As a result, it was several years before the company was able to again produce the 144,118 kL that it had brewed domestically in 1944. In 1945, Dai Nippon's total production volume at all of its factories was roughly 66,000 kL – a figure that would continue to slide over the next several years. In 1946, Dai Nippon brewed just 43,983 kL, followed by 41,702 kL in 1947 and 40,942 kL in 1948. Naturally, brewing technology in Europe and America had improved during the war, especially bottling machines, pasteurizing equipment, and other such systems. Japanese brewers had made no such progress during the war, and Kirin notes that due to the anticipated surge in postwar demand, it struggled to fill the gaps in its technical abilities and beef up its manufacturing equipment. In addition, the industry's production figures were depressed by the grave food shortage facing the nation, which will be explored in further detail below.[9]

Added to the ingredient and fuel supply crises was the expectation that the brewers would have to contribute to Japan's war reparations fund. Generally speaking, however, the beer industry was spared the need to pay the reparations imposed by the Allied powers. By late 1945, Japan's government had racked up an enormous tab through its wartime beer orders for Japan's armed forces, which it had purchased on a military credit account. At GHQ's insistence, this debt, together with debts owed to hundreds of other firms, was settled by means of a repayment that the government immediately taxed back at the rate of 100 percent and diverted toward the national reparations fund. This plan, which essentially erased the government's wartime procurement losses while simultaneously handing the nation's reparations bill to private industry, was accomplished through two laws that were reluctantly proposed by Finance Minister Ishibashi Tanzan in 1946. The first was the Company Accounting Special Measures Law, under which a special accounting company *(tokubetsu keiri kaisha)* was designated in August to assess Dai Nippon Beer's unpaid account. This was found to total ¥22.66 million. Then, in October, Japan's government enacted the Wartime Reparations Special Measures Law, which required companies to remit any payments received for war debts into the national war reparations fund. This was accomplished by imposing a Wartime Reparations Special Tax in the same amount as the payment issued.[10]

Dai Nippon records that while the process for paying its tax bill was established by the end of November 1946, the specific details of the payment remain "unclear" *(fumei)*. In fact, the details are not unclear: the tax was simply never paid, due to the costs incurred by the firm's loss of its overseas assets, which Dai Nippon valued at ¥42.6 million. Postwar operations and sales enabled the company to recoup ¥18.83 million of those losses by late 1947, and the remaining ¥23.77 million in early 1948. Given the significant weight of these sums, Dai Nippon submitted an application to the government in 1948, asking to be absolved of the ¥22.66 million special reparations tax. In late October, that application was accepted and the tax payment was indeed cancelled. Thus, along with Kirin, Dai Nippon was not required to contribute to Japan's national reparations fund, which was itself reduced substantially by the late 1940s. This turn of events aided the brewing industry's financial recovery significantly.[11]

Brewing for New Masters: The Allied Occupation, 1945-52

When interviewed in 1999, Asahi Breweries' former chair Seto Yūzō described the Occupation era as a period devoid of colour, save for the khaki green of the omnipresent US Occupation forces, which, he said, made the entire country resemble an "army camp."[12] Nevertheless, Japan's beer industry was the quickest to recover in the immediate postwar era, driven by the demand of Allied Occupation service personnel, who were stationed throughout the country. Although Japanese firms were in no position to turn a profit in late 1945, Occupation forces did offer a secure market for housing materials and a wide range of manufactured wares, including, of course, beer. Its supply, however, was extremely limited. The Japanese government had, quite rightly, anticipated the Allied soldiers' demands for alcohol, just as it had their need for sex. On the latter point, John Dower has already documented the government's detailed plans to recruit "new Japanese women" to service Allied soldiers stationed in Japan. Aiming to prevent widespread rapes, the government enlisted the aid of hundreds of Japanese women to service the sexual needs of the occupiers – a total of 1,360 women by 27 August.[13] At the same time, however, the Metropolitan Police refused to sanction the plans of the Tokyo Recreation and Amusement Association to purchase and convert the Mitsukoshi department store on the Ginza into an enormous beer hall, dance hall, and sexual "comfort station" for Allied personnel, fearing that such a conspicuous facility might generate further problems.[14] Instead, the Metropolitan Police permitted smaller beer halls and cabarets strictly for Occupation personnel to open throughout Tokyo and other major urban areas by late 1945, including locations in Asakusa, Ueno, and inside the former Yebisu Beer Hall on the Ginza.[15] Still, given the many pressing postwar reconstruction efforts that were under way, establishing or reopening these facilities took time, and the delays generated significant short-term tensions.

Already by early September 1945 the government received reports that Allied soldiers were approaching breweries throughout Japan and demanding beer. Sapporo records that Allied soldiers entered Dai Nippon's beer plants and attempted to communicate with the employees, who had a difficult time making themselves understood in return. At the outset, the brewery employees refused the soldiers' demands, but in order to avoid further trouble, they requested that Japanese defence soldiers *(keibihei)* be stationed at breweries. In order to protect its plant at Meguro, Tokyo, Dai Nippon issued a request to the former Imperial Navy Technical Research Centre (Kaigun gijutsu kenkyūsho) for the Allies to send troops to guard the plant. In response, one American and one Australian soldier were dispatched and stood guard in a passageway leading to the brewery's elevator entrance. They guarded the facility in shifts, taking turns napping on a cot placed inside the entryway. Sapporo notes that the American soldier sometimes brought along a can of American-made beer, but the Japanese staffers thought it tasted terrible and refused to drink it.[16]

Generally speaking, the immediate postwar security situation at Dai Nippon's breweries was good, except at its plant in Kawaguchi, Saitama prefecture. On 24 September, the firm records that one American and one British soldier appeared carrying weapons and demanded that the brewery sell them beer, which the factory staff refused to do. The next day, a larger group of Allied soldiers came, and just as the atmosphere grew dangerous, the plant's public relations representative agreed to sell them beer from the guardhouse at the plant's side service entrance. The factory managers requested that Japanese MPs *(kenpei)* be dispatched to guard the plant, but even still, the situation remained tense through 21 October. As a result, the plant managers petitioned *(chinjō suru)* that a Japanese military unit be stationed in the company dormitory at the nearby Kawaguchi Piston Ring Company. That unit dispatched patrols of defence soldiers every two hours to monitor the brewery. Dai Nippon also offered the security forces lodgings on the second floor of its factory assembly hall, but whether any troops actually stayed there the company does not say. Either way, the above situations are both remarkable and anomalous, for the literature on the Allied Occupation of Japan generally contends that the conduct of Allied forces during the early days of the Occupation was admirably peaceful. Most sources assert that Allied personnel concluded within a matter of weeks that their own personal security situation was good enough to warrant carrying no rifles or even side arms as they went about their business.[17]

In response to the Allied demand for beer, the Tax Bureau of the Ministry of Finance issued an ultimatum *(tsūchō)* to the heads of its regional tax offices, exempting Allied military units (but not civilian staffers) from paying the Alcohol Tax. This order was treated as top secret *(gokuhi)* because the nation's finances were in ruin and Japan could scarcely afford to curtail its own revenues.[18] Nevertheless, based on this order, Occupation forces took delivery of between one-third and one-half of Japan's total beer production in 1946. Between December 1946 and November 1947, Dai Nippon and Kirin together produced roughly 90,000 kL of beer, out of which 19,667 kL, or 22 percent, was consumed by Occupation forces. The untaxed portion of this sold to military units was 12,815 kL, or 14 percent of the total volume produced. The beer issued to US forces by Kirin bore labels that read "BEER – FOR USE OF

ALLIED FORCES ONLY – Free of Tax – Please return all empty bottles – The loss of bottles means that much less beer for you."[19] In order to keep up with the Allied demand, both Kirin and Dai Nippon made efforts to improve and expand their production equipment, and after 1947, they increased their capital investments. Still, as urban populations rose and demand began to increase, production could not keep up because of the severe shortage of both manufacturing ingredients and bottles. As a result, Japan's brewers continued their wartime bottle collection effort, and also issued special beer coupons aimed at ensuring the return of empties. Each coupon was issued to a particular US army; those issued to the US Eighth Army read: "Good for twenty five (25) full bottle cases of Japanese beer on presentation to any authorized Japanese brewery in exchange for twenty five (25) empty bottle cases."[20] Much more ominous than dwindling bottle supplies, however, was the threat of famine that faced Japan in late 1945.

Brewing Beer amidst Starvation: GHQ and Alcohol Production Policy

The immediate and greatest hardship for the Japanese populace immediately following the war was food shortages. The 1945 rice-growing season yielded just two-thirds of the usual crop – already a dark omen. The total 1945 wet- and dry-land rice harvest was 39.15 million koku, or 7.06 million tonnes, which was a level not seen since 1905. Worse still, during the Occupation era, roughly seven million soldiers and civilians from throughout Japan's former overseas empire were repatriated, intensifying the already grave food shortage. This combination of circumstances reportedly drove ten million Japanese to the brink of starvation during the early years of the Occupation.[21] In October 1945, in order to increase the food supply, the government ordered that rice production was compulsory for all farmers with the appropriate land, and in February 1946, it began enforcing emergency food supply measures. Although Allied Occupation General Headquarters was interested in preventing widespread famine, GHQ was not especially concerned by the food supply crisis. The Occupation was intended to serve as a punishment for Japan's wartime conduct, so some degree of misery and starvation was deemed justified. GHQ's correspondence with the civilian government was stern, and faced with a global food supply that was already strained, Japan's government learned soon enough that it could expect limited assistance with its food supply problem from the Allied powers.[22]

On a policy level, however, the United States was prepared to intervene. On 6 February 1946, US president Harry Truman enacted a beer and alcohol production stoppage in occupied European countries as a relief plan to combat their food supply crises. The plan placed an emphasis on the economical use of US wheat, and it not only banned alcohol production using wheat, it also required the local governments to manage both flour milling and any wheat exports. When this news was reported in the American media, Japan's beer manufacturers took it as a serious blow, for Germany's brewing industry was already shuttered, and even British breweries were operating under tight restrictions. Kirin and Dai Nippon therefore anticipated that the same restrictions would inevitably reach Japan as well. Already in 1945, Kirin's production volume had fallen 48 percent from the previous year.[23] Importantly, given the beer industry's association with the nation's food supply, allowing new market entrants was impossible. The Ministry of Finance controlled the issuance of brewing licences, and for the next fifty years it would keep all but three new firms out of the industry altogether. This situation stands in sharp contrast to that in many other postwar industries, in which remarkably few barriers to entry enabled huge numbers of companies to try their hands in unfamiliar manufacturing sectors, such as pharmaceuticals, radios, and motorcycles.[24]

In May 1946, the food shortage reached crisis proportions, and in Tokyo, activists like Seda Tani led demonstrations before the Imperial Palace. Outraged and frightened by the looming spectre of starvation, Tokyoites staged protests entitled "Ward Residents' Send Rice Rally" *(Kome yokose kumin taikai)* and "Food May Day" *(Shokuryō mēdē)* in order to capture the government's attention.[25] Kirin and Dai Nippon were rightfully concerned, for immediately after the Food May Day rally, GHQ ordered the Japanese government to issue a total halt to all brewing operations nationwide. Thereafter, the Ministry of Finance ordered that from 1 June, all brewing materials in stock, including sweet potatoes, barley, and rice, were to be compulsorily delivered to the government, and prohibited the delivery of further ingredients or supplies to the brewers for two months afterward. Dai Nippon had 4,937 tonnes of brewing barley on hand from the 1945 production year, which it delivered to the government as ordered. Between 20 and 30 percent of its stocks were already laid in as beer, so that volume was omitted. Soon thereafter, however, GHQ's Interior Department softened its rigid policy, and the beer industry's biggest fear – a total stoppage of production – was avoided. Both Kirin and Dai Nippon succeeded in riding out the crisis, and in July 1946, the importation of ingredients from overseas began. In September and October 1947, full-scale beer production resumed, and a good crop of rice was at last harvested in that year. The industry's formerly productive relationship with agriculture appeared to be opening up once more.[26]

Contract farming for beer barley had been suspended in 1940, and in 1941 beer barley had become a regulated commodity as Japan's government sought tighter control over the nation's food supply. This suspension continued until the shortages began to ebb, but in the interim, the Japan Beer Ingredients Company discussed converting to a barley allocation quota system regulated by the Ministry of Finance. Postwar production of the best variety, known as "Golden Melon" barley, had fallen to just 50 or 60 percent of prewar levels, and the brewers had long since been forced to rely on lower-quality native species. Between 1945 and 1949, the Ministry of Finance allotted 74.5 percent of available beer barley to Dai Nippon, the larger firm, and just 25.5 percent to Kirin – a decision that effectively fixed the two companies' market shares. During that period, acquiring ingredients required approval first from the Ministry of Finance, then the Ministry of Agriculture and Forestry, as well as the city and prefectural authorities, and finally the Food Distribution Public Corporation. From 1949, the brewers mixed Golden Melon barley with native species in a 50:50 ratio. Finally, contract farming of beer barley resumed in 1952.[27]

As for hops, due to the stoppage of beer production by the military government in May 1945, just 10 percent of the nation's hops fields were still in production in July of that year. As only beer requires hops, the bulk of the nation's hops farms were naturally slated to be converted to food production. Domestic stocks were exhausted by November 1946, and in that year Dai Nippon agreed to sell 40,050 kg of hops to Kirin Brewery at ¥13 per kilogram in order to enable Kirin to continue operating. Two years later, in October 1948, Kirin purchased another 1,000 kg of hops at ¥150 per kilogram – over ten times the price.[28] Following a petition by the Japan Beer Ingredients Company, Japanese brewers were permitted to import hops starting in 1949, and the first shipment of 18,000 kg came from the United States. In 1950, Japan imported 336,000 kg of hops from both America and Germany, paid for through a foreign exchange currency allowance granted to the industry by the Ministry of Finance. By then, Kirin was encouraged by a sudden increase in Japan's domestic hops supply. Improvements in cultivation techniques led to greater domestic output, and the quality also improved, curbing the demand for imports. By the late 1950s, the beer ingredients supply problem was resolved entirely. Until that time, however, beer production and distribution remained under very tight control.[29]

Postwar Beer Recipes, Rationing, and Black Marketeering

The deprivation of the wartime era had unexpected consequences for Japan's beer brewers – especially the way in which it transformed consumer preferences. The era of controlled distribution and supply shortages had put pressure on brewers to produce a lighter, less flavourful product, and the availability of just one general-household-use beer had influenced beer drinkers' tastes significantly. The single government-directed brand known simply as *"Bakushu"* (Beer) had been shipped to most corners of the country during the war, and it was widely available for army and navy use, as well as at special events like send-off ceremonies. Kirin notes that wartime beer's necessarily lighter taste became preferred by consumers, and lighter-tasting beers were therefore regarded more favourably than before the war. This transformation was not limited to Japan; during the war years there was an international tendency for beer's flavour to grow lighter due to the shortages of grains, hops, and flavouring ingredients like bitters. Western authors of business case studies have described Kirin lager as a bitter, strong-tasting beer that postwar consumers enjoyed because the national diet was meagre and bland, especially during the Occupation, but this assertion must be qualified in two ways.[30] First, all Japanese beer was significantly less bitter and flavourful following the war, and second, postwar Kirin lager may be described as strong and bitter only in comparison to the even lighter-tasting products issued in more recent decades. Due in large part to the privations of the war era, what was thought of before the war as a beverage for getting drunk came to be thought of more as a clean, alcoholic soft drink. Given its lighter taste, women and young people began to demand beer like never before.[31] The war thus left an indelible mark not only on the beer industry but on consumers' tastes for the product itself. In the early years of the postwar era, however, beer distribution remained a significant challenge.

Throughout the Occupation era, and especially after 1946, beer was sold to consumers at official prices both in neighbourhood liquor shops and commercial establishments, though few could afford such a luxury at the outset. From 1947, slightly less expensive rationed beer was sold to agricultural workers as well as workers in designated key industries. Just as during the war, taxes on beer production and sales remained crucial sources of revenue for Japan's postwar government, which struggled to improve the nation's economy and its industrial productivity. Beer shipments therefore remained the responsibility of the Beer Distribution Control Company and continued to be supervised by the Ministry of Finance, which assigned the task to the Tax Bureau and its local offices. The state of the economy rendered it impossible for the beer industry to convert immediately to a system of free sales, so beer distribution controls remained in effect for much of the Occupation period. Slowly, however, the management of the distribution network was taken over by a series of independent, nongovernment agencies *(minkan dantei)* in preparation for the eventual return of free sales.

This conversion process began early with a GHQ memorandum on 6 August 1945, which stated that the many laws and ordinances on which Japan's wartime systems were based were now invalidated. This memo effectively broke up all former production and distribution control associations and paved the way for control by private industry. The changes were incremental, however. In the beer industry, the Beer Distribution Control Company merely dropped the word "Control" from its name in October 1945. Thereafter, in October 1946, a new Special Materials Supply and Demand Regulation Law wrested other material distribution controls away from the military and gave them formally to the civilian government. In December 1947, beer distribution authority was transferred to the Alcohol Distribution Public Corporation under the newly promulgated law of the same name. The wartime distribution network was then shut down completely in 1948, beginning with the Japan Beer Brewers Association, which was abolished in January. On 1 March, sales under the new public corporation officially began, and in May the Japan Beer Ingredients Company too was dissolved. Its long-time control over the distribution of beer ingredients ended by July, after which the former Japan Beer Association umbrella group was converted into the Beer Discussion Group.[32]

Added to the challenges of distribution were the great costs of repairing and replacing war-damaged facilities and equipment, and while bank lending increased, personal savings and deposits were withdrawn, triggering a severe, dangerous imbalance between money and goods. This led, of course, to crippling inflation. This inflation affected Kirin and Dai Nippon deeply, as the costs for payroll, ingredients, energy, and so on likewise rose sharply higher. From 1945 to 1949, the wholesale and retail prices for beer rose an astonishing sixty and seventy-nine times, respectively. The official maximum price for beer was raised by the Ministry of Finance in January 1946, and beer was taxed together with other alcoholic beverages through a basic Alcohol Tax. During the Occupation era, however, the government's poor finances and anemic tax yields prompted both tax increases and the introduction of a variety of new taxes. The basic Alcohol Tax rate was therefore raised in September 1946, and again in April and December 1947, and once more in July 1948. Then, in August 1948, the government began requiring beer retailers to charge an Alcohol Consumption Tax, ranging from 2.5 percent in smaller cities to 5 percent in Tokyo. In September 1948, this was converted to a 1 percent tax for brewers, a 2 percent tax for distributors, and a 3 percent tax for retailers.[33] Throughout this period, the official prices for beer reached remarkable heights. For the average consumer, the price of a large bottle of

Table 25

Consumer beer prices and those of other commodities, 1949-63

Item	Approximate date		
	1949	1955	1963
Large bottle of beer	¥126.50	¥125	¥115
1 serving of soba noodles	¥15	¥25-30 (1954)	¥50 (1964)
1 serving of curry rice	¥50 (1948)	¥100	¥120
1 cup of coffee	¥20 (1948)	¥50	¥80 (1965)
1 bottle of quality whisky	¥562	¥730 (1953)	¥750 (1962)
1 package of Peace cigarettes	¥60 (1948)	¥40 (1956)	¥40
Starting monthly salary, banker	¥3,000	¥5,600 (1956)	¥21,000
Salary can purchase x bottles of beer	23.7 bottles	44.8 bottles	182.6 bottles

Source: Sapporo biiru KK, *Sapporo 120 nenshi* [120-year history of Sapporo Breweries] (Tokyo: Sapporo biiru KK, 1996), 380. Data based on "Nedan no Meiji–Taishō–Shōwa no fūzokushi" [Manners and customs: Prices in Meiji, Taishō, and Shōwa], *Shūkan Asahi* [Asahi weekly].

beer reached ¥75.70 by September 1948, while a bottle of commercial-use beer sold for an incredible ¥162.20.[34]

Still, these prices could not begin to compare to the black market *(yami-ichi)* prices for beer. Emerging, as John Dower writes, almost simultaneously with Japan's capitulation, the black market was virtually *the* economy for many Japanese during the early Occupation era.[35] Along with a cheap, noxious *shōchū* liquor made from sake lees *(kasutori)*, beer sold briskly to hurried consumers at street stalls run by enterprising *tachiuri* (stand and sell) vendors, but only to those who could afford it. According to Sapporo's records, for those consumers who wished to purchase more than their allotted beer rations, the cost was truly dear. In late 1945, the black market price for beer was ten times higher than the official rationed price, and by 1947 it was four times higher than the official price, which had itself more than doubled. As time passed, the difference between the prices decreased, and by May 1949, the black market price of ¥150 for a large bottle of beer was much closer to the official price of ¥130. With time, black marketeering was sidelined both by government controls and market forces, which rendered unofficial beer sales less and less profitable.[36] (For comparative prices for beer and other common purchases, see Table 25.)

Still, while the economy had begun to stabilize, actual beer distribution remained a complicated, managed process. After 1949, it worked as follows. First of all, every quarter, the beer brewers had to report their planned production volumes. Then, the brewers drew up a list of proposed alcohol sales by type for Japan's forty-seven administrative districts, and the projected sales amounts were decided in consultation with the Alcohol Distribution Public Corporation. Then, the corporation's various branch offices, which fell within the jurisdiction of the local areas' Financial Affairs Bureaus, made their rulings, and based on their written decisions, local brewing companies were permitted to ship their products within their respective jurisdictions. This process was rather simple compared to the wartime production and distribution system, but it was still a top-down and carefully managed affair, rather than a free-market arrangement.

In time, as ingredients and revenues began to stabilize, Japan's government began to move toward a reformed beer distribution and taxation system, one that aimed to cut out the middleman. On 6 May 1949, the commercial-use beer tax and the special beer tax were abolished and replaced with a new tax on beer sales – a Free Sales Added Tax. This tax benefited workers in key designated industries as well as farm labourers, who continued to receive beer rations. Under the new tax structure, the price of beer fell for the first time since the end of the war; one bottle now sold for ¥130, while rationed beer cost ¥75. Finally, on the last day of June 1949, the Alcohol Distribution Public Corporation was abolished, and in mid-July, the three-tiered sales structure that had functioned since before the war (composed of manufacturers, wholesalers, and retailers) was changed to a two-tier structure comprising only brewers and regional networks of retailers. With this, the two surviving brewers began to sell beer independently, though lingering shortages and price controls would force them to deliver allotted shipments for the remainder of the year. Before that free market system materialized, however, Japan's leading beer producer, Dai Nippon, was split into two smaller firms – and not by GHQ.[37]

(In)Voluntary Divide: The Postwar Breakup of Dai Nippon Beer

Adding to the beer industry's physical and financial recovery was a third dimension of complexity, namely its division from two major firms into three. Under Douglas MacArthur, GHQ directed the Japanese government to break up the leading industrial conglomerates in an effort to achieve economic democratization *(keizai minshuka)*.[38] SCAP concluded that the war's outbreak and direction stemmed in large part from the excessive control over industry, trade, and national policy wielded by Japan's most powerful, family-controlled corporations, which were long referred to critically by the press as *zaibatsu,* or money cliques. As a result, Japan's government passed Law 207, the Law for the Elimination of Excessive Concentration of Economic Power (otherwise known as the Anti-Monopoly Law), which was promulgated on 18 December

1947.[39] Based on Article 3 of this statute, both Kirin and Dai Nippon received orders from the government to liquidate their shares and submit reorganization plans. Kirin's fate was much less arduous than that of its giant rival, Dai Nippon. Kirin was ordered simply to liquidate its shares, and even that order was cancelled on 17 December 1948, saving the firm and keeping it fully intact.[40]

Dai Nippon's fate was much more dramatic, but it also involved a degree of managerial autonomy and control, which is something that the literature on Occupied Japan tends to overlook, preoccupied as it is with GHQ's significant authority and predominant role in reorganizing Japan's political and economic systems. Japanese-language sources on this issue are less focused on GHQ's role, and deal instead with the impact of the Allies' decisions on Japanese companies and individuals.[41] Kirin records that because Dai Nippon Beer was Japan's largest brewer, it was targeted by the government and ordered to be divided into two firms. However, the successors of Dai Nippon Beer offer quite a different perspective. These sources show that its management, faced with the prospect of liquidation, undertook a voluntary (if anticipatory) effort to split the firm into two companies ahead of any such order from GHQ. That effort was led by Dai Nippon's second-in-command and managing director, Yamamoto Tamesaburō, who was spurred into action when Japan's government formed the Holding Company Liquidation Commission in August 1946. In 1983, the commission's president, Noda Iwajirō, authored a volume entitled *Reminiscences on Zaibatsu Dissolution,* in which he identified Yamamoto as the initiator of Dai Nippon's partition plan: "Yamamoto-san has a plan to undertake this independently *[dokuji].* That is, to divide the firm into two beer branches. Yamamoto-san has made this request both to GHQ and to the Holding Company Liquidation Commission."[42]

Since the start of formal government controls in 1938, it had been Yamamoto's job to single-handedly negotiate with the ruling authorities, and by 1945 it appears that he was already sounding out the staff at GHQ to see if such a partition was possible. Yamamoto was a commanding figure, whom former Asahi intranet designer Miyamoto Kotarō described as rather charismatic.[43] On the other hand, former Asahi chair Nakajō Takanori described Yamamoto as a "dictator president" *(wan-man shachō).*[44] Yamamoto's autocratic management style is also taken up in the *History of the Asahi Labour Union,* which records that in 1946, "The move toward voluntary division had already been decided, and the preparations were being made even as GHQ and the Ministry of Finance were being contacted."[45] Management's plan to partition the firm ahead of GHQ's orders can, therefore, be confirmed by the fact that it had already shared the details with its labour union. Dai Nippon's workers and management negotiated the partition problem in February and March 1947, and at a management conference on 12 May, the two sides agreed to form a separation measures committee. That body was assigned such logistical tasks as deciding how to divide operations, products, brands, equipment, and personnel. At Dai Nippon's eighty-third shareholders' meeting on 28 July, the president, Takahashi Ryūtarō, announced, "Concerning the gossip *[uwasa]* about the division problem, we have been conducting negotiations in that direction since December of last year."[46]

Events related to the company's partition thus unfolded very rapidly, offering us a unique case study, for major Japanese companies seldom split into two lesser entities, even in circumstances as dire as those that faced Dai Nippon Beer. By November 1947, the separation measures committee had ironed out most of the details and issued a report. The key points included the distribution of funds and equipment, and which of the two successor companies, termed "A" and "B," should inherit which facilities, and what brands they should produce. The report involved two options, which it likewise named "A" and "B," but which are referred to here as options 1 and 2. Under option 1, Company A would produce the "Sapporo," "Yebisu," and "Sakura" brands, and Company B would issue "Asahi" and "Union" beers. Although the five beer brands were split unevenly, the production volumes were nearly equivalent and the two flagship brands, "Asahi" and "Sapporo," were shared evenly. Alternatively, option 2 proposed to give both flagship brands to Company B and relegate the three lesser brands, "Yebisu," "Union," and "Sakura," to Company A. Both firms would continue to produce soft drinks as well – sharing the "Mitsuya Cider" and "Ribbon Citron" brands. The rationale for option 1 was that the two new companies would each produce one of the strongest brands in order to balance the marketplace. The rationale for option 2 involved the geographical locations of the new companies' manufacturing plants, some of which produced "Asahi" and "Sapporo" exclusively. Dai Nippon's successors identify Yamamoto as the principal author of the two proposed plans. Ultimately, a modified version of option 1 was chosen (see Table 26).[47]

Due to the groundwork that Dai Nippon had already laid, the company was not among the fifty *zaibatsu* firms officially slated for dissolution by SCAP in January 1949. Instead, the *New York Times* reported that Dai Nippon was among just three firms to receive approval of their own reorganization plans.[48] The official notice of Dai Nippon's partition was issued on 7 January 1949, and the official founding of the new firms is recorded as 1 September of that year. Dai Nippon was capitalized at ¥97.75 million, but by adding 45,000 shares, the two new firms were able to split an even ¥100 million in

Table 26

Final division plan pursued by Dai Nippon Beer, 1949

Company (brands)	Plants	Production capacity		
		Beer (kL)	Malts (kg)	Soft drink (boxes)
Nippon Beer	Meguro	30,666	4,400,000	
(Sapporo, Yebisu,	Kawaguchi	18,039	2,100,000	400,000
Sakura Ribbon	Nagoya	17,137	2,400,000	
Citron)	Sapporo	10,823	2,900,000	
	Moji	13,709	3,900,000	
Subtotal	5 plants	90,374	15,700,000	400,000
		(49%)	*(64%)*	*(29%)*
Asahi Breweries	Nishinomiya	19,482		
(Asahi, Union,	Azumabashi	22,187		
Mitsuya Cider)	Suita	34,187	6,400,000	900,000
	Hakata	17,137	2,400,000	100,000
Subtotal	4 plants	92,993	8,800,000	1,000,000
		(51%)	*(36%)*	*(71%)*
Total	9 plants	183,276	24,500,000	1,400,000
		(100%)	*(100%)*	*(100%)*

Source: Data compiled from Sapporo biiru KK, *Sapporo 120 nenshi* [120-year history of Sapporo Breweries] (Tokyo: Sapporo biiru KK, 1996), 341, 352.

capital stock. Named Nippon (Japan) Beer, and Asahi (Rising Sun) Breweries, they shared the former company's total beer production volume 49/51 percent, respectively. The name Nippon Beer revived the identity of one of the three firms that had merged to form Dai Nippon in 1906. Although Nippon controlled 64 percent of Dai Nippon's former malts production, Asahi was compensated by its receipt of 71 percent of total soft-drink capacity. Nippon and Asahi also shared Dai Nippon's former bottle-making operations, which were spun off as Nippon Glass and Asahi Beer Pax, each with operations in nearby regions throughout Japan. Overall, the separation plan was rather equitable, given Dai Nippon's great stable of brands and the geographical breadth of its operations. Despite their shared managerial heritage, the two firms were expected to act as rivals.[49] On its official founding on 1 September 1949, Asahi Breweries, Ltd., set sail with Yamamoto Tamesaburō at the helm as its first president, while Takahashi Ryūtarō carried on as the president of Nippon Beer Co., Inc., until a successor was named. At a special shareholders' meeting on 6 December, Nippon Beer's managing director, Shibada Kiyoshi, was promoted to the position of president-director.[50]

Shortly after its founding, Nippon Beer gave careful consideration to re-naming its flagship brand, "Sapporo Beer," because both the Asahi and Kirin breweries were selling eponymous brands. Furthermore, former Asahi Breweries president Matsui Yasuo recalled that following their split, Nippon and Asahi had effectively become "local brand makers" in Japan's eastern and western regions, respectively, whereas Kirin remained a "nationwide brand maker."[51] This necessitated rebranding strategies for both of the new firms. Nippon Beer therefore elected to merge its "Sapporo," "Yebisu," and "Sakura" brands into a single new brand, "Nippon Beer," which launched in December 1949. The new brand featured a star on its label (★), which was carried over from the original Sapporo trademark label. In September 1949, Nippon and Asahi each controlled 36.2 percent of Japan's beer market, while Kirin held on to 27.6 percent (see Table 27), although Kirin would very soon eclipse its rivals and become Japan's leading brand.[52] In fact, by 1953, Japan's newly founded *Jōzō Sangyō Shimbun* (Brewing industry newspaper) reported that the three companies were sharing the market almost perfectly, at 33.5 percent Nippon, 33.3 percent Asahi, and 33.2 percent Kirin.[53] As for the former firms' new sales operations, they will be explored in further detail below.

"Labour Democratization" and the Postwar Beer Industry

Both Dai Nippon and Kirin had lost many of their workers during the war, especially late in the conflict. In late May 1945, Kirin's regular employees numbered 1,414, but shortly afterward, 358 of them were drafted by Japan's military. A further 34 were drafted from Kirin's facilities in occupied China and Southeast Asia, and an additional 30 men from various other overseas offices were pressed into service. At war's end, many of these trained employ-ees returned, but Kirin had to lay off a number of them for several years due to the sharp decline in manufacturing. As the economy improved, these men were able to return to work, and Kirin also recovered over 320 employees who had been transferred to various other overseas companies or to heavy industry during the war. Kirin's payroll grew steadily, as shown in Table 28.

Before and during the war, any kind of labour organization or activism was actively suppressed, but among the newfound freedoms of the postwar era came the possibility of forming labour unions – known more commonly in Japan as labour federations *(rōdō kumiai)*. This development dovetailed neatly with GHQ's efforts to break up industrial monopolies, for in SCAP's estima-tion, enfranchised workers represented much-needed labour democratization *(rōdō minshuka)*. Consequently, workers at Kirin, as well as at Dai Nippon Beer, soon established independent labour federations. The Kirin Beer Labour Union Association was formed in May 1946. In August, the company and

Table 27

Scale of Japan's three brewing companies, September 1949

	Kirin Brewery	Nippon Beer	Asahi Breweries
Capital stock	¥80 million	¥100 million	¥100 million
Beer production by plant	Yokohama: 109,000 koku/ 19,663 kL Amazaki: 161,000 koku/ 29,043 kL Sendai: 68,000 koku/ 12,267 kL Hiroshima: 57,000 koku/ 10,282 kL	Meguro: 170,000 koku/ 30,666 kL Sapporo: 60,000 koku/ 10,823 kL Kawaguchi: 100,000 koku/ 18,039 kL Nagoya: 5,000 koku/ 902 kL Moji: 76,000 koku/ 13,710 kL	Azumabashi: 125,000 koku/ 22,549 kL Fukeda: 189,000 koku/ 34,094 kL Nishinomiya: 108,000 koku/ 19,482 kL Hakata: 95,000 koku/ 17,137 kL
Total beer production	395,000 koku/ 71,254 kL	501,000 koku/ 90,375 kL	515,000 koku/ 92,901 kL
Soft-drink production by plant (4 dozen/box)	Yokohama: 250,000 boxes Hiroshima: 250,000 boxes	Kawaguchi: 510,000 boxes Moji: 120,000 boxes	Nishinomiya: 630,000 boxes
Total soft-drink production	500,000 boxes	630,000 boxes	630,000 boxes
Bottle production	Yokohama: 36 million Hiroshima: 18 million	n.d.	n.d.
Major brands	Kirin Beer Kirin Lemon	Nippon Beer Ribbon Citron	Asahi Beer Mitsuya Cider

Note: Nippon and Asahi aligned the production of their respective soft-drink brands, Ribbon Citron and Mitsuya Cider, following their division in 1949.

Source: Kirin biiru KK, *Kirin biiru KK gojū nenshi* [Kirin Brewery Company, Ltd.: Fifty-year history] (Tokyo: Kirin biiru KK, 20 March 1957), 157.

the association reached an agreement that the firm would run a "union shop" and permit no employees other than union members. Over the next few years, the union advocated for higher wages, raising the retirement age, adding a year-end bonus, and the provision of personal loans for workers in

Table 28

Number of employees by type, Kirin Brewery, 1946-56

Fiscal year-end	Office and sales staff	Factory workers	Total
May 1946	542	1,139	1,687
May 1947	408	1,251	1,659
May 1948	437	1,204	1,641
May 1949	469	1,349	1,818
May 1950	632	1,702	2,334
May 1951	649	1,821	2,470
May 1952	679	1,806	2,485
June 1953	688	1,738	2,426
June 1954	712	1,751	2,463
June 1955	756	1,819	2,575
June 1956	772	1,819	2,591

Source: Kirin biiru KK, *Kirin biiru KK gojū nenshi* [Kirin Brewery Company, Ltd.: Fifty-year history] (Tokyo: Kirin biiru KK, 20 March 1957), 193.

debt. Through concerted effort, the association managed to achieve the above revisions to its labour agreement, as well as substantial welfare and recreational facilities on the factory grounds. More importantly, Kirin notes that these negotiations did not trigger substantial discord within the company, which is why the union broke away from its affiliated labour association and formed a single-enterprise union, the Kirin Beer Labour Union, in April 1951.[54]

As was the trend in other industries, however, Kirin's labour union soon began considering a merger with its peer organization at Dai Nippon Beer. Dai Nippon's employees had begun organizing in December 1945, and in November 1946, representatives from both unions sat down to discuss the possibility of forming an industry-wide league. In May 1949, the two groups formed the All Japan Beer Industry Labour Union Association. At first, this umbrella group was unable to set policy for the affiliated labour unions at its two, then three, member firms (Kirin, Nippon, and Asahi), but later it became the chief negotiating force for its members through the adoption of collective bargaining. Remarkably, it was not the union association that encouraged its membership to bargain collectively – that suggestion came from Kirin Brewery's senior management. The relationship between the two sides was not always so amicable, however; the tensions between Japanese workers and management often boiled over into strikes and lockouts during the early 1950s.[55]

By 1950, the three brewing unions found themselves mired in a dispute over their varying agendas concerning wages and working conditions, which posed headaches not only for the workers, but also for the breweries' management. This episode is documented by Kirin and Sapporo only in part, so we must turn also to reports from such newspapers as the *Asahi* and the *Jōzō sangyō* in order to contextualize and qualify the brewers' accounts. Because each of Japan's three brewers faced similar market challenges, production quotas, and labour conditions, Kirin's chair, recognizing an opportunity, sat down with the three component unions in group mediation. In August 1952, the employees' working hours were indeed cut and the retirement age was increased at each of the three firms, but the unions remained unable to achieve wage concessions from management. By May 1954, just as the issue of a wage increase was being considered by the entire labour association for the first time, a serious labour dispute broke out. The conflict became quite heated between May and June 1955, which was a time of rising tension and even pitched battles between workers and management in other industries across Japan. What began as a strike at three beer plants in Tokyo soon escalated into a seventy-two-hour walkout at all thirteen plants nationwide, prompting the *Asahi* to suggest that the impasse might result in a beer shortage by late summer.[56]

Once again, however, Kirin's senior managers got involved and worked to refine and present the labour association's demands for wage increases to the three brewing companies. They also encouraged the three firms to open up simultaneous "diagonal negotiations" between themselves and the labour association. Kirin's initiative encouraged the labour association to consider each union's data on hours and wages, as well as on retirement, holiday, and vacation benefit criteria, as a whole across the three companies. Although this effort clearly benefited the companies by streamlining theretofore fractured labour negotiations, it is nevertheless a remarkable example of management sponsorship of collective bargaining by its own workers. Naturally, the role played by Kirin's senior leaders was not entirely selfless. In return for encouraging Japan's brewery workers to bargain as a group, Kirin, as the emerging postwar market leader, essentially took on the role of lead labour negotiator, setting the tone for its new marketplace hegemony.[57]

By the mid-1950s, the working conditions for Japan's brewery employees had improved significantly, certainly when compared to the hardships experienced by most factory employees during the war years. Kirin, like its peers, began providing a range of benefits and recreational facilities for its male and rising number of female workers at its various plants. These included a 241-unit company residence, eight apartment buildings featuring 94 units, and a 6-unit family housing building, plus twelve more buildings to house up to a hundred unmarried employees. These units housed roughly

17 percent of Kirin's total workforce by 1956. Additional facilities provided to all employees and their families included cafeterias, sundry shops, recreation rooms, medical clinics, burial service benefits, and even lush offices for company retreats. At its many plants across Japan, Nippon Beer also constructed a series of tennis courts, baseball diamonds, volleyball courts, pools, and clubhouses, which it credits with expanding the popularity of sport ahead of the coming 1958 Pan Asian Games and the 1964 Tokyo Olympiad.[58] Taking care of workers was not a uniquely postwar phenomenon, for several major Japanese firms had boasted such benefits during the 1920s and 1930s, but the 1950s certainly witnessed a return to providing such comforts for company employees. Asahi Breweries' former chair Nakajō Takanori writes in his memoir of the difficulty that many young men like himself experienced in making the transition from wartime life as a young officer cadet to the role of a company "salaryman" in the late 1940s and early 1950s.[59] Such company amenities were therefore a welcome diversion. For most working families in Japan during the 1950s, urban housing was very basic and household amenities were few, which is why the company's provision of something as simple as a television or a Ping-Pong table improved employees' daily lives.[60] Still, living standards, like beer sales, were poised to climb rapidly through the 1950s, and wages would not be far behind.

The Ministry of Finance and Japan's Informal Postwar Beer Cartel

Returning to an era of truly free sales proved a lengthy and complex process, due chiefly to the total control that the Ministry of Finance had exerted over the beer industry during the war. Before the brewers could once again manage beer distribution, they had to rebuild their shattered national distribution networks. First, they recalled the staffers who had been transferred to the regional distribution offices in 1943 and assigned them to their own sales networks. As the companies were once again selling their products under their own brand names, Kirin swiftly reopened five shops, in Nagoya, Yokohama, Kobe, Sendai, and Hiroshima, as well as three district sales offices in Kyoto, Takematsu, and Fukuoka. Kirin thus returned to its special contract sales system, quickly establishing a nationwide sales network everywhere but in southern Kyushu and in Hokkaido. For the first time since 1943, beer distribution was again the product of the industry's own competitive initiative, and Kirin notes that the controlled distribution system "vanished like a bad dream" *(ichijō no akumu).*[61]

Naturally, most of the human relationships between Kirin and its former retailers had been severed during the war years, but the firm pressed ahead with a plan to revive those partnerships wherever possible. Touting its

Table 29

Kirin production figures rise, 1949-55

Date	Beer	Soft drinks (24 bottles per box)
1949	395,000 koku/71,254 kL	1,000,000 boxes
1952	600,000 koku/108,234 kL	1,540,000 boxes
1955	880,000 koku/158,743 kL	2,000,000 boxes

Source: Kirin biiru KK, *Kirin biiru KK gojū nenshi* [Kirin Brewery Company, Ltd.: Fifty-year history] (Tokyo: Kirin biiru KK, 20 March 1957), 162.

commitment that "Kirin's sole agents will certainly prosper" *(Kirin no tokuya-kuten kanarazu sakaeru),* the firm sought to rekindle former business partnerships.[62] The directors dispatched sales personnel throughout the country to locate former agents. This was a monumental task in a country that, as both Western and Japanese scholars underline, had lost large swaths of 215 war-damaged cities to Allied air raids.[63] Nevertheless, Kirin reestablished much of its former contract sales network, and its production levels rose in concert with the country's steadily improving economy (see Table 29).

By 1953, the three surviving firms were sharing the national market almost evenly, but the next year Asahi Breweries eclipsed its rivals, and led the way in sales with 37 percent of market share. In 1955, Kirin reopened its sales office in Sapporo – the company's first foray into Hokkaido since the war ended. Former Asahi Breweries chair Seto Yūzō described a frantic pace kept up by his company's many young sales managers, who travelled constantly from small shops to taverns and bars, conducting vigorous sales promotion activities. One of these campaigns involved encouraging retailers and bar owners to suggest "Asahi Beer" to those patrons who simply called out for "beer." Much of this friendly cajoling involved taking a personal approach, and Seto recalled that the very first thing new sales hires were taught was "Don't sell beer, sell yourself" *(Biiru o uru na, jibun o ure).*[64] In 1955, Japanese consumed 4.5 litres of beer per capita, more than the 4.4 litres consumed in 1939. Despite a brief recession following the end of the Korean War in 1953, industry-wide beer production and consumption per capita increased steadily, leading by 1956 to an annual production volume of over 2.56 million koku, or 462,000 kL (see Table 30).[65]

Japan's beer exports also recovered modestly during the early 1950s, boosted principally by the Korean War (1950-53) and the increasing numbers of US service personnel being transferred to Okinawa during the 1950s (see Table 31). Tracking the exact volumes of beer consumption and exports became much easier and more accurate once the 1951 Weights and Measures

Table 30

National population and domestic beer production per person, 1945-56

Year	National production (kL)	Population (000s)	Production per person (mL)
1945	83,299.8	72,200	1,152
1946	96,000.5	75,800	1,264
1947	93,113.7	78,101	1,190
1948	91,075.1	80,010	1,136
1949	138,937.5	81,780	1,696
1950	170,883.4	83,200	2,050
1951	271,511.1	84,600	3,202
1952	293,324.1	85,900	3,447
1953	390,984.0	87,000	4,484
1954	398,857.1	88,300	4,507
1955	408,623.9	89,276	4,567
1956	462,984.1	90,172	5,123

Source: Kirin biiru KK, *Kirin biiru KK gojū nenshi* [Kirin Brewery Company, Ltd.: Fifty-year history] (Tokyo: Kirin biiru KK, 20 March 1957), 235.

Table 31

Japan's postwar regional beer exports (kL), 1949-55

Year	United States	Okinawa	Korea	Taiwan	Southeast Asia	Other	Total
1949	461.1	0.9	1.4	0.0	97.6	5,413.3	597.5
1950	138.5	112.2	1,816.3	1,711.9	418.7	4,529.8	4,208.9
1951	51.6	1,177.2	7,953.9	0.0	399.0	4,001.6	9,678.8
1952	53.6	3,072.0	12,284.4	0.0	262.1	3,288.5	16,104.9
1953	147.2	1,917.5	13,639.1	0.0	127.4	3,234.6	16,375.4
1954	208.2	2,035.7	7,013.6	0.0	213.8	2,380.8	9,972.1
1955	274.9	2,557.7	3,627.3	15.9	307.7	2,391.1	7,321.5

Source: Kirin biiru KK, *Kirin biiru KK gojū nenshi* [Kirin Brewery Company, Ltd.: Fifty-year history] (Tokyo: Kirin biiru KK, 20 March 1957), 233.

Law, which regulated all metric units precisely, took effect in March 1952. The large 3.5l gō beer bottle, which was 633.17 mL, thereby became 633 mL, the small bottle was standardized at 334 mL, and the 720 mL bottle became obsolete. In July 1956, authorized bottles began featuring the kanji *tadashii* in a circle (㊣, for "correct"), denoting their metric accuracy.[66]

Although sales were increasing, Japan's postwar beer brewers remained subject to the powerful influence of the Ministry of Finance, which is a significant consequence of the government's wartime reorganization efforts.

Economist Joseph Schumpeter defines nonprice competition as that driven by new commodities, technologies, or sources of supply, as distinct from simple price-point competition.[67] More recently, Tim Craig has characterized Japan's postwar beer industry as "a stable oligopoly in which competition had traditionally been limited to well understood nonprice dimensions."[68] John Sutton and Richard Boyd are even more explicit, and refer to the relationship between the four large brewers operating today as a regulatory cartel managed by the Ministry of Finance. In exchange for being the gatekeeper and ensuring that no domestic competitors could enter the industry without a licence (for which a market entrant would have to apply and be approved to produce over 2,000 kL annually), the ministry permitted the leading brewers to set prices in consultation with its own officials.[69]

As a result, despite periodic and coordinated price rises, the retail price of different brands of beer would remain nearly identical for more than thirty years. Moreover, in exchange for continuing tariff protection against foreign imports, Japan's brewers agreed to use three tonnes of domestically grown barley (which is priced at roughly four times the world average) for every tonne of cheaper, imported barley that they brew. Importantly, this continuing regulatory agreement is tacit, renegotiated annually, and unwritten. If it appeared in writing, the deal would violate the former General Agreement on Tariffs and Trade (GATT) and the rules of today's World Trade Organization (WTO). In essence, Japan's postwar brewers acquiesced to very high beer production and consumption taxes in exchange for the ability to negotiate beer prices, provided that they also participated in a secondary barley cartel, itself managed by the Ministry of Finance. Beer prices, while not *directly* controlled, thus reflect an implicit understanding between the firms and the government. This arrangement was and remains a significant continuation of the prewar beer cartel, albeit with a much greater degree of government involvement.[70]

Cabarets and Celebrities: Beer Marketing and Emerging Postwar Consumerism

Not only did the brewing firms and their retail shops reemerge after the war, they began to reach out to beer consumers in new and varied ways. Importantly, the surviving companies began to showcase their product not as a European commodity, but as a domestic Japanese one. They therefore advertised their brands alongside images of Japanese celebrities, art forms, and wild vistas. Asahi began making important forays into new advertising media following its creation of a PR department in 1950. Its chair, Nakajō Takanori, summarized the urgent postwar embrace of modern advertising with the simple slogan "Product Out, Marketing In."[71] This shift meant that emphasis on beer recipes, ingredients, or brewing techniques was decidedly "out" and Japan's beer consumers were definitely "in." Sapporo likewise records that beer, formerly regarded as a high-status beverage, came to be thought of in the postwar era as a "public commodity," which greatly fuelled demand.[72]

Quickly, the brewers recognized that beer sales were influenced by the product's image, and beer thus had to be portrayed as bright, fun, and refreshing. As the Occupation drew to a close, the brewers therefore started sponsoring a wide array of entertainment and sporting events. Asahi began by sponsoring radio programs in 1951, and the next year it agreed to a promotional tie-in with the film *Gone with the Wind (Kaze to tomo ni sarinu)*, which returned to Japanese theatres. Further efforts included sponsorship of the much anticipated world flyweight boxing championship match between Shirai Yoshio and Hawaiian Dado Marino, which was broadcast by radio from Tokyo in May 1952. This was followed the next year by Asahi's first television commercials, which sponsored the Nihon Terebi (Japan Television, or NTV) program *Nandemo yarimashō* (Let's do anything). Other efforts included the promotion of an Asahi Beer Concert in Tokyo's Hibiya Park in 1954, as well as expensive full-page newspaper ads.[73] By the mid-1950s, the struggle for Japan's beer market required all three firms to reach out to consumers with true multimedia platforms.

The newly reopened beer halls became symbols of Japan's recovery, and beer was one of its most successful consumer products. Dai Nippon Beer had operated four beer halls in Tokyo until its division in 1949, but they were strictly for Allied forces personnel and did not serve Japanese. Two of those halls were located along the famed Ginza shopping street at 7-chōme, and bore the names Ginza Beer Hall and Kobe Beer Hall. The Sapporo Beer Hall had operated in Tokyo's Chūō ward since 1899, and the Lion Beer Hall was in Shinjuku. In 1950, Nippon Beer opened another Lion Beer Hall on the Ginza, which featured a huge neon sign of an overflowing beer glass (see Figure 10).[74] Known as the "Ginza Lion" and the "Shinjuku Lion" (see Figure 11), these shops contributed to the enduring image of rest and relaxation that US service personnel enjoyed in those parts of Tokyo (see Figure 12). The Ginza remained synonymous with fun and entertainment for American officers and GIs through the Occupation and well into the 1970s.[75] In May 1949, however, GHQ granted permission for bars and restaurants to reopen to Japanese patrons, followed by beer halls in June, which lit a fire under Japan's beer industry (see Figure 13).

On 1 June 1949, the *Asahi* newspaper reported happily that "Starting Today We Can Drink Draft Beer" *(Kyō kara nomeru nama biiru)*. The article featured

Figure 10 The Lion Beer Hall at Ginza 4-chōme, Tokyo, April 1954.
Courtesy of the Mainichi Newspapers.

Figure 12 Allied soldiers in a beer hall for Occupation personnel, Ginza, Tokyo, 30 June 1951. *Courtesy of the Mainichi Newspapers.*

Figure 13 Beer halls in Tokyo reopen to Japanese patrons, 1 June 1949. *Courtesy of the Mainichi Newspapers.*

◄ *Figure 11* The much-remodelled Shinjuku Lion Beer Hall, which opened in Shinjuku 3-chōme, Tokyo in 1939. *Photo by the author, July 2011.*

a photograph of workers lining up rows of wooden beer casks and noted that "the breweries have large, 2,000-litre tanks standing by" and "the beer halls will be open 2-8 p.m. The price for a half-litre is ¥156."[76] That price was very steep; as Sapporo notes, the official minimum price for a 633 mL bottle of beer was ¥126.50 in 1949, leaving the entire salary of the average banker unable to purchase more than twenty-three bottles a month (see Table 25).[77] Beer prices may have remained under official control, but the resumption of free beer sales at last permitted the beer companies to meet the growing demand profitably. Dai Nippon soon closed its smaller GI taverns along the Ginza and began opening shops and beer halls for Japanese patrons instead. Following the company's partition in September 1949, separate companies, named Nippon kyōei KK (Japan Mutual Prosperity Co., Inc.) and Asahi kyōei KK, were hived off in order to manage these businesses. Each was capitalized with ¥1.5 million, and Nippon kyōei assumed control over all of Dai Nippon's beer shops and halls east of Nagoya, while Asahi kyōei managed those to the west.[78] Beer halls became such a familiar place for postwar Japanese to while away the hours after work that a fictional hall even became the setting for director Uchida Tomu's 1955 film *Twilight Beer Hall (Tasogare sakaba)*. Scholars of Japanese cinema Joseph L. Anderson and Donald Richie explain that *Twilight Beer Hall* depicted a single day in a cheap beer hall, from opening to closing. "The film," they write, "was episodic in character with various little stories about the employees and the patrons, representing a cross section of postwar life as viewed by Uchida after ten years' absence from Japan."[79]

Beer sales were also driven very strongly by Japan's many postwar night-clubs, cabarets, and "neon bars," which were the most popular spot for Occupation personnel to drink and watch dancing girls. Many Japanese citizens were upset by these cabarets, especially when the newspapers re-ported on disreputable establishments that were frequented by criminals or that employed young schoolgirls as dancers.[80] Further reports involving cabaret-related social problems appeared almost every week throughout the 1950s, but the brewers were concerned with selling beer, not policing social mores. In 1950, the price of a large draft beer fell from ¥132 to just ¥115, which fuelled even greater demand.[81] Asahi Breweries' former chair Seto Yūzō noted that at one cabaret in Osaka named Crown Yukari, his company sold roughly 120 wooden crates (of twenty-four bottles) of beer each night. That totalled an entire truckload of beer per day and over forty-three thousand crates of beer per year, which made Crown Yukari by far Asahi's top-selling cabaret.[82] Kirin Brewery too operated a subsidiary company called Kinkō shokai KK (Golden Harbour Company, Inc.) that operated crowded beer halls in Tokyo, Yokohama, Nagoya, Osaka, Kobe, Hiroshima, and Sendai.[83] Tokyo alone was home to several hundred bars and nightclubs, many of which burned down during the 1950s and 1960s, as evidenced by frequent headlines reporting fatal cabaret fires.[84] Even the Sapporo Lion beer hall on the Ginza would burn in a fire in May 1964, which attests to the poor-quality construction and inadequate fire safety measures that plagued Japan's cities for decades after the war.[85]

Reaching out to beer consumers necessitated more than simply stocking Japan's bars. New technologies, especially television, offered powerful new marketing tools, and Nippon Beer led the way by launching its first radio commercial in 1951, followed by its first ad on NTV in 1953. Demand for "Nippon Beer" fell briefly during the Korean War, however, due to rapidly intensifying marketplace competition, which forced its directors to take different approaches toward strengthening its brand. The Nippon Beer Company therefore prioritized newspaper, magazine, and poster ads that showcased the work of young artists and writers, so as to appeal to younger consumers. Nippon began to copy the styles of ads found in American magazines, and faced with ink shortages, it produced monochrome posters that its artists coloured by hand. In 1954 it moved in truly novel directions by creating a new illustrated character called the Beer King *(Biiru ōsama)*. Until that point, Japanese beer ads were generally one-time phenomena, but the Beer King was a serial effort linked with special events, such as drinking contests. Nippon staged competitions to see who could recognize the "Nippon Beer" brand when blindfolded, or drink the most beer, or drink it the fastest *(nomippuri)*. Naturally, the winners were crowned Beer King and featured in Nippon's next Beer King advertisement. Thus by 1954, beer marketers were already cultivating the social acceptability of drinking to excess, which was clearly equated with power and masculinity.[86]

In 1955, as Japan's economic recovery picked up speed, Nippon Beer issued a poster that marked "10 Years since the War." This simple but symbolic effort aimed to remind consumers just how far the country, and the beer industry, had come since the period when the brewers were forced to produce generic, brandless beer.[87] Despite relentless advertising, however, Nippon Beer remained in second place behind Kirin. Faced with the impasse, Nippon's directors decided to try reviving their original "Sapporo" brand. In March 1955, just as Kirin began to penetrate the Hokkaido marketplace, Nippon brewed twelve thousand boxes of "Sapporo Beer" for test release throughout the northern island. When the iconic brand's return met with positive reviews, Nippon drew up plans to reintroduce it nationwide, beginning in Tokyo in September 1956. In that year, Nippon's other plants, led by those in Tōhoku, also began brewing "Sapporo Beer," and the firm's advertising budget reached an impressive ¥74.5 billion, fully seven times the sum spent in 1949. Backed by a major advertising campaign in print, on radio, on leaflets, and in films, as well as in posters hung in stores and on trains, sales accelerated very quickly, and national consumption set new records each year.[88] Importantly, Nippon's new ad slogan was *"Honba no aji – Sapporo"* (Authentic taste – Sapporo). Here, the word "authentic" *(honba)* also means "home," which gave the ad campaign a nostalgic tone. "Home" clearly implied Japan, not Europe or Germany, and the response from consumers was so enthusiastic that by February 1957, the firm decided to retire the "Nippon Beer" brand and issue the "Sapporo Beer" brand nationwide once more.[89]

The following year, Sapporo launched one of Japan's most famous ad campaigns. It featured a map of the world with a red line at forty-five degrees latitude connecting the three beer-brewing cities "München–Sapporo–Milwaukee."[90] Importantly, the ad identified the cities in an empirical fashion as industry peers, rather than in any particular rank order or historical chronology. Its catchphrase was hugely successful, and as the three-stage beat resonated strongly with consumers, this phrasing pattern became standard in Sapporo ad copy of the era. Iain Gately writes that this slogan "was a clever bridge between the pre-World War II perception of beer in Japan as a traditional Teutonic brew and the new and desirable Yankee dynamism."[91] Naturally, the company received many complaints that "München is at 48 degrees, while Sapporo and Milwaukee are at 43," but Sapporo rephrased the copy to read "45 degrees is home," once more underscoring the theme of "home." Clearly, beer was no longer a foreign or Western commodity in the minds of Japanese consumers, but a global commodity that had been brewed proudly in Japan for generations.[92]

Supported by beer's transformation into a nostalgic Japanese commodity, Kirin, Asahi, and Sapporo advertisements of the late 1950s and early 1960s also began featuring famous Japanese personalities. This was a far cry from the ads that featured stodgy German brewmasters in the 1880s and beautiful but anonymous women in the 1920s and 1930s. In 1954, an ad for "Nippon Beer" resulted in the company's first commercial hit song, sung by Miki Torirō (1914-94), which was followed by a series of hanging train posters *(nakazuri)* featuring glamorous but real Japanese women dressed in modern evening wear. Targeting women as much as men, these ads featured the actresses Maki Hiroko in 1957, Tsukasa Yōko in 1958, and Enami Kyōko in 1961. By 1958, the brewers' annual ad budgets had each surpassed ¥100 billion, and not only did the number of television sets in Japan surpass five million in 1960, broadcasters like NTV and NHK (Nippon hōsō kyōkai [Japan Broadcasting

Corporation]) soon began broadcasting in colour. In 1961, beer makers began running five-second television commercials.

Sapporo's ads featured *rakugo* (comedy) legend Kokontei Shinshō, Yomiuri Giants famed third-baseman Nagashima Shigeo, and *kabuki* icon Onoe Shōroku II, who was a designated Living National Treasure of Japan. Further entertainment figures included the four members of the male chorus group the Dark Ducks, which formed in 1951, as well as the actors from the hit NHK television drama *Basu dori ura* (Behind Bus Street), which ran from 1958 to 1963. Ads featuring television stars proved popular with consumers, and additional Sapporo posters included actors from such hit programs as *Jiken kisha* (Police reporters) and *Owarai sannin gumi* (The comic trio). In 1963, Sapporo even showcased Ishihara Yūjirō, who was a movie star and singer dubbed the "Japanese Elvis." (At the time of writing, his brother is the often controversial governor of Tokyo, Ishihara Shintarō.) Beer ads for this generation were clearly designed to speak directly to consumers' interests, and Japan's homegrown entertainment figures were at the top of the list.[93]

Kirin naturally followed suit by issuing posters, newspaper ads, and television commercials featuring a who's who of the Japanese sporting and entertainment worlds. Although Hollywood stars, such as the cast of the hit television western *Laramie* (1959-63), were sometimes the focus, the vast majority of the ads featured Japanese themes and celebrities exclusively.[94] In order to prevent a costly advertising war, however, the three firms agreed to limit their spending by not purchasing full-page newspaper ads. Even so, their advertising budgets approached ¥350 billion annually. In summer 1964, Tokyo hosted the world at the eighteenth Olympiad, and the beer producers, like legions of other consumer product makers, were quick to capitalize on the sensation. Five-second television commercials for beer ran frequently during NHK's Olympic broadcasts and reached a record number of television owners, many of whom had purchased their first TV sets in order to see the games at home.[95] Hosting the Olympics was arguably Japan's proudest moment of the postwar era to date, and Japan's beer producers succeeded in putting their brands before millions of consumers' eyes. Fuelled by all of this advertising, and given beer's widespread availability in department stores, groceries, liquor shops, and beer gardens, its popularity soared.[96] By the 1960s, beer was regarded as a thoroughly domestic, Japanese product that could stand proudly alongside the nation's most iconic personalities.

In 1965, however, the rate of increase began to slow, and though overall consumption continued to rise steadily, the brewers resorted to novel packaging and clever ad campaigns in order to catch consumers' eyes and boost sales. Sapporo had already started the trend in 1963 by releasing a large, fat bottle called "Sapporo Giant," which it promoted in newspaper ads on five consecutive pages for three days, rather than in a full-page ad. The campaign was so successful that retailers quickly sold out, so Asahi responded with its own unique package – a small bottle called "Steiny," which was also a big hit with consumers. Before Kirin could act, Sapporo returned fire with a twist-off bottle cap called "Sapporo Strike," sold under the slogan *"Te de akerareru"* (You can open it by hand). This campaign backfired, for the cap was affixed so tightly that many consumers were unable to open it. Some even cut their hands in the attempt, and their complaints forced Sapporo to make light of the whole affair in an ironic follow-up ad entitled *"Akehō no setsumei"* (Opening instructions). Still trailing Kirin, which controlled over half of the marketplace, Sapporo ran a blind taste test in 1965, which it took on the road in a nationwide caravan. Inspired by the American car rental company Avis, which was itself the second-place firm in its market, Sapporo launched ads for the return of its "Yebisu" brand in 1971 that copied the Avis slogans of "We are No. 2" and "We try harder." The results were positive, and Sapporo's market share rose, but rather than reach for the top, the company records that it "chose to cooperate with our competitors."[97]

Korean War Boom: Plant and Market Expansion in the 1950s and 1960s

In order to keep pace with the expanding postwar beer market, Japan's brewers reinvested their profits every year into improved equipment, technology, and manufacturing efficiency. As Kirin was the smallest of the three brewers in 1949, the firm's management was particularly eager to improve the firm's operations, but the expansion costs rendered it unprofitable. Each year, engineers recommended new machines, especially European systems, in order to avoid being left behind by Nippon and Asahi. Kirin revamped virtually all of its systems in anticipation of expanded mass production, and researched improved malts production, better quality-control mechanisms, and innovative approaches to storage, shipping, and delivery. Additionally, in response to rising consumer demand for once unthinkable products like fruit juice, Kirin began selling "Kirin Juice" brand orange juice in the Kansai region in June 1954 and nationwide by April 1955.

All of this expansion, however, came amidst an era of unprecedented inflation, during which the value of Japan's currency fell sharply, leaving Kirin's once adequate supply of capital stock gravely diminished. The new machinery and production systems required vast sums of capital, and by 1956, Kirin's fixed assets had risen dramatically in both number and value. When the government passed the Full Capitalization Law in that year, the firm collected its unpaid capital – giving it a total of over ¥18 billion. From the ¥2.5 million that Kirin possessed at its founding, its capital stock had increased 738 times if adjusted for inflation.[98] In the meantime, due to the rising consumer demand fuelled by the Korean War boom, Kirin's directors began to plan the construction of a new plant in Tokyo. Like Dai Nippon, which had purchased a warplane hangar from Nakajima Aircraft in 1947, Kirin came across a surplus factory site in 1953. The Oriental Prince Spinning Company, which had produced textiles for the Imperial Japanese Army, had gone out of business after its operations were suspended in 1945, and the plant had been shuttered ever since. Located near Ōgyū station, overlooking Arakawa, the site was an ideal location from which to supply the Tokyo market, and Kirin's directors purchased it on 1 September 1953. Their timing was key, for just six months prior the *Asahi* newspaper had reported that beer sales had at last surpassed their peak prewar levels.[99]

Both Nippon and Asahi Breweries were also developing plans for new breweries, and a new firm, Takara (Treasure) Brewing Company, also sought to enter the market.[100] As a distiller, Takara possessed the experience and the capacity necessary to produce 2,000 kL of beer per year, which the Ministry of Finance maintained as the minimum output required to qualify for a brewing licence. All four companies thus submitted plans for new plants to the National Tax Office, and each received approval in September 1955, given the forecast for rising beer sales in the coming years. Kirin had already held a Shinto groundbreaking ceremony *(jichinsai)* in August 1954, ahead of the tax office verdict, and prepared the foundation pilings in order to proceed as rapidly as possible. The new plant was ready the following year, with an annual production capacity of 180,390 kL and two brand-new bottling lines. Its brewmasters aimed to start shipping product from the plant in July 1957. Takara too launched its new brand in 1957, but the little firm faced an uphill battle against the growing production power of the established brands, and of Kirin in particular.[101]

During the construction, the *Nihon Keizai Shimbun* reported in February 1955 that the "equilibrium between the 3 beer firms had been shattered" and "Kirin alone was proud of its performance," while Asahi and Nippon were "building cautiously."[102] Sapporo records that this was due to "Kirin"'s rising popularity in the marketplace, for it had been a national brand before the war. "Asahi," meanwhile, led the way in markets west of Kansai, where it had been a popular brand prior to the 1906 merger that had created Dai Nippon Beer. Meanwhile, although Nippon Beer controlled significant territory, "Nippon" was, essentially, a new brand. Its label bore the star of the former "Sapporo," but its name had no such prewar legacy. For all of these reasons,

Kirin's sales continued to grow, and its expansion therefore came with strong support from the Mitsubishi *keiretsu* family of companies. Kirin's significant relationship with the Mitsubishi conglomerate benefited the company in very visible ways. Due to their relationship, Mitsubishi-group employees typically ordered "Kirin" beer whenever they went out drinking together after work (which was almost nightly), giving Kirin a built-in support system. Fuelled by this form of patronage, as well as its foray into the Hokkaido marketplace in 1955, Kirin's expansion continued to gather momentum, and it built more new plants in the late 1950s and early 1960s.

Eclipsing Sake: Beer Again Becomes Japan's Top Alcoholic Beverage

National demand for beer continued to skyrocket through the 1950s. By December 1956, the single-colour labels of the prewar era at last gave way to multicoloured labels, and sales began to reach altogether new heights.[103] Industry-wide, annual production rose from 400,000 kL in 1955 to 1.99 million kL in 1964 – a fivefold increase. During that time, the production of other alcoholic drinks rose as well, meaning that beer producers faced greater competition for consumers' tastes and purses. Sales of other alcoholic beverages rose 2.5 times from 510,000 kL to 1.28 million kL over the same period. Sales of whisky rose 1.3 times from 41,000 kL to 55,000 kL, giving beer the most conspicuous growth, while sales of cheap shōchū spirits fell 0.8 times, from 280,000 kL to 220,000 kL – all indicative of rising incomes and changing consumer preferences.[104] Soon thereafter, beer became available in new formats, including the 500 mL bottle, which was introduced by the new market entrant Takara in 1957.[105] The half-litre bottle sold for the low price of just ¥100, and strong sales prompted the young firm to go public in January 1958.[106] Also making its debut in that era was the 350 mL steel can, which was first issued by Asahi in 1958, followed by Nippon in 1959 and both Kirin and Takara in 1960. Sapporo notes that the taste of beer sold in cans was inferior because steel cans smelled badly inside, but the can nevertheless presented brewers with a photogenic marketing tool, for beer spurted from shaken cans when they were opened. Sapporo chose to market canned beer as a masculine option, and male consumers responded enthusiastically. Sapporo's manly ad campaign delivered a solid 10 percent increase in monthly sales.[107]

Significantly, while sake had held a 36.9 percent market share in 1955, while beer held just 29.3 percent, these figures were reversed by 1959, and by 1964, beer claimed a 53.9 percent share while sake held just 34.6 percent. In 1962, the English-language magazine *Tokyo Mail* described this epic shift in consumer preferences:

Summer and beer – the two are inseparable. Beer is certainly a thing of season [sic]. Rather, to be exact, it was a thing of season. For beer has new [sic] become popular in Japan throughout the year. The representative of alcoholic beverages in Japan, needless to say, was *sake*, Japanese rice wine. However, the taste of the Japanese is changing greatly. The total output of alcoholic beverages in Japan regained the pre-war level in 1952 and doubled the pre-war volume in 1960. At this point, however, a notable phenomenon differing from the pre-war days emerged: the consumption of *sake* decreased markedly and that of beer and whisky increased greatly. The pre-war consumption of *sake* took up 71 per cent of all alcoholic beverages combined and that of beer no more than 16 percent. In 1952, however, *sake* fell to 40 per cent while beer rose 29 per cent, and in 1956, *sake* fell further to 37 per cent while beer reached 32 percent and has finally exceeded *sake*. This tendency has continued since, beer coming to 44 per cent and *sake* 29 per cent in 1959, a complete reverse of the pre-war situation.[108]

Explaining this shift came down to a handful of key market trends. According to the *Asahi Almanac (Asahi nenkan)* of 1961, Asahi's market researchers gave four chief reasons for this rapid increase:

1 Japanese living standards were rising more quickly.
2 The number of female consumers of beer was increasing.
3 Consumers' tastes in alcoholic beverages were shifting.
4 More Japanese homes were equipped with heaters.

The last of these reasons seems incongruous on its face, but it was deeply significant. Because Japanese homes were not well heated in the winter (few homes have central heating even today), demand for beer had always fallen off during the cold winter months, when few consumers fancied drinking cold beverages indoors. As more homes came to own gas or electric heaters, however, more consumers could continue to drink beer even during wintertime – a trend that boosted beer sales throughout the 1960s.[109] On points 2 and 4, *Tokyo Mail* elaborated as follows:

Beer consumption increases annually. One reason is that the yearly prevalence of heating facilities in homes and offices has mended the unbalance of beer demand between the summer and winter seasons. Another reason reportedly is that beer, different from *sake*, has obtained greatly increased popularity with the fair sex. In most of Japan's beer halls, few tables are without women customers. Still another thing we cannot overlook is that the younger generation likes beer. Formerly, bars and cabarets did not serve beer. Foreign liquors such as whisky and brandy or cocktails were usually sold exclusively. Nowadays, however, every bar or cabaret furnishes beer, and moreover is in great demand. The fact is that no cabaret can flourish without beer, however attractive hostesses may be employed.[110]

Of course, drinking cold beer also requires refrigeration, and the manufacture of refrigerators also rose dramatically. In 1955, Japan produced just 30,000 fridges, but already by 1960 this figure hit 900,000, followed by 2.3 million in 1965 and 3.5 million in 1970.[111] As more postwar Japanese households boasted the essential "three Cs" (car, cooler, and colour TV), beer consumption at home became increasingly commonplace.

The demand for beer also increased greatly during the postwar era due to the rapid increase in the number of bars and restaurants. Competition between the brewers increased as hotel bars, cafeterias, Japanese-style restaurants (kappō ten), salons, sushi shops, neighbourhood taverns (izakaya), and so on opened in huge numbers, fuelled by consumers' increasing spending power. In 1944, there were 25,600 such businesses nationwide, but 23,700 more opened between 1945 and 1949, followed by 49,700 more in 1950-54, and then 112,700 between 1955 and 1959. Coupled with this was a trend toward less expensive Western-style menu items (yōfū), the proliferation of which also increased demand for beer.[112] The Tokyo Mail pointed out that the large and growing number of bars and cabarets was being watched closely by the government:

> Of these, bars and cabarets are concentrated in the Ginza as should be expected, and many of them are first-rate establishments. Some say that these facilities are necessary for business society purposes. The so-called expense account spenders are the best customers for bars and cabarets, but they were called in question recently by the Government on the grounds that their excessive spending practices disturb the consumer economy of Japan, and the Government reportedly intends to control them. In any event, it is these shops where alcoholic drinks, beer in particular, are consumed in large quantities.[113]

No strict control over these excessive spending practices would actually materialize for some time, but by the 1970s, company employees were required to limit the time that they spent in bars and cabarets during their many "business meetings" in order to be eligible to expense their hefty tabs (see Figure 14). Frequent news reports bemoaned the fate of many salarymen,

Figure 14 A Japanese hostess serving beer to businessmen in a cabaret, January 1954. *Courtesy of the Mainichi Newspapers.*

whose stressful jobs led to heavy drinking, womanizing, and even financial entanglements with the loan sharks who sometimes ran such nightclubs.[114] This did nothing, however, to curb the practice of entertaining clients at these establishments, where the hostess trade continued to flourish, fuelled by lavish corporate accounts for "entertainment expenses" *(settaihi)*.

For many of these men, who worked from morning until night and saw little of their own families, such interaction was often the closest thing to intimacy that they typically experienced. Anne Allison writes that hostesses plying salarymen with alcohol also nurtured and took care of them, thereby humanizing their work and enabling them to interact less formally with both junior and senior colleagues.[115] Brian Moeran likewise points out that the "wet" conversations that took place while drinking were very different than the more formal, ritualized "dry" exchanges that occurred during business hours.[116] Certainly, as beer was typically poured from large bottles into small glasses by others, patrons could lose track both of the time and of the volumes that they had consumed. It was thus not uncommon to see salarymen drinking to excess, stumbling home late or sleeping in capsule hotels, passing out on trains, and even vomiting in the streets during Japan's era of high-speed economic growth and into the 1980s. University students too held frequent "drinking gatherings" *(nomikai)* after sporting or club events, often with their professors, and many participated in drinking contests in which they were egged on by upperclassmen.[117] Steadily, Japan would unhappily welcome rising alcoholism, alcohol-related fatalities, and the familiar patterns of social distortion caused by alcohol abuse – diseases of affluence that affected virtually all developed nations that boasted rising postwar standards of living.[118]

No matter how drunk they became, however, loyal salarymen were careful to drink the "correct" brand of beer. Due to their corporate affiliation, those in the Mitsubishi group of companies drank "Kirin" exclusively; employees of Mitsui group companies typically drank "Sapporo," though not quite as selectively; and those who worked for members of the Sumitomo corporate family often drank "Asahi." Although Kirin and Sapporo each had lengthy corporate relationships, the bond between Sumitomo and Asahi began much later, when the Sumitomo group purchased Asahi shares to defend against the possibility of a hostile takeover in the 1960s. Asahi's export sales in many countries were managed by Mitsui and Company, which enabled some flexibility for its corporate affiliates. Still, whether hosting a dinner party, a wedding, or a business luncheon, wise hosts did well to ensure that the correct beer was on offer, for the wrong brand could send a chill through the most jovial atmosphere, or even derail a business negotiation. Given this intricate web of corporate loyalties, major hotels in Japan learned to serve all major brands of domestic beer at their banquets and conference events, lest these lavish properties inadvertently show any hint of favouritism, which would be awkward for certain clients.[119]

During the first two postwar decades, beer became the most ubiquitous of alcoholic beverages, prompting Sapporo to assert that beer had become the "beverage of the masses" *(taishūtekina nomimono)*.[120] Beer consumption had long since surpassed its prewar levels, and it now appealed to a much broader spectrum of Japanese than during the 1930s, when its chief consumers had been men. Younger Japanese were an especially important target market, for the brewers soon recognized that younger consumers' desire for sake was falling off very sharply. In 1958, Kirin's sales manager, Takeichi Masumi, told market reporters, "The younger generation does not like sake. They like beer because the alcoholic content is not high. Sake is usually consumed with a small snack, such as raw fish. Drinking beer is more pleasurable because a snack is not necessary. Last year, beer sales increased in 47 of the 48 prefectures in Japan."[121]

As incomes rose, seasonal beer gardens located in parks and even atop major urban buildings grew increasingly popular with both male and female patrons during the hot summer months (see Figure 15). As more women entered the workforce through the 1950s, they increasingly took advantage of the opportunity to visit beer gardens together after work, or even during their lunch hours (see Figure 16). In July 1957, the *Yomiuri* newspaper published a report entitled "Women and Beer Halls" *(Josei to biya-hōru)*, which observed that while one might have found perhaps two or three women in a prewar beer hall, modern outdoor, rooftop beer gardens were much more appealing to female professionals. The report noted that the "postwar generation of new women" *(atarashii sedai no josei)* had a great deal of free time, and that they were visiting beer gardens without male escorts, in groups of four, five, and six. The accompanying photo captured a group of women hoisting large glasses *(jokki)* of draft beer, with no men in sight.[122] As patterns of alcohol consumption continued to shift, corporate-run beer halls along the Ginza began to be replaced in the early 1960s by smaller, privately owned bars, many of which were owned by women.[123] The wartime pressures that had forced beer's flavour to become lighter clearly attracted many new female consumers, and as incomes rose and leisure time increased, so too did their beer consumption.

The Return of Free Pricing and the Launch of "Suntory Beer"

By 1959, beer's remarkable market expansion at last encouraged the government to amend part of the Alcoholic Beverages Industry Group Control Law and abolish controlled pricing. On 1 October 1960, a system of standard sale pricing was instituted, which was essentially a measured step closer toward free pricing, although the brewers could not set their own prices just yet. While the system did not prevent brewers from selling beer at higher or lower prices, it featured strongly recommended price levels, such as ¥125 for a large bottle. The new pricing system was rolled out slowly, in order to aid retailers who had a great deal of product on hand to convert to the new pricing regime. The Ministry of Finance later issued a notice that the standard pricing would remain in effect only on large bottles, in order to test whether the market for other size containers would remain stable, and not suffer rapid price swings in either direction. By this time, Kirin had become the industry leader. Early in the new pricing regime, in 1961, Japan's four brewing companies held the following market shares:

Figure 15 Rooftop beer garden atop the Dai-ichi Seimei building, Osaka, 5 July 1955. *Courtesy of the Mainichi Newspapers.*

Figure 16 Japanese women drinking at a beer garden in the summer of 1957.
Courtesy of the Mainichi Newspapers.

- Kirin Brewery: 41.7 percent
- Asahi Breweries: 27.9 percent
- Sapporo Breweries: 27.8 percent
- Takara Brewing: 2.6 percent.[124]

The next year, however, a fifth company joined the industry. In December 1962, Suntory announced that it would reenter the beer market, despite the already solid competition in the industry.[125] Founded in 1899, the company had produced whisky at its Yamazaki distillery in Shimamoto, Osaka, since 1923, but by the early 1980s, President Saji Keizō felt that his managers needed a greater challenge in order to maintain their competitive edge. The company, formerly known as Kotobuki-ya, had taken control of the troubled Japan-English Brewing Company in 1928 (see Figure 1 above), but operations were sidelined during the war and the brewery was broken up in 1948. When interviewed in 1983 about his bold decision to return to the beer market, Saji told the *Tōyō Keizai Shimpō* newspaper:

When we decided to get into the beer industry in 1963, I started with a feeling that our future in the whiskey market may not be that bright. The reaction I got was, "Our share in the whiskey market is high; why take the risk of crossing over to challenge this new market?" Somehow, I didn't think we could be so complacent. We could not just keep doing what we were doing. It was a lot different from the current conditions when we can hold our own with the foreign brands. At that time, Japanese whiskey was protected from the strong import competition in many ways. I thought that the company could not survive and prosper if it remained only in this whiskey industry. Getting into the beer business would certainly present problems, but we had to develop a field other than whiskey, and I also hoped this would stimulate the company, giving it new vitality.[126]

Saji was less interested in succeeding in the beer market than in sharpening his company's approach to the whisky industry. Suntory's management had to refocus its energies in order to compete in a well-established market, which in turn stimulated organizational changes that likewise benefited the firm's whisky division. Thus, whereas Japan's beer industry had three firms with a total of thirteen plants in 1952, by 1963 it boasted five firms with twenty-one plants in all.[127]

Japan's beer industry was thus enjoying an unprecedented growth phase just as the country embarked on Prime Minister Ikeda Hayato's ambitious national "income doubling" plan. The government's system of standard beer pricing was abolished on 1 June 1964, and control over pricing, negotiated with the Ministry of Finance, was left to the brewers involved.[128] Prices did creep upward steadily thereafter, and often in lockstep, but typically by less than ¥10 per year. Modest price increases were reported almost annually in the *Asahi* newspaper through the 1960s and later, usually in September or October, lest the price rises inhibit summer sales. Kirin, as the largest brewer, led the way in effectively setting prices, and through a concerted campaign to persuade its network of distributors and retailers to sell only "Kirin Beer," it wielded considerable clout in the marketplace. While all three of the top brewers built new breweries, Kirin did so almost every other year through the 1960s and 1970s.[129] This enabled the firm both to lead the way in low-cost production and to maintain the freshest products in Japan's rapidly increasing numbers of convenience stores and drink vending machines, where a new beer sales war was heating up (see Figure 17).[130]

Combined with relentless advertising that claimed to deliver "real beer taste," Kirin continued to eclipse its competitors through the achievement of economies of scale in manufacturing, as well as a powerful, dedicated nationwide distribution network. This enabled Kirin to set prices that would

Figure 17 Customers at food and drink vending machines, 24 July 1966. *Courtesy of the Mainichi Newspapers.*

(usually) enable its rivals to cover their costs, while at the same time ensuring steady profitability for Kirin's shareholders.[131] Thus the beer cartel of the prewar era carried on in the postwar, albeit informally. Unable to secure a viable position in the marketplace, Takara Brewing pulled "Takara Beer" from the market and sold its plant to Kirin in 1967.[132] Takara's departure left Sapporo, Asahi, and Suntory to face mighty Kirin alone. By the mid-1980s, Kirin's market share topped 60 percent, with Sapporo holding 20 percent, Asahi 11 percent, and Suntory 7 percent. Although foreign brands were often available in major urban hotels and commercial establishments, as costly premium imports they attracted little consumer interest. Foreign brewers were also unable to distribute their products uniformly throughout Japan due to the regional nature of its beer retail networks, which were dominated by Japan's domestic brewers. The networks could thus simply refuse to carry imports, and foreign brands never accounted for more than 3 percent of the domestic market.[133]

Conclusions

The beer industry led Japan's postwar industrial recovery, and was one of the first sectors to return to productivity and profitability, but it was a fundamentally changed industry. From experimental grain cultivation, to bottle-return programs, to the enfranchisement of a newly organized labour federation, the business of brewing was deeply transformed by the war and Occupation. During the two decades before the war, Japan's brewers had learned how to control their retailers, prohibit underselling, and eliminate the once-essential middle tier of beer wholesalers. After the war, the brewers gradually untangled themselves from the controlled beer distribution networks and industry associations set up by the Ministry of Finance, but they retained many of the more fundamental changes wrought by the exigencies of the war years. Bottle shapes remained consistent, beer recipes remained lighter, and Japan's mandatory bottle-return program has carried on to this day. So too has the beer cartel that standardizes prices and negotiates all increases, albeit in an unwritten fashion. Another fundamental change was the end of the industry's prewar dependence on German ingredients, brewmasters, and product identity. Beer's ties to its European heritage were shattered by the war, and the surviving brewers were liberated from the pretense that quality beer must meet foreign specifications. Japan's brewers thus broke with their German roots and resumed making beer as a fully domestic, if not indigenous, commodity.

The industry's quick recovery was aided significantly by the demands of Allied personnel during the early postwar era, but it also resumed sales to Japanese consumers by the late 1940s. Importantly, millions of Japanese soldiers, sailors, and airmen to whom beer had been served during the war years returned home with a taste for it – and their demands were soon satisfied. In June 1949, Japan's beer halls, which were initially open only to Allied personnel, were at last reopened to Japanese patrons. This symbolic event marked a turning point for Japan's postwar economy, and with the boom triggered by the Korean War, Japanese began or resumed their consumption of beer in earnest in the 1950s. Free to advertise their brands alongside images of Japanese celebrities and indigenous cultural forms rather than accompanied by claims of German authenticity, Japan's brewers were able to target smaller segments of the beer market, and to reach out to individual groups of consumers in more direct ways. Although Japanese beer consumers certainly existed prior to the war, they were almost never portrayed in beer advertisements. Ad campaigns of the 1950s grew increasingly complex and costly as the age of television dawned, and the themes and imagery conveyed by commercials helped to identify and cultivate new subsets of beer drinkers.[134] These trends were not unique to mainland Japan. Similar patterns of industrial development and the prioritization of domestic products and indigenous cultural forms were also unfolding in neighbouring Okinawa, as will be seen in the next chapter. In both markets, beer advertising now focused on the consumer of beer, rather than the product itself, and approaches to those consumers prioritized Japanese themes and personalities. Postwar beer advertising highlighted beer's "image" and showcased Japanese celebrities, sports heroes, culture, and indigenous art forms.

Not only did beer consumption return to its prewar levels by 1955, the sources also identify the specific economic, demographic, and even cultural reasons for the increase of beer sales in the postwar era. Facilitated by the advent of such amenities as indoor heating and home refrigeration, once luxuries for most households, beer steadily became a beverage that consumers could comfortably enjoy at home year-round. In addition, Japanese women began to consume much more beer than they had prior to the war. This shift occurred for a variety of reasons, not the least of which was the deprivation of the war era itself, when material shortages forced brewers to change the taste of their product. Once a stronger, bitterer drink, lighter postwar Japanese lagers took the form of alcoholic soft drinks, which appealed greatly to younger, often female consumers, as well as those simply looking to quench their thirst after work. As salaries rose, going out for beer became an activity unto itself for both men and women, especially when visiting Japan's growing number of outdoor and rooftop beer gardens. Furthermore, for Japan's growing number of salarymen, individual beer brands became powerful symbols of professional identity and affiliation. Those who did business with or worked inside the brewing firms' respective corporate families expressed their loyalties through their beer orders. In this way, the focus of beer's authenticity shifted from the product to the consumer. No longer were Japan's brewers concerned with demonstrating their loyalty to German recipes; instead, many of Japan's postwar beer consumers were careful to demonstrate their loyalties to particular brewers. Fuelled by all of the above changes in the marketplace, beer consumption eclipsed that of sake by the early 1960s, and then proceeded to leave sake far behind.

5 Learning from Japan: "Orion Beer" and Okinawan Consumer Identity, 1945-72

This chapter explores the establishment and growth of Okinawa's Orion Breweries, Ltd., and the experiences of its founding president, Gushiken Sōsei. Gushiken's pioneering efforts as an entrepreneur, promoter, salesman, and company manager closely reflect the struggles of the mainland Japanese beer industry, especially as both markets were challenged by powerful foreign imports at the outset. Selling domestically produced beer was considerably difficult in postwar Okinawa, which was both ravaged by the war and flooded after 1945 with foreign-made goods aimed squarely at the wealthiest island demographic – US military personnel. This situation mirrored the mainland Japanese experience of the late nineteenth century, when Japan welcomed new Western products, such as beer, that could be afforded only by the comparatively rich. In postwar Okinawa, manufacturers had to struggle in order to overcome long-standing local prejudices against *shima-guaa,* or "island-made" products, which islanders themselves traditionally viewed as inferior to foreign imports. Here too, Orion Beer travelled a path well worn by its mainland Japanese predecessors, which for decades advertised their product as domestically produced German beer rather than local Japanese beer.

Similarly, in order to brew a successful, quality product, Gushiken often sought the advice of outside advisers and experts, just as his mainland Japanese predecessors had done years earlier. Further complicating matters for Orion Beer, however, was the difficulty of integrating the disparate Ryūkyūan archipelago into a unified sales district. This required more than simply improving distribution routes; it necessitated considerable work aimed at forging a new and distinctly Ryūkyūan consumer identity spanning over a hundred islands. For many centuries, Okinawa's culture had been influenced more deeply by China and Southeast Asia than by Japan, giving it a unique blend of Japanese and local customs, dialects, and lifestyles.[1] Firms like Orion Beer were therefore tasked not simply with cultivating new postwar consumers, but, in a sense, unified postwar islanders. Not content with repeat sales, Orion Beer would also labour very actively to change Okinawan attitudes toward youth, recreation, and women, and even help to launch the island's sexual revolution. While it grew up amidst unprecedented circumstances, Orion's early growth parallels that of its mainland Japanese predecessors in many respects, and its development is deserving of investigation.

The Founding of the Okinawa Beer Company, Inc.

Gushiken Sōsei was born in 1896 in what is today the Kakibana district of Naha City, Okinawa's largest metropolis. Like many of the entrepreneurs who had participated in mainland Japan's Meiji-era beer industry, Gushiken had no formal business training or manufacturing experience. Instead, before the Pacific War, he had a promising career in law enforcement. Following the Battle of Okinawa, he was interned by the US military until February 1946, when he resumed his role as a police chief in Okinawa's Chinen district (modern Nanjō).[2] At that time, the prospects for ordinary Okinawans were beyond bleak. Those who had survived the American invasion were unable to return to homes or businesses in the capital city of Naha, for it had been absolutely obliterated. Home to 68,000 people before the war, almost all civilian dwellings and most facilities in Naha had been destroyed by intensive American air raids. After Okinawa fell, the islands southwest of the thirtieth parallel were cut off from the Japanese mainland, and Washington resolved that the severed region would be managed by a US military government.[3] The mainland Japanese government, itself lacking sovereignty until the end of the Allied Occupation in 1952, had no jurisdiction in the Ryūkyū Islands until their reversion to Japan in 1972.

As the US military gradually withdrew from Naha, the population swelled rapidly to 26,000 by 1948 and to 109,000 by 1949.[4] To support economic growth, the United States established the Bank of the Ryūkyūs in May 1948, which gradually extended its authority as the central bank of the entire archipelago. In November, Okinawa's three main island chains, Miyako, Yaeyama, and Amami, were combined into a single economic sphere wherein free enterprise was to be the norm. The next year, the US military government installed Gushiken Sōsei as the head of the provisional government of the Miyako island chain. Despite his aptitude for the role, Gushiken knew that he was not cut out for government service. Privately, he planned to end his political career after just a single two-year term of office. In 1950, he sent his younger brother, Gushiken Sōhatsu, ¥B30,000 and together they founded a miso and soy sauce brewing company in Naha, which they named Aka (Red) Marusō.[5] (The B-yen, a military scrip with a fixed value of one US dollar to ¥B120, was Okinawa's currency between 1945 and 1958, at which point the US dollar became the official currency until Okinawa's reversion in 1972.)

In 1951, Gushiken Sōsei moved to Naha to serve as the firm's president, while his brother worked as the factory manager. (Hereafter, the elder Gushiken will be referred to only by his family name.) The company's sales and technical skill grew steadily, especially after Gushiken asked the civilian government to curb imports of miso and soy sauce from mainland Japan.[6] Although a civilian Ryūkyūan government was formally established on 1 April 1952, it still had to "comply with the ordinance and command of USCAR," the US Civil Administration of the Ryūkyūs. Gushiken's request was approved in April 1953 because it aligned with a larger set of US military and civilian government policies aimed at reviving the Okinawan economy.[7] In addition, miso and soy sauce were produced chiefly for the civilian populace, and not the growing population of US military base personnel. As a result, such a trade restriction hardly concerned USCAR. After a total ban on imported miso and soy sauce went into effect in September 1954, Aka Marusō's miso production rose 10 percent and its soy sauce production rose 20 percent in the following months.[8]

Fuelled by the growing military bases, a thriving scrap metals trade, and the Korean War production boom, Okinawa's economy improved significantly by the mid-1950s. This brought a gradual rise in living standards for islanders, enabling them to acquire radios, electric fans, refrigerators, and durable consumer goods like their mainland Japanese peers. Beer and sake remained imported commodities, but as the standard of living rose in a similar pattern to that in mainland Japan, many islanders were able to enjoy these former luxuries on a regular basis. However, many saw the economic stimuli from base-related activity as one-time developments, rather than a secure economic foundation for future growth. Some suggested that dependence on the unstable military base economy should be limited in favour of building a self-sufficient island industrial base to supply export industries. Along these lines, in 1956, US brigadier general and USCAR civil administrator Vonna F. Burger (1956-59) gave an address to a general meeting at the Ryūkyū Commerce and Industry Assembly Hall entitled "Next, Okinawa Must Promote the Beer and Cement Enterprises."[9]

The general's timely address resonated strongly with the Gushiken brothers, who wished to found and equip a large-scale beer brewing firm. They thus aimed to capitalize on the experience they had earned as brewers of miso and soy sauce, just as many of Japan's earliest brewers had tried to do. All three products begin as cultivated foodstuffs fermented with yeast, which gave their company a solid technical foundation. Gushiken knew that the capital investment needed to found a beer brewery would be immense, and he anticipated that generating sufficient sales would be a major challenge.

Fortunately, the potential success of the venture was tied ultimately to the continuing growth of the Ryūkyūan economy, and therefore the military and civilian governments offered significant aid and support. In 1956, representatives from USCAR's Economic Development Section met with civilian government officials and Tomihara Moriyasu, the governor of the Bank of the Ryūkyūs (established in May 1948), to discuss their support for a domestic beer brewing venture. The result was an agreement to commission a comprehensive prefectural market analysis.

The investigation concluded that an Okinawan beer industry would likely succeed financially, provided that the necessary refrigeration equipment could also be produced locally. However, in a decision that paralleled the era of Japan's early Western *oyatoi gaikokujin* (hired foreigners), the market analysis recommended that Gushiken seek the opinion of a brewing expert from mainland Japan. These additional studies indicated that with the right advice, technicians, and machinery, success was possible. Following these recommendations, the first brewery-promoters' meeting was held on 13 September 1956 at a restaurant in Tsuboya, Naha. The promoters' committee consisted of twenty-eight members, among them representatives of an array of key Okinawan firms and agencies. These included the governor and president of the Bank of Okinawa (established in June 1956), the head of the Ryūkyū Government Domestic Affairs Agency, and the president and the senior managing director of the Dai-ichi Mutual Savings Bank. Their affiliations closely resemble the firms that were involved in the purchase of The Japan Brewery from British Hong Kong in 1885, which included Mitsubishi, the Ōkura Group, and the Dai-ichi Bank. Also present in 1956 were the presidents of Okinawa's leading cigarette, shipping, feed, oil, milling, marine, and trading companies, plus the head of the Ryūkyū Federation of Agricultural Cooperative Associations. Other committee members represented smaller Okinawan trading, manufacturing, and warehousing firms. Far from acting alone, the Gushiken brothers sought the input, advice, and counsel of their industrial and commercial peers, all of whom had a role to play in the promotion of island industry.[10]

The group of Okinawan industrialists concluded that the current annual demand for beer by Ryūkyūan civilians was 2,900 kL, and demand by US military personnel was estimated to be about 1,800 kL. Therefore, with the expectation of increasing sales, the planners called for a brewery with an annual production rate of 5,400 kL. Potential sites for the plant were discussed, and the candidates were narrowed down to two, pending studies of their water availability and quality: Kanatake and Nago, both cities located on the main island of Okinawa. Then, as another indication of how closely the planners had studied the founding of Kirin Brewery, the preparatory committee recommended that the new company seek Kirin's technical support. The group also took the surprising step of naming the new company the Okinawa *Kirin* Beer Company, Inc. On this count, the planners were overconfident, for Kirin would demonstrate significant reluctance to work with the new Okinawan venture.

Nevertheless, Gushiken sent an invitation to Kirin Brewery, asking for its technical cooperation. Kirin agreed to open discussions, and water samples were collected from each of the candidate sites. However, the talks with Kirin turned out to be much tougher sledding than expected. The veteran firm made it clear that its own water tests would take over a year to complete, and, in exchange for its technical assistance, Kirin reserved the right to designate the machinery manufacturers with which the junior firm must do business. Despite several counterproposals, Kirin's directors would not modify their conditions, so the Okinawan entrepreneurs broke off the discussions. Consequently, the name Kirin was dropped; when the company's founding was reported in the press, it was named simply the Okinawa Beer Company, Inc. Although the negotiations with Kirin Brewery had ended in failure, the group quickly refocused their efforts and, ironically, stumbled on an even more fortunate solution.[11]

Through a referral from a professor at Tokyo University, Gushiken's team was introduced to the former factory manager *(kōjōchō)* of Kirin Brewery's Yokohama plant, Sakaguchi Jūji. Sakaguchi was a graduate of the agricultural science program at Tokyo University, and after serving as Kirin's Yokohama plant chief, he had gone to work as a technician for the Ocean Brewing Company. The latter was a small postwar start-up firm in Tokyo founded by a company called Tokyo Laver, but the firm failed to launch and Ocean was planning to close its doors. Gushiken therefore sent Sakaguchi an invitation to come to Okinawa, and after encouraging negotiations, secured his agreement to work for the new firm. Furthermore, through Sakaguchi the Okinawans met several more of Ocean Brewing's experienced technicians, each of whom, facing imminent unemployment, agreed to move to Okinawa and take up positions with the Okinawa Beer Company. At a stroke, Gushiken's fledgling brewery recruited an entire team of engineers.[12]

Meanwhile, the founders of Okinawa Beer were making preparations to purchase extensive production machinery from overseas suppliers. They ultimately purchased an American-made bottle-making machine called the Semiko 50, a German-made device for culturing yeast, and other machines that were some of the newest and most powerful in Japan. Determined to support Okinawan industry as well, Gushiken purchased several pieces of equipment locally, such as storage tanks, which were ordered from Nago City Ironworks. Not only did this bring the local ironworks unexpected profits, the brewery's flexibility in sourcing equipment managed to limit the total cost to just over ¥200 million. Nevertheless, the planned brewery would not only be the largest privately managed construction project in Okinawan history, it would also be one of the costliest. Given the reliance on foreign machinery and technical experts, the entire project has close parallels to the Meiji-era founding of Sapporo, Kirin, and their contemporaries on the Japanese mainland.[13]

Going Door to Door: Recruiting Okinawan Shareholders

On 27 February 1957 the new brewery received a Temporary Alcohol Manufacturers Licence *(Shurui seizō karimenkyō)*, and the executives began their effort to recruit shareholders from 1 March. As the firm planned to erect a plant that could produce 5,400 kL annually, their business plan called for a minimum of ¥B180 million ($1.5 million) in capital. The founders resolved to seek ¥B50 million ($420,000) in capital stock and the rest in the form of a bank loan for ¥B130 million ($1,080,000). The civilian government also agreed to authorize the initial public offering, based on the understanding that the members of the promoters' committee would not only invest themselves, but would do their utmost to encourage others to do likewise. On 1 March Okinawa Beer ran an advertisement in the *Ryūkyū* newspaper announcing the IPO. The ad provided details on the company's mission, its proposed importance to the Okinawan economy, and a look at its prospectus. Prospective investors were invited to purchase ten shares at ¥B500 ($4.17) each. The advertisement conveyed the enthusiasm and the confidence of the firm's president, and it emphasized the promoters' desire for the Okinawa Beer Company to contribute to the development of the local economy.

In support of the IPO, Gushiken travelled across the island on a personal pilgrimage by bus, car, and even on foot in search of shareholders. Investors were convinced by the company's careful preparations, and the target of ¥B50 million in shares was sold within a month. The buyers, who numbered more than four hundred, included everyone from leading representatives of the financial world to small-time investors. The sale attracted the attention of *Pacific Stars and Stripes*, which reported:

> Sosei Gushiken, prominent Okinawa businessman, already has raised almost all of the required 50 million yen through the sale of stock. Shares, costing 500 yen each, have sold rapidly in blocks of from 10 to 4,000. There are some 200 shareholders at present representing all levels of the Okinawan population.

Okinawans, says Gushiken, spend about $800,000 annually on beer, and this is increasing at the rate of 10 percent each year. He has promotional plans of his own to still further increase beer consumption on the island.[14]

Significantly, when an unnamed Dutch beer company offered to buy close to 50 percent of the shares, Gushiken refused the offer, as he was committed to selling shares solely to Okinawan investors.[15] In addition to the monies generated by the IPO, the US government and the Bank of the Ryūkyūs together furnished the start-up company with a loan of $970,000 through the Ryūkyū Recovery Loan Fund *(Ryūkyū fukkō kinyū kikin)*.[16] Such loans were used to help construct individual homes, build manufacturing and commercial enterprises, repair agricultural and water-related infrastructure, and improve shipping, as well as repair damage to cities, towns, and villages.[17]

Eight months after the meeting of the promoters' committee in Tsuboya, the officials of the Okinawa Beer Company at last convened their founding shareholders' meeting on 9 May 1957. Notably, the general meeting that established Okinawa Beer was held in the Ryūkyū Movie Theatre *(Ryūkyū eiga honkan)*, in Asato, Naha. Fully a dozen years after the end of the war, very few meeting halls had yet been constructed in the city, and for that reason general assemblies were usually held in theatres or schools. On the day of the meeting, crowds of people affiliated with the Okinawan business and economic world turned up, as interest in Okinawa's first beer company was very high. During the meeting, the founders deliberated the articles of association and fifteen company officers were elected: one senior managing director, three managing directors, ten regular directors, and the president, Gushiken Sōsei. Eight of those chosen were Okinawan.[18] At the meeting, Gushiken introduced himself to the crowd and gave the following address:

> With the nomination of all of the shareholders, I, Gushiken Sōsei have been elected president, something that is both a pleasure and at the same time bears a strong sense of responsibility. I am the same as all of you, and during the war I tried to avoid being hit by shells, and when I was captured by US forces, I was determined to kill myself with my pistol. However, for better or for worse, because my pistol was wet and rusty, the bullet did not fire, and for that reason, my life has continued until today. Since that time, it has been my desire to devote the remainder of my life to society and to my company. As a result, at today's establishment there is an enthusiastic spirit of "let those outside see Okinawa stand up and take its place in the world," which is the driving desire of the management here today. However, my strength as an individual has its limits. With the support of all of you shareholders, and the military-civilian

government, and all the citizens, I am convinced that we can succeed in this great undertaking. Please give us your guidance.[19]

With this, Gushiken earned the endorsement of his new shareholders. As for the rest of the management team, their diverse backgrounds illustrate the firm's determination to include local Okinawan civic leaders. The senior managing director, Mr. Ijū, was the principal of Shuri High School. One of the regular directors, Mr. Tominaga, was the vice-director of the Ryūkyū Transportation Engineering Bureau, and another, Mr. Tamoyori, was the trade section chief of the Ryūkyū Government Economic Bureau. Unlike traditional Okinawan business executives, the directors of this new company gave a fresh impression that inspired discussion in the local media for days after the founding assembly.[20]

Staking a Claim: Okinawa Beer versus the Ryūkyū Government

Finding a suitable location for their brewery presented Okinawa Beer's directors with challenges very similar to those that had faced Sapporo and Kirin at the outset of their own operations. From a cost standpoint, the ideal location would be close to the capital, Naha, but an ample supply of clean water was essential, for roughly 15 kL of water is required in order to produce 1 kL of beer. The test results indicated that a site just outside of Nago City, in the north end of the island, was ideal. Led by Mayor Ōjirō Kamesuke, Nago's city government was hoping to attract manufacturing enterprises to facilitate the town's economic development. Ōjirō cooperated enthusiastically with the company directors, and negotiations over the purchase of 13,200 square metres of public land proceeded well. However, the Nago Agricultural Experimental Farm *(Nago nōgyō shikenjō hobō)* was adjacent to the chosen site, which presented a significant obstacle. Several additional tests indicated that the ideal water source sprang from the farm, which would necessitate the division of the farm and the sale of some of the component lots to the brewery. Permission for such a sale, however, required an application to the Economic Bureau of the Ryūkyū Government, which responded, "The development of a beer company is also very important to the Ryūkyū economy, but we do not approve of the need to divide the land of the experimental farm, as requested by the town mayor."[21]

For weeks, the local Nago papers ran editorials with titles like "From the Perspective of Industrial Promotion, We Urge the Economic Bureau of the Ryūkyūan Government to Reconsider." Nevertheless, the Ryūkyūan government refused to listen to appeals to divvy up the experimental farm. In the meantime, other preparations for the establishment of the plant were progressing well, which placed added pressure on the management team to resolve the land dispute. Gushiken and a team of fellow directors went to Tokyo in May to purchase the necessary machinery, but they returned hurriedly amidst the ongoing site controversy. Several times they petitioned the government, asking the Economic Bureau to relent, and their demands were echoed by Governor Tomihara of the Bank of the Ryūkyūs and President Nakamura of the Dai-ichi Mutual Bank, but to no avail. On 4 June, the people of Nago held a mass meeting in support of dividing the land, and the group moved to filed suit against the government, but with no effect. Finally, a compromise was reached by the citizens of Nago at a meeting on 25 June, after three months of continued disagreement. The city agreed to permit the construction of the brewery on the land next to the experimental farm, but the farm's land was not divided, leaving the company obliged to dig a well on its own lot. The site problem would linger on for several years and was not in fact resolved until it came time to expand the facility. In the end, the growing brewery would essentially bulldoze its way through the Economic Bureau's agricultural priorities.[22]

On 29 July 1957, just a month after the site compromise was reached, operations to clear the land began. As was also customary in mainland Japan, a Shinto ceremony was held to purify the site in preparation for the construction of a 6,600-square-metre factory building. Wisely, the firm also consulted the US Army Corps of Engineers in order to be absolutely certain that the earth was solid enough to support the weight of a factory building. This was the first such geologic test to precede the construction of a factory building in Okinawa's history, but the plan demanded caution due to the unique complexity and cost of the project. Just as Kirin's contractor had done at the site of its new plant at Namamugi, Yokohama, in 1925, the US Army Corps of Engineers drilled holes at the Nago site to check the quality of the soil. Rather than finding bedrock, as Kirin's team had done, the engineers at Nago discovered a stratum of liquefied earth at a depth between 4.5 metres and 9.1 metres. The engineers recommended that the company drive five hundred concrete posts into the earth to support the structure – a costly but essential requirement. The company enlisted Japanese design authority Itō Chiemon to draw up the architectural plans, and he and his designers studied the Kirin Brewery plant in Sendai very carefully. The construction job was a boon for local Okinawan contractors, and by the fall of 1957, Okinawa's largest-ever private construction project was well under way.[23]

The construction of the plant proceeded smoothly, but early in 1958, Gushiken was diagnosed with a severe stomach ulcer. Then, on 22 September, the company's factory manager, Sakaguchi Jūji, died suddenly. Having just recovered from stomach surgery, a stunned Gushiken called an emergency directors' meeting the next day. There the management team decided ultimately to invite Sawada Takeji to come and fill the late factory manager's shoes. A graduate of Tokyo University's engineering department who had studied applied chemistry, Sawada had also worked in business affairs with Mitsubishi before the war. Importantly, he had also been the factory manager for Kirin Brewery's plant in Manchuria, so he too was an authority on brewing beer and had an intimate understanding of Kirin's processes. Once more, the new brewery tapped Kirin's former talent when Sawada joined the firm. In addition, the directors managed to recruit the former foreman of Kirin's Sendai plant, along with several other experienced men, which increased the new firm's technical capabilities substantially. Sawada assumed his post as factory manager on 29 November, and the next year he became its senior managing director. By late 1958, research into product manufacturing was well under way, but the firm still had three issues to resolve: accessing water, equipping the factory, and cultivating suitable brewing yeast. Only about 10 percent of the needed machinery had yet arrived, and the plant still had no water supply. While the firm set about digging a well on the factory site, the directors had a yeast culture flown in from Germany, research with which began in a temporary lab at the plant.[24]

The Branding and Launch of "Orion Beer"

During the construction of its plant, Okinawa Beer recruited factory workers from the local Nago area, but it advertised broadly throughout the Ryūkyū Islands for office employees. As the economy was then in recession and finding a job was especially difficult, the company received seven hundred applications for office jobs, from which it shortlisted just thirteen candidates. Okinawa still faced significant infrastructural challenges, so in order to conduct interviews, two meeting halls had to be rented – the Nago elementary school and the Naha commercial high school. At the same time, hoping to curry interest, the company launched a public campaign to name its new beer. A naming contest was announced in the local newspapers on 1 November 1957, requesting entries by postcard by the end of the month. The selection was to be made in mid-December, with prizes of ¥B10,000 ($83.30) for first place, ¥B3,000 ($25) for second, and ¥B2,000 ($16.70) for third. The effort to create a media stir ahead of the launch of the product was creative and effective, and 2,500 entries were received bearing 823 unique names. The judging committee, which comprised the ten company directors as well as the president of the *Okinawa Shimpō* and the chief editor of the *Okinawa Times*, chose "Orion" as the winning entry. The constellation Orion is made up of southern stars, so the judges saw it as a good parallel for the Ryūkyū Islands. Also, the corresponding symbol designed for the product label, a row of three stars, was then the rank of the USCAR high commissioner, Lieutenant General James E. Moore (1957-58). The results of the contest were announced in the newspaper on 29 January 1958. The second-place name was "Golden," and the third-place name was "Sun."[25]

The next decision involved what type of beer to brew. A variety of beers were imported to Okinawa at that time, such as "Kirin," "Sapporo," "Asahi," "Miller," "Budweiser," "Heineken," and a brand from the Philippines called "San Miguel." The directors settled on brewing a traditional German lager beer, and for this reason they chose to import all of their malts and hops from Germany, just as Japan's earliest breweries had done.[26] Orion's directors anticipated (correctly) that the hot Okinawan climate would make brewing extremely challenging. Nevertheless, through repeated trials, the firm's technicians gradually developed the original form of what would soon become known as "Orion Beer." In January 1959, the team conducted a satisfactory test run of its new machinery, and on 4 February, factory chief Sawada declared that it was time to brew the first large batch. The yeast culture was ready, the well was flowing, and the brewing preparations were complete. The first batch matured for three months, and on 9 May, the technicians conducted a trial run of the bottling line. Every company employee came out to watch the filling, capping, sterilizing, and labelling operation. The volume of the main storage tank was 18 kL, and the entire bottling process took four and a half hours, but if there were delays it was not uncommon for the operation to take from morning to night. New factory employees were trained in groups of ten by a single instructor in what were called "practice operations" *(jishū sagyō)*. Before long, the operations were running smoothly, and the first batch of Orion Beer was scheduled to ship on 17 May.

Not coincidentally, 17 May was also the date of Okinawa's Nanminsai festival (波上祭), which marks the beginning of summer and is seen as an auspicious day for the launch of any new product. Nanminsai is a gathering traditionally held in May at Naminoue Gu Shrine on the shore of Naha, at what is today Naminoue Beach and Park. It is an old religious event that predates the arrival of Shinto on the island. The atmosphere during Nanminsai is one of revelry and large crowds often gather, so it was seen by the brewery directors as an ideal time to launch a new island-made beer. To mark the occasion, the firm invited nearly a thousand citizens and government figures to an "Orion Beer" party to be held the day before the festival, 16 May, at the Okinawa Electric Hall *(Okinawa haiden hōru)* in Naha. When planning the party, Gushiken and his management team clearly followed in the footsteps of Magoshi Kyōhei, who had marketed "Yebisu Beer" so cleverly in the early twentieth century. Just as Magoshi had often done, fireworks were set off as a seventeen-truck convoy departed the brewery with thirty-eight hundred cases of "Orion Beer," bound for Naha. Every employee and hundreds of local citizens came out to bid the caravan farewell. Flags were hoisted aloft, a lantern procession was organized to bless the travellers, and even the band from the Northern Region Agriculture and Forestry High School was hired to play as the trucks pulled away.

As the parade travelled through neighbouring towns along the western coast of Okinawa, locals gathered along the roadside. When the convoy arrived in Naha, Gushiken addressed the attendees and underlined the local character of his company, which was both staffed and owned by people from throughout the Ryūkyūs. He stated his conviction that a company should be a public institution, and he asked for their support for this new and unprecedented Okinawan venture, saying, "We bought all machinery and equipment from Japan and the United States. In addition to providing people here with beer at cheaper prices, we are providing employment for more than 50 residents in the Nago and Naha areas."[27] The next day, on the occasion of Nanminsai, the firm began to sell "Orion Beer" throughout the island. At the end of the summer season, Okinawa Beer joined roughly forty other companies in a lavish, hundred-car parade during the Okinawan Commerce Festival *(Shōkō matsuri)*, which marked the final act in the formal debut of "Orion Beer."[28]

Reality Check: The Struggle against Mainland Japanese Brewers
On 26 May 1959, the *Okinawa Times* reported that the shareholders had passed a resolution changing the company's name from Okinawa Beer to Orion Breweries Ltd.[29] As the brewing industry was a global business, the firm's directors felt that the company name should reflect the brand name, rather than the firm's geographic location. The next day, an elaborate ceremony was held to mark the official completion of the Nago plant. The complex was equipped with a 2,309-square-metre warehouse, a fermentation room of the same dimensions, a bottle-making plant, a bottle-sterilizing machine, and a hops warehouse. It also boasted a three-storey refrigerated primary tank, a four-storey settling tank, and tanks for both malts and water. Okinawa's most ambitious private manufacturing venture was complete, and to celebrate, Nago's main street was decorated with an archway of sago palm leaves, and a huge red and white banner was hung like a gate at the entrance of the plant.

The tall white factory buildings were draped on all sides with flags from every country, and the ordinarily quiet streets of Nago were transformed into public beer gardens. To mark the event, Orion chartered seven buses to bring in the USCAR civil administrator, General Burger; his deputy; and various leading government figures. In all, about fifteen hundred attendees representing the military-civilian government gathered. At the beginning of the ceremony, Sawada, the plant manager, gave an address, after which Gushiken presented letters of thanks to General Burger and others involved with the plant's construction.[30]

Celebrating the brewery's completion was simple, but squaring off against Orion's powerful Japanese rivals was a significant challenge. The key lay in securing sales agents, so in anticipation of its product launch, Orion had concluded contracts with sales agents in early May. At that time, Okinawa's beer market was composed of three tiers: large wholesalers and medium- and small-sized retailers. The wholesalers, which had long been used by Kirin Brewery, were the Okinawa Trading Company, the Okinawa Industrial Business Affairs Company, and the joint stock firm Marunaka Company. A fourth firm, Kokusai bussan kaisha (International Products Trading Company), principally sold whisky to the US military. Together, these large firms acted as importers and in turn sold products to the island's medium and small retailers. These shops typically sold both Japanese and foreign beers, but each brewer tended to control its own territories, where customer loyalty was strongest. For example, "Kirin" was sold and consumed all over the Ryūkyūs, "Asahi" was sold chiefly in the civilian bar districts of Naha, and the foreign imports were generally sold in the bar districts frequented by US military personnel. For "Orion Beer"'s first foray into the market, the company planned initially to take advantage of the strength of Kirin's Ryūkyū-wide network of small retailers. However, those retailers wished to remain loyal to Kirin and feared being regarded as disloyal if they sold another brand. Orion was able to make use of the existing network of stores selling Aka Marusō soy sauce and miso, but there really was no array of shops that would sell "Orion Beer" exclusively.[31]

Orion's first sales campaign was a lively, showy affair, but the firm's directors soon realized that the front lines were where serious combat took place. Despite a price difference versus the imports that favoured Orion, Orion's early sales were poor and they grew only slowly. The big three beer companies, Kirin, Asahi, and Nippon, had enormous capital reserves, which they poured into advertising. Orion possessed roughly 10 percent of the capital of these rivals, and simply could not outgun them in the marketplace. Furthermore, in an ironic and unnecessary parallel to mainland Japanese beers of the *prewar* era, "Orion Beer" initially took the form of a heavily hopped, stronger-tasting German lager. Frequent criticisms heard at Orion's promotional tasting parties included "the hops are too strong," and "the hops have a strong, bitter taste." Like mainland Japanese, Okinawans had grown accustomed to lighter-tasting Japanese and American beers, and had little familiarity with stronger-tasting, traditional German brews. In response to these reviews, the brewers took steps to lighten the flavour somewhat by using less hops, but still the sales did not improve.[32]

Complicating the situation was the deep-rooted idea among Okinawan consumers that imported products were first-class, while island-made things were judged to be second-class. This affinity for imported products was observed in bars, cabarets, and especially in fancier restaurants, where imported products commanded consumers' respect and higher prices. This lingering sentiment was summed up by the phrase *yasukarō warukarō,* literally "cheap things, bad things," or "You get what you pay for." "Orion Beer" did, in fact, sell for less than its competitors, which did not help consumers to overcome their prejudice. In 1959, a 633 mL bottle of imported beer sold for $0.55, whereas the same-sized bottle of "Orion Beer" sold for $0.45. Ironically, Orion was a large-volume, local producer that could take advantage of economies of scale, but the additional import-regulation measures in effect at that time actually worked against Orion in the marketplace. Imported beer was taxed at a rate of 200 percent as a protective measure, to aid the recovery of the Okinawan economy, while "Orion Beer" was taxed at just $21 per 100 litres. But widening the price differential between "Orion" and its imported rivals only intensified the existing prejudice. In short, "Orion" was just too affordable, and therefore appeared markedly inferior.[33]

As Orion's poor sales continued, many islanders began to think that the company had little chance against its imported foes, and so the directors sat down to speak with Orion's chief wholesaler and a group of mid-sized retailers. The theme of the discussion was positive sales cooperation, and the attendees discussed a variety of marketing initiatives, including radio and television advertising, which had grown hugely important for beer makers in Japan. Also, the company extended invitations to attend a beer quality contest in the summer of 1959 that pitted the various brands against each other. In the blind taste test, the judges agreed that "Orion Beer" was the best, and the company advertised on television and in the newspapers that "Orion"'s taste was better than imported Japanese rivals. In the meantime, however, Orion's bank debt loomed large and, unable to make its first payment, the firm had to ask for an additional loan, which strained relations with its creditors.

Calls to support the Okinawan beer industry through increased import regulation had filled the local newspapers during the 1950s, but negotiations between the military and civilian governments had ultimately collapsed. By September 1959, Orion was on the verge of taking another loan from the Bank of the Ryūkyūs when, suddenly, General Burger and the American military government finally agreed to Orion's long-standing petition to restrict imports of foreign beer. The Ryūkyū government too considered Orion's situation, and in the interest of nurturing and protecting island industry, it moved to support the policy. The head of the Ryūkyū Government Economic Bureau, Nishime Junji, even published an unofficial editorial about import regulation.[34] Just as Orion's struggle against imported beer seemed to take a turn, however, General Burger took back his pledge to regulate beer imports. His successor, Brigadier General John C. Ondrick, terminated the policy initiative shortly afterward. Ondrick told Orion's managers, "I don't know anything about my predecessor's policy, but I don't think there will be any beer import regulations."[35] In the two years since Orion's establishment, the Okinawan economy had improved dramatically, and the principle of free trade *(bōeki jikyūkai)* had at last come to pass.

The issue attracted significant public attention from September 1959 until April 1960, during which period Orion and USCAR met ninety-five times, underscoring the seriousness of the situation. In the end, however, General Ondrick could simply not be persuaded. He met with Gushiken and summed up his position in the bluntest possible terms:

> I think that you may have heard my ideas about this, but I will discuss the details of my decision. A beer industry specialist will come from America via Manila to Orion Breweries to analyze your company. Based on that analysis, he will recommend the best sales and advertising approaches. You must show your subordination to him. This will last a minimum of six months. After that, I'll give beer some thought. Until then, we won't even talk about beer. I will not prohibit beer imports. I will not provide financial aid. Or any other kind of aid. You will have to give this your very best effort. In order for me to conserve funds, the best thing for you to do is borrow $1,000,000 from the Bank of the Ryūkyūs and from private banks ... beyond that, we won't discuss this problem again.[36]

As the US military government sternly refused to compromise, the responsibility for getting Orion out of its sales slump fell single-handedly to its directors. Even more awkwardly, Gushiken and his fellow directors had always assured the Bank of the Ryūkyūs that it was possible to persuade USCAR to restrict beer imports by 10 percent, and it was based on that premise that the bank had agreed to support the new firm. Once the negotiations collapsed, therefore, Gushiken expressed his intention to resign out of a sense of responsibility. He told his executives that "the thing about this problem is that the struggle is actually a dispute between commander Ondrick and the newspapers. For that reason too, I want to free [the firm] from this situation in which its active president is ineffectual."[37] However, Orion's directors insisted unanimously that Gushiken stay on as president. Bolstered by their support, he turned to face the sales crisis.

Targeting Consumers in Naha's Pleasure Districts

In its debut year, "Orion Beer" sold just 797 kL, giving it a market share of 21 percent, but company records show that its goal was to sell an incredible 2,160 kL. When the hoped-for beer import restrictions were refused, Orion's management felt that the company had been cornered *(happo fusagari)*. Consequently, the directors decided that they would have to reform their sales system and use "human wave tactics" *(jinkaisenjutsu)* in a "do-or-die effort" *(haisuinojin)*.[38] As noted above, Orion's sales system comprised the three main "Kirin Beer" distributors, plus the whisky distributor Kokusai bussan, as well as its own network of Aka Marusō shops. The first three of these were also required to sell "Kirin Beer" at their stores, which was the key obstacle to the expansion of Orion's sales. As a result, Orion's directors decided to cancel their sales agency contract and found their own sales division, just as Kirin Brewery had done when it cancelled its contract with Meidi-ya and poached its entire beer sales staff in 1927.

The new sales division, named the Orion Beer Distributing Company, was established on 15 June 1960. Capitalized at $30,000, it comprised five regional agencies and a home office, to which a series of Orion employees were soon transferred. The president, Zamami Yōshin, who was chosen by the chief of the Ryūkyū Labour Bureau *(Ryūkyū rōdō kyokuchō)*, was the former executive director of the Ryūkyū Asphalt Company.[39] When Zamami assumed office, he greeted the staff with a very grave address: "Of course our first task is to fix Orion Breweries' sales problems and raise sales and realize excellent results, but this is also a test of whether or not Okinawans have the enterprise management ability to run a beer company. Therefore, let's just say that the success or failure of Orion Beer is tied to the broader subject of all Okinawan businesses, industries, and its economy."[40] Zamami concluded his address by underscoring that the company was on the verge of life or death.

The new sales company quickly commissioned a comprehensive market expansion study and determined that, just as the Japanese beer sales system revolved around Tokyo, the Okinawan system must revolve around Naha, and its entertainment districts must be captured. Therefore, despite the significant red ink already facing the firm, Orion launched a $50,000 sales campaign in Naha's Sakurazaka social district. At that time, the Sakurazaka district had over three hundred little bars, most of which were squeezed into a two-kilometre stretch of road called Kokusai-dori (International Street). The district took on the name Sakurazaka (Cherry Hill) in about 1952 when it came to life and became known to locals as a "social paradise" *(shakō tengoku)*. It was there that Orion waged a sales war with a rolling operation *(rōrā sakusen)* of salesmen on foot.

During the operation, Gushiken and all of the men and boys who worked for the company called at all of the bars, cabarets, and drinking stands to leave samples of "Orion Beer." At the places where imported beer was very popular and their sales campaign was refused point-blank, the salesmen returned day after day, even in bad weather. In the daytime they would make their pitch from back doors, where kitchen staff could hear them, and in the evening they would combine their sales pitches with advertising, in order to appeal directly to the patrons. Each Orion staffer typically visited seven or eight establishments each night, and often a dozen, until two or three in the morning. Even Gushiken visited over a dozen establishments each night, despite the fact that he was forbidden to drink or smoke after his stomach surgery. Each morning, the sales staff would assemble and report on their business dealings, the results of their visits with the customers, what brands of beer the patrons happened to drink, and so on. If any of the customers were well-known members of the Okinawan community, Gushiken would later telephone them to recommend "Orion Beer" to them personally.

Through this campaign, which the company referred to as its "carpet bombing strategy" *(jūtan bakugeki senryaku)*, Orion Breweries was able to persuade both bar owners and patrons to try its product.[41] The effectiveness of Gushiken's personal telephone offensive against well-known patrons also played a significant role, and the campaign was a resounding success. Together with the leadership of Orion Breweries' head office, the sales company managed to make significant inroads at both medium and small retailers, as well as at bars, cabarets, and upscale Japanese-style businesses. This too parallels the early inroads made by Orion's mainland Japanese rivals, which sold staggering quantities of beer to cabarets and hostess bars in Tokyo and Osaka during the 1950s. Orion also employed an additional marketing tactic that sat very well with both patrons and bar employees. In 1960, each bottle of Orion began featuring a coupon in the form of a trademark seal affixed to the neck of the bottle. Each seal was worth 2 cents off the next bottle of

"Orion Beer," which increased the pocket change of patrons as well as host-esses, busboys, bartenders, and bar-owning "mama-sans."[42] At that time, a bowl of soba noodles in Okinawa cost between 10 and 13 cents, the price of a typical lunch set was 25 cents, and the initial fare for a taxi was 13 cents, so Orion's decision to knock 2 cents off the price of its beer was no small incentive. The promotion was a great success, and as more and more custom-ers began collecting the "Orion Beer" seals, the company's sales rose accord-ingly. Having captured the Sakurazaka entertainment district handily, Orion began pouring its efforts into other districts of Naha, such as Sakaemachi and Maejima, and as its sales campaigns widened, the firm generated in-creased brand recognition throughout the island. In the meantime, in February 1960, Orion also began selling a smaller 341 mL bottle, which had become the leading format on the Japanese mainland and was also popular with American consumers. When it made its debut in cities throughout Okinawa, it sold for 25 cents.

Through these combined efforts, by September 1960 Orion at last managed to surpass its monthly production goal of 180 kL. Never ones to miss an op-portunity to celebrate, the firm's directors threw street parties in Nago, Naha, and Koza to commemorate the milestone. The company's sales for 1960, which spanned the period from April 1960 to March 1961, reached 1,446 kL – nearly double the figure of 1959. Despite improved performance in 1960, Orion noted that its sales appeared to plateau at 30 percent of market share, and the company was falling behind on its loan payments. This outcome parallels the experience of the firms that competed in the mainland Japanese beer market during the 1920s, when the "beer sales war" spurred ever rising production, but rendered the business virtually unprofitable. Out of the $970,000 loan received by the Okinawan brewer at its founding, $349,000 remained unpaid and was long overdue. Its creditors reported the default to the US military government, which, for the sake of Orion's credit rating, demanded an investigation.[43]

Calling in Foreign Experts: The Falstaff Assessment

In response to Orion's rising tide of red ink, the USCAR high commissioner, Lieutenant General Paul W. Caraway (1961-64), maintained his predecessor's directive by ordering an inspection of the brewer's operations by American beer company executives in early February 1961. Just as foreign experts had often aided mainland Japanese brewers in the past, Orion's enterprise inspec-tion was entrusted to the Falstaff Brewing Corporation of St. Louis, Missouri. At the request of the Ryūkyū Development Corporation, three Falstaff execu-tives arrived on 12 March to inspect Orion's operations: the company's vice-president in charge of planning, Karl K. Vollmer; the vice-president in charge of brewing, Louis J. Walther; and the firm's special planning section man, Ferdinand J. Gutting. Over six days they analyzed Okinawa's beer market, the firm's accounting situation, its factory location, its ingredients and water quality, its manufacturing techniques and quality control, and its sales and marketing systems. Their report began with a detailed breakdown of the regional beer market, which totalled 4.45 million litres sold in 1960, fully 72.2 percent of which were foreign imports, with Orion holding 10 percent of the US military marketplace. These figures underline the overwhelming dominance of imported beer in the Ryūkyūs, which was just one of many markets controlled by foreign imports at that time.[44]

Based on their findings, the team from Falstaff proposed a series of solutions to some of Orion's key operational problems. Concerning product quality, the report found that "Orion Beer" and American-type beers were not terribly different, but that Orion's effort to brew a German-type beer left an unnecessarily strong and bitter aftertaste that did not really rouse consumer interest. For the sake of sales, the team suggested specific changes to the brewing temperature, the proportion of hops, and so on, to improve the taste of the product. Concerning sales, the investigators agreed that Orion's newly formed sales division and related network of small retailers were an improvement over its former contract agencies. However, the Falstaff team recommended that Orion trim its costs in order to lower its sale price. Despite the inherent prejudice against cheap, island-made products, Falstaff agreed with Gushiken that lower prices would better target Okinawa's working-class market, which was then drawn overwhelmingly toward the purchase of the cheap, strong, rice-based liquor known as *awamori*. (Brewed in Okinawa for several hundred years, the taste of good-quality awamori registers somewhere between a strong sake and a mild whisky. The most refined awamori brands use black Thai rice exclusively, but the least expensive are noxious, and are known simply as *shima* or "island.") The Falstaff report also recommended that Orion seek the advice both of experienced retailers and a Tokyo-based PR consultancy. Finally, they concluded that a cut in the Okinawan beer tax was required. The taxes on "Orion Beer" were found by the Falstaff team to be extraordinarily high compared to the beer taxes in the United States (see Table 32) or even the taxes on other kinds of alcoholic beverages sold in Okinawa.[45]

The inspectors from Falstaff concluded that beer consumption was being kept low by the inordinately high beer taxes then in effect.[46] Each year, Okinawans drank 1.56 gallons of liquor per capita, compared to 1.3 gallons per

Table 32

Okinawan and US annual beer consumption and tax rates, 1960

Location	Annual consumption per capita in US gallons	Consumption tax Per 31-gallon barrel	Per 100 litres
Okinawa	1.33	$24.60	$21.00
United States	15.30	$9.00	$7.67

Note: Imported beer in Okinawa, whether made in Japan or overseas, was charged a 200 percent ad valorem tax, which is reflected in the price shown.
Source: Falstaff Brewing Company, *Enterprise Assessment Report on Orion Breweries Co., Inc.,* in Orion biiru KK, *Orion yonjūnen no ayumi* [Forty-year history of Orion Breweries] (Naha: Orion biiru KK, 28 July 1998), 46.

capita in the United States, but Americans drank 15.3 gallons of beer per person, while Okinawans drank just 1.33 gallons. Falstaff therefore advised that Okinawa's beer tax be reduced. Although "Orion Beer" received a measure of protection through the 200 percent tax on imported beers, the Falstaff team pointed out that if the taxes were lowered, it would drive demand for "Orion Beer" and generate further profit for the firm. The government would see an immediate drop in tax revenue, but the demand for "Orion Beer" would be stimulated, so the increased sales would offset this loss. Also, the Falstaff team pointed out that because beer has more vitamins and nutrients than strong liquor, suppressing the consumption of strong liquor might improve the health of the population over time. On completing their investigation, the investigators sent their assessment report, along with a letter, to the high commissioner. They pointed out that if their recommendations were implemented, Orion Breweries had a potentially bright future, and that the firm could indeed be profitable.[47]

Making and Connecting New Ryūkyūan Consumers through Beer Advertising

The Falstaff report noted that Orion supplied just 10 percent of the beer sold to US military bases on Okinawa, which were 90 percent dominated by foreign beer imports. Due to the hostile market competition in the rest of the islands, Orion recognized that improving its sales to the US base market was vital. In May 1962, Orion therefore signed a contract with a military supply firm in Ginowan City called Gilbert and Hart, which further drove demand for "Orion Beer" in the military market, and the company's sales jumped as a result. This quasi-export market was lucrative for Orion because the company did not actually need to deliver its product by ship. In 1964, sales to military

Table 33

Sales of "Orion Beer" to US military bases, 1959-72

Year	Volume (kL)	Year	Volume (kL)	Year	Volume (kL)
1959	9.53	1964	944.72	1969	570.06
1960	12.67	1965	1,039.50	1970	499.40
1961	63.75	1966	1,177.16	1971	372.25
1962	387.94	1967	989.17	1972	34.15
1963	921.59	1968	761.29		

Source: Orion biiru KK, *Orion yonjūnen no ayumi* [Forty-year history of Orion Breweries] (Naha: Orion biiru KK, 28 July 1998), 49.

bases accounted for 10 percent of Orion's total volume, and contributed to a steady upward trend in sales (see Table 33).[48]

In 1964, sales to military base clubs, including army, navy, and air-force clubs for both officers and enlisted personnel, accounted for 15 percent of Orion's overall market share. Such numbers were by no means overwhelming, but with roughly thirty foreign beers jostling for market share amidst tight competition, Orion put up a good fight. Over the next few years, however, the United States initiated a "Buy American" policy, and US beers were imported in greater volume. From that point, Orion's volumes declined, and its market share on the US bases began to slide.

In the meantime, however, Orion managed by July 1961 to surpass its long-sought monthly sales goal of 270 kL, and in August the firm sold 324 kL. On 15 August 1961, the anniversary of Japan's surrender in 1945, *Pacific Stars and Stripes* reported that Nago had become a thriving industrial city, due in large part to Orion Breweries, which was issuing sixty thousand gallons of beer per month.[49] This production was a result of the steady sales offensive that it had continued since 1960, which greatly boosted its reputation among small retailers. The company threw additional parties as its sales reached subsequent milestones, and each time it invited beer industry affiliates and clients from Naha, Koza, Nago, Miyako, and Yaeyama to its manufacturing plant. The company also arranged to give a complimentary "service" (*saabisu)* bottle of its draft-style beer to clients at specified small retailers and beer halls, which was naturally very popular. However, as sales of "Orion Beer" continued to grow, the three major mainland Japanese brewers, Kirin, Asahi, and Nippon, began to fight back. They launched a stream of newspaper, television, and radio advertisements, and the beer war among the four companies grew very fierce. The new market entrant, "Takara Beer," had also joined the fray in

1957, but Orion managed to ride out this storm and its sales continued to rise steadily. Orion managed to sell 2,862 kL of beer in 1961.[50]

As Orion's sales increased, the product spread all over the Ryūkyū Islands, which required the establishment of new and consistent sales routes across the archipelago. Permanent distribution routes were set up in Yaeyama in November 1961, Miyako in December 1961, and the northern, central, and southern regions of the main island in January 1962. In more remote areas, Orion organized a central wholesalers group. Orion's three slogans were "market expansion" *(hanro kakuchō)*, "unified sales price to promote mutual profits" *(hanbai kakaku no tōitsu ni yoru sōgo rieki zōshin)*, and "mutual friendship" *(sōgo shinboku)*. Above all, Orion emphasized friendship and cooperation among its partners as it pressed to increase sales. The firm therefore established the Orion Beer Federation in February 1962 in order to foster a closer relationship between its head office, the Orion Beer Distributing Company, and the wholesaler network. At the same time, Orion restructured its business operations, established a business planning and investigative section, and launched further advertising and service promotions, including an Orion Beer Hall on Naha's busy International Street.[51]

As a result of these promotions, "Orion" enjoyed not only increased popularity in the island's pleasure districts, but also increasing sales among ordinary Okinawans. In November 1962, *Pacific Stars and Stripes* reported:

> Beer, once a drink for men in the moneyed class of the Ryukyu Islands, is finding its way into ordinary homes and gaining increasing patronage among men and women here with the rapid development of a local brewery. "Before World War II nobody would have imagined a beer company being established here and people enjoying the drink as they do now," said Yoshimi Yamada, chief of the Planning and Investigation section of Orion Breweries Ltd. in this northern Okinawan commercial center ... "By the end of next March, we will be meeting about 70 per cent of the total demand," Yamada said.[52]

Orion's researchers found that retailers and bar owners were beginning to think more positively about selling "Orion Beer" because they felt that it was to their advantage. For example, one promotional campaign aimed at retailers was called "Sell Orion Beer, Buy a Car." This campaign profiled a dealer close to an American military base at Koza, where the big sellers were large bottles of "Nippon" and small bottles of "San Miguel." The US base personnel generally preferred the small bottle format, so "San Miguel" was the biggest seller. At that time, stocking one case of "San Miguel" cost the retailer $8.70, but a case of "Orion Beer" cost just $5.00, providing a solid profit margin of $3.70. Therefore, if a small retailer who sold one case per day switched from "San Miguel" to "Orion Beer," they would see a profit of $1,350 over the course of a year, enough to buy a new car. Consequently, "Sell Orion Beer, Buy a Car" became the company's catchphrase.[53]

In May 1962, Orion celebrated its fifth anniversary, by which time its market had expanded to every corner of the Ryūkyūs and its annual production surpassed 5,400 kL. The scale of the celebration was unprecedented in postwar Okinawan history, and it coincided with both the annual Nanminsai Festival and also the Sakurazaka Festival. On 16 May, Gushiken and fellow company executives began by visiting fourteen state facilities across the Ryūkyūs, including a tuberculosis clinic, a school for the blind, a school for the handicapped, and a children's hospital, where they distributed gifts. On the eve of Nanminsai, the company put on a fireworks display to usher in the festival, and the next day Orion took part in a seventy-float festival parade that began in Naha. Additionally, Orion staged a sumo wrestling tournament; the crowd of sixty thousand people who gathered to watch the matches was the largest of the postwar era to date. Finally, on May 18, Orion hosted over two thousand guests at its fifth anniversary party at Okinawa Electric Hall. In his address, Gushiken told the crowd that Orion Breweries and a series of partner firms would donate $33,000 over the next three years to restore the inner sanctum of Naminoue Gu Shrine.[54]

At this point, Orion launched its most successful island-wide PR vehicle. In spring 1962, the company borrowed a page from the playbook of the mainland distiller Suntory Whisky and began publishing a newsletter called *Tipsy Heaven* (*Horoyoi Tengoku,* or *Horoten* for short). The well-known Suntory version was *Western Liquor Heaven* (*Yōshu Tengoku*), and Orion intended this similar small newspaper to be filled with stories about "Orion Beer" and beer-related conversation. It featured no hard news, aiming instead to be something that customers would read for enjoyment, with topics such as the brewing of beer at the plant, beer etiquette, and hobbies. Orion shipped copies of its new paper to little beer stands in public squares, as well as to small shops and sellers of *otsumami* (tidbits). Orion was already distributing another newsletter called *Orion Information* (*Orion Jōhō*) to shareholders, retailers, and bar owners, but that paper featured a businesslike tone for hard news about sales reports and marketing campaigns. To produce the new paper, Orion hired a newspaper reporter named Yamada Hiroshi to be the section chief of the planning and investigative section. Under Yamada's direction, *Tipsy Heaven* published articles on customer loyalty, Western advertisements, and women's issues, as well as interviews, aphorisms about drunkenness, *tanka* poems, graphics, essays, politics, manga, and jazz reviews. It had regular columns by an economist as well as an actress, plus features like "Music beer idealism" and "What do you do when drinking Orion Beer?"[55] The gazette was published monthly in a four-page tabloid format, and while the news and editorial features were printed in various pale colours, the beer-related stories were always printed in soft pink text. The initial circulation began at 2,500 copies, but as its reputation spread by word of mouth and people began demanding subscriptions, regular subscribers quickly reached 1,500. *Tipsy Heaven* became far more popular than Orion had dared to hope, prompting readers to send in their own contributions, which encouraged communication between Orion dealers, affiliates, and consumers throughout the Ryūkyūs. Much more than a marketing vehicle, Orion's newspaper helped to cultivate a shared identity among the inhabitants of the vast and often disconnected archipelago. The publication's purpose and tone were recreational, but before long, the circulation of *Tipsy Heaven* was second only to the major Okinawan newspapers. The paper remained in circulation for nine years, until March 1971, publishing 110 issues, during which time Orion's sales made tremendous progress. When publication began in 1962, Orion sold 5,494 kL, but its sales climbed over 300 percent to 17,787 kL in 1970, giving Orion a 90 percent share of the Okinawan prefectural market. Rather inexplicably, *Tipsy Heaven* was discontinued as part of a broader effort toward reducing expenses and implementing enterprise rationalization *(kigyō no gōrika)*.[56]

Gendered Marketing: Women, Beer, and Sexual Revolution in Okinawa

In 1961, Gushiken Sōsei visited Tokyo in order to investigate the local beer market. During his trip, he visited several beer gardens and halls, where he was surprised to see that many women were drinking beer. In fact, Gushiken noted that 20 to 30 percent of the beer garden patrons were women – and the popularity of rooftop summer beer gardens was rising in major cities throughout Japan (see Figure 15, above). Not only were women drinking in groups by themselves, there were female workers drinking with male colleagues after work, as well as women out on dates. A popular Japanese phrase after the Second World War observed that "women and stockings became stronger" *(josei to kutsushita ga tsuyokunatta)*, and Gushiken observed that in Tokyo, the women who got stronger also drank beer (see Figure 16, above).[57] On his return, he immediately gathered his staff together and told them to develop Okinawa's female market for beer. Gushiken proclaimed, "From now on, the beer market must also serve women. Men and women have equal rights under the law. The women of the world will also drink a lot of beer."[58]

Soon, Orion's marketing team began to plan an event called "Giving Young People an Orion Beer Evening" *(Wakoudo ni okuru Orion biiru no tabe)*. For Okinawans, this evening would turn out to be nothing short of a sexual revolution.

Until that time, all of the guests invited to Orion's parties and anniversary celebrations had always been men. The very subject of women was considered by Okinawan men to be a private matter, and women were generally hidden away during public events. Orion's chief of planning and investigation, Yamada Yoshimi, told *Pacific Stars and Stripes* that many Okinawans even had negative feelings about the idea of women drinking alcohol.[59] In order to abolish these old customs, Orion's marketers decided not only to invite women to accompany men to a beer party, but to make the women the guests of honour. The company therefore sent carefully crafted invitations to women only, inviting the men to come as their companions. The first such event was held on 31 August 1962 at the Okinawa Electric Hall in Miebashi, Naha. Six hundred invitations were sent to the "business girls" *(bijinesu garu)* or "BGs" of Naha (the equivalent of mainland Japan's "office ladies" or "OL"). The hall had a large stage, and Orion hired two bands from the Sakurazaka district to play for the evening. The doors opened at six, and, as expected, the ladies came in very slowly and anxiously. The hall soon filled. The guests of honour, a large group of young office ladies, were waited on by male bartenders, service boys, and male hosts, and nearly a thousand young people attended in all.[60] Women and men danced together, and reporters from the newspapers, television, and radio stations turned out to cover the event.[61] Orion's female company representative, Ms. Takeno, greeted the media and gave a rather bold statement:

> It is said that the position of postwar women has improved, but it was not until today that this honour was truly achieved. We haven't planned a novel function like this until now – isn't this a great way to start abolishing old-fashioned customs like parties for men only? We've just leaped over our goal of 30,000 koku [5,400 kL], so it is significant that the status of women should rise up too.[62]

Due to the success of the first Orion Beer Evening, the company made it an annual event. The next year's party was held outdoors at the Bank of the Ryūkyūs Club on 19 July 1963, and drew a crowd of fourteen hundred young people. The third, even larger beer evening was held on 20 May 1964, in Yasuri, Naha, at the Shōwa Hall *(Kaikan)*, and brought in two thousand attendees.

Every year, more women and their escorts came out than before, and Naha at last had the infrastructure to accommodate such large gatherings. Although Gushiken was nearing seventy years of age, he always joined the young women on the dance floor. As a PR event, Orion's beer evenings were a great success, and the company observed that the demand for beer increased as a result. One thing was certain – women were growing accustomed to being the guests of honour at public parties, and with each passing year they became more and more unlikely to step back into the shadows.

Rivalling the West: Expanding Facilities and Cutting Prices

In 1962, Orion sold a record 5,494 kL, which required that its Nago plant operate at peak capacity. As a result, Orion earmarked $500,000 in capital to double its production capacity to 10,800 kL. The first phase of expansion involved the construction of a two-storey beer storage room. The 495-square-metre facility was equipped with twenty new pure-aluminum storage tanks capable of holding 18 kL apiece, plus eight tanks, each with a 27 kL capacity. At the same time a new two-floor bottling room was erected and fitted with machines from the United States. The new line was capable of filling twenty thousand bottles per hour. In addition, Orion installed a series of Swedish-made machines, including water purifying equipment, an automated boiler, and a centrifuge vessel for the production of barley mash. The construction work was completed by October 1962, and on 6 November the firm threw yet another party inside the new facilities. The event brought together fifteen hundred people, and the company rented eight buses to transport guests from the central and southern districts of Okinawa. Several days before the party, Gushiken had returned from a trip to Western Europe and the United States, where he inspected various beer industries and economies. He boasted to his party guests that "on this trip to Europe and America, [I discovered that] there is no beer in the world against which Orion Beer cannot hold its own. From now on, I want to provide a good, inexpensive beer to Okinawa's beer halls. This new beer factory is a clear step in that direction."[63]

As Orion Breweries approached its sixth anniversary, the company issued its first price cuts. Sales had grown steadily for four years, and motivated by Gushiken's policy of reducing profit for the sake of society, the company at last delivered on its commitment to give back. Orion took out large ads in the local newspapers, announcing "gratitude price cuts" *(hōon nesage)* effective 17 May 1963 – the anniversary of its first product launch. The price of 633 mL bottles was cut by 5 cents to a minimum retail price of 40 cents, while the price of 354 mL bottles was cut by 2 cents to 23 cents. The price of draft beer was reduced as well; small- and medium-sized glasses were cut by 5 cents, and a large mug fell by 15 cents. This was a steep reduction of between 10 and 20 percent in Orion's retail prices that was expected to cut the company's profit by over $500,000 annually. Orion notes that, due to rising standards of living, consumer prices had increased throughout the Ryūkyūs, which magnified the impact of its price cuts. Just as Japan's early brewers had done in the Meiji era, PR trucks bearing loudspeakers and hand-painted billboards were sent out to spread the news to consumers in both urban and rural areas. The company had come a long way in overcoming consumers' prejudices against island-made products, and its directors therefore opted to further widen the price differential between "Orion Beer" and its imported rivals.[64]

Orion's price cuts were naturally met very positively, especially by Ferd Gutting and the investigative team at the Falstaff Brewing Corporation, who sent Gushiken the following letter on 19 July 1963:

> It was a real pleasure to receive your letter of July 5 and to learn of the excellent progress of your company. You certainly have every reason to be proud of the accomplishments, especially since they were brought about in such a short period of time.
>
> Of particular interest is the fact that you have now been able to reduce the price of your product to the consumer. As I recall, you had this in mind at the time of our visit two years ago so that your product would be more competitive with the higher alcoholic content "Awa-More," which enjoyed a lower excise tax rate and consequently a greater share of the working class market. The continued increases in your sales volume (and I hope in your profits) would seem to indicate that it was a proper course of action.[65]

Orion's decision to lower its prices was followed by a new advertising campaign featuring the catchphrase "Orion Beer is the beer at our house" *(Orion biiru wa waga ie no biiru)*. This PR effort targeted consumers' sense of family status and encouraged them to keep up with their neighbours. Sales continued to rise, and Orion sold 8,999 kL in 1963, giving the company an 83 percent share of total prefectural sales. As a consequence of the increased production, Orion's new 10,800 kL plant was soon rendered insufficient, and an even larger plant was begun in 1964. Orion raised the capacity of its beer fermentation and storage rooms, which increased its brewing capacity by 1.6 times. Construction was finished in March 1965. On 28 March the company once again invited fifteen hundred people to its third expansion celebration, and among the dignitaries in attendance were the head of the US military civilian government, the local parliamentary representative, the mayor of Nago, and the head of the company's labour union. Significantly, the presidents of Kirin Brewery and Suntory Holdings, and the chair of the Mitsubishi Trading Company, flew to Okinawa to attend the event. A huge red and white curtain was again draped around the periphery of the plant grounds, and an enormous wreath from Orion customers, dealers, and affiliates was set up on the dais. By 1965, Okinawa's largest privately managed industrial enterprise had begun to command genuine respect, even from Japan's top three brewers. Orion's sales to the US military were also rising, and demand outside of the prefecture was beginning to grow. The company began exporting beer to Taiwan in March 1966. In that year, sales rose again, topping 14,721 kL and triggering the need for further expansion.[66]

Cutting prices while reforming its operations and enduring foreign competition was a bold initiative for Orion, but as the cuts came at a time when most other prices were continuing to rise, they were received very well by consumers. Orion's sales rose to 9,873 kL in 1964, and it captured 89 percent of the prefectural market in that year. The firm also netted $170,000 in profit, and its share price rose 20 percent. Orion's determination to limit its own profit margin thus generated no backlash from shareholders, who were pleased with the firm's steadily increasing sales figures. Close on the heels of its first price cut, Orion hoped to lower its prices yet again on 1 August 1964, but this effort suffered from significant complications. Firstly, because the firm had already increased its brewing capacity to 18,000 kL in that year, there was no more room in its budget for further expansion. Furthermore, Okinawa's legislature had recently reformed the prefectural income tax system in response to public demands, and individual income tax rates fell in 1964. In order to compensate for the decreased revenue from income taxes, legislators opted to increase the alcohol consumption tax, and the tax on "Orion Beer" thus rose from $21.00 to $22.50 per 100 litres.[67]

Coincidentally, however, the new higher alcohol-consumption tax was also due to take effect on 1 August, and it would raise the tax on 100 litres of beer by $3.50, from $22.50 to $26.00. This would increase Orion's tax liability to nearly $450,000 per year, which was roughly equivalent to the rate paid in Japan by its domestic brewers. Orion's appeals to the government, the deliberative tax council, and the legislature had no effect. Further obstacles included poor summer weather in 1964, the steady rotation of a number of US troops to Vietnam, and a prefectural ban on the late-night sale of alcohol that was scheduled to begin on 24 September 1964. The ban would prohibit bars and cabarets from selling alcohol after midnight (known in Japan as zero hour) in order to curb rowdiness and late-night carousing by military base personnel. Faced with these headwinds, and unable to devise a solution before the coming tax hike took effect, Orion reluctantly cancelled its plans for a second price cut and instead raised the price of a large bottle by two cents and by one cent for a small. Nevertheless, the company's sales continued to climb. By 1965, Orion dominated an impressive 93 percent of the prefectural beer market, and it shipped a full 1,040 kL to its US military consumers.[68]

At the ninth annual shareholders' meeting on 11 May 1966, Gushiken announced suddenly that he intended to move from the office of president to that of chairman, in order to make way for younger directors. He appointed senior managing director Tominaga Kanji as his successor. Soon afterward, in November 1967, Japanese prime minister Sato Eisaku and US president Lyndon Johnson announced their plan for the eventual return of the administration of Okinawa to Japan. Representatives from the United States, Japan, and the Ryūkyūs formed an advisory committee *(shimon iinkai)* in March 1968 to draft a plan for Okinawa's economy under Japan's administration. In November 1969, Satō visited the White House for talks with President Richard Nixon, and it was finally announced in a joint communiqué that Okinawa would revert to Japanese control in 1972. As anticipated, the reversion had an enormous impact on the Okinawan economy.

Already by 1974, Naha's once bustling International Street had grown quiet, prompting reporters from the Taiwan Bureau of *Stars and Stripes* to report that Kokusai-dori, once known as the "Miracle Mile," had become a "Street of Broken Dreams":

> The Orion Beer hall stood across from the Naha police station, but there was headier fare up the street. The Hollywood Nightclub was the first of a string of pleasure palaces – like the Latin Quarter, Ginbashi, the New Comet – to bring what was chic then in nightlife to Kokusai. All have passed into oblivion now. The Hollywood, torn down last year to make room for a restaurant, was the last to go – replaced by a covey of cellar clubs and all-night "snacks."[69]

Orion's directors knew that the changes were unavoidable, especially after Japanese tourists in search of deep discounts on foreign goods stopped flocking to Okinawa, which was now simply ordinary Japanese territory. Fortunately for Orion's employees, the brewery was granted a vital concession during the prefecture's complex reversion negotiations; as a protective measure, imports of Japanese beers would not be permitted to increase, and a can of "Orion Beer" would continue to be priced at just 23 cents, compared to

35 cents for Japanese brands. Shielded by this significant concession and supported by a loyal Ryūkyūan consumer base, Orion had a solid foundation for its future operations.[70]

Conclusions

May 1967 marked the tenth anniversary of Orion's founding, by which point only four mainland Japanese brewers remained: Kirin, Sapporo, Asahi, and Suntory. Even Takara Brewing, founded in 1957, was bought out by Kirin a decade later due to slumping sales.[71] For ten years, Orion had struggled against the powerful brands and lavish advertising budgets of its mainland Japanese rivals, and its survival is a significant achievement. Postwar economic conditions in Okinawa trailed those in mainland Japan, but gradually its standard of living improved, and the demand for beer in average households began to rise. When "Orion Beer" first went on sale in 1959, the total prefectural beer consumption rate in Okinawa was an estimated 5,533 kL. Seven years later, in 1966, it had reached 15,452 kL – a nearly threefold increase. In the interim, Orion's market share rose from 14 percent in 1959 to a staggering 95 percent in 1966. Importantly, while generations of US military personnel have since become familiar with "Orion Beer," Gushiken Sōsei did not endeavour merely to capitalize on the growth of American military bases. Instead, he aimed to cultivate a successful island manufacturing enterprise targeted toward indigenous Okinawan consumers, who had historically shunned island-made products in favour of foreign imports.

Orion Breweries thus spearheaded "island industry" against tough postwar competition from both foreign and Japanese brands – an effort that very much reflected the experiences of mainland brewers in the Meiji era. From its purchase of foreign machinery, to its search for foreign talent, to its importation of German ingredients in order to brew a traditional German lager, Orion's early operations closely parallel those of its mainland predecessors. Like Kirin and Sapporo before it, Orion also had to teach many Okinawan consumers about beer, and through extensive PR and marketing campaigns the company promoted both the unity of the Ryūkyūan archipelago and a new Ryūkyūan consumer identity. It also championed industrial self-sufficiency, economic reconstruction, public welfare, and even a sexual revolution. Orion's first public parties for women, to which they could choose to bring escorts or not, were much more than just marketing events. They were a determined challenge to Okinawa's traditional male culture that was triggered by Gushiken's revelatory trip to Tokyo in 1961, where he witnessed women drinking beer in public, unescorted by men. Orion's histories thus

222 Learning from Japan

provide valuable details not just on the themes of entrepreneurship and industrialization, but on daily life for ordinary Okinawan consumers.

Orion Breweries is still in operation today, and at the time of writing it controls roughly 50 percent of the Okinawan beer market. In 2002, the firm entered into a development partnership with Asahi Breweries, under which Asahi's beers are produced in Nago alongside "Orion Beer." In exchange, Asahi supports the sale of "Orion Beer" in mainland Japan, where it holds a roughly 1 percent share of the national Japanese market and has begun to enjoy some popularity in Tokyo. The arrangement appears mutually beneficial, but symbolic reminders of Asahi's dominant position are not difficult to spot. While a statue of Gushiken Sōsei stands in front of the Orion Breweries offices in Nago, the first thing that visitors see on entering the lobby is an Asahi soda vending machine – a reminder of the Japanese brewing giant's powerful influence.

6 Indigenous Brews: Innovation, Entrepreneurship, and Beer's Continuing Evolution since the 1970s

For over sixty years now, beer has been thought of as a foreign beverage only when Japanese consumers consciously choose foreign imports over domestic brands. Moreover, just as Japanese automobiles are today built in Ontario, Kentucky, and Derbyshire, many of those foreign beers are themselves produced in Japan. "Guinness" and "Heineken" are brewed under licence by Sapporo and Kirin, respectively, while Asahi brews "Coors." "Sapporo" is likewise produced in Ontario, Canada, by its subsidiary brewer, Sleeman, which ships the brand all over North America.[1] Asahi too has licensed Molson-Coors to brew its products in Canada and Miller-Coors to do so in the United States. Naturally, all of Japan's leading brewers have acquired or signed production agreements with brewers in China.[2] Indeed, the global reach of modern megabrewing conglomerates has so blurred the lines between what is domestic and what is imported that the labels are sometimes the only means of telling them apart.

By 1970, the evolutionary process that had transformed beer from a transplanted German beverage into a domestic Japanese one was complete. There have, however, been several subsequent innovations that make Japanese beers unique on the world stage, the creativity of which underscores just how completely the industry and its product have evolved since the war. In order to avoid the very high production taxes that reflect a recipe's proportion of malted barley, which is itself very costly, all of Japan's leading brewers today issue "beer-like" beverages that are produced from very little or even no barley malts. Some of these unusual brews are even flavoured without hops, which are likewise costly. These cold beverages often look and taste somewhat like beer, and they are certainly packaged and marketed like beer, but whether they are actually beer is a matter of perspective. More importantly, such innovations underscore what Japan scholars and management theorists have long known: while the Japanese are very good at absorbing and imitating foreign products, they are equally good at adapting them to their own needs and preferences. This ability has enabled a great deal of innovation in the beer sector, most of which has been very popular with Japanese consumers, but very little of which has been exported or adopted overseas. This pattern of unique innovation that fails to catch on elsewhere, which Japanese commentators have dubbed their country's "Galápagos syndrome," is perhaps most apparent in Japan's highly evolved but equally isolated cellphone market.[3] Nevertheless, beer's transformation is clearly not yet complete, and Japanese brewers have made many indigenous contributions to the industry's development. This chapter briefly examines the beer market's continuing evolution and the distance that its participant firms are putting between contemporary beer and its early foreign origins.

Playing by the Rules: Competition within Japan's Informal Beer Cartel of the 1970s

Kirin Brewery controlled over 40 percent of domestic sales by 1961 and dominated fully 60.1 percent of the market by 1972. This period, marked by rapid economic growth, rising consumer affluence, and increased spending on luxury items, witnessed huge and sustained increases in annual beer sales among both men and women. Kirin's rivals also adopted new approaches to consumers, paid increasing attention to beer's "image," and launched innovative efforts to reach out to deeper and more diverse segments of the market. However, they did not seek to challenge Kirin's marketplace hegemony during the 1970s. Pricing remained carefully choreographed by the brewers and the Ministry of Finance, which was reminiscent of the wartime era of centralized sales and distribution. As none of the brewers were permitted to engage in a price war to undercut the leader, Kirin's market share hovered between 60 and 64 percent throughout the 1970s. The once explicit cartel arrangement thus persisted on an informal level, and Sapporo continued to share most of the remainder of the market with third-place Asahi, followed by little Suntory.[4]

As economist Joseph Schumpeter has argued, however, nonprice competition remains possible even in an oligopoly, and indeed significant competition occurred in arenas other than pricing through the 1970s. All four brewers continued to experiment with new flavours, creative packaging, and trendy ad campaigns in an effort to target key consumer groups. They also marketed new products in more stratified ways to smaller segments of the consumer market, such as heavy-drinking men, women interested in taste and image, younger consumers who wanted fresh, healthy products, and men concerned with increasing their prestige. Seasonal, regional, and light beers also emerged in this era, and their ads targeted consumers with images from nature, including alpine peaks, open skies, and mountain streams. In December 1971,

Sapporo announced the return of its historic "Yebisu" brand, which used no rice or cornstarch in its brewing process. "Yebisu" served both as a premium, all-malt beer and an opportunity to recapture the industry's prewar golden years – minus the German affectations.[5] Other campaigns emphasized macho, tough-guy imagery, such as Sapporo's 1970-72 Silent Man ad campaign, which starred samurai film icon Mifune Toshirō. In these television commercials, Mifune appeared at the bow of a ship, said nothing, and blew the head off his glass of beer before drinking it. His voiceover said, "Otoko wa damatte Sapporo biiru" (Men drink Sapporo Beer silently). In the corresponding posters, Mifune simply stared into the distance, flanked by the catchy slogan. The Silent Man ad campaign and its macho theme was a huge hit, and when the Olympic Winter Games were held in Sapporo in 1972, Sapporo Breweries followed up by reviving its famous "München–Sapporo–Milwaukee" campaign.[6] In 1976, Sapporo celebrated the hundredth anniversary of its eponymous brand with a nostalgic newspaper ad featuring an antique beer poster, which was an intentional anachronism.[7] By that time, beer branding and marketing had matured into a carefully articulated, targeted process, which was a far cry from the industry's prewar focus on German recipes and *reijin posters*.

All four surviving brewers continued to experiment with clever gimmicks throughout the decade, the most significant of which took the form of a "draft beer war" *(nama biiru sensō)* that began in Tokyo in 1977.[8] Until the 1970s, the bulk of Japan's beer was sold in bottles or cans, which were not only convenient for home consumption, but also enabled drinkers to pour beer for one another when dining out. This classic Japanese drinking etiquette, however, began to give way during the 1970s to the popularity of ordering a single draft beer for oneself, which was typically the way it was served at Japan's many beer halls and beer gardens.[9] The convenience of draft beer for restaurant owners was also undeniable, for it was much easier to take delivery of a few small kegs than several dozen bottles. Restaurant patrons soon grew accustomed to seeing a single brand of inexpensive draft beer on tap, and the modern beer posters in casual *izakaya* taverns, typically featuring bikini-clad Japanese women, left no confusion as to which brand was on offer. Draft beer certainly never replaced bottled beer, which often represented an establishment's premium or imported selections. However, in 1977 the brewers rushed to capitalize on the new trend of *bottling* "draft-style" beer for home consumption, and the response from consumers was very positive. Soon, all of the brewers offered bottled "draft beer," and well beyond basic lagers. The draft beer war finally culminated in Asahi's colossal two-litre bottle of "Black Draft," which sold for ¥1,300 when it debuted in May 1982.[10]

Given Kirin's steady marketplace dominance through the 1970s, its management began to consider diversifying the company's operations. "Kirin Lager" was securely positioned as the company's flagship brand, but when the Ministry of Finance intervened in 1972 and urged Kirin to actually stop growing, Kirin's directors turned to new markets.[11] As it branched out, Kirin made forays into a variety of other beverage and even food sectors, as well as the agri-bio, pharmaceutical, and life-science markets.[12] This process had already begun in 1971, when Kirin announced plans to enter the whisky market, just as its junior rival and long-time whisky maker Suntory had entered the beer market ten years earlier. Through an industry tie-up with the Seagram Co., Ltd., Kirin collaborated to form Kirin-Seagram KK, which began selling "Robert Brown" brand whisky in Japan the following year.[13] In order to sell its new whisky, Kirin even slowed production of "Kirin Lager" and required desperate wholesalers to purchase "Robert Brown" if they wished to also take delivery of its beer.[14] Next, Kirin teamed up in 1976 with Nagano Tomato KK of Nagano prefecture in order to produce and sell tomato juice. In the same year, the firm entered into the manufacture and sale of food products, including Kirin-brand butter and cheese.[15] Kirin's long-time rivals Asahi and Sapporo likewise diversified their operations and kept their hands in Japan's soda market as well.

As for the core beer market, product innovation in the 1970s was less revolutionary. Aside from the flurry of popularity in the bottled "draft beer" sector, the brewers maintained a stable of lagers, as well as a few stouts and dark lagers known as "black beers." The brewers also released light beers in order to keep pace with the trend toward light products, such as "Mild Seven" cigarettes. Still, despite such novelties and the rising tide of consumer affluence that prompted them, the business of beer *manufacturing* experienced little real change beyond the construction of more, larger, and increasingly automated breweries. The beer *marketplace*, however, had undergone significant transformation since the 1950s. As Andrew Gordon notes, the proportion of Western alcoholic beverages consumed by Japanese rose from 17 percent in 1950 to fully 63 percent by 1975, the bulk of which was due to the rising popularity of beer.[16] Importantly, the consumers were not solely men. As Tanaka Yukiko writes, by the mid-1970s, women were more often seen drinking in both television dramas and commercials, and health workers had begun to observe a rising number of women with alcohol dependency. Japan's alcoholic beverage producers had by that time spent more than twenty years targeting women's increased earnings and leisure time, and younger women were already accustomed to visiting bars, with or without male companions.[17] Meanwhile, middle-aged women still influenced by more traditional views on alcohol consumption drank alone at home in the daytime, earning them the popular moniker "kitchen drunks."[18] In 1982, the Mitsubishi Economic Research Institute reported that 85 percent of Japanese men and 60 percent of Japanese women were regular beer drinkers.[19] This represents a significant shift from prewar patterns of beer consumption.

Yet, as far as the industry's structure was concerned, from the local neighbourhood *izakaya* to the upscale hotel bar, Kirin remained on top, and none of its juniors was permitted to challenge the market leader with a price war. By 1985, Asahi had less than 10 percent market share. Faced with the growing popularity of flavoured, carbonated alcoholic beverages known as *chū-hai* (a name derived from the phrase *shōchū-highball*), Asahi was in danger of losing even more of Japan's alcoholic beverage market.[20] Nevertheless, while the Ministry of Finance did not wish to see any of the country's brewers actually fail, it remained adamantly opposed to price competition. Barred from undercutting Kirin's prices, Asahi was forced to take radical steps.

Coup d'État: Asahi Launches Japan's "Dry Beer" Wars

Frustrated by his company's fossilized market share and product lineup, Asahi chair Nakajō Takanori decided that it was time to revolutionize his company from the inside. In order to stimulate and promote transformative new ideas, Nakajō made a series of structural changes in 1985 designed to encourage innovation both inside and outside of the firm.[21] The company's top and middle management were reorganized in order to challenge the "elders group," thus giving junior managers greater input on product development, which soon gave the firm a new strategic direction.[22] These changes stemmed from Nakajō's belief that Asahi was capable of challenging Kirin's marketplace dominance through product innovation. When interviewed in 2009, he reflected on his motivations, recalling:

When I entered my company in 1952, I decided to always think over a point three times before making a statement about it. That usually took me about two seconds, so I quickly became known as quite outspoken. Anyone over the age of 35 should not have a say in new product development. Older people are too opinionated and they tend to believe that they are always right, even when proven otherwise. More importantly, younger staff members are too scared to argue with such seasoned professionals, which leaves a lot of young talent and fresh ideas untapped. Young people must be encouraged to make products that they enjoy ... In 1986, Kirin Beer had 63 percent of the domestic beer market. After Sapporo Beer, we were a distant third in the running. Back then, a Harvard University study predicted that if one company had such huge advantage in a market, the second and third companies would find it impossible to change the status quo. I listened carefully and disagreed. Sure, it was true that to increase the company's market share by one percent we had to sell 97 million bottles. Even so, we all believed that we could make Asahi number one.[23]

Kirin, meanwhile, had grown complacent as the market leader, and its directors focused squarely on maintaining the status quo as the brewer of a classic pasteurized lager. Without warning, Asahi transformed Japan's beer market in 1987 by introducing a revolutionary new product with a very different taste – Asahi "Super Dry."[24] This breakthrough beer had a sharper flavour and no aftertaste, which consumers found accompanied the increasingly heavy flavours of Japanese cuisine very well. The pairing of beer with particular dishes, as well as the observance of proper glassware and serving etiquette, had been the subject of much popular publishing since the 1950s.[25] Although postwar Japanese lagers were already much lighter than prewar beers, the crisp, clean taste of "Super Dry" complemented modern cuisine so well that suppliers could barely keep it in stock. Industry writers called the new product a "home run."[26] Within a year, Asahi's market share doubled to 20 percent, and Kirin's fell sharply to 50 percent, prompting observers to dub this turn of events the "Super-Dry shock."[27]

Naturally, Kirin responded in 1988 by releasing Kirin "Draft Dry Beer," but Asahi successfully forced its rival to limit the similarity of its packaging, which reinforced the authenticity of "Super Dry" as the "true" dry beer. As the two firms struggled over this new market segment, commentators wrote that the industry had once again entered a "warring states era" *(biiru sengoku jidai)*.[28] Kirin fought to regain its footing in 1990 by releasing "Kirin Ichiban" (Number One), which was brewed with 100 percent malts and boasted a milder, smoother flavour than the firm's leading lager. Kirin also fought back with star power, hiring Hollywood actor Harrison Ford for a series of campy television ads promoting "Kirin Lager" in the early 1990s. Significantly, however, rather than simply showcasing their brand next to a famous foreign movie star, these commercials featured Ford speaking Japanese and encouraging fictitious male colleagues to leave the office, saying, "Kirin ragā, ikimashō" ("Let's go for a Kirin Lager"). When offered a generic beer by their local tavern owner, Ford corrects him and asks specifically for "Kirin Lager" once more, thus demonstrating his sophisticated understanding of Japan's domestic beer market. Although advertising efforts like these halted Kirin's overall market decline until 1995, within two years Kirin announced that it would close some of its fifteen plants and increase productivity at its remaining breweries in order to cut costs.[29] Asahi ultimately eclipsed its long-time rival in 2001, capturing 37 percent of the domestic market in that year.[30] By 2009, Kirin and Suntory had entered into merger talks – the first such talks since Dai Nippon Beer was formed in 1906 – but the discussions were scrapped in 2010 when the two sides failed to agree on a market ownership ratio.[31]

Importantly, the market takeover by Asahi was achieved through product innovation, rather than a price war, which meant that Asahi was still playing within the informal cartel rules and the boundaries of oligopolistic competition. Kirin, which had grown complacent and invested the bulk of its energies into maintaining the dominance of its flagship lager, had clearly been upstaged. A younger generation of consumers, bored by the available brands and oppressed by the collusive pricing regime, embraced "Super Dry" enthusiastically and ended Kirin's marketplace dominance in short order. Not only did the "dry beer war" intensify quickly, the phenomenon also marked the first time that a Japanese product influenced beer flavours worldwide, triggering similar dry beer wars in markets around the world.[32] Indeed, in a rare instance of American firms copying Japanese beverage innovations, by 1990 over twenty dry beers were competing for US consumers' attention.[33] Although the trend passed quickly from foreign markets, Asahi "Super Dry" remains the company's flagship brand, and in 2007, the firm launched a marketing blitz to commemorate its twentieth anniversary.[34] Figure 18 traces the evolving market shares held by the country's leading firms in Japan's combined postwar beer *and* beer-type beverage market.[35]

Continuing Evolution: Entrepreneurship and the Craft-Beer Phenomenon

Until the mid-1990s, the only domestic beers available to Japanese consumers were those produced by Asahi, Kirin, Sapporo, and Suntory. Although consumers began to rail against the country's collusive beer pricing regime, the Japan Fair Trade Commission investigated the industry in 1990 and failed to find evidence of a cartel. This left the four firms to continue dominating the market, and their combined output peaked at a record 7,135,020 kL in 1994. In that year, Japan's top four supermarket chains – Daiei, Jusco, Ito-Yokado, and Seiyu – began to fight back by offering their customers discounts on beer, and they further announced that they would not pass along the price increases announced recently by the breweries.[36] Discounting was the only weapon that major retailers could use to challenge the unofficial cartel, and as Japan's post-bubble economy continued to slide, consumers responded enthusiastically. This offers a clear historical parallel to the pattern of underselling by retailers during the 1920s, when Japan's economy was also experiencing significant deflation. It was in an effort to combat that underselling

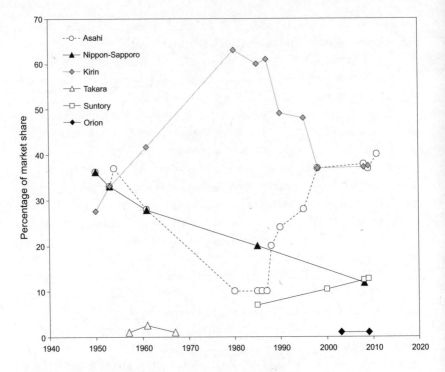

Figure 18 Shares held by major firms in Japan's postwar beer-type market,
1949-2011
Source: Data compiled by the author from: Sapporo Beer K.K., *Sapporo 120 nenshi [120-year
History of Sapporo Beer]* (Tokyo, JP: Sapporo Beer K.K., 1996); Kirin Beer K.K., *Kirin biiru
K.K. gojū nenshi [Kirin Beer Company, Incorporated: 50-Year History]* (Tokyo, JP: Kirin Beer
K.K., 20 March 1957); David A. Aaker, *Brand Relevance: Making Competitors Irrelevant*
(San Francisco, CA: John Wiley and Sons, 2011); and *The Japan Times.*

that Japan's brewers formed their first production and pricing cartel in the
1930s. In 1994, however, the grocers' representatives voiced no fear of being
cut off by the brewers because they had recently undergone a series of mergers
that enabled them to deal in very large volumes. Toyama Haruko, a spokes-
woman for Daiei, stated that her firm believed it could use its considerable
size to negotiate new lower prices from the breweries. A similar retail rebellion had also begun to threaten the authority of Japan's cosmetics makers,
which was further evidence that dealers and consumers alike were frustrated
by the long-running ability of major corporations to fix prices.[37]

Given the significant new discounting trend, which even the brewers realized was unavoidable, Japan's Ministry of Finance at last decided to open up
the beer market to modest additional competition. In 1994, the ministry
lowered the minimum annual output required for a brewing licence from

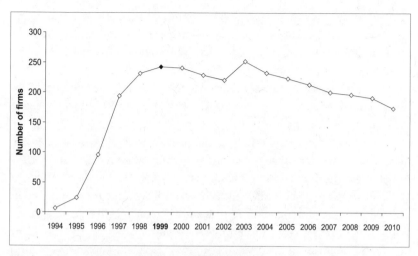

Figure 19 Licensed *jibiiru* brewers, 1994-2010
Source: Japan National Tax Agency, as appearing in Bryan Baird, "Japan's Beer Revolution: The Birth, Death, and Resurrection of Japanese Craft Beer," a lecture at the Japan Society, New York, 5 October 2011. Unpublished paper given to the author.

2,000 kL to just 60 kL.[38] This sharp policy shift eliminated a significant barrier to entry that had for decades bolstered Japan's informal beer cartel by thwarting the launch of craft breweries.[39] Under this new regime, indigenous innovation in Japan's beer industry exploded and local entrepreneurship took flight. Two "local beer" *(jibiiru)* firms were awarded brewing licences in December 1994, and in February 1995 the Echigo Brewery opened in Niigata, Japan's first microbrewery in nearly a century. Significantly, the company was founded by sake brewer Uehara shuzōshō KK, which paralleled the ownership trends of Japan's Meiji-era beer brewing industry, many participants in which were also sake or miso brewers. The first five licensed *jibiiru* brewers were as follows:

1 Echigo Beer: Uehara shuzōshō KK, Niigata prefecture, 16 February 1995
2 Brewery-pub Sumidagawa: Asahi Breweries, Asakusa, Tokyo, 1 March 1995
3 Ohotsuka Beer: Suimoto Kensetsu et al., Kitami, Hokkaido, 17 March 1995
4 Umenishiki Beer: Umenishiki yamakawa KK, Ehime prefecture, 26 March 1995
5 Jibiiru sandaya: Steak House Sandaya, Hyōgo prefecture, 26 April 1995.

Before the end of the year, the number of *jibiiru* firms reached 24. From there, growth in this beer market sector continued exponentially, reaching 95 firms in 1996, then 194 in 1997, 231 in 1998, and peaking at 242 in 1999 (see Figure 19). The number of individual brands produced by these companies topped a thousand in that year, introducing Japanese consumers to a wide array of new products, many of which were named for local regions or cities.[40]

In the same year that Japan's jibiiru operations began, entrepreneur Oda Ryōji founded the Japan Craft Brewing Association (JCBA). Hardly a challenge to Japan's leading beer makers, who continued to dominate over 95 percent of the domestic market, the JCBA's member firms aimed chiefly to foster informed appreciation for the craft brewing industry and its wares. Accordingly, the organization staged Japan's first *jibiiru* festival in Tokyo in 1995, showcasing twelve local beers from across Japan, and in 2000 it founded the Beer Tasters Organization in order to train and certify qualified beer tasters. The latter initiative was prompted by the industry's recognition that, because home-brewed beer was illegal, most Japanese consumers had no knowledge of craft beers, and therefore did not appreciate their complex, handmade flavours. In postwar Japan, small-scale brewing and distilling were considered "social problems" *(shakai mondai)*, and Japan's Liberal Democratic government banned the practices in 1975.[41] It remained possible to brew beer at home, typically from kits, but because the final product could not exceed 1 percent alcohol by volume, very few Japanese actually bothered to attempt it.

Due to these legal restrictions, Japanese consumers have long since become accustomed to the taste of Japan's leading beer brands, which are either heat pasteurized or filtered to eliminate the yeast from the finished product. In contrast, *jibiiru* brands often contain beer yeast, which Japanese drinkers of traditional brands found strange. Moreover, some craft brewers took their creativity to extreme lengths, issuing products like the Nasu-Kogen Beer Company's "Ichigo [strawberry] Ale," and even "Wasabi [horseradish] Ale" by the Miyamori Brauhaus in Iwate. Such novelty brews are, of course, not designed to capture the mainstream market, and are generally eclipsed by darker craft beers such as ambers, pale ales, and stouts.[42] The production costs are high, however, and can often exceed those of Japan's major brewers. Despite their small sizes, *jibiiru* makers typically pay more for their select ingredients than do the major brewers, and they pay equivalent production taxes. In recent years, a grace period has allowed brewers producing less than 1.3 kL of beer per year to pay just ¥176 per litre on their first two hundred litres, but this applies only to their first five years of operation. Afterward, they pay the same production tax rate as the industry leaders: over ¥200 per litre of beer, or as much as 45 percent of the sale price.[43]

Faced with these costs and the continuing struggle to build a consumer base, the number of participants in the *jibiiru* industry has contracted 28 percent since 2000 (see Figure 19, above).[44] Significantly, however, those brands that were driven out of the industry have been described by economists as "poor imitations of German-style beers" that failed due to a lack of product differentiation.[45] Their founders' skill at producing traditional German lagers may have been adequate, but too few consumers were interested. In response to their demands, the surviving craft brewers have continued to produce darker, bitterer, and more complex recipes that they now refer to only as "craft beers" – fuelling a steady increase in their annual production volumes. Between 2003 and 2009, annual output of craft beers more than doubled, rising from 14,672 kL to 34,000 kL. The successful firms include a joint venture called the Baird Brewing Company that was founded in Numazu by American entrepreneur Bryan Baird and his wife, Sayuri, in 2000. At the outset, the Ministry of Finance would issue the start-up company only a temporary brewing licence. Despite the company's success and its expanding stable of brewpubs stretching from Numazu to Tokyo, the ministry refused to award Baird Brewing a permanent brewing licence for a full ten years, but finally did so in 2010.[46]

Much of the sales growth in the craft beer sector is due to a boom in online beer retailing, which gives Japanese consumers an ideal means of perusing, discussing, and purchasing new craft beer products. Online and mail-order distribution accounted for roughly 41 percent of all craft beer sales in Japan in 2010, as compared to 27 percent in specialty bars and pubs, and 18 percent in restaurants owned by the microbreweries. For this reason, consumption of craft beers at home is almost as popular with consumers as their consumption in licensed establishments. Although entrepreneurship in the craft brewing sector has clearly faced challenges, especially from Japan's extremely high brewing taxes (discussed below), the market's revival and growth has enabled significant creativity by new entrants. These brewers' abilities to showcase their local regions, techniques, and unusual recipes have given consumers an escape from Japan's monolithic domestic lager-brewing industry that, although the maker of a firmly indigenous product, had faced no real outside market stimuli in decades. Domestic beer production by the four market leaders has also fallen sharply since 1994. The total volume turned out by Asahi, Kirin, Sapporo, and Suntory declined nearly 23 percent to 5,521,473 kL in 2000, driven downward in part by a combination of Japan's lingering economic recession and a younger generation of consumers looking to lead healthier lifestyles.[47]

Innovation and the Race to the Bottom: *Happoshu* and "Third Beer"

Notably, the decline in beer production volume has not been due in any significant way to competition from craft beers. Instead, the major brewers have curbed sales of their own "real beers" by producing a series of beer-like products, beginning in the mid-1990s with *happoshu,* or "sparkling spirit." Under Japan's tax code, beer-related products are taxed according to their malt content as a proportion of the recipe's fermentable ingredients by weight. To be considered beer by the Ministry of Finance, which borrowed its defin- ition from the Reinheitsgebot (German Beer Purity Law) of 1516, a beverage was then required to have at least 67 percent malted barley by grist weight. If the brew had less than 67 percent malts, it was not considered beer, and it was taxed at a lower rate.[48] In 1994, Suntory was the first to market a beer- like product called "Hop's Draft," which had just 65 percent malts, and was therefore taxed at the lower rate – enabling it to be priced 30 percent less than beer in stores. Kirin soon followed with its own *happoshu* brand called "Tanrei," which quickly overtook Suntory's brand, due chiefly to its taste, which quite resembled that of Asahi "Super Dry." By 2001, *happoshu* sales accounted for over 30 percent of the domestic beer market, and Asahi was forced to launch a *happoshu* of its own.[49] Asahi, of course, did not wish to imitate "Super Dry," lest it damage its leading beer brand, and it was therefore unable to dislodge Kirin's "Tanrei."[50] In 2005, by which point *happoshu* had seized over 40 percent of the beer market, the Ministry of Finance moved to tax all beer-like products containing 50 to 67 percent malts at the same rate as full-fledged beer, ¥222 per litre.[51]

From this point, the beer-like market became a race to the bottom, with the brewers introducing a series of brands with lower and lower malt content, leading ultimately to a sub-25 percent malt category. Known as "third-category beers" or "third beers" *(dai-san no biiru),* these brands are sometimes fla- voured by peas and soybeans instead of hops, or are *happoshu* fortified by unmalted barley spirits. Because these ultra-low-malt third beers enjoyed a tax rate of just ¥69 per litre, and therefore cost roughly ¥50 less per bottle, they captured 10 percent of the market by 2005. Even more importantly, they have, together with *happoshu,* come to be consumed at home almost as often as beer.[52] Whereas "real" beer consumption at home accounted for 60.1 percent of Japan's total production volume in 2001, pressure on household incomes reduced that rate to just 53.5 percent of the total volume in 2009.[53] In December 2003, the *Japan Times* reported that *happoshu* sales for home consumption had eclipsed those of beer for the first time; nearly 177 million 12.6-litre cases of *happoshu* shipped between January and November 2003, versus just 156 million same-sized cases of beer.[54]

This continuing trend drove production volume of "real" beer down to 3,560,578 kL by 2005, and to 3,018,400 kL by 2009 – less than half of the 1994 production level of 7,135,020 kL. Significantly, beer's chief rivals were the major brewers' own creations – fully indigenous, beer-like beverages brewed partly from malted barley, but growing less recognizable as beer with each passing year. With new recipes, creative flavours, seasonal packaging, and names like Asahi's "Ajiwai" (Flavour), Sapporo's "Off to Zeitaku" (Off and luxury), and Kirin's "Nodogoshi" (Going down smoothly), these products may *look* like beer, but they are totally original and uniquely Japanese. In no other global beer market has so much product innovation taken place since 1995. Indeed, there has been so much innovation that the beer market is now difficult to assess, and market share for the leading firms must be measured by their sales of "beer-type" products, rather than just beer.

Although Asahi's control of the "real" beer market topped 50.5 percent in the latter half of 2008, the numbers look very different when all beer-type products are included. In that case, Asahi controlled just 37.8 percent, while Kirin commanded 37.2 percent of the domestic beer-type beverage market. Significantly, Suntory's range of brands eclipsed Sapporo's for the first time in that period, and commanded 12.4 percent of the market, leaving Sapporo in fourth place with 11.8 percent. Although domestic beer sales fell dramatically following the March 2011 earthquake and tsunami disasters in Tōhoku and have not recovered fully, Asahi is seeing significant growth in its sales in China, which bodes well for the future.[55] China's rising demand for beer is offsetting the increasingly fickle domestic marketplace. Like fashion, consumer tastes in beer and beer-like beverages have become seasonal, and the major brewers must play a leading role in directing consumers' interests to the next big market trend – even to the detriment of their oldest brands.

Full Circle: A German Brewmaster in Japan

In Chapter 1, I noted that Sapporo's first shipments of beer from Hokkaido to Tokyo went by ship from a little harbour town called Otaru. Lined with quaint stone warehouses, canals, and other period fittings, Otaru remains the picture of Meiji-era modernization and commerce. It is also home to a start-up brewpub called Otaru Beer, which was opened by a local entrepreneur in 1995. The brewmaster, Johannes Braun, was located by a headhunter in 1994 and invited to move to Japan at the age of twenty-seven in order to lead the new firm. Born in a small village near Frankfurt, Braun began studying brewing at his family's *brauhaus* when he was twelve and worked as an apprentice before studying to become a brewing engineer at the prestigious Technische Universität München Weihenstephan in Munich. After graduation, he worked for Henninger and Löwenbräu before moving to Scotland to study whisky distilling at Heriot-Watt University in Edinburgh. When approached in 1994, Braun not only agreed to take the job in Otaru, he took care to bring with him the copper brewing kettles and other equipment necessary to produce beer that abides strictly by the Reinheitsgebot of 1516. A copy of the law hangs on the wall in the company's Soko No. 1 brewery, situated in a canalside stone warehouse, where each year he brews 150 kL of regular ales such as dunkel, pilsner, and weiss, as well as seasonal ales. Like his Meiji-era predecessors, Braun uses only barley, wheat, and hops imported from Germany, and he cultivates his own yeast. His experience and brewing philosophy are indeed as pure as the law that he follows, but this only underscores just how much Japan's brewing industry has changed since the nineteenth century.[56]

Despite Otaru Beer's success and the opening of a second brewery at nearby Zenibako that issues a further 2,000 kL per year, the very nature of Braun's craft is what prevents it from reaching more Japanese consumers. His carefully cultured yeast does not travel well, and thus his product cannot ship further than a hundred kilometres from Otaru. When interviewed in 2011, Braun said:

> I brew beer – real beer, using only natural ingredients. Many breweries in Germany still abide by a law governing beer production that dates back almost 500 years. I follow that law to the letter. Until [1995] there were only four big makers offering two types of beer in Japan. So I thought this was a fantastic opportunity to bring in a wider variety to such a highly developed country. My aim was to produce genuine German ale and, like in Germany, people have to visit the brewery or nearby to drink it. Our beer contains a lot of yeast, minerals and vitamins, meaning they have a short shelf life and don't travel well. Bigger breweries filter out the yeasts and the proteins and so the beer is longer lasting, but consequently much lighter.[57]

Braun's attention to his craft does indeed produce a product that abides by the Reinheitsgebot, but that law serves as a barrier to mass-production and nationwide sales. Moreover, Braun argues that beer's steady loss of market share to its beer-like cousins, *happoshu* and "third beer," shows that for most consumers, beer is merely a beverage for clearing the throat, and because the beer-like beverages taste similar to Japanese beer, customers naturally choose the cheaper option. Thus, despite the interest shown by Japan's leading brewers in the quality and purity of his craft, none of them could deliver a comparable product to their many consumers. Furthermore, even if it were possible, due to its higher cost and traditional taste it is very unlikely that many Japanese consumers would buy it. On this point, Braun noted, "Every year, Asahi Breweries sends staff here for research purposes and they often say they would like to do what we do, but couldn't get it to the customer in decent enough shape. Neither could I, and that's why I don't try. What's important for microbreweries is not to expand to other areas, but to brew decent beer that will lure more customers and improve understanding of what real ale is all about."[58] While Braun's craft may have been rendered something of an anachronism, over 170 additional beer makers are today producing craft beers throughout Japan, many of them in the same traditional manner. Their products are highly unlikely to ever begin to rival the leading domestic brands, but the individuality of their recipes highlights just how distinct the mainstream Japanese beer industry has become.

Conclusion:
Biiru no Nihonka – The "Japanization" of Beer

From the earliest domestic brews to the rapidly shifting market for beer-like beverages, Japan's beer industry has evolved significantly since the late nineteenth century. The country has now had its own unique beer culture for decades, which the traditional German brewmaster of Otaru Beer, Johannes Braun, recognizes as very different from his own. The beer industry offers us a remarkably detailed example of the way in which new technologies and products, initially seen as foreign and exotic, gradually make themselves at home in Japan. Although disposed in 1870 to view Western material goods as strange, Japanese consumers proved to be incredibly receptive, and they had adopted a wide array of imported items for everyday use and domestic production by 1930. Unlike pastries, confections, or soft drinks, however, beer proved difficult to produce with entirely domestic ingredients. Due also to the insistence of early German brewmasters on adhering rigidly to traditional recipes and manufacturing techniques, beer's identity as a foreign product endured for several decades.

Japan's surviving beer brewers also spent the first seven decades of their existence struggling to overcome significant financial, logistical, and systemic obstacles. Each time they cleared a major hurdle, such as when Japan's government agreed to begin taxing foreign imports in 1897, they faced another – a new production tax, in that instance. And the hurdles continued. The reduced foreign competition of the First World War era was followed by a significant domestic price war during the 1920s. The subsequent peace brokered through the establishment of a beer cartel in the 1930s was beset by continued underselling by "locust" shops. The final defeat of the undersellers in 1937 was followed almost immediately by Japan's plunge into war in China. And so on. Throughout much of their histories, even the largest and seemingly most powerful of Japan's beer brewers could hardly win for losing.

However, a remarkable thing happened on the way to achieving industrial self-sufficiency during the Second World War era: beer became a thoroughly domestic consumer product. Throughout this book I have argued that it was the trying experiences of total war, extensive government reorganization, foreign occupation, and economic recovery that transformed Japan's beer industry into the proud maker of a domestic Japanese product rather than a transplanted Western one. These pressures

- demanded the material and agricultural self-sufficiency necessary to brew beer during the Second World War, when importing European ingredients was impossible
- prompted a total and lasting reorganization of the industry by the wartime Ministry of Finance in order to secure access to the vital tax revenues that it generated
- suspended not only access to German technical advisers and equipment, but also any postwar incentive to advertise them as product strengths
- changed the taste of beer from a bitterer, heavily hopped brew to a lighter-tasting beverage that was much more popular with women and young people
- prompted Japanese and Okinawan consumers to identify domestically made beer as distinct from, rather than inferior to, Western recipes and imported brands
- encouraged Japan's brewers to advertise their product to consumers in manifold new ways that showcased Japanese vistas, celebrities, and indigenous cultural forms.

Some may ask whether, in the absence of these transformative pressures, this industry would still have evolved, eventually, into the maker of a domestic Japanese beverage, as beer has been viewed by consumers since 1950. The answer is unclear, especially given Kirin's lengthy and determined prewar effort to distinguish itself from its then giant rival, Dai Nippon, by promoting the authenticity of its flagship German brew, "Kirin Lager." In any event, the point is moot, for the historical record offers no evidence of transformative pressures that rivalled the influence of Japan's wartime bureaucrats and their urgent demands for secure tax revenues and manufacturing self-sufficiency. Furthermore, nothing short of Japan's defeat and its seven-year occupation by the Allied powers could have severed Japan's relationship with Germany so completely. The seven-year hiatus freed Japan's brewers from the influence of their German engineers and, no longer obsessed with showcasing the calibre of their European hops, they soon returned to modest profitability as the producers of a domestic Japanese beverage. In the meantime, contract farming resumed and domestic production of barley and hops rose, and sales increased steadily through the 1950s.

In 2002, anthropologist Stephen R. Smith asserted that, along with the postwar Westernization of Japanese drinking customs and preferences, "one could argue that the Japanese have domesticated the alcoholic beverages they have imported and borrowed from the West."[1] With respect to beer, his assertion is absolutely correct. By the 1950s, Japan's beer industry was brewing lighter recipes for a wider, younger, and increasingly female consumer marketplace that no longer cared for heavier European lagers or dark ales. Men, women, and young people soon grew accustomed to drinking lighter-tasting beers with their colleagues at halls and cabarets, and home consumption likewise increased as postwar living standards improved. Through the 1960s and 1970s, Japan's leading brewers, Kirin, Sapporo, Asahi, and Suntory, settled into a comfortable, managed pattern of modest annual price rises, steady factory expansion, and constant domestic demand for their products. Instead of showcasing their loyalty to foreign recipes or brewing laws, the brewers were free to focus on cultivating loyalty to their brands, and beer consumers responded positively. Japanese tastes had changed substantially, and in a postwar era marked by swift economic recovery and rising beer sales, the brewers no longer had any reason to remind their customers of beer's prewar flavours, recipes, or fastidious German processes. By the 1970s, few people cared that beer was once an imported or exotic foreign beverage, and beer marketing seldom even focused on the product at all. Instead, it focused on beer's consumers, who were Japanese and Okinawan. Naturally, like consumers everywhere, they wished to look into the mirror of beer advertising and see themselves.

No.	Brand	Enterprise head	Location	Company type	Initial capitalization (¥ unless specified)	Brewmaster	Founding	Initial sale	Final sale	Reason for closure	Initial annual production (koku)	Notes
1	Amanuma Beer	William Copeland & Emil Wiegand	Yokohama	Unlimited partnership (later sole proprietor)	Unclear	William Copeland	1869~70	1869~70	1885	Bankruptcy, factory disposal sale, acquired by Japan Brewery	Unclear	Became individually managed under Copeland in roughly 1880
2	Mitsuuroko (Three Scales) Beer	Noguchi Masaaki	Kōfu	Sole proprietor	40,000	Murata Kichigorō & Yokoyama Sukejirō	1872	1874	1881	Unbalanced books	200	Transferred to Noguchi Masaaki
	Mitsuuroko Beer	Noguchi Masaaki	Kōfu	Sole proprietor	Unclear	Yokoyama Sukejirō	1881	1881	1901	Enforcement of the new Beer Tax	Unclear	
3	Shibutani Beer	Shibutani Shōzaburō	Osaka	Sole proprietor	Unclear	Furst & Kanazawa Kazō	1872	1872	1881	Unbalanced books, death of Shōzaburō	250	
4	Sapporo Beer	Kaitakushi (Hokkaido Colonization Office)	Sapporo	Government-managed	15,000	Nakagawa Seibei	1876	1877	1886	Sold to the Ōkura Group	100~300	
5	Sakurada (Cherry Field) Beer	Kanazawa Mitsuemon et al.	Tokyo	Joint-stock	20,000	Unclear	1877	1877	1883	Reorganized as Tokyo Beer	2,500	

No.	Brand	Enterprise head	Location	Company type	Initial capitalization (¥ unless specified)	Brewmaster	Founding	Initial sale	Final sale	Reason for closure	Initial annual production (koku)	Notes
6	Tegata (Draft) Beer	Miyauchi Fukumitsu	Tokyo	Sole proprietor	Unclear	Yokoyama Sukejirō	1881	1881	1888	Factory disposal sale to Teikoku Beer	2,000	
7	Naniwa (former name for Osaka) Beer	Araki	Osaka	Sole proprietor	Unclear	Kanazawa Kazō	1881	1881	1882			
8	Urokoin (Scale marque) Pale Ale	Hashimoto Seizaburō	Osaka	Sole proprietor	Unclear	Kanazawa Kazō	1882	1882	Unclear		Unclear	
9	Yebisu Beer	Shibatani Yoshisaburō & Ōmura Sukejirō	Osaka	Sole proprietor	Unclear	Kanazawa Kazō	1884	1884	1891		Unclear	
10	Asahi (Morning Sun) Beer	Konishi Gisuke	Osaka	Sole proprietor	20,000	Kanazawa Kazō	1884	1884	1888		Unclear	

11	Mitsuboshi (Three Stars) Beer	Morita Kyūzaemon	Aichi	Sole proprietor	Unclear	Staff from Sakurada Beer	Unclear	1884	1885	Unclear	
12	Handa Beer	Takemoto	Aichi (Handa)	Sole proprietor	Unclear	Staff from Sakurada Beer	Unclear	1884	1885	Unclear	Perhaps left the industry due to rising beer taxes
13	Washi (Eagle) Beer	Unclear	Aichi (Washidzuka)	Sole proprietor	Unclear	Staff from Sakurada Beer	Unclear	1884	1885	Unclear	
14	Asada Beer	Asada Jin'emon	Tokyo	Sole proprietor	Unclear	Murata Kichigorō & Kubota Hatsutarō	1884	1885	1912	700 — Could not fulfill the production restriction of 1,000 koku	Purchased Copeland's equipment; Copeland's apprentice, Murata, went to work for Kubota
15	Kirin Beer	Japan Brewery	Yokohama	Limited liability company	HK$50,000	Hermann Heckert	1885	1888	1906	1,890 — Succeeded to Kirin Beer Co.	
16	Ōkura Beer	Ōkura Kuratarō	Tokyo	Sole proprietor	Unclear	Yokoyama Sukejirō	1885	1885	1888	150	
17	Sapporo Beer	Ōkura Group	Sapporo	Sole proprietor	26,672	Nakagawa Seibei	1886	1887	1888	Unclear — Sold to Sapporo Breweries	

No.	Brand	Enterprise head	Location	Company type	Initial capitalization (¥ unless specified)	Brewmaster	Founding	Initial sale	Final sale	Reason for closure	Initial annual production (koku)	Notes
18	Yebisu Beer	Nippon Beer Co., Inc.	Tokyo	Limited liability company	150,000	Katsura Jirō	1887	1890	1906	Merged to form Dai Nippon biiru	1,750	Reorganized as an incorporated company in 1903
19	Asahi Beer	Osaka Beer Co., Inc.	Osaka	Incorporated company	150,000	Ikuta Hide and Max Pormann	1889	1892	1906	Merged to form Dai Nippon biiru	1,000	
20	Marusan Beer	Morita	Aichi	Sole proprietor	Unclear	Nameki	1887	1888	1896	Reorganized as Marusan Beer Co., Inc.	100	
21	Sapporo Beer	Sapporo Beer Co., Inc.	Sapporo	Incorporated company	70,000	Nakagawa Seibei	1888	1888	1906	Merged to form Dai Nippon biiru	700	Nippon biiru
22	Daikoku (Big Black) Beer	Daikoku Sha (Andō Sotō)	Tokyo	Joint-stock	Unclear	Kubota Hatsutarō	1892	1895	1898		600	Refilled Sakura Beer bottles at the outset
23	Teikoku (Imperial) Beer (Kaiser Beer)	Teikoku Beer Co., Inc.	Osaka	Incorporated company	50,000	Yokoyama Sukejirō	1889	1889	1891	Broken up	Unclear	Purchased and moved into the Tegata Beer plant

24	Tokyo Beer	Tokyo Beer Co., Inc.	Kanagawa	Incorporated company	200,000 (in 1898)	unclear	1893	1898	1907	Disposal sale to Dai Nippon biiru		Descended from Sakurada Beer
25	Kabuto Beer	Marusan Beer Co., Inc.	Aichi	Incorporated company	600,000	Von Gore?	1896	1898	1922	Merged with Dai Nippon biiru	Unclear	Changed its name from Marusan Beer to Nippon Dai-ichi (Japan #1) Beer in 1906, and to Kabuto Beer in 1908
26	Sakura (Cherry) Beer	Teikoku Beer Co., Inc.	Moji	Incorporated company	2 million		1912	1913	1943	Merged with Dai Nippon biiru	15,000	
27	Cascade Beer	Japan-English Brewing Co., Inc.	Tsurumi	Incorporated company	2 million		1919	1920	1928	Sold to Kotobuki-ya Co., Inc.	Unclear	
28	Fuji Beer	Orient Brewing Company Co., Inc.	Sendai	Incorporated company	2 million	Streichel	1919	1921	1923	Merged with Kirin Brewery		

No.	Brand	Enterprise head	Location	Company type	Initial capitalization (¥ unless specified)	Brewmaster	Founding	Initial sale	Final sale	Reason for closure	Initial annual production (koku)	Notes
29	Takasago Beer	Takasago	Taihoku (Taipei, Taiwan)	Incorporated company	2 million		1919	1920	1945	Requisitioned by the Allies at war's end	2,500	
30	Union Beer	Japan Beer Springs Co., Inc.	Aichi	Incorporated company	9 million		1922	1922	1933	Merged with Dai Nippon biiru	38,373	
31	New Cascade Beer, and Oraga Beer	Kotobuki-ya	Tsurumi	Incorporated company	Unclear		1928	1929	1943	Closed due to enterprise equipment measures, bought out by Dai Nippon	18,275	Began selling Oraga Beer in 1930; renamed Tokyo Beer Co., Inc, in 1934
32	Yebisu Beer, Sapporo Beer, Asahi Beer	Dai Nippon Beer Co., Inc.	Tokyo	Incorporated company	5 million		1906	1906	1949	Divided amidst the enterprise reconstruction equipment plan		Formed by 1906 merger of Nippon Beer, Sapporo Beer, and Osaka Beer
33	Kirin Beer	Kirin Brewery Co., Ltd.	Yokohama	Incorporated company	2.5 million		1907	1907	Continuing			

34	Nippon Beer	Nippon Beer Co., Inc.	Tokyo	Incorporated company	100 million	1949	1949	Continuing	Formed out of Dai Nippon biiru in 1949; changed name to Sapporo in 1964
35	Asahi Beer	Asahi Breweries Co., Ltd.	Tokyo	Incorporated company	100 million	1949	1949	Continuing	Formed out of Dai Nippon biiru

Data available for Meiji-era (1868-1912) companies listed below is more limited than data for those listed above

No.	Brand	Enterprise head	Location	Notes
36	Hosaka Beer	Hosaka Norikazu	Yokohama	Sales began in 1875
37	Yokohama Beer	Shibatani Tomesaburō	Honmoku, Yokohama	Another version of Ryūgorō
38	Daikoku (Big Black) Beer	Shibatani Ryūkichi	Maedabashi dōri, Yokohama	Another version was on Makitabashi dōri, roughly 1892-92; various other companies' products named Daikoku were sold; in 1892 the trademark was sold to Daikoku-sha.
39	Kōki (Brilliant) Beer	Unclear	Yokohama	
40	Nakatani Beer	Unclear	Honmoku, Yokohama	
41	Tēburu (Table) Beer	Isogai Zenbei	Yushima, Tokyo	Began selling Lion Beer in roughly 1877; was still in existence in 1887
42	Fuki Beer	Fūki Beer Co., Inc.	Shinagawa, Tokyo	Began selling beer in roughly 1877
43	Nisshin Beer	Hata Kichigorō	Yodobashi, Tokyo	Began selling beer in roughly 1877
44	Araganema Beer	Unclear	Shinbashi, Tokyo	Began selling beer in roughly 1877

No.	Brand	Enterprise head	Location	Notes
45	Koishikawa Beer	Unclear	Koishikawa, Tokyo	Began selling beer in roughly 1877
46	Janome (bullseye) Beer	Unclear	Kyōbashi, Tokyo	Began selling beer in roughly 1877
47	Katō Beer	Katō Group	Tokyo	
48	Daruma (Dharma Doll) Beer	Daruma Beer Brewing	Tokyo	
49	Mitsubishi Beer	Mitsubishi Brewing	Tokyo	
50	Hinomaru Beer	Unclear	Tokyo	
51	Miyako Beer	Sold by a shop named Fuba shōten	Sudachō, Tokyo	
52	Nishiki Beer	Nishikiori	Motomachi, Tokyo	Different from Nishiki Beer brewed by Osaka Beer in 1893
53	Asahi Beer	Sold by a shop named Ōkura shōten	Tokyo	
54	Arauma (Wild Horse) Beer	Sold by a shop named Hirano shōten	Nihonbashi, Tokyo	
55	Hotei (One of the Seven Gods of Good Luck) Beer		Tokyo jōzōshō	Tokyo
56	Kinkei (Golden Cock) Beer			
57	Kōyō (Maple/Autumn Leaves) Beer	Sold first by Hibino	Tokyo	
58	Mori Beer	Samejima Moriyoshi Brewery	Tokyo	
59	Tonbo (Dragonfly) Beer	Tonbo Beer Brewery	Nippori, Tokyo	
60	Sakura (Cherry) Beer	Kondō Brewery	Tokyo	
61	Sanegawa Beer	Hōryū Co.	Hongō, Tokyo	
62	Ajima Beer	Higashi Co.	Yotsuya, Tokyo	
63	Nippon (Japan) Beer	Ishigawa Brewery	Nishida Magōri Kumagawa	

No.	Name	Maker/Seller	Location	Notes
64	Maruko Beer	Maruko Co.	Musashi	
65	Tōyō Beer	Tōyō	Nippori, Tokyo	
66	Kujaku (Peacock) Beer	Tenma Brewery	Osaka	
67	Osaka Beer	Hashimoto Brewery	Osaka	Named for Hashimoto Seizaburō (see #8)
68	Raion (Lion) Beer	Lion Beer Brewery	Osaka	
69	Yamana Beer	G. Yamana	Osaka	
70	Kujaku (Peacock) Beer	Ōhashi	Osaka	
71	Namihana Beer	Unclear	Osaka	
72	Kokku (Cock) Beer	Unclear	Osaka	
73	Kiku (Chrysanthemum) Beer	Unclear	Kawaguchi, Osaka	
74	Senzai (Millennium) Beer	S. Yokoyama	Osaka	Perhaps a product of Yokoyama Sukejirō (see #2, 6, 16, 23)
75	Aoi (Hollyhock) Beer	Sold by a shop named Oda shōten	Osaka	
76	Meiji Beer	Unclear	Tenma, Osaka	
77	Tōyō Beer	Sold by a shop named Esuena shōten	Osaka	
78	Fuji Beer	Yajima	Osaka	
79	Kikumi Beer	Sold by a shop named Minami shōten	Kawauchi	
80	Kokonoe (Imperial Court) Beer	Isohata Brewery	Kyoto	
81	Lager Beer	Unclear	Kyoto	
82	Kokonoe (Imperial Court) Beer	Ōda Genzō	Kyoto	
83	Itō Beer	S. Itō	Kiya-machi, Kyoto	
84	Hinomaru Beer	Unclear	Kyoto	
85	Kimaru Beer	Kimaru Co.	Nada, Settsu	
86	Nunobiki Beer	Nunobiki Co.	Nada, Settsu	
87	Kitsune Beer	Ōmi (Ōgai?)	Hyōgo, Settsu	

No.	Brand	Enterprise head	Location	Notes
88	Yotsume (Four Eyes/Squares) Beer	Shikata Jōkichi & Shimobe Heizō	Kobe	
89	Gunkan (Battleship) Beer	Ikeda Isaburō	Wakayama prefecture	
90	Bokku (Bock) Beer	Hakodate Beer Brewery	Hakodate	
91	Hakodate Beer	Watanabe Kumashirō	Hakodate	
92	Shachihoko (Mythical Lion-headed Fish) Beer	Unclear	Aichi prefecture	
93	Shiroyama (White Mountain) Beer	Makino	Kanazawa	
94	Fuji Beer	Hokuriku Beer Brewery	Niigata	
95	Kiraku Beer	Shinyo Beer Co., Inc.	Nagano	
96	Shinano Beer	Yamakishi Chōjirō	Nagano	
97	Yamato Beer	Orii/Orei Eitarō	Nagano	
98	Sakura (Cherry) Beer	Nakamura Kanpei	Nagano	
99	Uebishi? Beer	Sekiguchi Hachibē	Hatosaki, Ibaraki	
100	Noda Beer	Maru Maru & Co.	Chiba	
101	Chikari Beer	Haga Yūsuke	Yamagata	Also brewed Sakura Beer
102	Tsuruoka Beer	Saitō Shichirō	Yamagata	
103	Yamato Beer	Uno	Toyokunimura, Shiga	
104	Kamito? Beer	Nishida	Yamada, Ise	
105	Chikiri Beer	Banshima	Gifu	
106	Ryū Beer	Kuno	Nagato	
107	Tengu (Goblin) Beer	Unclear	Hiroshima	
108	Nippon (Japan) Beer	Unclear	Hiroshima	
109	Iroho Beer	Nanamori Yasubē	Fukuyama City	

110	Himematsu Beer	Tomita, Himematsu shōten	Ehime prefecture	
111	Yotsuboshi (Four Stars) Beer	Miyauchi, Yotsuboshi-kan	Uchiwajima	
112	Fuku Beer	Fuku Group Brewing	Tokushima prefecture	
113	Honda Beer	Honda	Nagasaki	
114	Lager-Beer	Nakatomi Brewing	Unclear	
115	Kame (Turtle) Beer	Shimabara	Unclear	
116	Yūshutsu (Export) Beer	South Seas?	Unclear	
117	Yamaguchi Beer	Yamaguchi shōten	Unclear	
118	Noda Beer	Noda shōten	Unclear	
119	Tōkai Beer	Tōkai Beer Brewery	Unclear	
120	Kanamizu Beer	Kanamizu Co.	Unclear	
121	Katō Beer	Kato Group	Unclear	
122	Botan Beer	Nakatomi	Unclear	
123	Tama Beer	Tamajima	Unclear	
124	Unclear	Kyoto Chemistry Department	Kyoto	Established in 1877, engineer named Wagner

Source: Kirin biiru KK, *Kirin biiru KK gojū nenshi* [Kirin Brewery Company, Ltd.: Fifty-year history] (Tokyo: Kirin biiru KK, 20 March 1957), 244-47.

Glossary

Units of Measure

1 gō (合) = 0.18 litres

1 kan (貫) = 3.75 kilograms

1 kin (斤) = 600 grams

1 koku (石)= 180.39 litres

1 shō (升) = 1.8 litres

1 tsubo (坪) = 3.306 square metres

Historical Eras

Edo, 1603-1867, named for the capital city of Edo, modern-day Tokyo; also known as
the Tokugawa era for the Tokugawa family of shoguns

Meiji, 1868-1912, named for the reign of the Meiji emperor, Mutsuhito (1852-1912)

Taishō, 1912-26, named for the reign of the Taishō emperor, Yoshihito (1879-1926)

Shōwa, 1926-89, named for the reign of the Shōwa emperor, Hirohito (1901-89)

Heisei, 1989-present, named for the reign of the Heisei emperor, Akihito (b. 1933)

Major Japanese Brewing Companies and Affiliated Firms

Anglo-German Beer Co., Inc. (Ei-Doku bakushu kabushiki kaisha [KK])

Asahi Breweries, Ltd. [Morning Sun Breweries, Ltd.] (Asahi biiru KK)

Asia Beer Co., Inc. (Ajia bakushu KK)

Chōsen Beer Co., Inc. (Chōsen bakushu KK). Subsidiary of Dai Nippon Beer

Dai Nippon Beer Co., Inc. [Greater Japan Beer Co., Inc.] (Dai Nippon bakushu KK)

Harbin Beer

Japan Beer Springs Co., Inc. (Nippon bakushu kōsen KK)

Japan Brewery Co., Ltd.

The Japan Brewery Co., Inc.

Japan-English Brewing Co., Inc. (Nichi-Ei jōzō KK)

Kabuto Beer Co., Inc. [Helmet Beer Co., Inc.] (Kabuto bakushu KK)

Kirin Brewery Co., Ltd. (Kirin biiru KK)

Kotobuki-ya Beer Co., Inc. (Kotobuki-ya bakushu KK)

Manchuria Beer Co., Inc. (Manshu bakushu KK). Owned by Dai Nippon and Kirin

Marusan Beer Brewery Co., Inc. (Marusan bakushu KK)

Mitsubishi Corporation (Mitsubishi KK)

Mitsui Trading Co. (Mitsui bussan kaisha)

Nippon Beer Co., Inc. [Japan Beer Co., Inc.] (Nippon bakushu KK)

Ocean Brewing Co. (Taiyō shōzō KK)

Okinawa Beer Co., Inc. (Okinawa Beer KK)

Ōkura Group (Ōkura gumi), later Ōkura Trading Co. (Ōkura shōji KK)

Orient Brewing Co., Inc. (Tōyō shōzō KK)

Orion Breweries, Ltd. (Orion biiru KK)

Osaka Beer Co., Inc. (Osaka bakushu KK)

Peking Beer Co., Inc. (Pekin bakushu KK)

Sakura Beer Co., Inc. [Cherry Beer Co., Inc.] (Sakura bakushu KK)

Sapporo Breweries, Ltd. (Sapporo biiru KK)

Shōwa Kirin Beer Co., Inc. (Shōwa Kirin bakushu KK)

Spring Valley Brewery (Izumi no tani)

Suntory Holdings, Ltd. (Santori hōrudingusu KK)

Takara Brewing Co., Inc. [Treasure Brewing Co., Inc.] (Takara shuzō KK)

Takasuna Beer Co., Inc. (Takasuna bakushu KK)

Teikoku Beer Co., Inc. [Imperial Beer Co., Inc.] (Teikoku bakushu KK)

Tokyo Beer Co., Inc. (Tōkyō bakushu KK)

Beer Research, Supply, and Distribution Companies

Alcohol Distribution Public Corporation (Shurui haikyū kōdan)

Beer Distribution Control Co., Inc. (Bakushu haikyū tōsei KK)

Central Beer Sales Co., Inc. (Chūō bakushu hanbai KK)

Cooperative Beer Sales Co., Inc. (Bakushu kyōdō hanbai KK)

Japan Beer Ingredients Co., Inc. (Nihon bakushu genryō KK)

Japan Malts Manufacturing Co., Inc. (Nippon bakuga kōgyō KK)

Orion Beer Distributing Co., Inc. (Orion biiru hanbai KK)

Sakura Beer Sales Co., Inc. (Sakura bakushu hanbai KK)

Brewing-Related Associations, Federations, Leagues, and Organizations

All Japan Agricultural Business Association (Zen Nihon nōgyō keizai kai)

All Japan Beer Industry Labour Union Association (Zen Nihon bakushu sangyō rōdō kumiai rengōkai)

Beer Discussion Group (Biiru konwakai)

Incorporated Beer Association (Shadan hōjin bakushu konwakai)

Japan Beer Association (Nihon bakushu kyōkai)

Japan Beer Brewers Association (Nihon bakushu shuzō kumiai)

Japan Beer Ingredients Association (Nihon bakushu genryō kyōkai)

Japan Craft Brewing Association (JCBA)

Kantō Brewing Company League (Kantō no ichi fu jūku shōzōya rengōkai)

Kirin Beer Labour Union (Kirin biiru rōdō kumiai)

Orion Beer Federation (Orion biiru rengōkai)

Retail Sales Association (Kōri shubai kumiai)

Tokyo Alcoholic Beverage Sales Association (Tōkyō shuruisho kumiai)

Tokyo Alcoholic Beverage Wholesalers League (Tōkyō yōshu kessai renmeikai)

Tokyo Beer Cooperative Association (Tōkyō bakushu kyōchōkai)

Laws and Taxes

1873 Alcohol Tax Law. *Shuzeihō*

1893 Commercial Code. *Shō hō* (first drafted in 1890, enacted in 1893)

1899 Corporate Law (also known as the Company Law). *Kaisha hō*

1901 Alcohol Manufacturing Tax Law. *Shūzō zeihō*

- Alcohol and Alcohol Beverage Container Law. *Shūsei oyobi shūsei ganyū inryō zeihō*

- Beer Tax Law. *Bakushu zeihō*

- Yeast Mash, Main Fermenting Mash, and Malt Director Law. *Shūbo moromi oyobi kiku torishimari hō*

1904 Special Tax. *Tokubetsu zei*

1905 Special Emergency Tax. *Tokubetsu hijō zei*

1920 Road Law. *Dōro hō*

1937 Temporary Tax Increase Notification Law. *Rinji sozeizō chō hō*

- Import and Export Quality Temporary Measures Law. *Yushutsunyū hintō rinji sochi hō*

- Temporary Funds Adjustment Law. *Rinji shikin chōsei hō*

- Munitions Industry Mobilization Law. *Gunju kōgyō dōin hō*

- North China Incident Tax. *Hokushi jiken tokubetsu zei*

1938 National General Mobilization Law. *Kokka sōdōin hō*

- China Incident Special Tax Law. *Shina jihen tokubetsu zei hō*

1939 National General Mobilization Law. *Kokka sōdōin hō*, known as 9-18 Price Freeze Order (9-18 *bukka teishirei*)

1940 Alcohol Tax Law. *Shūzei hō*

- Storage and Shipping Tax. *Kura dashi zei*

1942 Food Provisions Control Law. *Shakuryō kanri hō*

1943 Alcoholic Beverages Industry Group Control Law. *Shuri gyō dantai hō*, known as the Alcohol Group Law *(Shudan hō)*

1945 Antitrust Law. *Dokusen kinshi hō*

1946 Special Materials Supply and Demand Regulation Law. *Rinji busshi jūkyū chōsei hō*

- Company Accounting Special Measures Law. *Kaisha keiri ōkyū sochi hō*

- Wartime Reparations Special Measures Law. *Senji hoshō tokubetsu sochi hō*
- Wartime Reparations Special Tax. *Senji hoshō tokubetsu zei*
1947 Alcohol Distribution Public Corporation Law. *Shurui haikyū kōdan hō*
- Law for the Elimination of Excessive Concentration of Economic Power. *Dokusen kinshi hō,* known commonly as the Anti-Monopoly Law
1948 Alcohol Consumption Tax. *Shu shōhi zei*
1949 Free Sales Added Tax. *Jiyū hanbai kasan zei*
1951 Weights and Measures Law. *Keiryō hō* (Took effect 1 March 1952)
1956 Full Capitalization Law. *Shihon jūjitsu hō*

Government Ministries and Agencies

Economic Development Section [USCAR]. *Keizai kaihatsu bu*
Food Distribution Public Corporation. *Shokuryō haikyū kōdan*
Hokkaido Colonization Office. *Kaitakushi*
Holding Company Liquidation Commission. *Mochikabu kaisha seiri iinkai*
Home Office. *Naimukyō*
Imperial Household Ministry. *Kunaishō*
Japan Fair Trade Commission. *Nihon kōsei torihiki iinkai*
Ministry of Agriculture and Commerce. *Nōshōmushō*
Ministry of Agriculture and Forestry. *Nōrinshō*
Ministry of Commerce and Industry (MCI). *Shōkōshō*
Ministry of Finance. *Ōkurashō*
Ministry of Justice. *Shihōshō*
National Tax Office. *Koku zeichō*
Ryūkyū Government Economic Bureau. *Ryūkyū seifu keizai kyoku*
Ryūkyū Transportation Engineering Bureau. *Ryūkyū kōmu kōtsūkyoku*

Notes

Introduction

1 For a discussion of beer's early origins and its gradual adoption by various world cultures, especially those in Europe, see Haruyama Yukio, *Biiru bunka shi* [The history of beer culture] (Tokyo: Tōkyō shobōsha, 1972).

2 For excellent Japanese-language sources on the science of brewing and the chemistry of yeast fermentation, known as "zymurgy," see Matsuyama Mosuke, *Biiru wisuki* [Beer, Whisky] (Tokyo: Kyōwa seihon KK, 1951); and Matsuyama Mosuke, *Biiru jōzōgaku* [Beer zymurgy] (Tokyo: Tōyō keizai shimpō-sha, 1970).

3 See especially Murakami Mitsuru, *Biiru denrai: Mori Ōgami to doitsu biiru* [Imported beer: Mori Ōgami and German beer] (Tokyo: Sogensha, 2006).

4 For a comprehensive, annotated bibliography of English-language works on the development of Japan's automobile industry, see Sheau-Yueh J. Chao, *The Japanese Automobile Industry: An Annotated Bibliography* (Westport, CT: Greenwood Press, 1994).

5 See Harald Fuess, "Investment, Importation, and Innovation: Genesis and Growth of Beer Corporations in Pre-war Japan," in *Institutional and Technological Change in Japan's Economy: Past and Present,* ed. Janet Hunter and Cornelia Storz (London: Routledge, 2006), 43-59; Penelope Francks, "Inconspicuous Consumption: Sake, Beer, and the Birth of the Consumer in Japan," *Journal of Asian Studies* 68, 1 (February 2009): 135-64; passages in Chapters 4 and 5 of Penelope Francks, *The Japanese Consumer: An Alternative Economic History of Modern Japan* (Cambridge: Cambridge University Press, 2009); and Stephen R. Smith, "Drinking Etiquette in a Changing Beverage Market," in *Re-Made in Japan: Everyday Life and Consumer Taste in a Changing Society,* ed. Joseph J. Tobin (New Haven, CT: Yale University Press, 1992), 143-59. Beyond these works, there is a lengthy but unpublished doctoral dissertation that sheds light on the theme of entrepreneurship in Japan's prewar beer industry, but it focuses largely on individual brewers and their many start-ups and relationships. Its introduction is also heavily influenced by postwar Marxist scholarship, which steers the author's approach toward the themes of protocapitalism and entrepreneurial incentive. See Joseph Alphonse Laker, "Entrepreneurship and the Development of the Japanese Beer Industry, 1872-1937" (PhD diss., Indiana University, 1975).

6 Kōno Shōzō, *Bijinesu no seisei: Seiryō inryō no Nihonka* [Business creation: The Japanization of cool beverages] (Tokyo: Bunshindō, 2002).

7 Industry histories include Miyake Yūzō, *Biiru kigyō shi* [A history of the beer industry] (Tokyo: Mitakisha, 1977); Inagaki Masami, *Nihon no biiru* [Japanese beer] (Tokyo: Chūō kōronsha, 1978); Kirin biiru KK, ed., *Biiru to Nihonjin: Meiji/Taishō/Shōwa fukyūshi* [Beer and the Japanese: A broad Meiji/Taishō/Shōwa history] (Tokyo: Sanseidō, 1984); Endo Kazuō, *Nihon no gijutsu, 10: Biiru no 100 nen* [Historical technology in Japan, vol. 10: 100 years of beer] (Tokyo: Daiichi hōki shuppansha, 1989); Kaidō Mamoru, *Yōshū, biiru* [Western liquor, beer] (Tokyo: Jitsumu kyōiku shuppansha, 1989); Naitō Hiroshi, "Meijiki biiru gyōkai ni okeru gaikokujin gijutsusha no keifu: Yebisu biiru no baii ni" [The geneaology of

foreign engineers in the Meiji-era Japanese beer industry: The case of Yebisu Beer], *Keiei shigaku* [Japan business history review] 29, 4 (January 1995): 58-75; and Tanji Yuichi, "Dai Nippon bakushu no keiei to hanbaimo, 1906-1939" [The marketing policy of Dai Nippon Brewery Co., 1906-1939], *Shakai keizai shigaku* [Socioeconomic history] 67, 3 (January 2001): 3-26. Memoirs include Nakajō Takanori, *Risshi no keiei: Asahi biiru fukkatsu no genten to waga bijinesu jinsei* [Management success: The starting point of Asahi Breweries' comeback and my business life] (Tokyo: Chichi shuppansha KK, 1993); Nishimura Akira, *Asahi biiru no keiei senryaku* [Asahi Breweries' management strategy] (Tokyo: Tachibana shuppansha KK, 1999); Nakajō Takanori, *Asahi biiru kishi kaisei no keiei senryaku to jinsei tetsugaku* [The management strategies and the philosophy of life behind the revival of Asahi Breweries], Heihō ni manabu: Katsu tame ni nasubeki koto [Lessons in the art of war: What must be done in order to win] (Tokyo: Keizaikai KK, 2002); Miyamoto Kotarō, *Asahi biiru seikōsuru kigyō fūdo: Uchigawa kara mita fukkatsu no hosoku* [Asahi Breweries' successful corporate culture: An inside view of its comeback principles] (Tokyo: Shodensha KK, 2002); Matsui Yasuo, *Takaga biiru saredo biiru: Asahi sūpā dorai 18 nenme no shinbi* [It's only beer, but it's beer all the same: Asahi Super Dry's eighteenth beautiful year] (Tokyo: Nikkan kōgyō shimbun-sha KK, 2005); and Inokuchi Osami, *Kirin no ryūgi: Kane ni tayoru na, jibun ni tayore!* [The Kirin way: Don't rely on money, rely on yourself!] (Tokyo: Puresidento-sha KK, 2007).

8 The key *shashi* (company histories) used in this study are Kirin biiru KK, *Kirin biiru KK gojū nenshi* [Kirin Brewery Company, Ltd.: Fifty-year history] (Tokyo: Kirin biiru KK, 20 March 1957); Orion biiru KK, *Jūnen no ayumi: Orion biiru KK* [Ten-year history of Orion Breweries] (Naha: Orion biiru KK, 18 May 1967); Orion biiru KK, *Orion yonjūnen no ayumi* [Forty-year history of Orion Breweries] (Naha: Orion biiru KK, 28 July 1998); Sapporo biiru KK, *Sapporo 120 nenshi* [120-year history of Sapporo Breweries] (Tokyo: Sapporo biiru KK, 1996); Suntory KK, *Hibi ni arata ni: Santori hyakunenshi* [Fresh every day: 100-year history of Suntory] (Osaka: Suntory KK, 1999); and Asahi biiru KK, *Asahi 100* (Tokyo: Asahi biiru KK, 1990).

Chapter 1: Foreign Influences

1 See especially the introduction and Chapters 1 and 2 of Miyake Yūzō, *Biiru kigyō shi* [A history of the beer industry] (Tokyo: Mitakisha, 1977), 28-63.

2 When Osaka's "Naniwa Beer" went on sale in 1882, it was advertised by Western liquor wholesalers throughout the Kansai region. See *Asahi Shimbun* [Asahi newspaper, Osaka], 4 July 1883, 4. (Note that the newspaper was not related to the Osaka Beer Company, which brewed "Asahi Beer.")

3 Kirin biiru KK, *Kirin biiru KK gojū nenshi* [Kirin Brewery Company, Ltd.: Fifty-year history] (Tokyo: Kirin biiru KK, 20 March 1957), 1.

4 Kirin biiru KK, ed., *Biiru to Nihonjin: Meiji/Taishō/Shōwa fukyūshi* [Beer and the Japanese: A broad Meiji/Taishō/Shōwa history] (Tokyo: Sanseidō, 1984), 40-41.

5 Ueda Toshirō, *Biiru tengoku* [Beer heaven] (Tokyo: Bokusho, 1963), 47.

6 Takebe Seian and Sugita Genpaku, *Oranda iji mondō* [Questions and answers on Holland], first published 1795, quoted in Kirin biiru, *Kirin biiru gojū nenshi*, 2.

7 Umesao Tadao, Yoshida Shūji, and Paul Gordon Schalow, *Alcoholic Beverages*, Japanese Civilization in the Modern World, vol. 18 (Osaka: National Museum of Ethnology, 2003), 55.

8 Millard Fillmore, President of the United States of America, to His Imperial Majesty, the Emperor of Japan, 13 November 1852, in Francis L. Hawks, compiler, *Narrative of the Expedition of an American Squadron to China and Japan, Performed in the Years 1852, 1853, and 1854, under the Command of Commodore M.C. Perry United States Navy, by Order of the Government of the United States*, vol. 1. (Washington, DC: A.O.P. Nicholson, 1856), 256-59.

9   Kirin biiru, *Kirin biiru gojū nenshi,* 4.

10 Fukuzawa Yukichi, *Seiyō jijō* [Conditions in the West], first published 1867, quoted in Kirin biiru, *Kirin biiru gojū nenshi,* 5.

11 Kirin biiru, *Kirin biiru gojū nenshi,* 4-6.

12 The overwhelming dominance of German brewing techniques and German brewmasters, which quickly eclipsed English beer imports, is explored in depth in Chapter 4 of Miyake, *Biiru kigyō shi,* 159-75.

13 See Edward E. Pratt, *Japan's Proto-Industrial Elite: The Economic Foundations of the Gōnō* (Cambridge, MA: Harvard University Press, 1999).

14 Ibid., 176.

15 See especially Chapter 3 in Joseph Alphonse Laker, "Entrepreneurship and the Development of the Japanese Beer Industry, 1872-1937" (PhD diss., Indiana University, 1975).

16 See Chapters 1-4 of Jeffrey W. Alexander, *Japan's Motorcycle Wars: An Industry History* (Vancouver: UBC Press, 2008).

17 See Chapter 4 of Miyake, *Biiru kigyō shi,* 85-101; and Kirin biiru, *Kirin biiru gojū nenshi,* 6.

18 *Japan Weekly Mail: A Review of Japanese Commerce, Politics, Literature, and Art* (Yokohama), 15 February 1902, 185.

19 Kayama Michinosuke and Hotta Shōzō, *Yokohama-shi shi kō* [The written history of Yokohama City], 11 vols. (Yokohama: Yokohama City, 1931-33), cited in Kirin biiru, *Kirin biiru gojū nenshi,* 17.

20 Kayama and Hotta, *Yokohama-shi shi kō,* cited in Kirin biiru, *Kirin biiru gojū nenshi,* 8, 13; Kirin biiru, *Biiru to Nihonjin,* 59, 65.

21 Kirin biiru, *Kirin biiru gojū nenshi,* 14-15.

22 Satō Kenji, *Nihon no biiru seisuishi* [The rise and fall of Japanese beers] (Tokyo: Tokyo shobōsha, 1985), 30.

23 Quoted in Kirin biiru, *Kirin biiru gojū nenshi,* 11.

24 Quoted ibid., 7.

25 For further details on Copeland's second wife, her family, their time in Guatemala, and images of several of Copeland's handwritten letters, see Kirin biiru KK, *Biiru to bunmei kaika no Yokohama: Kōpurando seitan 150-nen kinen* [Beer and Yokohama's civilization and enlightenment: Commemorating 150 years since Copeland's birth] (Tokyo: Kirin biiru KK, 1984), 34-39.

26 Paraphrased in Kirin biiru, *Kirin biiru gojū nenshi,* 17-19.

27 Quoted ibid., 18.

28 Quoted ibid., 19-20.

29 *Japan Weekly Mail,* 15 February 1902, 185.

30 Paraphrased in Kirin biiru, *Kirin biiru gojū nenshi,* 20.

31 For a photo of Copeland's grave, see Kirin biiru, *Biiru to bunmei kaika no Yokohama,* 37.

32 Yanagita Kunio and Charles S. Terry, *Kaikoku hyakunen kinen bunka jigyōkai* [Japanese manners and customs in the Meiji era] (Tokyo: Ōbunsha, 1957), 48-51.

33 Fujimoto Taizō, *The Nightside of Japan* (London: T. Werner Laurie, 1914), 7; see also Kamiya Bar's website, http://www.kamiya-bar.com.

34 See "A vendor selling amazake," no. 711, Metadata Database of Japanese Old Photographs in Bakumatsu-Meiji Period, Nagasaki University Library, http://oldphoto.lb.nagasaki-u.ac.jp.

35 For further detail on the Rokumeikan, see especially Dallas Finn, "Reassessing the Rokumeikan," in *Challenging Past and Present: The Metamorphosis of Nineteenth-Century Japanese Art,* ed. Ellen P. Conant (Honolulu: University of Hawai'i Press, 2006), 227-39; and Toby Slade, *Japanese Fashion: A Cultural History* (London: Berg, 2009), 95-96.

36 Gendai kigyō kenkyūkai (Modern Enterprise Research Association), *Kirin biiru* [Kirin Brewery] (Tokyo: Meiji Shoin, 1962), 32.

37 The title of the finished document was "Preliminary Prospectus. Yokohama June 26th, 1885." Kirin biiru, *Kirin biiru gojū nenshi*, 17, 21-22.

38 Ibid., 17, 23-24.

39 These expenses, including 10 percent depreciation of the building and 7.5 percent depreciation of the equipment, totalled HK$11,150, while the necessary brewing materials were expected to cost HK$17,496. Taken together, projected costs totalled HK$28,646. The company's plan to refit the brewery to its own specifications under the supervision of an architect helped to secure inexpensive rates on fire insurance. Ibid., 25.

40 Minus the projected establishment and operating costs, this revenue was expected to yield a profit of HK$18,101. However, because the company's projected paid-in capital would total HK$35,000, or HK$6,354 more than the projected costs, the accountants projected a 52 percent net profit for the year. The term "paid-in capital" *(haraikomishihon)* refers to the actual payments received for all shares of a company sold to date, while "capital stock" *(shihonkin)* refers to the par value of the shares, which was generally higher than the actual payments received. As Steven Ericson notes, before the implementation of the Commercial Code in 1893 there were no laws or regulations detailing the proportion of the par value of shares that buyers had to pay for in full at the time of a company's incorporation, and later requirements were generally lenient. Until the practice was banned in 1948, payments were typically scheduled in gradual instalments in order to avoid the accumulation of unnecessary funds. See Steven J. Ericson, "Railroads in Crisis: The Financing and Management of Japanese Railway Companies during the Panic of 1890," in *Managing Industrial Enterprise,* ed. William D. Ray (Cambridge, MA: Harvard University Press, 1989), 124; and Kirin biiru, *Kirin biiru gojū nenshi,* 25-26.

41 Kirin biiru, *Kirin biiru gojū nenshi,* 26-30.

42 Ibid., 31.

43 Morris Low, *Building a Modern Japan: Science, Technology, and Medicine in the Meiji Era and Beyond* (New York: Palgrave Macmillan, 2005), 170.

44 Harald Fuess notes that contemporary German brewing equipment makers indicated strong demand from Japanese firms, to the delight of German diplomats. Fuess, "Investment, Importation, and Innovation: Genesis and Growth of Beer Corporations in Pre-war Japan," in *Institutional and Technological Change in Japan's Economy: Past and Present,* ed. Janet Hunter and Cornelia Storz (London: Routledge, 2006), 51.

45 Kawashima Tomou, "Kindai Nihon ni okeru shuzō kenchiku no hensen – shuzōsho, biiru kōjō" [The changing architecture of breweries in modern Japan – Sake breweries and beer factories], research paper published online by Asahi Breweries, 2006, http://www.asahibeer. co.jp/csr/philanthropy/ab-academic/image/pdf/report2006/cul_03.pdf.

46 Katō Kazuyasu, "Growing in a World of Change," in *Rediscovering Japanese Business Leadership: 15 Japanese Managers and the Companies They're Leading to New Growth,* ed. Hasegawa Yōzō (Singapore: John Wiley and Sons, 2011), 96.

47 Kirin biiru, *Kirin biiru gojū nenshi,* 33-34. Asahi Breweries also notes the overwhelming influence of German brewing tradition on Japan's brewing industry during its formative years. Asahi biiru KK, *Asahi 100* (Tokyo: Asahi biiru KK, 1990), 203.

48 *Japan Weekly Mail* (n.d.), reprinted in *Chinese Times* (Tianjin), 15 June 1889, 372.

49 *Board of Trade Journal* (London) 21 (1896): 729-30.

50 Kirin biiru, *Kirin biiru gojū nenshi,* 35.

51 *Yokohama Mainichi Shimbun* [Yokohama daily newspaper], 29-31 May 1888, quoted in Kirin biiru, *Kirin biiru gojū nenshi,* 36.

52 Kirin biiru, *Kirin biiru gojū nenshi,* 37-38.

53 Extensive detail on the vast number of defunct Japanese beer brands, labels, and logos is found throughout Satō, *Nihon no biiru seisuishi.* For further discussion, see Ishiguro

Keishichi, *Biiru monogatari* [The history of beer] (Tokyo: Shinmaisho, 1961), 43-54; and Miyake, *Biiru kigyō shi*, 62-65.

54 "Japan Brewery Company (Limited)," *London and China Telegraph* (London), 28 March 1891, 2.

55 Basil Hall Chamberlain and W.B. Mason, *A Handbook for Travellers in Japan*, 4th ed. (London: John Murray, 1894), 86.

56 "Japan Brewery Company (Limited)," *London and China Telegraph* (London), 8 June 1896, 2.

57 Kirin biiru, *Kirin biiru gojū nenshi*, 32, 38.

58 Miyake, *Biiru kigyō shi*, 37; Kirin biiru, *Kirin biiru gojū nenshi*, 39.

59 *Japan Weekly Mail*, 4 February 1905, 134.

60 The Japan Brewery's official capital stock totalled ¥600,000; however, to that point, only ¥500,000 had been paid in on nine thousand shares, which was deemed insufficient. After some deliberation, it was decided at a special shareholders' meeting on 25 June 1906 to issue another nine thousand shares, raising the company's capital stock to ¥1,200,000.

61 Morikawa Hidemasa, *Zaibatsu: The Rise and Fall of Family Enterprise Groups in Japan* (Tokyo: University of Tokyo Press, 1992), 102.

62 From a biographical plaque accompanying a statue of Magoshi Kyōhei at the Yebisu Beer Museum, 4-20-1 Ebisu in Ebisu Garden Place, Tokyo. Yebisu is intentionally spelled with a silent Y. The Japanese spelling similarly uses the now-obsolete *we* kana character as an intentional anachronism. Tokyo's Ebisu neighborhood and its train station were both named for the Yebisu beer brand, which was once produced nearby. The beer brand, in turn, was named for the god Yebisu, also known as Hiruko, who is one of the Seven Gods of Fortune. In Japanese mythology, he is the god of prosperous fishing and business.

63 Kirin biiru, *Kirin biiru gojū nenshi*, 42. Regrettably, on the tantalizing subject of Dodds's antiquing, Kirin offers no further details.

64 The *Japan Weekly Mail* (4 February 1905, 134) reported that James Dodds had sailed home to England in January 1905, but according to Kirin, he continued to represent The Japan Brewery in negotiations. This may be an editorial oversight on Kirin's part, because James was both Dodds's first name and his successor's surname.

65 Kirin biiru, *Kirin biiru gojū nenshi*, 45. While The Japan Brewery had shares worth ¥50, and ¥25 paid in on every two of them, the new company would have ¥25 paid in on each share, for a total of ¥1,012,500 in shares delivered, with the balance to be paid in cash by 1 March.

66 Known formally as the "Memorandum of Association and the Companies Ordinances 1865 to 1890 of the Colony of Hong Kong."

67 Kirin biiru, *Kirin biiru gojū nenshi*, 46.

68 *Japan Weekly Mail*, 17 October 1908, 473.

69 *Japan Weekly Mail*, 7 November 1908, 561.

70 Kirin biiru, *Kirin biiru gojū nenshi*, 45-61.

71 Ibid., 46-47, 61. When The Japan Brewery's assets were transferred, the liquidator arranged for its shareholders, whose names were unlisted, to each receive 1.5 shares in Kirin Brewery Co. for every share that they had held of The Japan Brewery.

72 *Japan Weekly Mail*, 3 June 1905.

73 For the seminal work on this theme, see Richard J. Samuels, *Rich Nation, Strong Army: National Security and Ideology in Japan's Technological Transformation* (Ithaca, NY: Cornell University Press, 1994).

74 Sapporo biiru KK, *Sapporo 120 nenshi* [120-year history of Sapporo Breweries] (Tokyo: Sapporo biiru KK, 1996), 34.

75 For further discussion of foreign experts assisting in Japan's early brewing industry, see Naitō Hiroshi, "Meijiki biiru gyōkai ni okeru gaikokujin gijutsusha no keifu: Yebisu biiru

no baii ni" [The geneaology of foreign engineers in the Meiji-era Japanese beer industry: The case of Yebisu Beer], *Keiei shigaku* [Japan business history review] 29, 4 (January 1995): 58-75.

76 William D. Wray, *Mitsubishi and the N.Y.K., 1870-1914: Business Strategy in the Japanese Shipping Industry* (Cambridge, MA: Harvard University Press, 1984), 138. Note that the Hokkaido Colonization Office *(Kaitakushi)* has been translated into English into various ways, and sometimes appears as the "Hokkaido Development Commission," or the "Hokkaido Colonization Commission."

77 Horace Capron, *Reports and Official Letters to the Kaitakushi* [Hokkaido Colonization Office] (Tokyo: Kaitakushi, 1875), 309. For further detail on Horace Capron and the early efforts at hops cultivation in Hokkaido, see Tanaka Kazuo, *Monogatari Sapporo biiru* [The History of Sapporo Breweries] (Sapporo: Hokkaido shimbun-sha, 1993), 9, 14-17, 81-81, 177.

78 Sapporo biiru, *Sapporo 120 nenshi,* 34-35.

79 "Address of the Emperor to Commissioner Capron" (28 March 1875), in Capron, *Kaitakushi,* 736-37.

80 For a detailed biography of Nakagawa Seibei (whose name is sometimes romanized as Seibē) featuring photographs, see Kikuchi Takeo and Yanai Saki, *Nakagawa Seibē deni biiru-zukuri no senjin* [The life of Nakagawa Seibē: Beer-making pioneer] (Tokyo: Yashio shup-pansha, 1982). For further discussion, see Tanaka, *Monogatari Sapporo biiru,* 17-19.

81 For further detail on Nakagawa's time in Fürstenwalde, as well as a colour reproduction of his diploma, see Kikuchi and Yanai, *Nakagawa Seibē,* 37-39, 51.

82 Sapporo biiru, *Sapporo 120 nenshi,* 36-38, 51.

83 At that time, the top grade (1) paid ¥650 per month, and the bottom grade (15) paid ¥12 per month. Sapporo biiru, *Sapporo 120 nenshi,* 38n.

84 Sapporo biiru, *Sapporo 120 nenshi,* 39-40.

85 Discussion of the development plan and the designers' first trip to Hokkaido appears in Tanaka, *Monogatari Sapporo biiru,* 28-41.

86 Sapporo biiru, *Sapporo 120 nenshi,* 40-42.

87 Ibid., 43n.

88 For diagrams of the developing brewery site, see Tanaka, *Monogatari Sapporo biiru,* 36, 85, 101.

89 For further discussion of Sapporo's early operations, see Kikuchi and Yanai, *Nakagawa Seibē,* 58-70.

90 *Japan Times* (Tokyo), 24 September 2005.

91 Sapporo biiru, *Sapporo 120 nenshi,* 45-48.

92 Ibid., 45-46.

93 "Notes," *Nature* 19 (27 February 1879): 397.

94 Sapporo biiru, *Sapporo 120 nenshi,* 46-47.

95 Kirin biiru, *Kirin biiru gojū nenshi,* 7-8.

96 Ibid., 51-52.

97 The brewery's early efforts at public relations and sales are discussed in Kikuchi and Yanai, *Nakagawa Seibē,* 71-76.

98 Sapporo biiru, *Sapporo 120 nenshi,* 47-51.

99 Penelope Francks, *The Japanese Consumer: An Alternative Economic History of Modern Japan* (Cambridge: Cambridge University Press, 2009), 220.

100 For further discussion of early Western-style saloons and beer salons, see Ishiguro, *Biiru monogatari,* 62-63.

101 "History of Hokkaido," in *Gurafu Hokkaidō (Hokkaidō graph),* Sapporo: Public Relations and Opinions Division, Hokkaido Government. Sapporo: 2011, 2.

102 "The History of Sapporo Breweries," Sapporo Holdings, Ltd., http://www.sapporoholdings. jp/english/history/; and "Chronology of the Life of Shibusawa Eiichi," Shibusawa Eiichi Memorial Foundation, http://www.shibusawa.or.jp/english/eiichi/chronology.html.

103 Osaka Beer Company, Inc., began selling its "Asahi Beer" brand in Osaka in 1892 and merged into Dai Nippon Beer in 1906. The modern Asahi Breweries, Ltd., however, dates its founding to 1949, when it was created out of the partition of Dai Nippon Beer (see Chapter 4). Asahi biiru, *Asahi 100,* 90.

104 Sapporo biiru KK, *Dai Nippon biiru sanjūnenshi* [Thirty-year history of Dai Nippon Beer] (Tokyo: Dai Nippon biiru KK), 26 March 1936, unpaginated photographic companion volume.

105 Sapporo biiru, *Sapporo 120 nenshi,* 769. Penelope Francks also deals with the subject of beer's steadily rising popularity among those who could afford such luxuries during the Meiji era in "Inconspicuous Consumption."

106 Henry Theophilus Finck, *Lotos-time in Japan* (New York: Charles Scribner's Sons, 1895), 219.

107 The sake industry was also burdened by a centuries-old koku production tax. In 1890, the members of the Kantō Brewing Company League, which represented the city of Tokyo and nineteen surrounding prefectures, drew up a petition of complaint against the excessively heavy brewing tax and submitted it to both houses of parliament.

108 Kirin biiru, *Kirin biiru gojū nenshi,* 49-50.

109 Quoted ibid., 51.

110 Mizukawa Susumu, *Nihon no biiru sangyō* [Japan's beer industry] (Tokyo: Senshu University Press, 2002), 8.

111 Kirin biiru, *Kirin biiru gojū nenshi,* 53.

112 Ibid., 51.

113 Osaka Beer had hosted thirsty patrons at the previous year's exhibition, prompting Kirin to follow suit. Ibid., 50; Asahi biiru, *Asahi 100,* 141.

114 "Beer Brewing in Japan," *American Brewers' Review* 21, 8 (1 August 1907): 385.

115 For an extensive collection of food and drink, including beer, advertisements from the Meiji, Taishō, and Shōwa eras, see Hajima Tomoyuki, *Shimbun kōkoku bijutsu taikei* [Compendium of newspaper advertisement artwork], 17 vols., (Tokyo: Ōzorosha, 2003-7), especially vols. 2, 7, and 12, which feature advertisements for food, drink, and luxury items.

116 Ishiguro, *Biiru monogatari,* 65.

117 For a discussion of the words "biiru" versus "biya," see Ueda, *Biiru tengoku,* 56-60. For further discussions of Japan's early beer halls, see Ishiguro, *Biiru monogatari,* 61; and Miyake, *Biiru kigyō shi,* 112.

118 *Yomiuri Shimbun,* 6 August 1899, 4.

119 Asahi biiru, *Asahi 100,* 142; Sapporo biiru, *Sapporo 120 nenshi,* 770.

120 *Asahi Shimbun,* 9 November 1899, 8.

121 *Asahi Shimbun,* 14 November 1899, 7.

122 *Asahi Shimbun,* 29 March 1904, 8.

123 Arthur Lloyd, *Every-Day Japan: Written after Twenty-Five Years' Residence and Work in the Country* (London: Cassell, 1909), 227.

124 Kirin biiru, *Kirin biiru gojū nenshi,* 73; Asahi biiru, *Asahi 100,* 138-41, 146.

125 Sapporo's histories freely admit that Magoshi's approach to advertising made "Yebisu" product launches entertaining events, and that Sapporo's own ads were lacking by comparison. Sapporo biiru, *Sapporo 120 nenshi,* 770. For further discussion of early beer advertising in Japan, see Francks, *Japanese Consumer,* 85-86.

126 *Strand Magazine* 27, 157 (February 1904): 118.

127 Sapporo biiru, *Sapporo 120 nenshi,* 770.

128 The majority of works dealing even in part with the Meiji and Taishō eras generally characterize Japan's industrial, technological, and economic growth as "rapid" or "swift," and Japanese industrial progress was indeed quick in many respects. I aim here simply to qualify this broad characterization by identifying important examples of growth and innovation that were rather slow, and often hamstrung by technological or logistical challenges, which were manifold. A comprehensive list of relevant titles is not possible here, but for a good assortment of important works, see Tessa Morris-Suzuki, *The Technological Transformation of Japan: From the Seventeenth to the Twenty-First Century* (Cambridge: Cambridge University Press, 1994); Samuels, *Rich Nation, Strong Army*; Dirk Pilat, *The Economics of Rapid Growth: The Experience of Japan and Korea* (Brookfield, VT: Edward Elgar, 1994); Christopher Howe, *The Origins of Japanese Trade Supremacy: Development and Technology in Asia from 1540 to the Pacific War* (London: Hurst, 1996); William M. Tsutsui, *Manufacturing Ideology: Scientific Management in Twentieth-Century Japan* (Princeton, NJ: Princeton University Press, 1998); and David G. Wittner, ed., *Technology and the Culture of Progress in Meiji Japan,* Routledge/Asian Studies Association of Australia (ASAA) East Asian Series (Cambridge, UK: Routledge, 2007).

129 *Japan Times Year Book,* 1930 edition (Tokyo: Japan Times, 1 January 1931), 205.

130 Johannes Hirschmeier, *The Origins of Entrepreneurship in Meiji Japan* (Cambridge, MA: Harvard University Press, 1964), 148, 246.

Chapter 2: Keeping Up Appearances

1 *Asahi Shimbun,* 8 January 1905, 6.

2 *Asahi Shimbun,* 1 November 1905, 2.

3 Alice Teichova and Maurice Lévy-LeBoyer, *Historical Studies in International Corporate Business* (Cambridge: Cambridge University Press, 2002), 185.

4 For an excellent discussion of industrial rationalization and the pursuit of industrial self-sufficiency, see especially Chapters 2 and 3 of William M. Tsutsui, *Manufacturing Ideology: Scientific Management in Twentieth-Century Japan* (Princeton, NJ: Princeton University Press, 1998).

5 For a good examination of the merger process not issued by the companies involved, see Miyake Yūzō, *Biiru kigyō shi* [A history of the beer industry] (Tokyo: Mitakisha, 1977), 66-77.

6 Kirin biiru KK, *Kirin biiru KK gojū nenshi* [Kirin Brewery Company, Ltd.: Fifty-year history] (Tokyo: Kirin biiru KK, 20 March 1957), 133.

7 Sapporo biiru KK, *Sapporo 120 nenshi* [120-year history of Sapporo Breweries] (Tokyo: Sapporo biiru KK, 1996), 66.

8 Kirin biiru, *Kirin biiru gojū nenshi,* 55-57, 66, 133.

9 Ibid., 55.

10 Similarly today, "Sapporo Beer" is sold in the United States as an "imported" brand, but it is brewed and shipped under licence by Sapporo's subsidiary Canadian brewer, Sleeman, from its plant in Guelph, Ontario. Such arrangements were no less practical in 1906.

11 Mizukawa Susumu, *Nihon no biiru sangyō* [Japan's beer industry] (Tokyo: Senshu University Press, 2002), 8.

12 Kirin biiru, *Kirin biiru gojū nenshi,* 57-58.

13 Ibid., 59-60.

14 Katō Kazuyasu, "Growing in a World of Change," in *Rediscovering Japanese Business Leadership: 15 Japanese Managers and the Companies They're Leading to New Growth,* ed. Hasegawa Yōzō (Singapore: John Wiley and Sons, 2011), 97.

15 Kirin biiru, *Kirin biiru gojū nenshi,* 65.

16 Ibid., 68-69.

17   Ibid., 71-73. The subject of the popping corks is also noted by Harald Fuess, who points out that another problem was that hand-blown glass bottles were too irregularly shaped to permit the use of aluminum caps. See Fuess, "Investment, Importation, and Innovation: Genesis and Growth of Beer Corporations in Pre-war Japan" in *Institutional and Technological Change in Japan's Economy: Past and Present*, ed. Janet Hunter and Cornelia Storz (London: Routledge, 2006), 54.

18   For details on Japan's expanding rail network, see Steven J. Ericson, *The Sound of the Whistle: Railroads and the State in Meiji Japan* (Cambridge, MA: Harvard University Press, 1996).

19   Kirin biiru, *Kirin biiru gojū nenshi*, 68-69, 73, 78.

20   Ibid., 64; Sapporo biiru, *Sapporo 120 nenshi*, 775.

21   Nihon jidōsha kōgyōkai (Japan Automobile Manufacturers Association), "Dōro kōtsū no rekishi" [The history of road traffic], in *Mōtāsaikuru no Nihon shi* [Japan motorcycle history], ed. Nihon jidōsha kōgyōkai (Tokyo: Sankaidō Press, 1995), 137.

22   Kirin biiru, *Kirin biiru gojū nenshi*, 64-67.

23   *Asahi Shimbun*, 15 July 1912, 7.

24   *Asahi Shimbun*, 12 April 1912, 2.

25   Kirin biiru, *Kirin biiru gojū nenshi*, 64-71.

26   See William D. Wray, "Opportunity vs Control: The Diplomacy of Japanese Shipping in the First World War," in *The Merchant Marine in International Affairs, 1850-1950*, ed. Greg Kennedy (London: Frank Cass, 2000), 59-83; and see also Frederick R. Dickinson, *War and National Reinvention: Japan in the Great War, 1914-1919* (Cambridge, MA: Harvard University Press, 1999).

27   *Asahi Shimbun*, 6 February 1915, 4.

28   "Tsingtao Beer," *North China Herald*, 23 December 1916, 31.

29   *Japan Advertiser* (Tokyo), quoted in US Bureau of Foreign and Domestic Commerce, *Commerce Reports* 157 (6 July 1916): 50.

30   Kirin biiru, *Kirin biiru gojū nenshi*, 66-68, 75, 104.

31   *Straits Times* (Singapore), 18 October 1916, 10.

32   *Japan Chronicle* (Kobe), reproduced in US Bureau of Foreign and Domestic Commerce, *Commerce Reports* 280 (28 November 1916): 790.

33   *Straits Times* (Singapore), 18 October 1916, 10.

34   "Japan's Production of Beer and Sake," *Western Brewer: and Journal of the Barley, Malt and Hop Trades* 45, 4 (October 1915): 144.

35   US Bureau of Foreign and Domestic Commerce, *Commerce Reports* 321 (June 1917): 159.

36   Amos P. Wilder, "Christianizing America's Contacts through Political Relations," in *Men and World Service: Addresses Delivered at the National Missionary Congress, Washington, D.C., April 26-30, 1916* (New York: Laymen's Missionary Movement, 1916), 173.

37   Kirin biiru, *Kirin biiru gojū nenshi*, 134.

38   Ibid., 134.

39   Ibid., 82-83, 136.

40   Ibid., 84.

41   *Brewer's Journal: and Barley, Malt and Hop Trades Reporter* 41, 3 (January 1917): 131.

42   Jeff Haas, phone conversation with the author, 22 May 2012.

43   Quoted in Jeff Haas, "They Have No Idea What It Is to Run a Malthouse: A Wisconsin Beer Maker in Japan," *Wisconsin Magazine of History* 87, 2 (Winter 2003-4): 14-29. Mr. Haas is Groeschel's great-grandson, and my thanks go to him for kindly sharing his family's photos of Groeschel's tenure in Yokohama.

44   Kirin biiru, *Kirin biiru gojū nenshi*, 84.

45   Haas, "They Have No Idea," 14-29.

46   Kirin biiru, *Kirin biiru gojū nenshi*, 80. The Kanzaki plant was renamed the Amazaki plant on 1 January 1949.

47 Ibid., 78-81.

48 Ibid., 81-82.

49 Ibid., 74-75, 79, 84, 104.

50 Ibid., 97-98, 136-37.

51 Yasutake Rumi, "Transnational Women's Activism: The Woman's Christian Temperance Union in Japan and the United States," in *Women and Twentieth-Century Protestantism*, ed. Margaret Lamberts Bendroth and Virginia Lieson Brereton (Chicago: University of Illinois Press, 2001), 98. For further details on the WCTU in Japan, see Elizabeth Dorn Lublin, *Reforming Japan: The Woman's Christian Temperance Union in the Meiji Period* (Vancouver: UBC Press, 2010).

52 See Chapter 5, "The Struggle to Create a Sober Society," in Lublin, *Reforming Japan*, 126-48.

53 *Japan Advertiser*, 9 January 1920, 3.

54 *Asahi Shimbun*, 15 October 1921, 2.

55 *Japan Advertiser*, 13 September 1922, 7.

56 For further data on export sales, which rose between 1898 and 1922, but fell sharply from 1922 to 1938, consult Tetsudō shō Un'yukyoku (Railway Department, Transportation Office), *Cha, tabako, seishu, biiru, seiryō inryō ni kansuru chōsa* [Investigation concerning the tea, cigarette, sake, beer, and cold drink markets] (Tokyo: Tetsudō shō Un'yukyoku, 1926), 12-14.

57 Kirin biiru, *Kirin biiru gojū nenshi*, 76-78, 84-85.

58 "Japan's Beer Industry Makes Notable Strides," *Japan Advertiser*, 8 October 1921, 7.

59 Kirin records that Streichel worked for Orient Beer under contract, but had left the firm by the time of its merger with Kirin in 1923. Years later, he returned to Japan and visited Kirin, at which point he recalled his years in Japan fondly. Kirin biiru, *Kirin biiru gojū nenshi*, 86.

60 In the purchase contract, Orient's shareholders were given 1 share of Kirin in return for every 2.5 of their own, which netted them ¥5 profit per share. Ibid., 85-87.

61 *North China Herald*, 17 February 1923, 12.

62 See the many reports from the Associated Press and United Press International published in newspapers worldwide, 3-6 September 1923.

63 See especially the introduction to Gregory K. Clancey, *Earthquake Nation: The Cultural Politics of Japanese Seismicity, 1868-1930* (Berkeley: University of California Press, 2010).

64 Kirin biiru, *Kirin biiru gojū nenshi*, 88.

65 Ibid., 89.

66 Ibid., 64, 89-92, 106.

67 Ibid., 92.

68 Ibid., 76-77, 92-93.

69 Ibid., 94.

70 Ibid., 93-95.

71 Tetsudō shō Un'yukyoku, *Cha, tabako*, 23-25.

72 The company's Namamugi plant is still in operation today, but the location remains infamous for the eponymous "Namamugi Incident" of 1862. Observant visitors who walk to the brewery from the nearby rail station will spot the modest stone marker identifying the site where Richardson met his sudden, untimely fate. Kirin biiru, *Kirin biiru gojū nenshi*, 74, 94-95, 104-6.

73 Kendall H. Brown and Sharon Minichiello, *Taishō Chic: Japanese Modernity, Nostalgia, and Deco* (Honolulu, HI: Honolulu Academy of Arts, 2001), 163.

74 "Some Posters from Japan," *National Lithographer: Devoted to the Interests of Lithography and the Graphic Arts* 24, 9 (September 1917): 43-44.

75   For further discussion of the uses of the "modern girl" in advertising and sales promotions, see Barbara Hamill Sato, *The New Japanese Woman: Modernity, Media, and Women in Interwar Japan* (Durham, NC: Duke University Press, 2003), 46.

76   See especially Miriam Silverberg, "The Modern Girl as Militant," in *Recreating Japanese Women, 1600-1945*, ed. Gail Bernstein (Berkeley: University of California Press, 1991), 239-40; the 1920s Kabuto and Union beer posters featuring modern Japanese youth reproduced in Ajioka Chiaki, *Modern Boy Modern Girl: Modernity in Japanese Art, 1910-1935* (Sydney, AU: Art Gallery of New South Wales, 1998); and Sapporo biiru, *Sapporo 120 nenshi*, 779.

77   Katarzyna J. Cwiertka, *Modern Japanese Cuisine: Food, Power and National Identity* (London: Reaktion Books, 2006), 23.

78   Donald Keene, "Memories of Edward Seidensticker," *International House of Japan Bulletin* 27, 2 (December 2007): 26. For further details on Kirin's posters, see Ōhashi Masafusa, *Kirin biiru no takakuka senryaku* [Kirin Brewery's diversification strategy] (Tokyo: Shibata shoten, 1979) 127; and Hotta Masayasu, *Kirin biiru* [Kirin Brewery](Tokyo: Asahi sonoramu, 1980), 50.

79   "Taishō posutaa no onna" [Taishō poster women], *Nihon Keizai Shimbun* [Japan economic times]. Articles in this series that focused specifically on beer poster advertising appeared on 28 June 2012 and 4 July 2012.

80   For details on "Kirin Lemon" and rival brands of soda produced by other brewers, see Ōhashi, *Kirin biiru no takakuka senryaku*, 125-49; Hotta, *Kirin biiru*, 150; and Kirin biiru, *Kirin biiru gojū nenshi*, 106-7.

81   Kirin biiru, *Kirin biiru gojū nenshi*, 107-9.

82   Ibid., 109.

83   Hazama Hiroshi, "Historical Changes in the Life Style of Industrial Workers," in *Japanese Industrialization and its Social Consequences*, ed. Hugh Patrick with Larry Meissner (Berkeley: University of California Press, 1976), 39.

84   See Penelope Francks, *The Japanese Consumer: An Alternative Economic History of Modern Japan* (Cambridge: Cambridge University Press, 2009), 166.

85   Kirin biiru, *Kirin biiru gojū nenshi*, 75, 98, 106, 111.

86   Ibid., 99-100.

87   Ibid., 98.

88   Ibid., 99.

89   Ibid., 112.

90   *Asahi Shimbun*, 20 February 1926, 4.

91   Kirin biiru, *Kirin biiru gojū nenshi*, 100.

92   Ibid., 102.

93   Ibid., 105.

94   In 1927, Kirin's branch stores were located at

   • Tokyo, Kōjimachi-ku, Eirakumachi, 1-chōme, 1
   • Yokohama, Kitanaka-dōri, 1-chōme, 2
   • Osaka, Higashi-ku, Hiranomachi, 413
   • Nagoya, Naka-zu, Teppomachi, 1-chōme, 18
   • Fukuoka, Shimonishi-machi, 2
   • Sendai, Odawara, Chōchō-dōri, 15
   • Keijō, Nandaimon-dōri, 2-chōme, 33.

95   Kirin biiru, *Kirin biiru gojū nenshi*, 101-6.

96   Ibid., 111, 136.

97   When Suzuki Shōten went out of business in 1929, it sought to dispose of its subsidiary company at Moji, Sakura Beer. Suzuki Shōten sent a representative named Akashi Shotarō

to offer Kirin the opportunity to purchase about 10 percent of Sakura Beer's bank debt. However, Kirin had recently built its new Yokohama plant, so the discussions did not proceed well. Akashi then went along to Dai Nippon Beer, which agreed to buy the troubled firm. Ibid., 117-18.

98 Ibid., 77, 106, 111.
99 Ibid., 112-13.
100 For details on "Oraga Beer," see Miyake, *Biiru kigyō shi*, 94-98.
101 Kirin biiru, *Kirin biiru gojū nenshi*, 113.
102 Ibid., 113.
103 Ibid., 114.
104 Foreign Affairs Association of Japan, *The Japan Year Book, 1928* (Kenkyusha Press, 1929), 55.
105 Further to the figures above, Dai Nippon's actual paid-in capital was ¥50,000,000, and Japan Beer Springs' was ¥14,000,000, which at a merger ratio of 10:7 resulted in ¥59,800,000 of paid-in capital and a total capital stock of ¥94,000,000 for Dai Nippon Beer, after settling all consolidation-related costs. Kirin biiru, *Kirin biiru gojū nenshi*, 115.
106 Nakamura Takafusa, "Depression, Recovery, and War, 1920-1945," in *The Economic Emergence of Modern Japan*, vol. 1, ed. Yamamura Kōzō (Cambridge: Cambridge University Press, 1997), 124-26, 129, 139.
107 Kirin biiru, *Kirin biiru gojū nenshi*, 115-16.
108 Tanji Yuichi, "Dai Nippon Bakushu no keiei to hanbaimo, 1906-1939" [The marketing policy of Dai Nippon Brewery Co., 1906-1939], *Shakai keizai shigaku* [Socioeconomic history] 67, 3 (January 2001): 20.
109 A. Hamish Ion, *The Cross in the Dark Valley: The Canadian Protestant Missionary Movement in the Japanese Empire, 1931-1945* (Waterloo, ON: Wilfrid Laurier University Press, 1999), 49.
110 Kirin biiru, *Kirin biiru gojū nenshi*, 78, 117.
111 *Asahi Shimbun*, 6 July 1904, 4.
112 Jeffrey W. Alexander, "Nikon and the Sponsorship of Japan's Optical Industry by the Imperial Japanese Navy, 1917-1945," *Japanese Studies* 22, 1 (2002): 19-31.

Chapter 3: Brewing Self-Sufficiency

1 Grant K. Goodman, "Japan and Philippine Beer: The 1930s," *Journal of Southeast Asian Studies* 1, 1 (January 1970): 54-59.
2 See Chalmers Johnson, *MITI and the Japanese Miracle: The Growth of Industrial Policy, 1925-1975* (Stanford, CA: Stanford University Press, 1982).
3 Nakamura Takafusa, *Nihon keizai: Sono seichō to kōzō* [The Japanese economy: Its development and structure], 3rd ed. (Tokyo: Tokyo University Press, 1993), quoted in Bai Gao, *Economic Ideology and Japanese Industrial Policy: Developmentalism from 1931 to 1965* (Cambridge: Cambridge University Press, 1997), 122.
4 Paul Preston, Michael Partridge, and Antony Best, *British Documents on Foreign Affairs – Reports and Papers from the Foreign Office Confidential Print: From 1946 through 1950*, Series E: Asia, Part 4: From 1946 through 1950 (Frederick, MD: University Publications of America, 2000), 94; Sapporo biiru KK, *Sapporo 120 nenshi* [120-year history of Sapporo Breweries] (Tokyo: Sapporo biiru KK, 1996), 296.
5 Sapporo biiru, *Sapporo 120 nenshi*, 297.
6 Kirin biiru KK, *Kirin biiru KK gojū nenshi* [Kirin Brewery Company, Ltd.: Fifty-year history] (Tokyo: Kirin biiru KK, 20 March 1957), 139.
7 See especially Louise Young, *Japan's Total Empire: Manchuria and the Culture of Wartime Imperialism* (Berkeley: University of California Press, 1998).

8   Nihon nikkeru jihōkyoku (Japan Nickel Information Bureau), *Biiru jōzō to nikkeru oyobi sono gōkin* [Nickel and its alloys in beer brewing] (Tokyo: Nihon nikkeru jihōkyoku, 1938), 3-11.

9   Sapporo biiru, *Sapporo 120 nenshi,* 296-97.

10 Kirin biiru, *Kirin biiru gojū nenshi,* 139.

11 Sheldon Garon, "Fashioning a Culture of Diligence and Thrift: Savings and Frugality Campaigns in Japan, 1900-1931," in *Japan's Competing Modernities: Issues in Culture and Democracy, 1900-1930,* ed. Sharon A. Minichiello (Honolulu: University of Hawai'i Press, 1998), 312-34.

12 Kirin biiru, *Kirin biiru gojū nenshi,* 139.

13 Sapporo biiru, *Sapporo 120 nenshi,* 297-301; Kirin biiru, *Kirin biiru gojū nenshi,* 139-40.

14 Foreign Affairs Association of Japan, *Japan Year Book, 1939-40* (Kenkyusha Press, 1940), 513.

15 Kirin biiru, *Kirin biiru gojū nenshi,* 140-41.

16 Saitō Osamu and Shimbo Hiroshi, "The Economy on the Eve of Industrialization," in *Emergence of Economic Society in Japan, 1600-1859,* ed. Hayami Akira, Saitō Osamu, and Ronald P. Toby, vol. 1 of *The Economic History of Japan: 1600-1990* (Oxford: Oxford University Press, 1999), 344.

17 Sapporo biiru, *Sapporo 120 nenshi,* 297-301; Kirin biiru, *Kirin biiru gojū nenshi,* 139-40.

18 Sapporo biiru, *Sapporo 120 nenshi,* 301.

19 Specifically, these were the Alcohol Manufacturing Tax Law, the Alcohol and Alcohol Beverage Container Law, the Beer Tax Law, and the Yeast Mash, Main Fermenting Mash, and Malt Director Law, all of which dated from 1901.

20 Kirin biiru, *Kirin biiru gojū nenshi,* 141.

21 Sapporo biiru, *Sapporo 120 nenshi,* 298.

22 The cultivation of "new" or "secret" fields was an age-old activity in Japan's countryside, where peasants had long tried to turn a profit in the face of withering tax rates on rice production, especially during the Edo age. See Nakane Chie and Ōishi Shinzaburō, *Tokugawa Japan: The Social and Economic Antecedents of Modern Japan* (Tokyo: Tokyo University Press, 1990), 65.

23 For discussions of wartime food control laws, see Erich Pauer's own fifth chapter in Pauer, ed., *Japan's War Economy* (London: Routledge, 1999); Bruce F. Johnston, *Japanese Food Management in World War II* (Stanford, CA: Stanford University Press – Stanford Food Research Institute, 1953), 82, 156; and Sapporo biiru, *Sapporo 120 nenshi,* 305.

24 *Yomiuri Shimbun,* 29 April 1943, 2.

25 Sapporo biiru, *Sapporo 120 nenshi,* 305.

26 Ibid., 305-8.

27 See the discussions of the Rikagaku kenkyūsho (Institute for Physical and Chemical Research, or "Riken") in Michael A. Cusumano, "'Scientific Industry': Strategy, Technology, and Entrepreneurship in Prewar Japan," in *Managing Industrial Enterprise: Cases from Japan's Prewar Experience,* ed. William D. Wray (Cambridge, MA: Harvard University Press, 1989), 269-315; and Tessa Morris-Suzuki, *The Technological Transformation of Japan: From the Seventeenth to the Twenty-First Century* (Cambridge: Cambridge University Press, 1994), 127-28.

28 See William M. Tsutsui, *Manufacturing Ideology: Scientific Management in Twentieth-Century Japan* (Princeton, NJ: Princeton University Press, 1998); Kyoko Sheridan, *Governing the Japanese Economy* (Cambridge, UK: Polity Press, 1993); and Nakamura Takafusa, "Depression, Recovery, and War, 1920-1945," in *The Economic Emergence of Modern Japan,* vol. 1, ed. Yamamura Kōzō (Cambridge, UK: Cambridge University Press, 1997), 116-58.

29 See Nakamura, "Depression, Recovery, and War," 116-58; Hara Akira, "Wartime Controls," in *The Economic History of Japan, 1600-1900,* vol. 3: *Economic History of Japan, 1914-1955,*

A Dual Structure, ed. Nakamura Takafusa and Odaka Kōnosuke, trans. Noah S. Brannen (New York: Oxford University Press, 1999), 247-86; Michael A. Barnhart, *Japan Prepares for Total War: The Search for Economic Security, 1919-1941* (Ithaca, NY: Cornell University Press, 1987), 74-76; and Sasaki Satoshi, "The Rationalization of Production Management Systems in Japan," in *World War II and the Transformation of Business Systems,* ed. Shiba Takao and Sakadō Jun (Tokyo: Tokyo University Press, 1994), 30-58.

30 For a discussion of the development of old and new zaibatsu, industrial zaibatsu, and the four leading conglomerates – Mitsui, Mitsubishi, Sumitomo, and Yasuda – see Odagiri Hiroyuki and Goto Akira, *Technology and Industrial Development in Japan: Building Capabilities by Learning, Innovation, and Public Policy* (New York: Oxford University Press, 1996), 74-81.

31 Sapporo biiru, *Sapporo 120 nenshi,* 299.

32 *Asahi Shimbun,* 20 September 1939.

33 Sapporo biiru, *Sapporo 120 nenshi,* 299-300.

34 Sapporo biiru, *Sapporo 120 nenshi,* 299.

35 *Asahi Shimbun,* 2 June 1940.

36 Kirin biiru, *Kirin biiru gojū nenshi,* 141.

37 Sapporo biiru, *Sapporo 120 nenshi,* 301.

38 Ibid., 300.

39 Ibid., 301.

40 *Yomiuri Shimbun,* 26 May 1943, 2. Japan's Weights and Measures Law of 1895 was updated in 1921 as the Revised Weights and Measures Law, which went into effect on 1 July 1924. In that year, Japan adopted the metric system, though traditional units of measurement survived and were used commonly for many years.

41 *Yomiuri Shimbun,* 16 May 1943, 2.

42 *Asahi Shimbun,* 5 May 1944, 3.

43 Although the sake brewing industry was shuttered during the war, the existing supply of sake was sufficient to enable rationed consumption through 1945. Many thanks to Steven Ericson for referring me to the discussion of "people's bars" in wartime Japan found in Thomas R.H. Havens, *Valley of Darkness: The Japanese People and World War Two* (New York: W.W. Norton, 1978), 152-53; and *Biiru no jiten: Tanoshisha ichiban minna de kanpai!* [The beer encyclopedia: Cheers to number one enjoyment!] (Tokyo: Sanseidō, 1984), 122. Today, the term "kokumin sakaba" survives as the ironic name of several trendy pubs and restaurants throughout Japan.

44 For a study of Japanese cuisine and the impact of the wartime command economy on dining and the restaurant trade, see Chapters 5 and 6 of Katarzyna J. Cwiertka, *Modern Japanese Cuisine: Food, Power and National Identity* (London: Reaktion Books, 2006); and Kirin biiru, *Kirin biiru gojū nenshi,* 142-43.

45 Dennis L. McNamara, *The Colonial Origins of Korean Enterprise, 1910-1945* (Cambridge: Cambridge University Press, 1990), 180, 186.

46 Sapporo biiru, *Sapporo 120 nenshi,* 302.

47 Kirin biiru, *Kirin biiru gojū nenshi,* 145-46.

48 *Biiru no jiten,* 122.

49 "Fujikawa Maru," PacificWrecks.com, last modified 23 January 2012, http://www.pacificwrecks.com/ships/maru/fujikawa.html. Similar finds of Kirin and Dai Nippon bottles are often reported on land throughout Japan's wartime Pacific holdings, such as Saipan and Guam, and posted online by amateur archaeologists.

50 Sapporo biiru, *Sapporo 120 nenshi,* 302-3.

51 Ibid., 303; Kirin biiru, *Kirin biiru gojū nenshi,* 144-45.

52 Sapporo biiru, *Sapporo 120 nenshi,* 300-1.

53 *Yomiuri Shimbun,* 30 November 1944, 2; 6 June 1944, 2.

54   For further discussion of Kirin's experience of controlled wartime production, see Gendai kigyō kenkyūkai (Modern Enterprise Research Association), *Kirin biiru* [Kirin Brewery] (Tokyo: Meiji Shoin, 1962), 70-74.
55   Kirin biiru, *Kirin biiru gojū nenshi*, 147.
56   *Asahi Shimbun*, 22 April 1943, 2; 29 April 1943, 3.
57   Sapporo biiru, *Sapporo 120 nenshi*, 303-4.
58   Ibid., 304.
59   Kirin biiru, *Kirin biiru gojū nenshi*, 147-48.
60   *Nihon gaji kyōkai*, or *The Japan Year Book*, is subtitled *Complete Cyclopaedia of General Information and Statistics on Japan and Japanese Territories*. Published between 1908 and 1952, its editors included Takenobu Yoshitarō, K. Inahara, and the Foreign Affairs Association of Japan. Its various publishers included the Japan Year Book Company, Kenkyūsha Press, and the *Japan Times*. There was also a *Japan-Manchukuo Yearbook* between 1934 and 1941, published in Tokyo by the Japan-Manchukuo Yearbook Company.
61   See especially Young, *Japan's Total Empire*.
62   Norman Smith, *Intoxicating Manchuria: Alcohol, Opium, and Culture in China's Northeast* (Vancouver: UBC Press, 2012), 74-77.
63   Young, *Japan's Total Empire*, 77-78.
64   *Osaka Mainichi Shimbun*, cited in Kirin biiru KK, ed., *Biiru to Nihonjin: Meiji/Taishō/Shōwa fukyūshi* [Beer and the Japanese: A broad Meiji/Taishō/Shōwa history] (Tokyo: Sanseidō, 1984), 219; Young, *Japan's Total Empire*, 77.
65   For a contemporary report on the farming of grain and hops in Manchukuo, see Matsūra Susumu, *Biiru ni kansuru chōsa hōkokusho* [Investigative report concerning beer] (Manchuria: Government of Manchukuo, 1936), 11-14. See also Kirin biiru, *Kirin biiru gojū nenshi*, 131-32.
66   *The Japan-Manchukuo Year Book: Cyclopedia of General Information and Statistics on the Empires of Japan and Manchukuo* (Tokyo: Japan-Manchukuo Year Book, 1939), 428, 431. During the period 1932-36, the yen traded at an average of US$0.29.
67   Kirin biiru, *Kirin biiru gojū nenshi*, 122.
68   Ibid., 123.
69   Chūgai shōgyō shimpōsha (Foreign and Domestic Business Newspaper Company), *Industrial expansion of Japan and Manchoukuo*, 1935 ed. (Tokyo: Chūgai shōgyō shimpōsha, 1936), 39.
70   Kirin biiru, *Kirin biiru gojū nenshi*, 123-25.
71   Tetsudōin (Department of Railways), *An Official Guide to Eastern Asia: Chōsen and Manchuria, Siberia*, vol. 1 (Tokyo: Department of Railways, 1920), xcii n.
72   For one manufacturing company's discussion of the city, the plants there, and the Allied bombing campaign, see Miyata seisakusho (Miyata Manufacturing), ed., *Miyata seisakusho shichijūnenshi* [Seventy-year history of Miyata Manufacturing] (Tokyo: Miyata seisakusho KK, 1959), 144-45. For a discussion of the liberation of the camp by Allied soldiers in 1945, see Ronald H. Spector, *In the Ruins of Empire: The Japanese Surrender and the Battle for Postwar Asia* (New York: Random House, 2008), 11-14.
73   *Contemporary Manchuria* (Minami manshū tetsudō KK [South Manchuria Railway Co., Inc.]) 3 (1939): 72-76.
74   Kirin biiru, *Kirin biiru gojū nenshi*, 125-28.
75   Ibid., 128.
76   Matsūra, *Biiru ni kansuru chōsa hōkokusho*, 2-10.
77   Miyake Yūzō, *Biiru kigyō shi* [A history of the beer industry] (Tokyo: Mitakisha, 1977), 135.

78 Daqing Yang, *Technology of Empire: Telecommunications and Japanese Expansion in Asia, 1883-1945* (Cambridge, MA: Harvard University Asia Center, Harvard University Press, 2010), 297-314.
79 *China Weekly Review* (Shanghai) 84-85 (1938): 184.
80 The phrase used by Kirin is *sesshū sareta* (requisitioned), which is a more passive way of saying "seized."
81 Kirin biiru, *Kirin biiru gojū nenshi*, 149-50.
82 See especially Saya S. Shiraishi and Takashi Shiraishi, eds., *The Japanese in Colonial Southeast Asia* (Ithaca, NY: Cornell University Press, 1993).
83 Shimizu Hiroshi and Hirakawa Hitoshi, *Japan and Singapore in the World Economy: Japan's Economic Advance into Singapore, 1870-1965* (London: Routledge, 1999), 138-39.
84 Frank N. Trager, *Burma: Japanese Military Administration, Selected Documents, 1941-1945* (Philadelphia: University of Pennsylvania Press, 1971), 97.
85 Kirin biiru, *Kirin biiru gojū nenshi*, 149-51.
86 Sapporo biiru, *Sapporo 120 nenshi*, 310.
87 Ibid., 309.
88 The merger ratio decided on was 10:7.5, where for every 10 shares of Sakura Beer stock delivered, Dai Nippon Beer had to deliver 7.5 shares. These terms increased Dai Nippon Beer's capital by ¥3.75 million as Sakura Beer added 100,000 shares, with ¥5 million.
89 Kirin biiru, *Kirin biiru gojū nenshi*, 148.
90 Asahi biiru KK, *Asahi 100* (Tokyo: Asahi biiru KK, 1990), 194-95; Sapporo biiru, *Sapporo 120 nenshi*, 310-11; Kirin biiru, *Kirin biiru gojū nenshi*, 148.
91 "Russians Strip Manchurian Industry," *Life* (New York), 20, 12 (25 March 1946): 32.
92 Kirin biiru, *Kirin biiru gojū nenshi*, 132-33.
93 Sapporo biiru, *Sapporo 120 nenshi*, 303.
94 Ibid.

Chapter 4: "The Taste of Home"

1 James J. Cooke, *Chewing Gum, Candy Bars, and Beer: The Army PX in World War II* (Columbia: University of Missouri Press, 2009), 159.
2 Kenneth B. Pyle, "Japan and the United States: An Unnatural Intimacy," *Journal of Japanese Studies* 37, 2 (Summer 2011): 377-95.
3 Andrew Gordon, *Postwar Japan as History* (Berkeley: University of California Press, 1993), 64, 245.
4 Sapporo biiru KK, *Sapporo 120 nenshi* [120-year history of Sapporo Breweries] (Tokyo: Sapporo biiru KK, 1996), 312.
5 Kirin biiru KK, *Kirin biiru KK gojū nenshi* [Kirin Brewery Company, Ltd.: Fifty-year history] (Tokyo: Kirin biiru KK, 20 March 1957), 161.
6 Ibid., 159-60.
7 Ibid.
8 Sapporo biiru, *Sapporo 120 nenshi*, 313.
9 Ibid.; Kirin biiru, *Kirin biiru gojū nenshi*, 161, 167.
10 Special thanks to Professor Masao Nakamura for his helpful explanation of this unique tax arrangement. "Sengō zeisei no sutāto" [Start of the postwar tax system], Kokuzeichō (National Tax Agency), 2012, http://www.nta.go.jp/ntc/sozei/shiryou/library/17.htm; Sapporo biiru, *Sapporo 120 nenshi*, 312-13.
11 Sapporo biiru, *Sapporo 120 nenshi*, 312-13.
12 Quoted in Nishimura Akira, *Asahi biiru no keiei senryaku* [Asahi Breweries' management strategy] (Tokyo: Tachibana shuppansha KK, 1999), 53.

13 John Dower, *Embracing Defeat: Japan in the Wake of World War II* (New York: W.W. Norton, 2000), 127.

14 Tanaka Yuki, *Japan's Comfort Women: Sexual Slavery and Prostitution during World War II and the US Occupation* (London: Routledge, 2002), 141-44.

15 *Asahi Shimbun*, 13 September 1945, 2; 25 October 1945, 2.

16 Sapporo biiru, *Sapporo 120 nenshi*, 317-18.

17 William P. Woodard, *The Allied Occupation of Japan 1945-1952 and Japanese Religions* (Leiden, Netherlands: Brill, 1972), 366.

18 Sapporo biiru, *Sapporo 120 nenshi*, 317.

19 Kirin biiru KK, ed., *Biiru to Nihonjin: Meiji/Taishō/Shōwa fukyūshi* [Beer and the Japanese: A broad Meiji/Taishō/Shōwa history] (Tokyo: Sanseidō, 1984), 264.

20 Sapporo biiru, *Sapporo 120 nenshi*, 317; Kirin biiru, *Kirin biiru gojū nenshi*, 161, 167; Kirin biiru, *Biiru to Nihonjin*, 265.

21 Takemae Eiji, *Inside GHQ: The Allied Occupation of Japan and Its Legacy* (London: Continuum International, 2002), 406.

22 Dower, *Embracing Defeat*, 89-93, 569n11.

23 *Asahi Shimbun*, 8 February 1946, article reproduced in Sapporo biiru, *Sapporo 120 nenshi*, 315; Kirin biiru, *Kirin biiru gojū nenshi*, 152.

24 Umemura Maki notes that companies entering the postwar pharmaceutical industry were formerly in unrelated sectors such as food, beverages, confectionery, brewing, and textiles. See Umemura, *The Japanese Pharmaceutical Industry: Its Evolution and Current Challenges* (New York: Routledge, 2011), 13; and Chapter 4 of Jeffrey W. Alexander, *Japan's Motorcycle Wars: An Industry History* (Vancouver: UBC Press, 2008).

25 A photo of the Food May Day protest appeared in the *Mainichi* newspaper (Tokyo) on 19 May 1946; reproduced in Sapporo biiru, *Sapporo 120 nenshi*, 316. For further commentary on the Food May Day and associated demonstrations, see Dower, *Embracing Defeat*, 267-71.

26 Sapporo biiru, *Sapporo 120 nenshi*, 315-16.

27 Ibid., 316-17; Kirin biiru, *Kirin biiru gojū nenshi*, 153.

28 Sapporo biiru, *Sapporo 120 nenshi*, 316-17.

29 Ibid.; Kirin biiru, *Kirin biiru gojū nenshi*, 154, 156.

30 Tim Craig, "The Japanese Beer Wars: Initiating and Responding to Hypercompetition in New Product Development," in "Hypercompetition," special issue, *Organization Science* 7, 3 (May-June 1996): 306.

31 For further discussion of the drinking patterns of Japanese women and men, see Julia Adeney Thomas, "Women and Wine in Japan," *Wine and Spirits* (March 1988); Kirin biiru, *Kirin biiru gojū nenshi*, 165.

32 Kirin biiru, *Kirin biiru gojū nenshi*, 152-53.

33 For a detailed table of beer prices and taxes from 1945 to 1965, see ibid., 248-49.

34 Sapporo biiru, *Sapporo 120 nenshi*, 319-20.

35 Dower, *Embracing Defeat*, 139.

36 Sapporo biiru, *Sapporo 120 nenshi*, 320.

37 Ibid., 318, 320, 356; Kirin biiru, *Kirin biiru gojū nenshi*, 153.

38 Dower, *Embracing Defeat*, 75, 82, 210, 546.

39 Yamamura Kozo, *Economic Policy in Postwar Japan: Growth versus Economic Democracy* (Berkeley: University of California Press, 1967), 14.

40 Iyori Hiroshi and Uesugi Akinori, *The Antimonopoly Laws and Policies of Japan* (Somers, NY: Federal Legal Publications, 1994), 59; Kirin biiru, *Kirin biiru gojū nenshi*, 156; Sapporo biiru, *Sapporo 120 nenshi*, 341.

41 Miki Yōnosuke, *Biiru sensō* [Beer war] (Tokyo: Sankei, 1974), 26-35.

42 Noda Iwajirō, *Zaibatsu kaitai shiki* [Reminiscences on zaibatsu dissolution], Watakushi no rirekisho [Personal histories] (Tokyo: Nihon keizai shimbun-sha, 1983), quoted in Sapporo biiru, *Sapporo 120 nenshi*, 339.

43 Miyamoto Kotarō, *Asahi biiru seikōsuru kigyō fūdo: Uchigawa kara mita fukkatsu no hosoku* [Asahi Breweries' successful corporate culture: An inside view of its comeback principles] (Tokyo: Shodensha KK, 2002), 23.

44 Nakajō Takanori, *Risshi no keiei: Asahi biiru fukkatsu no genten to waga bijinesu jinsei* [Management success: The starting point of Asahi Breweries' comeback and my business life] (Tokyo: Chichi shuppansha KK, 1993), 68.

45 Asahi bakushu rōdō kumiai (Asahi Labour Union), *Asahi bakushu rōdō kumiai no kumiaishi, 1945-1970* [History of the Asahi Labour Union, 1945-1970] (Tokyo: Asahi bakushu rōdō kumiai, 1974), quoted in Sapporo biiru, *Sapporo 120 nenshi*, 340.

46 Ibid.

47 Asahi biiru KK, *Asahi 100* (Tokyo: Asahi biiru KK, 1990), 198; Sapporo biiru, *Sapporo 120 nenshi*, 341.

48 The other two firms were Japan Iron and Steel, and Ōji Paper. Burton Crane, "Zaibatsu Breakup Nearly Completed: Decentralization Board Names Only 50 Japanese Companies on Its List Awaiting Action," *New York Times*, 15 January 1949.

49 Miki, *Biiru sensō*, 66.

50 Paul Preston, Michael Partridge, and Antony Best, *British Documents on Foreign Affairs – Reports and Papers from the Foreign Office Confidential Print*, Series E: Asia, Part 4: From 1946 through 1950, (Frederick, MD: University Publications of America, 2000), 94. By that point in his career, Takahashi had risen to become chair of the Japan Chamber of Commerce and Industry and a member of the House of Councillors (serving from 1947 to 1953). After leaving Nippon Beer, Takahashi served as minister of international trade and industry from 1951 to 1952, and president of the All-Japan Football Association, before getting involved in Japan's pharmaceutical industry.

51 Matsui Yasuo, *Takaga biiru saredo biiru: Asahi sūpā dorai 18 nenme no shinbi* [It's only beer, but it's beer all the same: Asahi Super Dry's eighteenth beautiful year] (Tokyo: Nikkan kōgyō shimbun-sha KK, 2005), 53.

52 Sapporo biiru, *Sapporo 120 nenshi*, 156, 317, 339, 351-59.

53 Jōzō sangyō shimbun-sha henshū kyokuhen (Brewing Industry Newspaper Company Editing Bureau), ed., *Shurui sangyo sanjūnen: Sengo hatten no kiseki* [Thirty-year history of the alcoholic beverage industry: The path of postwar development] (Tokyo: Yamazaki shuppansha, 1983), 6.

54 Kirin biiru, *Kirin biiru gojū nenshi*, 191-94.

55 Jōzō sangyō shimbun-sha, *Shurui sangyo sanjūnen*, 10.

56 *Asahi Shimbun*, 27-31 May 1955; 6 June 1955.

57 Kirin biiru, *Kirin biiru gojū nenshi*, 195; Sapporo biiru, *Sapporo 120 nenshi*, 321-23.

58 Hanbai Kyōikusha¨(Sales Instructor), *Sapporo biiru* [Sapporo Breweries] (Tokyo: Shuppan sābisu, 1983), 114-15.

59 Nakajō, *Risshi no keiei*, 68.

60 Kirin biiru, *Kirin biiru gojū nenshi*, 196-98, unpaginated photo insert, 198-99.

61 Ibid., 164.

62 Ibid., 166.

63 See especially Carola Hein, "Rebuilding Japanese Cities after 1945," in *Rebuilding Urban Japan after 1945*, ed. Carola Hein, Jeffry M. Diefendorf, and Ishida Yorifusa (New York: Palgrave Macmillan, 2003), 1-16.

64 Nishimura, *Asahi biiru no keiei senryaku*, 59-61.

65 Kirin biiru, *Kirin biiru gojū nenshi*, 164-65.

66 Ibid., 165; Sapporo biiru, *Sapporo 120 nenshi*, 382.
67 Joseph Schumpeter, *Capitalism, Socialism, and Democracy*, 3rd ed. (New York: Harper and Row, 1950), 84, quoted in Craig, "Japanese Beer Wars," 302.
68 Craig, "Japanese Beer Wars," 302, 306.
69 Richard Boyd, "Rents and Economic Outcomes in Japan and Taiwan," in *East Asian Capitalism, Conflicts, Growth, and Crisis*, ed. Luigi Tomba (Milan, Italy: Fondazione Giangiacomo Feltrinelli, 2002), 168-71; John Sutton, *Sunk Costs and Market Structure: Price Competition, Advertising, and the Evolution of Concentration* (Cambridge, MA: MIT Press, 1991), 530-31.
70 For further discussion of beer pricing and cartelism, see Boyd, "Rents and Economic Outcomes," 168-71; and Sutton, *Sunk Costs and Market Structure*, 530-31.
71 Nakajō, *Risshi no keiei*, 25, 102.
72 Sapporo biiru, *Sapporo 120 nenshi*, 785.
73 Matsui, *Takaga biiru saredo biiru*, 57, 60.
74 Miki, *Biiru sensō*, 201.
75 Tanaka, *Japan's Comfort Women*, 141-44.
76 *Asahi Shimbun*, 1 June 1949, 2.
77 Sapporo biiru, *Sapporo 120 nenshi*, 358.
78 Ibid., 352-53.
79 Joseph L. Anderson and Donald Richie, *The Japanese Film: Art and Industry* (Princeton, NJ: Princeton University Press, 1982), 288-89.
80 "Joseito kū, odorasete" [Schoolgirls forced to dance to survive], *Asahi Shimbun*, 10 September 1950, 3.
81 Miyamoto, *Asahi biiru seikōsuru kigyō fūdo*, 26.
82 Nishimura, *Asahi biiru no keiei senryaku*, 69.
83 Kirin biiru, *Kirin biiru gojū nenshi*, 191.
84 *Asahi Shimbun*, 27 December 1952, 7; 9 February 1953, 7; 14 February 1953, 3; 10 May 1960, 5.
85 *Yomiuri Shimbun*, 15 May 1964, 11; *Asahi Shimbun*, 15 May 1964, 7.
86 Sapporo biiru, *Sapporo 120 nenshi*, 781.
87 Author's personal collection. Many thanks to Teri Bryant for sending a scan of Nippon Beer's "10 Years since the War" poster.
88 Japanese consumed a record 1,605,000 koku (289,500 kL) of beer in the first half of 1956. *Asahi Shimbun*, 25 August 1956.
89 Sapporo biiru, *Sapporo 120 nenshi*, 381, 385-86.
90 Miyake Yūzō, *Biiru kigyō shi* [A history of the beer industry] (Tokyo: Mitakisha, 1977), 43.
91 Iain Gately, *Drink: A Cultural History of Alcohol* (London: Gotham Books, 2008), 443.
92 Sapporo biiru, *Sapporo 120 nenshi*, 781, 783.
93 Ibid., 785.
94 Asahi biiru, *Asahi 100*, unpaginated illustration section, part 4.
95 Albert Moran and Michael Keane, *Television across Asia: TV Industries, Programme Formats and Globalisation* (London: Routledgecurzon, 2004), 22.
96 Sapporo biiru, *Sapporo 120 nenshi*, 785, 787.
97 Ibid., 787, 789.
98 In 1947, nine years after its last increase in 1938, Kirin had raised its capital stock to ¥25 million; Kirin then raised it to ¥80 million in 1949, and to ¥202 million in 1950. Thereafter, the company reassessed all of its fixed assets and put the revalued amount into a separate reserve fund at a rate of 1:1, giving it a reserve of capital stock valued at ¥402.3 million. A small portion of this total came from the restoration of foreign-owned shares, which had been returned to the company in the interim. By 1952, Kirin's capital stock reached ¥602.27

million, fully half of which was paid-in, but even this was not sufficient to keep up with the cost of its expansion plans. Kirin biiru, *Kirin biiru gojū nenshi*, 161-62, 166-67.

99 *Asahi Shimbun*, 26 March 1953.
100 *Asahi Shimbun*, 2 September 1955; Jōzō sangyō shimbun-sha, *Shurui sangyo sanjūnen*, 8.
101 Mizukawa Susumu, *Nihon no biiru sangyō* [Japan's beer industry] (Tokyo: Senshu University Press, 2002), 22. For details on Takara Brewing Co.'s debut, see Tobita Etsujirō and Shimano Morio, *Biiru wa doko ga katsu ka: Gendai o ugokasu toppu riida* [Where are the beer market winners? Current shifts in the top leadership] (Tokyo: Daiyamondo-sha, 1992), 12-17.
102 *Nihon Keizai Shimbun*, 7 February 1955, reproduced in Sapporo biiru, *Sapporo 120 nenshi*, 381.
103 Jōzō sangyō shimbun-sha, *Shurui sangyo sanjūnen*, 13.
104 Sapporo biiru, *Sapporo 120 nenshi*, 379-80.
105 Jōzō sangyō shimbun-sha, *Shurui sangyo sanjūnen*, 13.
106 Takara shuzō KK stock was listed in mid-January 1958. *Japan Times* (Tokyo), 8 January 1958, 1.
107 For further discussion of the debut of canned beer in Japan, see Ishiguro Keishichi, *Biiru monogatari* [The history of beer] (Tokyo: Shinmaisho, 1961), 178-80; and Sapporo biiru, *Sapporo 120 nenshi*, 382-84.
108 *Tokyo Mail* 2, 6 (1962): 8. With thanks to the Tokyo Metropolitan Archives for permission to photograph this rare source.
109 *Asahi nenkan* [Asahi Almanac], cited in Sapporo biiru, *Sapporo 120 nenshi*, 380.
110 *Tokyo Mail* 2, 6 (1962): 9.
111 Suzuki Takashi, *Jihanki no jidai* [The era of vending machines] (Tokyo: Nikkei, 2007), 197.
112 Sapporo biiru, *Sapporo 120 nenshi*, 380.
113 *Tokyo Mail* 2, 6 (1962): 10.
114 See *Asahi Shimbun*, 25 August 1978, 23.
115 Anne Allison, *Nightwork: Sexuality, Pleasure, and Corporate Masculinity in a Tokyo Hostess Club* (Chicago: University of Chicago Press, 1994), 7-10.
116 Brian Moeran, "Drinking Country: Flows of Exchange in a Japanese Valley," in *Drinking Cultures*, ed. Thomas M. Wilson (Oxford: Berg, 2005), 25-43.
117 Amy Beth Borovoy, *The Too-Good Wife: Alcohol, Codependency, and the Politics of Nurturance in Postwar Japan* (Berkeley: University of California Press, 2005), 45.
118 For further discussions of the drinking culture of Japan's salarymen, see David W. Plath, *The After Hours: Modern Japan and the Search for Enjoyment* (Berkeley: University of California Press, 1964), 184-90; Gately, *Drink*, 443-45; Borovoy, *Too-Good Wife*, 46-47; Eyal Ben-Ari, "Sake and 'Spare Time': Management and Imbibement in Japanese Business Firms" (Papers in Japanese Studies, University of Singapore, 1993); and Kato Keiko, "Dysfunction of Functional Drinking: Voices of Japanese Alcoholics' Wives" (PhD diss., Washington State University, 2004).
119 Michael L. Gerlach, *Alliance Capitalism: The Social Organization of Japanese Business* (Berkeley: University of California Press, 1997), 173; John G. Roberts, *Mitsui: Three Centuries of Japanese Business* (New York: Weatherhill, 1973), 282.
120 Sapporo biiru, *Sapporo 120 nenshi*, 380.
121 "Japs Becoming Beer Drinkers," *Petersburg* (VA) *Progress-Index*, 7 September 1958, 20.
122 *Yomiuri Shimbun*, 9 July 1957, 6.
123 Tanaka Yukiko, *Contemporary Portraits of Japanese Women* (Westport, CT: Praeger, 1995), 79.
124 Matsui, *Takaga biiru saredo biiru*, 79.
125 Jōzō sangyō shimbun-sha, *Shurui sangyo sanjūnen*, 25; Tobita and Shimano, *Biiru wa doko ga katsu ka*, 12-17; Suntory KK, *Hibi ni arata ni: Santori hyakunenshi* [Fresh every day:

100-year history of Suntory] (Osaka: Suntory KK, 1999), 144-49; Mizukawa, *Nihon no biiru sangyō*, 22.

126   *Tōyō Keizai Shimpō* [Oriental economist newspaper] (Tokyo), 27 August 1983, cited in Itami Hiroyuki, *Mobilizing Invisible Assets*, with Thomas W. Roehl (Cambridge, MA: Harvard University Press, 1987), 136-37.

127   For background on Japan's whisky market, including the rise of Suntory and Nikka as whisky producers as well as Suntory's decision to enter the beer market, see Kaidō Mamoru, *Yōshū, biiru* [Western liquor, beer] (Tokyo: Jitsumu kyōiku shuppansha, 1989), 89-100, 140-46.

128   Sapporo biiru, *Sapporo 120 nenshi*, 380, 383; and Suntory, *Hibi ni arata ni*, 146. Penelope Francks also discusses the boom in beer sales enabled by rising Japanese salaries during the era of the "economic miracle." See Francks, *The Japanese Consumer: An Alternative Economic History of Modern Japan* (Cambridge: Cambridge University Press, 2009), 166.

129   Jōzō sangyō shimbun-sha, *Shurui sangyo sanjūnen*, 21-59.

130   Suzuki, *Jihanki no jidai*, 216-18.

131   Ron Sanchez, "Analyzing Internal and Competitor Competences: Resources, Capabilities, and Management Processes," in *The Oxford Handbook of Strategy*, ed. David O. Faulkner and Andrew Campbell (New York: Oxford University Press, 2006), 375-77.

132   *Asahi Shimbun*, 8 April 1967.

133   Sanchez, "Analyzing Internal and Competitor Competences," 375; Sutton, *Sunk Costs and Market Structure*, 530n.

134   For discussions of the evolution of television advertising in Japan, see Part 3 of Jayson Makoto Chun, *"A Nation of a Hundred Million Idiots"? A Social History of Japanese Television* (New York: Routledge, 2007).

Chapter 5: Learning from Japan

1   For further discussion of Okinawa's culture, see George H. Kerr, *Okinawa: History of an Island People* (Rutland, VT: C.E. Tuttle, 1958), which is one of the few monographs on Okinawa that does not deal chiefly with the Battle of Okinawa or the archipelago's role as an East Asian pawn on the Cold War chessboard.

2   Kuroyanagi Yasunori, "Miyako minseifu chiji toshite no Gushiken Sōsei" [Gushiken Sōsei as a governor of Miyako provisional government], *Okinawa hōgaku, Okinawa kokusai daigaku* [Journal of the Association of Law, Okinawa International University] 37 (2008): 83-102.

3   Leonard Weiss, "U.S. Military Government on Okinawa," *Far Eastern Survey* 15, 15 (31 July 1946): 234-38.

4   Ikeda Takayuki, "War Damage Reconstruction, City Planning and US Civil Administration in Okinawa," in *Rebuilding Urban Japan after 1945*, ed. Carola Hein, Jeffry M. Diefendorf and Ishida Yorifusa (New York: Palgrave Macmillan, 2003), 127, 130, 133.

5   Orion biiru KK, *Orion yonjūnen no ayumi* [Forty-year history of Orion Breweries] (Naha: Orion biiru KK, 18 May 1967), 5.

6   This significant issue is explored in an unpublished MA thesis; see Tomonori Genka, "Okinawa's Import Substitution Policy: A History and Evaluation" (University of Tennessee, 1971).

7   Ikeda, "War Damage Reconstruction," 132.

8   Orion biiru, *Orion yonjūnen no ayumi*, 6-7.

9   Ibid., 9.

10   Ibid., 9-11.

11   Jōzō sangyō shimbun-sha henshū kyokuhen (Brewing Industry Newspaper Company Editing Bureau), ed., *Shurui sangyo sanjūnen: Sengo hatten no kiseki* [Thirty-year history

of the alcoholic beverage industry: The path of postwar development] (Tokyo: Yamazaki shuppansha, 1983), 15; Orion biiru, *Orion yonjūnen no ayumi*, 10-12.

12 Orion biiru, *Orion yonjūnen no ayumi*, 12.

13 Ibid., 13.

14 "Okinawans to Build Brewery at Nago City," *Pacific Stars and Stripes* (Washington, DC), 3 April 1957, 26.

15 Ibid.

16 Such recovery funds had once been made available free through the Government and Relief in Occupied Areas (GARIOA) capital fund, but from 1949 they became loans that had to be repaid. This new Ryūkyū Recovery Loan Fund was managed by the Okinawa Development Promotion Loan Corporation *(Okinawa shinkō kaihatsu kinyūkōko)*. In April 1950, the military government also announced that it was establishing an Economic Recovery Fund *(Keizai fukkō kikin)*, the management of which was assumed by the Ryūkyū Development Corporation *(Ryūkyū kaihatsu kinyū kōkō)* in 1959. Orion biiru, *Orion yonjūnen no ayumi*, 45.

17 James B. Lampert, *Final Report of the High Commissioner to the Ryūkyū Islands* (Naha, Okinawa: High Commissioner of the Ryūkyū Islands, 14 May 1972), 12-13.

18 Orion biiru, *Orion yonjūnen no ayumi*, 15.

19 Quoted ibid., 16-17.

20 *Okinawa Times* (Naha), 13 May 1957.

21 Economic Bureau of the Ryūkyū Government, 22 May 1957, quoted in Orion biiru, *Orion yonjūnen no ayumi*, 19.

22 Orion biiru, *Orion yonjūnen no ayumi*, 19-20.

23 Ibid., 21-22.

24 Ibid., 22.

25 Ibid., 23-24.

26 "Okinawans to Build Brewery at Nago City," *Pacific Stars and Stripes* (Washington, DC), 3 April 1957, 26.

27 Quoted in "New Home Product: Okinawa Beer – Brewery Makes 1st Delivery," *Pacific Stars and Stripes,* 27 May 1959, 30.

28 Orion biiru, *Orion yonjūnen no ayumi*, 25-26.

29 *Okinawa Times* (Naha), 26 May 1959.

30 Orion biiru, *Orion yonjūnen no ayumi*, 28-32.

31 Ibid., 28.

32 Ibid., 33.

33 Ibid., 33-34.

34 Ibid., 34.

35 Ibid., 35.

36 Quoted ibid.

37 Ibid., 36.

38 Ibid.

39 Ibid., 37-38.

40 Ibid., 37.

41 Ibid., 41.

42 Ibid., 40-41.

43 Ibid., 41-42, 45.

44 Ibid., 45, 47.

45 Ibid., 48.

46 Beer taxes in mainland Japan were also the world's highest in the 1960s, composing 52.3 percent of beer's purchase price in 1964, as compared to 31.1 percent in Great Britain,

19.5 percent in Italy, 10.1 percent in the United States, and just 8.7 percent in West Germany. *Asahi Shimbun,* 3 May 1964. Japan's alcohol taxes remain the highest in the world today.

47   Orion biiru, *Orion yonjūnen no ayumi,* 47.
48   Ibid., 49.
49   "Nago Develops into a Thriving Industrial City: 15 Years Bring Big Changes," *Pacific Stars and Stripes* (Washington, DC), 15 August 1961, 36.
50   Orion biiru, *Orion yonjūnen no ayumi,* 51.
51   Ibid., 52.
52   "Nago Brewery Triples Output: In Ryukyus Now, It's Bring on the Beer," *Pacific Stars and Stripes* (Washington, DC), 18 November 1962, 35.
53   Orion biiru, *Orion yonjūnen no ayumi,* 52-53.
54   Ibid., 54-56.
55   Ibid., 57.
56   *Asahi Shimbun,* 30 May 1969; Orion biiru, *Orion yonjūnen no ayumi,* 57-58. Orion would maintain its 90 percent market share into the early 1970s.
57   Orion biiru, *Orion yonjūnen no ayumi,* 59.
58   Quoted ibid., 58.
59   "Nago Brewery Triples Output: In Ryukyus Now, It's Bring on the Beer," *Pacific Stars and Stripes* (Washington, DC), 18 November 1962, 35.
60   Orion biiru, *Orion yonjūnen no ayumi,* 59.
61   "Nago Brewery Triples Output: In Ryukyus Now, It's Bring on the Beer," *Pacific Stars and Stripes* (Washington, DC), 18 November 1962, 35.
62   Quoted in Orion biiru, *Orion yonjūnen no ayumi,* 61.
63   Ibid., 64-65.
64   Ibid., 65.
65   Letter from Falstaff Brewing Corporation to Orion Breweries, Ltd., 19 July 1963, reproduced in Orion biiru, *Orion yonjūnen no ayumi,* 48. Gushiken visited the Falstaff Brewery in June 1963.
66   Orion biiru, *Orion yonjūnen no ayumi,* 66-68.
67   Ibid., 68-69.
68   Ibid., 73.
69   "The 'Miracle Mile' Becomes 'Street of Broken Dreams,'" *Pacific Stars and Stripes* (Washington, DC), 15 June 1974, 25.
70   Phil Brown, "Revaluation Plagues Okinawa," Associated Press, 11 May 1972.
71   *Asahi Shimbun,* 8 April 1967.

Chapter 6: Indigenous Brews

1   Sleeman's brewing crew leader, Chris McCormick, reports that in triangle taste tests pitting Japan-brewed "Sapporo" against Sleeman's version, not even the firm's Japanese personnel can tell the difference. Email correspondence with the author, 4 July 2011.
2   Roger Farrell, *Japanese Investment in the World Economy: A Study of Strategic Themes in the Internationalisation of Japanese Industry* (Northampton, MA: Edward Elgar, 2008), 193-94.
3   Hiroko Tabuchi, "Why Japan's Cellphones Haven't Gone Global," *New York Times,* 19 July 2009.
4   Jōzō sangyō shimbun-sha henshū kyokuhen (Brewing Industry Newspaper Company Editing Bureau), ed., *Shurui sangyo sanjūnen: Sengo hatten no kiseki* (Thirty-year history of the alcoholic beverage industry: The path of postwar development) (Tokyo: Yamazaki shuppansha, 1983), 41-49.
5   Ibid., 43.

6　Sapporo biiru KK, *Sapporo 120 nenshi* [120-year history of Sapporo Breweries] (Tokyo: Sapporo biiru KK, 1996), 791.

7　*Yomiuri Shimbun,* 14 March 1976, 23.

8　Inokuchi Osami, *Anrāningu kakumei: Kirin bīru no asu o yomu* [Unlearning revolution: Reading Kirin Brewery's tomorrow] (Tokyo: Daiyamondo-sha, 1992), 26-27.

9　Stephen R. Smith, "Drinking Etiquette in a Changing Beverage Market," in *Re-Made in Japan: Everyday Life and Consumer Taste in a Changing Society,* ed. Joseph J. Tobin (New Haven, CT: Yale University Press, 1992), 143-56.

10　Jōzō sangyō shimbun-sha, *Shurui sangyo sanjūnen,* 65.

11　Richard Boyd, "Rents and Economic Outcomes in Japan and Taiwan," in *East Asian Capitalism, Conflicts, Growth, and Crisis,* ed. Luigi Tomba (Milan, Italy: Fondazione Giangiacomo Feltrinelli, 2002), 196.

12　For discussion of Kirin's diversification strategy, see Ōhashi Masafusa, *Kirin biiru no takakuka senryaku* [Kirin Brewery's diversification strategy] (Tokyo: Shibata shoten, 1979); and Nakada Shigemitsu, *Kirin biiru no henshin: Raifu indasutorii kakumei e no chōsen* [The transformation of Kirin Brewery: The start of a life-industry revolution] (Tokyo: Daiyamondo-sha, 1988), 129-35.

13　For details on the Kirin-Seagram tie-up, see especially Umezawa Shōtarō, *Dokusō Kirin biiru no ketsudan* [Solo decisions: Kirin Brewery in the lead] (Tokyo: Hyōgensha, 1983), 37; Ōhashi, *Kirin biiru no takakuka senryaku,* 215-53; and Hotta Masayasu, *Kirin biiru* [Kirin Brewery] (Tokyo: Asahi sonoramu, 1980), 151-58.

14　Boyd, "Rents and Economic Outcomes," 196.

15　Umezawa, *Dokusō Kirin biiru no ketsudan,* 39; Ōhashi, *Kirin biiru no takakuka senryaku,* 169-92; Hotta, *Kirin biiru,* 158-77.

16　Andrew Gordon, *Postwar Japan as History* (Berkeley: University of California Press, 1993), 275-77.

17　Tanaka Yukiko, *Contemporary Portraits of Japanese Women* (Westport, CT: Praeger, 1995), 79.

18　Weng-shing Tseng, *Handbook of Cultural Psychiatry* (San Diego, CA: Academic Press, 2001), 352.

19　*MERI's Monthly Circular: Survey of Economic Conditions in Japan* (Tokyo: Mitsubishi keizai kenkyūsho [Mitsubishi Economic Research Institute]), July 1982, 228-29.

20　Nakamura Yoshihei, *3-nengo no biiru, yōshu gyōkai fuchin no kōzu* [The composition of the beer and liquor market after three years of ups and downs] (Tokyo: Besuto bukku, 1993), 108-9. Shōchū is distilled from grain, sweet potatoes, or rice, and typically contains 25 percent alcohol by volume.

21　See especially Nakajō Takanori, *Risshi no keiei: Asahi biiru fukkatsu no genten to waga bijinesu jinsei* [Management success: The starting point of Asahi Breweries' comeback and my business life] (Tokyo: Chichi shuppansha KK, 1993); Nishimura Akira, *Asahi biiru no keiei senryaku* [Asahi Breweries' management strategy] (Tokyo: Tachibana shuppansha KK, 1999); Nakajō Takanori, *Asahi biiru kishi kaisei no keiei senryaku to jinsei tetsugaku* [The management strategies and the philosophy of life behind the revival of Asahi Breweries], Heihō ni manabu: Katsu tame ni nasubeki koto [Lessons in the art of war: What must be done in order to win] (Tokyo: Keizaikai KK, 2002); Miyamoto Kotarō, *Asahi biiru seikōsuru kigyō fūdo: Uchigawa kara mita fukkatsu no hosoku* [Asahi Breweries' successful corporate culture: An inside view of its comeback principles] (Tokyo: Shodensha KK, 2002); Matsui Yasuo, *Takaga biiru saredo biiru: Asahi sūpā dorai 18 nenme no shinbi* [It's only beer, but it's beer all the same: Asahi Super Dry's eighteenth beautiful year] (Tokyo: Nikkan kōgyō shimbun-sha KK, 2005); Nakajō Takanori and Kono Toyohiro, "Success through Culture Change in a Japanese Brewery," *Long Range Planning* 22, 6

(December 1989): 29-37; and Asahi biiru KK, *Asahi 100* (Tokyo: Asahi biiru KK, 1990), 72-76.

22 Takigawa Ayako, *Biiru sensō no butai ura: Dorai būmu no suitai* [Behind the scenes of the beer war: The decline of the dry boom] (Tokyo: Banseisha, 1992), 27.

23 "Words to Live By: Asahi Breweries Advisor Nakajo Takanori," *Japan Times* (Tokyo), 27 August 2009.

24 Matsui, *Takaga biiru saredo biiru*, 8; Malcolm S. Salter and Kokuryo Jiro, *Asahi Breweries Ltd.,* Harvard Business Case Study (Cambridge, MA: Harvard Business School Case Services, 23 February 1989).

25 For a lengthy discussion of beer and Japanese cuisine, as well as glassware and serving etiquette (complete with diagrams), see *Biiru no jiten: Tanoshisha ichiban minna de kanpai!* [The beer encyclopedia: Cheers to number one enjoyment!] (Tokyo: Sanseidō, 1984), 158-72.

26 Tobita Etsujirō and Shimano Morio, *Biiru wa doko ga katsu ka: Gendai o ugokasu toppu riida* [Where are the beer market winners? Current shifts in the top leadership] (Tokyo: Daiyamondo-sha, 1992), 84-87.

27 Inokuchi, *Anrāningu kakumei,* 173-77.

28 Nakada, *Kirin biiru no henshin,* 1.

29 "Kirin Brewery to Close Some Plants," *New York Times,* 29 July 1997.

30 Mizukawa Susumu, *Nihon no biiru sangyō* [Japan's beer industry] (Tokyo: Senshu University Press, 2002), 97.

31 Nagata Kazukai, "Kirin-Suntory Merger Talks Break Down: Deal Doomed by Discord over Share Ratio," *Japan Times* (Tokyo), 9 February 2010.

32 Andrew Feinberg, "And Now from Japan, the Hot New 'Dry' Beers," *New York Times,* 10 July 1988.

33 David A. Aaker, *Brand Relevance: Making Competitors Irrelevant* (San Francisco: John Wiley and Sons, 2011), 2-3; Steven P. Schnaars, *Managing Imitation Strategies* (New York: Free Press, 1994), 92-95; Dominique Turpin, Christopher H. Lovelock, and Joyce Miller, "Kirin Brewery Co., Ltd.: The Dry Beer War," case study. (Cambridge, MA: *Harvard Business Review,* 1 January 1992).

34 "Asahi Plans Super Dry Anniversary Blitz," *Japan Times* (Tokyo), 15 December 2006.

35 "Beer Sales Fall 2.7%, Lowest since '91," *Japan Times* (Tokyo), 16 January 2009.

36 James Sterngold, "Japanese Beer Drinkers Get Something New: Discounts," *New York Times,* 21 April 1994.

37 Ibid.

38 "Japanese Market Introduction," Japan Craft Beer Association, http://www.craftbeer association.jp/jpcraftbeermarket.html.

39 For recent sources on this subject see *Nippon jibiiru hyakka: Saishin jibiiru jigyō jittai chōsa shiryōshū: Jitsurei kara saguru Nihongata jibiiru jigyō seikō no shuhō* [Encyclopedia of Japanese craft beers: Document collection investigating the true state of the craft-brewing industry: Searching for examples of successful techniques from Japanese-style craft brewing businesses] (Tokyo: Sōgōyunikomu, 1997).

40 Ogata Fusako, "Breweries (Japan)," in *Alcohol and Temperance in Modern History: An International Encyclopedia,* vol. 1, ed. Jack S. Blocker, David M. Fahey, and Ian R. Tyrrell (Santa Barbara, CA: ABC-CLIO, 2003), 415.

41 Miyake Yūzō, *Biiru kigyō shi* [A history of the beer industry] (Tokyo: Mitakisha, 1977), 330.

42 Ogata, "Breweries (Japan)," 415.

43 OECD (Organisation for Economic Co-operation and Development) Centre for Tax Policy and Administration, "Table IV.3, Taxation of beer (2007)," Tax Database, http://www. OECD.org.

44 Bryan Baird, "Japan's Beer Revolution: The Birth, Death, and Resurrection of Japanese Craft Beer," lecture at the Japan Society, New York, 5 October 2011. Unpublished paper given to the author by Baird, co-owner of the Baird Brewing Company of Numazu, Japan, in which Baird cites figures on participant firms from the Japan National Tax Agency.

45 David Besanko, David Dranove, Mark Shanley, and Scott Schaefer, *Economics of Strategy,* 5th ed. (Boston, MA: Harvard Business School, 2009), 313.

46 Author's conversation with John Chesen, the Bairds' partner, at the Bashamichi Taproom, Yokohama, July 2011; see also Baird Brewing's website, http://www.bairdbeer.com.

47 Japan Craft Beer Association.

48 The ministry's 67 percent rule is partly inspired by Germany's strict Reinheitsgebot beer purity law of 1516, which is one lingering German influence that today makes a convenient tax criterion.

49 "Happoshu: A Sparkling Alternative," *Japan Times* (Tokyo), 30 June 2002.

50 Aaker, *Brand Relevance,* 4.

51 "LDP Eyes Putting Beer-Like Beverages in Same Tax Category as Beer," Kyodo News International, 9 December 2005.

52 Besanko et al., *Economics of Strategy,* 314.

53 "Japanese Market Introduction," Japan Craft Beer Association, http://www.craftbeer association.jp/jpcraftbeermarket.html.

54 "'Happoshu' to Eclipse Beer for First Time," *Japan Times* (Tokyo), 11 December 2003.

55 "April Beer Shipments at Record Low," *Japan Times* (Tokyo), 15 May 2012; "Asahi Eyes 60% China Beer Sales Boost," *Japan Times* (Tokyo), 25 February 2012.

56 Rob Gilhooly, "German Braumeister Puts Otaru Brewery on Map," *Japan Times* (Tokyo), 22 January 2011.

57 Ibid.

58 Ibid.

Conclusion

1 Stephen R. Smith, "Drinking Etiquette in a Changing Beverage Market," in *Re-Made in Japan: Everyday Life and Consumer Taste in a Changing Society,* ed. Joseph J. Tobin (New Haven, CT: Yale University Press, 1992), 143. See also Chapter 5 in Kōno Shōzō, *Bijinesu no seisei: Seiryō inryō no Nihonka* [Business creation: The Japanization of cool beverages] (Tokyo: Bunshindō, 2002).

Bibliography

Newspapers, Magazines, and Yearbooks
Note: Date ranges are given for current and defunct periodicals.

American Brewers' Review (US Brewer's Association). Chicago: Der Braumeister, 1891-1918.
Asahi Nenkan [Asahi almanac]. Osaka: Asahi Newspaper, annual.
Asahi Shimbun [Asahi newspaper]. Osaka: 1879-present.
China Weekly Review (later *China Monthly Review*). Shanghai: Millard Publishing House, 1923-41; 1945-50.
Chinese Times. Tianjin: 1886-91.
Contemporary Manchuria. 1939. Dairen: Minami manshū tetsudō KK (South Manchuria Railway Co., Inc.).
Japan Advertiser. Tokyo: 1905-40.
Japan Chronicle. Kobe: 1905-42.
The Japan-Manchukuo Yearbook: Cyclopedia of General Information and Statistics on the Empires of Japan and Manchukuo. Tokyo: Japan-Manchukuo Yearbook, 1934-41.
Japan Times. Tokyo: 1897-present.
The Japan Times Year Book, 1930 edition. Tokyo: Japan Times, 1 January 1931.
Japan Weekly Mail: A Review of Japanese Commerce, Politics, Literature, and Art (later *Japan Daily Mail*). Yokohama: Harper Collins, 1870-1915.
The Japan Year Book: Complete Cyclopaedia of General Information and Statistics on Japan and Japanese Territories for the Year [...] Tokyo: 1908-52.
Life. New York: 1883-2000.
London and China Telegraph. London: 1859-1921.
Mainichi Shimbun [Daily newspaper]. Tokyo: 1872-present.
MERI's Monthly Circular: Survey of Economic Conditions in Japan. Tokyo: Mitsubishi keizai kenkyūsho (Mitsubishi Economic Research Institute), 1923-present.
New York Times. 1851-present.
Nihon Keizai Shimbun [Japan economic times]. Tokyo: Nihon Keizai Shimbun KK, 1876-present.
North China Herald (later *North China Daily News*). Shanghai: 1850-1951.
Okinawa Times. Naha: 1948-present.
Osaka Mainichi Shimbun [Osaka daily newspaper]. Osaka: 1876-1911.
Pacific Stars and Stripes (a division of *Stars and Stripes* since 1945). Washington, DC: 1861-present.
Petersburg (VA) *Progress-Index.* 1865-present.
Straits Times. Singapore: 1845-present.
Strand Magazine. London: 1891-1946.
Tokyo Mail. Tokyo: Kyōdō seikei, 1961-63.
Tōyō Keizai Shimpō [Oriental economist newspaper]. Tokyo: 1895-present.

Western Brewer: and Journal of the Barley, Malt and Hop Trades (later *Brewer's Journal: and Barley, Malt and Hop Trades Reporter*). Chicago: 1876-1920.

Yokohama Mainichi Shimbun [Yokohama daily newspaper]. 1871-1940.

Yomiuri Shimbun [Yomiuri newspaper]. Tokyo: 1874-present.

Japanese-Language Sources

Asahi bakushu rōdō kumiai (Asahi Labour Union). *Asahi bakushu rōdō kumiai no kumiaishi, 1945-1970* [History of the Asahi Labour Union, 1945-1970]. Tokyo: Asahi bakushu rōdō kumiai, 1974. Quoted in Sapporo biiru, *Sapporo 120 nenshi*.

Asahi biiru KK. *Asahi 100*. Tokyo: Asahi biiru KK, 1990.

Biiru no jiten: Tanoshisha ichiban minna de kanpai! [The beer encyclopedia: Cheers to number one enjoyment!]. Tokyo: Sanseidō, 1984.

Endo Kazuō. *Nihon no gijutsu, 10: Biiru no 100 nen* [Historical technology in Japan, vol. 10: 100 years of beer]. Tokyo: Daiichi hōki shuppansha, 1989.

Fukuzawa Yukichi. *Seiyō jijō* [Conditions in the West]. Tokyo: Shōkodō, 1867. Quoted in Kirin biiru, *Kirin biiru gojū nenshi*.

Gendai kigyō kenkyūkai (Modern Enterprise Research Association). *Kirin biiru* [Kirin Brewery]. Tokyo: Meiji Shoin, 1962.

Hajima Tomoyuki. *Shimbun kōkoku bijutsu taikei* [Compendium of newspaper advertisement artwork]. Tokyo: Ōzorosha, 2003-7.

Hanbai kyōikusha (Sales Instructor). *Sapporo biiru* [Sapporo Breweries]. Tokyo: Shuppan sābisu, 1983.

Haruyama Yukio. *Biiru bunka shi* [The history of beer culture]. Tokyo: Tokyo shobōsha, 1972.

Hotta Masayasu. *Kirin biiru* [Kirin Brewery]. Tokyo: Asahi sonoramu, 1980.

Inagaki Masami. *Nihon no biiru* [Japanese beer]. Tokyo: Chūō kōronsha, 1978.

Inokuchi Osami. *Anrāningu kakumei: Kirin bīru no asu o yomu* [Unlearning revolution: Reading Kirin Beer's tomorrow]. Tokyo: Daiyamondo-sha, 1992.

–. *Kirin no ryūgi: Kane ni tayoru na, jibun ni tayore!* [The Kirin way: Don't rely on money, rely on yourself!]. Tokyo: Puresidento-sha KK, 2007.

Ishiguro Keishichi. *Biiru monogatari* [The history of beer]. Tokyo: Shinmaisho, 1961.

Jōzō Sangyō Shimbun-sha henshū kyokuhen (Brewing Industry Newspaper Company Editing Bureau), ed. *Shurui sangyo sanjūnen: Sengo hatten no kiseki* [Thirty-year history of the alcoholic beverage industry: The path of postwar development]. Tokyo: Yamazaki shuppansha, 1983.

Kaidō Mamoru. *Yōshū, biiru* [Western liquor, beer]. Tokyo: Jitsumu kyōiku shuppansha, 1989.

Kawashima Tomou. "Kindai Nihon ni okeru shuzō kenchiku no hensen – shuzōsho, biiru kōjō" [The changing architecture of breweries in modern Japan – Sake breweries and beer factories]. Research paper published online by Asahi Breweries, 2006, http://www.asahibeer.co.jp/csr/philanthropy/ab-academic/image/pdf/report2006/cul_03.pdf.

Kayama Michinosuke and Hotta Shōzō. *Yokohama-shi shi kō* [The written history of Yokohama City]. 11 vols. Yokohama: Yokohama City, 1931-33. Cited in Kirin biiru, *Kirin biiru gojū nenshi*.

Kikuchi Takeo and Yanai Saki. *Nakagawa Seibē deni biiru-zukuri no senjin* (The life of Nakagawa Seibē: Beer-making pioneer). Tokyo: Yashio shuppansha, 1982.

Kirin biiru KK. *Biiru to bunmei kaika no Yokohama: Kōpurando seitan 150-nen kinen* (Beer and Yokohama's civilization and enlightenment: Commemorating 150 years since Copeland's birth). Tokyo: Kirin biiru KK, 1984.

. –, ed. *Biiru to Nihonjin: Meiji/Taishō/Shōwa fukyūshi* [Beer and the Japanese: A broad Meiji/Taishō/Shōwa history]. Tokyo: Sanseidō, 1984.

–. *Kirin biiru KK gojū nenshi* [Kirin Brewery Company, Ltd.: Fifty-year history]. Tokyo: Kirin biiru KK, 20 March 1957.

Kokuzeichō (National Tax Agency). "Sengō zeisei no sutāto" [Start of the postwar tax system]. 2012. http://www.nta.go.jp/ntc/sozei/shiryou/library/17.htm.

Kōno Shōzō. *Bijinesu no seisei: Seiryō inryō no Nihonka* [Business creation: The Japanization of cool beverages]. Tokyo: Bunshindō, 2002.

Kuroyanagi Yasunori. "Miyako minseifu chiji toshite no Gushiken Sōsei" [Sōsei Gushiken as a governor of Miyako provisional government]. *Okinawa hōgaku, Okinawa kokusai daigaku* [Journal of the Association of Law, Okinawa International University] 37 (2008): 83-102.

Matsui Yasuo. *Takaga biiru saredo biiru: Asahi sūpā dorai 18 nenme no shinbi* [It's only beer, but it's beer all the same: Asahi Super Dry's eighteenth beautiful year]. Tokyo: Nikkan kōgyō shimbun-sha KK, 2005.

Matsūra Susumu. *Biiru ni kansuru chōsa hōkokusho* [Investigative report concerning beer]. Manchuria: Government of Manchukuo, 1936.

Matsuyama Mosuke. *Biiru jōzōgaku* [Beer zymurgy]. Tokyo: Tōyō keizai shimpō-sha, 1970.

–. *Biiru wisuki* [Beer, whisky]. Tokyo: Kyōwa seihon KK, 1951.

Miki Yōnosuke. *Biiru sensō* [Beer war]. Tokyo: Sankei, 1974.

Miyake Yūzō. *Biiru kigyō shi* [A history of the beer industry]. Tokyo: Mitakisha, 1977.

Miyamoto Kotarō. *Asahi biiru seikōsuru kigyō fūdo: Uchigawa kara mita fukkatsu no hosoku* [Asahi Breweries' successful corporate culture: An inside view of its comeback principles]. Tokyo: Shodensha KK, 2002.

Miyata seisakusho (Miyata Manufacturing), ed. *Miyata seisakusho shichijūnenshi* [Seventy-year history of Miyata Manufacturing]. Tokyo: Miyata seisakusho KK, 1959.

Mizukawa Susumu. *Nihon no biiru sangyō* [Japan's beer industry]. Tokyo: Senshu University Press, 2002.

Murakami Mitsuru. *Biiru denrai: Mori Ōgami to doitsu biiru* [Imported beer: Mori Ōgami and German beer]. Tokyo: Sogensha, 2006.

Naitō Hiroshi. "Meijiki biiru gyōkai ni okeru gaikokujin gijutsusha no keifu: Yebisu biiru no baii ni" [The geneaology of foreign engineers in the Meiji-era Japanese beer industry: The case of Yebisu Beer]. *Keiei shigaku* [Japan business history review] 29, 4 (January 1995): 58-75.

Nakada Shigemitsu. *Kirin biiru no henshin: Raifu indasutorii kakumei e no chōsen* [The transformation of Kirin Brewery: The start of a life industry revolution]. Tokyo: Daiyamondo-sha, 1988.

Nakajō Takanori. *Asahi biiru kishi kaisei no keiei senryaku to jinsei tetsugaku* [The management strategies and the philosophy of life behind the revival of Asahi Breweries]. Heihō ni manabu: Katsu tame ni nasubeki koto [Lessons in the art of war: What must be done in order to win]. Tokyo: Keizaikai KK, 2002.

–. *Risshi no keiei: Asahi biiru fukkatsu no genten to waga bijinesu jinsei* [Management success: The starting point of Asahi Breweries' comeback and my business life]. Tokyo: Chichi shuppansha KK, 1993.

Nakamura Takafusa. *Nihon keizai: Sono seichō to kōzō* [The Japanese economy: Its development and structure]. 3rd ed. Tokyo: Tokyo University Press, 1993. Quoted in Bai Gao, *Economic Ideology and Japanese Industrial Policy: Developmentalism from 1931 to 1965.* Cambridge: Cambridge University Press, 1997.

Nakamura Yoshihei. *3-nengo no biiru, yōshu gyōkai fuchin no kōzu* [The composition of the beer and liquor market after three years of ups and downs]. Tokyo: Besuto bukku, 1993.

Nihon jidōsha kōgyōkai (Japan Automobile Manufacturers Association), ed. *Mōtāsaikuru no Nihon shi* [Japan motorcycle history]. Tokyo: Sankaidō Press, 1995.

Nihon nikkeru jihōkyoku (Japan Nickel Information Bureau). *Biiru jōzō to nikkeru oyobi sono gōkin* [Nickel and its alloys in beer brewing]. Tokyo: Nihon nikkeru jihōkyoku, 1938.

Nippon jibiiru hyakka: Saishin jibiiru jigyō jittai chōsa shiryōshū: Jitsurei kara saguru Nihongata jibiiru jigyō seikō no shuhō [Encyclopedia of Japanese craft beers: Document collection investigating the true state of the craft-brewing industry: Searching for examples of successful techniques from Japanese-style craft brewing businesses]. Tokyo: Sōgōyunikomu, 1997.

Nishimura Akira. *Asahi biiru no keiei senryaku* [Asahi Breweries' management strategy]. Tokyo: Tachibana shuppansha KK, 1999.

Noda Iwajirō. *Zaibatsu kaitai shiki* [Reminiscences on zaibatsu dissolution]. Watakushi no rirekisho [Personal histories]. Tokyo: Nihon keizai shimbun-sha, 1983. Quoted in Sapporo biiru, *Sapporo 120 nenshi.*

Ōhashi Masafusa. *Kirin biiru no takakuka senryaku* [Kirin Brewery's diversification strategy]. Tokyo: Shibata shoten, 1979.

Orion biiru KK. *Jūnen no ayumi: Orion biiru KK* [Ten-year history of Orion Breweries]. Naha: Orion biiru KK, 18 May 1967.

–. *Orion yonjūnen no ayumi* [Forty-year history of Orion Breweries]. Naha: Orion biiru KK, 28 July 1998.

Sapporo biiru KK. *Dai Nippon biiru sanjūnenshi* [Thirty-year history of Dai Nippon Beer]. Tokyo: Dai Nippon biiru KK, 26 March 1936.

–. *Sapporo 120 nenshi* [120-year history of Sapporo Breweries]. Tokyo: Sapporo biiru KK, 1996.

Sapporo Holdings, Ltd. "The History of Sapporo Breweries." 2013. http://www.sapporo-holdings.jp/english/history/.

Satō Kenji. *Nihon no biiru seisuishi* [The rise and fall of Japanese beers]. Tokyo: Tokyo shobōsha, 1985.

Shibusawa Eiichi Memorial Foundation. "Chronology of the Life of Shibusawa Eiichi." 2013. http://www.shibusawa.or.jp/english/eiichi/chronology.html.

Suntory KK. *Hibi ni arata ni: Santori hyakunenshi* [Fresh every day: 100-year history of Suntory). Osaka: Suntory KK, 1999.

Suzuki Takashi. *Jihanki no jidai* [The era of vending machines]. Tokyo: Nikkei, 2007.

Takebe Seian and Sugita Genpaku. *Oranda iji mondō* [Questions and answers on Holland]. First published 1795. Quoted in Kirin biiru, *Kirin biiru gojū nenshi.*

Takigawa Ayako. *Biiru sensō no butai ura: Dorai būmu no suitai* [Behind the scenes of the beer war: The decline of the dry boom]. Tokyo: Banseisha, 1992.

Tanaka Kazuo. *Monogatari Sapporo biiru* [The history of Sapporo Breweries]. Sapporo: Hokkaido shimbun-sha, 1993.

Tanji Yuichi. "Dai Nippon Bakushu no keiei to hanbaimo, 1906-1939" [The marketing policy of Dai Nippon Brewery Co., 1906-1939]. *Shakai keizai shigaku* [Socioeconomic history] 67, 3 (January 2001): 3-26.

Tetsudō shō un'yukyoku (Railway Department, Transportation Office). *Cha, tabako, seishu, biiru, seiryō inryō ni kansuru chōsa* [Investigation concerning the tea, cigarette, sake, beer, and cold drink markets]. Tokyo: Tetsudō shō un'yukyoku, 1926.

Tobita Etsujirō and Shimano Morio. *Biiru wa doko ga katsu ka: Gendai o ugokasu toppu riida* [Where are the beer market winners? Current shifts in the top leadership]. Tokyo: Daiyamondo-sha, 1992.

Ueda Toshirō. *Biiru tengoku* [Beer heaven]. Tokyo: Bokusho, 1963.

Umezawa Shōtarō. *Dokusō Kirin biiru no ketsudan* [Solo decisions: Kirin Brewery in the lead]. Tokyo: Hyōgensha, 1983.

Yanagita Kunio and Charles S. Terry. *Kaikoku hyakunen kinen bunka jigyōkai* [Japanese manners and customs in the Meiji era]. Tokyo: Ōbunsha, 1957.

English-Language Sources
Note: Japanese names are presented here with family name first and given name second, as in the rest of the book.

Aaker, David A. *Brand Relevance: Making Competitors Irrelevant.* San Francisco: John Wiley and Sons, 2011.

Ajioka Chiaki. *Modern Boy Modern Girl: Modernity in Japanese Art, 1910-1935.* Sydney: Art Gallery of New South Wales, 1998.

Alexander, Jeffrey W. *Japan's Motorcycle Wars: An Industry History.* Vancouver: UBC Press, 2008.

–. "Nikon and the Sponsorship of Japan's Optical Industry by the Imperial Japanese Navy, 1917-1945." *Japanese Studies* 22, 1 (2002): 19-31.

Allison, Anne. *Nightwork: Sexuality, Pleasure, and Corporate Masculinity in a Tokyo Hostess Club.* Chicago: University of Chicago Press, 1994.

Anderson, Joseph L., and Donald Richie. *The Japanese Film: Art and Industry.* Princeton, NJ: Princeton University Press, 1982.

Baird, Bryan. "Japan's Beer Revolution: The Birth, Death, and Resurrection of Japanese Craft Beer." Lecture at the Japan Society, New York, 5 October 2011.

Barnhart, Michael A. *Japan Prepares for Total War: The Search for Economic Security, 1919-1941.* Ithaca, NY: Cornell University Press, 1987.

Ben-Ari, Eyal. "Sake and 'Spare Time': Management and Imbibement in Japanese Business Firms." Papers in Japanese Studies, University of Singapore, 1993.

Besanko, David, David Dranove, Mark Shanley, and Scott Schaefer. *Economics of Strategy,* 5th ed. Boston: Harvard Business School, 2010.

Board of Trade Journal (London) 21 (1896).

Borovoy, Amy Beth. *The Too-Good Wife: Alcohol, Codependency, and the Politics of Nurturance in Postwar Japan.* Berkeley: University of California Press, 2005.

Boyd, Richard. "Rents and Economic Outcomes in Japan and Taiwan." In *East Asian Capitalism, Conflicts, Growth, and Crisis,* edited by Luigi Tomba, 151-92. Milan, Italy: Fondazione Giangiacomo Feltrinelli, 2002.

Brown, Kendall H., and Sharon Minichiello. *Taishō Chic: Japanese Modernity, Nostalgia, and Deco.* Honolulu, HI: Honolulu Academy of Arts, 2001.

Capron, Horace. *Reports and Official Letters to the Kaitakushi* [Hokkaido Colonization Office]. Tokyo: Kaitakushi, 1875.

Chamberlain, Basil Hall, and W.B. Mason. *A Handbook for Travellers in Japan,* 4th ed. London: John Murray, 1894.

Chao, Sheau-Yueh J. *The Japanese Automobile Industry: An Annotated Bibliography.* Westport, CT: Greenwood Press, 1994.

Chūgai shōgyō shimpōsha (Foreign and Domestic Business Newspaper Company). *Industrial Expansion of Japan and Manchoukuo,* 1935 ed. Tokyo: Chūgai shōgyō shimpōsha, 1936.

Chun, Jayson Makoto. *"A Nation of a Hundred Million Idiots"? A Social History of Japanese Television.* New York: Routledge, 2007.

Clancey, Gregory K. *Earthquake Nation: The Cultural Politics of Japanese Seismicity, 1868-1930.* Berkeley: University of California Press, 2010.

Cooke, James J. *Chewing Gum, Candy Bars, and Beer: The Army PX in World War II.* Columbia: University of Missouri Press, 2009.

Craig, Tim. "The Japanese Beer Wars: Initiating and Responding to Hypercompetition in New Product Development." In "Hypercompetition." Special issue, *Organization Science* 7, 3 (May-June 1996): 302-21.

Cusumano, Michael A. "'Scientific Industry': Strategy, Technology, and Entrepreneurship in Prewar Japan." In Wray, *Managing Industrial Enterprise,* 269-315.

Cwiertka, Katarzyna J. *Modern Japanese Cuisine: Food, Power and National Identity.* London: Reaktion Books, 2006.

Dickinson, Frederick R. *War and National Reinvention: Japan in the Great War, 1914-1919.* Cambridge, MA: Harvard University Press, 1999.

Dower, John. *Embracing Defeat: Japan in the Wake of World War II.* New York: W.W. Norton, 2000.

Ericson, Steven J. "Railroads in Crisis: The Financing and Management of Japanese Railway Companies during the Panic of 1890." In Wray, *Managing Industrial Enterprise,* 121-82.

–. *The Sound of the Whistle: Railroads and the State in Meiji Japan.* Cambridge, MA: Harvard University Press, 1996.

Farrell, Roger. *Japanese Investment in the World Economy: A Study of Strategic Themes in the Internationalisation of Japanese Industry.* Northampton, MA: Edward Elgar, 2008.

Finck, Henry Theophilus. *Lotos-time in Japan.* New York: Charles Scribner's Sons, 1895.

Finn, Dallas. "Reassessing the Rokumeikan." In *Challenging Past and Present: The Metamorphosis of Nineteenth-Century Japanese Art,* edited by Ellen P. Conant, 227-39. Honolulu: University of Hawai'i Press, 2006.

Francks, Penelope. "Inconspicuous Consumption: Sake, Beer, and the Birth of the Consumer in Japan." *Journal of Asian Studies* 68, 1 (February 2009): 135-64.

–. *The Japanese Consumer: An Alternative Economic History of Modern Japan.* Cambridge: Cambridge University Press, 2009.

Fuess, Harald. "Investment, Importation, and Innovation: Genesis and Growth of Beer Corporations in Pre-war Japan." In *Institutional and Technological Change in Japan's Economy: Past and Present,* edited by Janet Hunter and Cornelia Storz, 43-59. London: Routledge, 2006.

Fujimoto Taizō. *The Nightside of Japan.* London: T. Werner Laurie, 1914.

Garon, Sheldon. "Fashioning a Culture of Diligence and Thrift: Savings and Frugality Campaigns in Japan, 1900-1931." In *Japan's Competing Modernities: Issues in Culture and Democracy, 1900-1930,* edited by Sharon A. Minichiello, 312-34. Honolulu: University of Hawai'i Press, 1998.

Gately, Iain. *Drink: A Cultural History of Alcohol.* London: Gotham Books, 2008.

Gerlach, Michael L. *Alliance Capitalism: The Social Organization of Japanese Business.* Berkeley: University of California Press, 1997.

Goodman, Grant K. "Japan and Philippine Beer: The 1930s." *Journal of Southeast Asian Studies* 1, 1 (January 1970): 54-59.

Gordon, Andrew. *Postwar Japan as History.* Berkeley: University of California Press, 1993.

Haas, Jeff. "They Have No Idea What It Is to Run a Malthouse: A Wisconsin Beer Maker in Japan." *Wisconsin Magazine of History,* 87, 2 (Winter 2003-4): 14-29.

Hara Akira. "Wartime Controls." In *The Economic History of Japan, 1600-1900,* vol. 3: *Economic History of Japan, 1914-1955, A Dual Structure,* edited by Nakamura Takafusa and Odaka Kōnosuke, translated by Noah S. Brannen, 247-86. New York: Oxford University Press, 1999.

Havens, Thomas R.H. *Valley of Darkness: The Japanese People and World War Two.* New York: W.W. Norton, 1978.

Hawks, Francis L., compiler. *Narrative of the Expedition of an American Squadron to China and Japan, Performed in the Years 1852, 1853, and 1854, under the Command of Commodore M.C. Perry United States Navy, by Order of the Government of the United States,* vol. 1. Washington, DC: A.O.P. Nicholson, 1856.

Hazama Hiroshi. "Historical Changes in the Life Style of Industrial Workers." In *Japanese Industrialization and Its Social Consequences,* edited by Hugh Patrick with Larry Meissner, 21-52. Berkeley: University of California Press, 1976.

Hein, Carola. "Rebuilding Japanese Cities after 1945." In *Rebuilding Urban Japan after 1945*, edited by Carola Hein, Jeffry M. Diefendorf, and Ishida Yorifusa, 1-16. New York: Palgrave Macmillan, 2003.

Hirschmeier, Johannes. *The Origins of Entrepreneurship in Meiji Japan*. Cambridge, MA: Harvard University Press, 1964.

Hokkaido Government. "History of Hokkaido." In *Gurafu Hokkaidō (Hokkaidō graph)*. Sapporo: Public Relations and Opinions Division, Hokkaido Government, 2011.

Howe, Christopher. *The Origins of Japanese Trade Supremacy: Development and Technology in Asia from 1540 to the Pacific War*. London: Hurst, 1996.

Ikeda Takayuki. "War Damage Reconstruction, City Planning and US Civil Administration in Okinawa." In *Rebuilding Urban Japan after 1945*, edited by Carola Hein, Jeffry M. Diefendorf, and Ishida Yorifusa, 127-55. New York: Palgrave Macmillan, 2003.

Ion, A. Hamish. *The Cross in the Dark Valley: The Canadian Protestant Missionary Movement in the Japanese Empire, 1931-1945*. Waterloo, ON: Wilfrid Laurier University Press, 1999.

Itami Hiroyuki. *Mobilizing Invisible Assets*. With Thomas W. Roehl. Cambridge, MA: Harvard University Press, 1987.

Iyori Hiroshi and Uesugi Akinori. *The Antimonopoly Laws and Policies of Japan*. Somers, NY: Federal Legal Publications, 1994.

Johnson, Chalmers. *MITI and the Japanese Miracle: The Growth of Industrial Policy, 1925-1975*. Stanford, CA: Stanford University Press, 1982.

Johnston, Bruce F. *Japanese Food Management in World War II*. Stanford, CA: Stanford University Press – Stanford Food Research Institute, 1953.

Katō Kazuyasu. "Growing in a World of Change." In *Rediscovering Japanese Business Leadership: 15 Japanese Managers and the Companies They're Leading to New Growth*, edited by Hasegawa Yōzō, 95-108. Singapore: John Wiley and Sons, 2011.

Kato Keiko. "Dysfunction of Functional Drinking: Voices of Japanese Alcoholics' Wives." PhD diss., Washington State University, 2004.

Keene, Donald. "Memories of Edward Seidensticker." *International House of Japan Bulletin* 27, 2 (December 2007): 20-29.

Kerr, George H. *Okinawa: History of an Island People*. Rutland, VT: C.E. Tuttle, 1958.

Laker, Joseph Alphonse. "Entrepreneurship and the Development of the Japanese Beer Industry, 1872-1937." PhD diss., Indiana University, 1975.

Lampert, James B. *Final Report of the High Commissioner to the Ryūkyū Islands*. Naha, Okinawa: High Commissioner of the Ryūkyū Islands, 14 May 1972.

Lloyd, Arthur. *Every-Day Japan: Written after Twenty-Five Years' Residence and Work in the Country*. London: Cassell, 1909.

Low, Morris. *Building a Modern Japan: Science, Technology, and Medicine in the Meiji Era and Beyond*. New York: Palgrave Macmillan, 2005.

Lublin, Elizabeth Dorn. *Reforming Japan: The Woman's Christian Temperance Union in the Meiji Period*. Vancouver: UBC Press, 2010.

McNamara, Dennis L. *The Colonial Origins of Korean Enterprise, 1910-1945*. Cambridge: Cambridge University Press, 1990.

Moeran, Brian. "Drinking Country: Flows of Exchange in a Japanese Valley." In *Drinking Cultures*, edited by Thomas M. Wilson, 25-43. Oxford: Berg, 2005.

Moran, Albert, and Michael Keane. *Television across Asia: TV Industries, Programme Formats and Globalisation*. London: Routledgecurzon, 2004.

Morikawa Hidemasa. *Zaibatsu: The Rise and Fall of Family Enterprise Groups in Japan*. Tokyo: University of Tokyo Press, 1992.

Morris-Suzuki, Tessa. *The Technological Transformation of Japan: From the Seventeenth to the Twenty-First Century*. Cambridge: Cambridge University Press, 1994.

Nakajō Takanori and Kono Toyohiro. "Success through Culture Change in a Japanese Brewery." *Long Range Planning* 22, 6 (December 1989): 29-37.

Nakamura Takafusa. "Depression, Recovery, and War, 1920-1945." In *The Economic Emergence of Modern Japan*, vol. 1, edited by Yamamura Kōnō, 116-58. Cambridge: Cambridge University Press, 1997.

Nakane Chie and Ōishi Shinzaburō. *Tokugawa Japan: The Social and Economic Antecedents of Modern Japan*. Tokyo: Tokyo University Press, 1990.

"Notes." *Nature* 19 (27 February 1879): 395-97.

Odagiri Hiroyuki and Goto Akira. *Technology and Industrial Development in Japan: Building Capabilities by Learning, Innovation, and Public Policy*. New York: Oxford University Press, 1996.

Ogata Fusako. "Breweries (Japan)." In *Alcohol and Temperance in Modern History: An International Encyclopedia*, vol. 1, edited by Jack S. Blocker, David M. Fahey, and Ian R. Tyrrell, 415. Santa Barbara, CA: ABC-CLIO, 2003.

Pauer, Erich, ed. *Japan's War Economy*. London: Routledge, 1999.

Pilat, Dirk. *The Economics of Rapid Growth: The Experience of Japan and Korea*. Brookfield, VT: Edward Elgar, 1994.

Plath, David W. *The After Hours: Modern Japan and the Search for Enjoyment*. Berkeley: University of California Press, 1964.

Pratt, Edward E. *Japan's Proto-Industrial Elite: The Economic Foundations of the Gōnō*. Cambridge, MA: Harvard University Press, 1999.

Preston, Paul, Michael Partridge, and Antony Best. *British Documents on Foreign Affairs – Reports and Papers from the Foreign Office Confidential Print*. Series E: *Asia*, Part 4: *From 1946 through 1950*. Frederick, MD: University Publications of America, 2000.

Pyle, Kenneth B. "Japan and the United States: An Unnatural Intimacy." *Journal of Japanese Studies* 37, 2 (Summer 2011): 377-95.

Roberts, John G. *Mitsui: Three Centuries of Japanese Business*. New York: Weatherhill, 1973.

Saitō Osamu and Shimbo Hiroshi. "The Economy on the Eve of Industrialization." In *The Economic History of Japan: 1600-1990*, vol. 1: *Emergence of Economic Society in Japan, 1600-1859*, edited by Hayami Akira, Saitō Osamu, and Ronald P. Toby, 337-68. Oxford: Oxford University Press, 1999.

Salter, Malcolm S., and Jiro Kokuryo. *Asahi Breweries Ltd.* Harvard Business School. Cambridge, MA: Harvard Business School Case Services, rev. ed., 1995.

Samuels, Richard J. *Rich Nation, Strong Army: National Security and Ideology in Japan's Technological Transformation*. Ithaca, NY: Cornell University Press, 1994.

Sanchez, Ron. "Analyzing Internal and Competitor Competences: Resources, Capabilities, and Management Processes." In *The Oxford Handbook of Strategy*, edited by David O. Faulkner and Andrew Campbell, 350-77. New York: Oxford University Press, 2006.

Sasaki Satoshi. "The Rationalization of Production Management Systems in Japan." In *World War II and the Transformation of Business Systems*, edited by Shiba Takao and Sakadō Jun, 30-58. Tokyo: Tokyo University Press, 1994.

Sato, Barbara Hamill. *The New Japanese Woman: Modernity, Media, and Women in Interwar Japan*. Durham, NC: Duke University Press, 2003.

Schnaars, Steven P. *Managing Imitation Strategies*. New York: Free Press, 1994.

Schumpeter, Joseph. *Capitalism, Socialism, and Democracy*. 3rd ed. New York: Harper and Row, 1950. Quoted in Craig, "Japanese Beer Wars."

Sheridan, Kyoko. *Governing the Japanese Economy*. Cambridge, UK: Polity Press, 1993.

Shimizu Hiroshi and Hirakawa Hitoshi. *Japan and Singapore in the World Economy: Japan's Economic Advance into Singapore, 1870-1965*. London: Routledge, 1999.

Shiraishi, Saya S., and Takashi Shiraishi, eds. *The Japanese in Colonial Southeast Asia*. Ithaca, NY: Cornell University Press, 1993.

Silverberg, Miriam. "The Modern Girl as Militant." In *Recreating Japanese Women, 1600-1945*, edited by Gail Bernstein, 239-66. Berkeley: University of California Press, 1991.

Slade, Toby. *Japanese Fashion: A Cultural History*. London: Berg, 2009.

Smith, Norman. *Intoxicating Manchuria: Alcohol, Opium, and Culture in China's Northeast*. Vancouver: UBC Press, 2012.

Smith, Stephen R. "Drinking Etiquette in a Changing Beverage Market." In *Re-Made in Japan: Everyday Life and Consumer Taste in a Changing Society*, edited by Joseph J. Tobin, 143-59. New Haven, CT: Yale University Press, 1992.

"Some Posters from Japan." *National Lithographer: Devoted to the Interests of Lithography and the Graphic Arts* 24, 9 (September 1917): 43-44.

Spector, Ronald H. *In the Ruins of Empire: The Japanese Surrender and the Battle for Postwar Asia*. New York: Random House, 2008.

Sutton, John. *Sunk Costs and Market Structure: Price Competition, Advertising, and the Evolution of Concentration*. Cambridge, MA: MIT Press, 1991.

Takemae Eiji. *Inside GHQ: The Allied Occupation of Japan and Its Legacy*. London: Continuum International, 2002.

Tanaka Yuki. *Japan's Comfort Women: Sexual Slavery and Prostitution during World War II and the US Occupation*. London: Routledge, 2002.

Tanaka Yukiko. *Contemporary Portraits of Japanese Women*. Westport, CT: Praeger, 1995.

Teichova, Alice, and Maurice Lévy-LeBoyer. *Historical Studies in International Corporate Business*. Cambridge: Cambridge University Press, 2002.

Tetsudōin (Department of Railways). *An Official Guide to Eastern Asia: Chōsen and Manchuria, Siberia*, vol. 1. Tokyo: Department of Railways, 1920.

Thomas, Julia Adeney. "Women and Wine in Japan." *Wine and Spirits* (March 1988): 26-30.

Tomonori Genka. "Okinawa's Import Substitution Policy: A History and Evaluation." MA thesis, University of Tennessee, 1971.

Trager, Frank N. *Burma: Japanese Military Administration, Selected Documents, 1941-1945*. Philadelphia: University of Pennsylvania Press, 1971.

Tseng, Weng-shing. *Handbook of Cultural Psychiatry*. San Diego, CA: Academic Press, 2001.

Tsutsui, William M. *Manufacturing Ideology: Scientific Management in Twentieth-Century Japan*. Princeton, NJ: Princeton University Press, 1998.

Turpin, Dominique, Christopher H. Lovelock, and Joyce Miller. "Kirin Brewery Co., Ltd.: The Dry Beer War." Case study. Cambridge, MA: *Harvard Business Review*, 1 January 1992.

Umemura Maki. *The Japanese Pharmaceutical Industry: Its Evolution and Current Challenges*. New York: Routledge, 2011.

Umesao Tadao, Yoshida Shūji, and Paul Gordon Schalow. *Alcoholic Beverages*. Japanese Civilization in the Modern World, vol. 18. Osaka: National Museum of Ethnology, 2003.

US Bureau of Foreign and Domestic Commerce. *Commerce Reports*. Washington, DC: Government Printing Office, 1916-17.

Weiss, Leonard. "U.S. Military Government on Okinawa." *Far Eastern Survey* 15, 15 (31 July 1946): 234-38.

Wilder, Amos P. "Christianizing America's Contacts through Political Relations." In *Men and World Service: Addresses Delivered at the National Missionary Congress, Washington, D.C., April 26-30, 1916*, 169-86. New York: Laymen's Missionary Movement, 1916.

Wittner, David G., ed. *Technology and the Culture of Progress in Meiji Japan*. Routledge/Asian Studies Association of Australia (ASAA) East Asian Series. Cambridge, UK: Routledge, 2007.

Woodard, William P. *The Allied Occupation of Japan 1945-1952 and Japanese Religions*. Leiden, Netherlands: Brill, 1972.

Wray, William D., ed. *Managing Industrial Enterprise: Cases from Japan's Prewar Experience*. Cambridge, MA: Harvard University Press, 1989.

–. *Mitsubishi and the N.Y.K., 1870-1914: Business Strategy in the Japanese Shipping Industry*. Cambridge, MA: Harvard University Press, 1984.

–. "Opportunity vs Control: The Diplomacy of Japanese Shipping in the First World War." In *The Merchant Marine in International Affairs, 1850-1950*, edited by Greg Kennedy, 59-83. London: Frank Cass, 2000.

Yamamura Kozo. *Economic Policy in Postwar Japan: Growth versus Economic Democracy*. Berkeley: University of California Press, 1967.

Yang, Daqing. *Technology of Empire: Telecommunications and Japanese Expansion in Asia, 1883-1945*. Cambridge, MA: Harvard University Asia Center, Harvard University Press, 2010.

Yasutake Rumi. "Transnational Women's Activism: The Woman's Christian Temperance Union in Japan and the United States." In *Women and Twentieth-Century Protestantism*, edited by Margaret Lamberts Bendroth and Virginia Lieson Brereton, 93-112. Chicago: University of Illinois Press, 2001.

Young, Louise. *Japan's Total Empire: Manchuria and the Culture of Wartime Imperialism*. Berkeley: University of California Press, 1998.

Index

sake, 6, 8, 9-12, 16-17, 40, 43, 51, 77-78,
93-94, 109, 11-12, 122, 127, 134, 140,
148, 158, 180-81, 184, 191, 194, 210,
231, 262n109, 269n43
Sakurazaka, Naha, 208-9, 214, 216
Sapporo City, 31, 34-37, 39, 41, 46(t), 59,
70, 73, 92, 117-18, 124, 162(t), 168,
241(t), 243(t), 244(t)
Sapporo Winter Olympiad (1972), 225
Satsuma Domain, 38-39, 85
Sawada Takeji, 201
Schumpeter, Joseph, 170, 224
Second World War (1939-45), 1-3, 54, 56,
73, 107, 109-45, 215, 238-39
Seidensticker, Edward, 87, 91
self-sufficiency (material/industrial), 2,
24, 57-58, 73, 108, 110, 115-19, 131, 139,
143-44, 147, 221, 238, 263n4
Sendai, 47(f), 80-81, 83, 94, 97, 124, 133,
149, 164(t), 167, 175, 200-1
Seoul, 97, 133, 267n94
Seto Yūzō, 151, 168, 174
Shandong Province, 46, 72, 138
Shanghai, 46, 48, 58, 72, 131
shareholders, 21, 25-27, 29-31, 67, 73-74,
81, 92, 97, 109, 161-62, 189, 197-99, 203,
214, 219, 220, 260n60, 260n71, 265n60
Shibusawa Eiichi, 27, 41
shōchū, 158, 180, 227, 279n20
Shōwa era (1926-89), 2, 109, 252, 262n117
Singapore, 24, 46, 69, 71, 80(t), 114(t),
137, 139
Sino-Japanese War (1894-95), 21, 46, 48
soda brands (*see* soft drinks, brands of)
soft drinks, 86, 91-92, 124, 138, 149, 156,
161, 162(t), 164(t), 168(t), 191, 215, 230
soft drinks, brands of: "Diamond Lemon,"
91; "Kirin Cider," 92; "Kirin Citron," 92;
"Kirin Lemon," 92, 164(t), 266n80; "Kirin
Tansan," 92; "Mitsuya Cider," 161, 162(t),
164(t); "Ribbon Citron," 161, 162(t),
164(t)
Soviet Union, 142-43, 147
soy sauce, 119, 138, 193-94, 204
starvation, postwar, 146, 153-54
Straights Colonies, 80(t), 114(t)
Suita City, 59, 70, 72, 92, 123(t), 162(t)
Sumida River, 49, 231
Sumitomo, 184, 269n30
supermarkets, 25, 229

Taishō era (1912-26), 2, 10, 64, 86, 91,
104, 111, 252, 262n117, 263n130
Taiwan, 46, 103, 111, 130, 137-38, 140,
148, 169(t), 219-20, 246(t)
Takahashi Ryūtarō, 102, 109-10, 117, 124,
126, 134, 137, 161-62, 273n50
tariffs, 19, 24, 43, 44(t), 45, 53, 170
taxes/taxation, xii, 4, 11, 13-14, 28, 30,
43-44, 45(t), 46, 53, 96(t), 99, 102, 108-9,
111, 113-15, 119-20, 121(t), 122, 128-30,
133, 135, 144-46, 149-50, 152-53, 156-
57, 159, 170, 179, 205, 209-10, 211(t),
218-20, 223, 232-34, 238-39, 241(t),
243(t), 254-55, 262n109, 268n19,
268n22, 271n10, 272n33, 278n46,
281n44, 281n48
temperance. *See* Japan Woman's Christian
Temperance Union (WCTU)
Thailand, 137
third-category beers (*dai-san no biiru*),
234-35
Tianjin, 24, 46, 138
Tipsy Heaven (Horoyoi Tengoku), 214-15
Tokyo, xi, 6, 8, 11, 17-18, 22, 26-27, 29,
32-40, 42-43, 46(t), 47(f), 49-52, 56, 59,
65, 69, 72-73, 78, 81-87, 94-95, 97-98,
100, 102, 105, 118-20, 122, 123(t), 124,
125(f), 126-29, 133, 141, 148-49, 151,
154, 157, 166-67, 171, 172(f), 173(f),
174-75, 177, 179, 196, 200-1, 208, 210,
215-16, 222, 225, 231-33, 235, 241(t),
242(t), 243(t), 244(t), 245(t), 246(t),
247(t), 248(t), 252-54, 260n62, 262n109,
266n94, 270n60
Tokugawa shogunate (1603-1867), 6, 8-10,
51, 252
trade, 6, 8-10, 19, 24-25, 42-43, 48, 54,
57, 69-72, 104, 111-12, 117, 130-31, 159,
170, 183, 194, 199, 206, 229, 255,
269n44, 270n65, 273n50
trains. *See* railways
trams, 11, 64, 83
trucks. *See* automobiles
Tsingtao/Tsingtau. *See* Qingdao
Twenty-One Demands, of China by Japan
(1915), 72

"unequal treaties," 6, 16-19, 21, 24, 28, 31,
43-44, 53
unions. *See* labour, federations